ITALY'S 500
BEST-EVER RECIPES

ITALY'S 500
BEST-EVER RECIPES

The ultimate collection of classic pasta, pizza, antipasto, risotto, meat, fish and vegetable dishes, and delicious desserts, with 500 photographs

CONTRIBUTING EDITOR: JENI WRIGHT

southwater

This edition is published by Southwater, an imprint of Anness Publishing Ltd,
Blaby Road, Wigston, Leicestershire LE18 4SE

Email: info@anness.com

Web: www.southwaterbooks.com; www.annesspublishing.com

If you like the images in this book and would like to investigate using them for publishing, promotions
or advertising, please visit our website www.practicalpictures.com for more information.

Publisher: Joanna Lorenz
Editorial Director: Helen Sudell
Editors: Doreen Gillon, James Harrison
Designer: Design Principals
Photographers: Karl Adamson, Edward Allwright, David Armstrong, Steve Baxter, Michelle Garratt,
    John Heseltine, Amanda Heywood, Janine Hosegood, William Lingwood, Patrick McLeavey
Contributors: Catherine Atkinson, Angela Boggiano, Carla Capalbo, Jacqueline Clark, Maxine Clark,
    Carole Clements, Roz Denny, Joanna Farrow, Christine France, Silvano Franco, Sarah Gates, Shirley
    Gill, Norma McMillan, Sue Maggs, Elizabeth Martin, Annie Nichols, Jenny Stacy, Liz Trigg, Laura
    Washburn, Steven Wheeler, Jenny White and Jeni Wright
Production Controller: Christine Ni

NOTES

Bracketed terms are intended for American readers.

*For all recipes, quantities are given in both metric
and imperial measures and, where appropriate, in
standard cups and spoons. Follow one set of
measures, but not a mixture, because they are not
interchangeable. Standard spoon and cup measures
are level. 1 tsp = 5ml, 1 tbsp = 15ml, 1 cup =
250ml/8fl oz. Australian standard tablespoons are
20ml. Australian readers should use 3 tsp in place of
1 tbsp for measuring small quantities of gelatine,
flour, salt, etc. American pints are 16fl oz/2 cups.
American readers should use 20fl oz/2.5 cups in
place of 1 pint when measuring liquids.*

*Electric oven temperatures in this book are for
conventional ovens. When using a fan oven, the
temperature will probably need to be reduced by
about 10–20°C/20–40°F. Since ovens vary, you
should check with your manufacturer's instruction
book for guidance.*

*The nutritional analysis given for each recipe is
calculated per portion (i.e. serving or item), unless
otherwise stated. If the recipe gives a range, such as
Serves 4–6, then the nutritional analysis will be for
the smaller portion size, i.e. 6 servings.
Measurements for sodium do not include salt added
to taste. Medium (US large) eggs are used unless
otherwise stated.*

Important: *Pregnant women, the elderly, the ill
and very young children should avoid recipes using
raw or lightly cooked eggs.*

ETHICAL TRADING POLICY
At Anness Publishing we believe that business should be conducted in an ethical and ecologically
sustainable way, with respect for the environment and a proper regard to the replacement of the
natural resources we employ.
As a publisher, we use a lot of wood pulp to make high-quality paper for printing, and that wood
commonly comes from spruce trees. We are therefore currently growing more than 750,000 trees
in three Scottish forest plantations: Berrymoss (130 hectares/320 acres), West Touxhill (125 hectares
/305 acres) and Deveron Forest (75 hectares/185 acres). The forests we manage contain more than
3.5 times the number of trees employed each year in making paper for the books we manufacture.
Because of this ongoing ecological investment program, you, as our customer, can have the pleasure
and reassurance of knowing that a tree is being cultivated on your behalf to naturally replace the
materials used to make the book you are holding.
Our forestry programme is run in accordance with the UK Woodland Assurance Scheme
(UKWAS) and will be certified by the internationally recognized Forest Stewardship Council
(FSC). The FSC is a non-government organization dedicated to promoting responsible
management of the world's forests. Certification ensures forests are managed in an
environmentally sustainable and socially responsible way. For further information about this
scheme, go to www.annesspublishing.com/trees

Main front cover image shows Fusilli with Tomato and Balsamic Vinegar Sauce – for recipe, see page 73

PUBLISHER'S NOTE
Although the advice and information in this book are believed to be accurate and true at the time
of going to press, neither the authors nor the publisher can accept any legal responsibility or
liability for any errors or omissions that may have been made nor for any inaccuracies nor for any
loss, harm or injury that comes about from following instructions or advice in this book.

Contents

Introduction

Italy is a country of great diversity. Its long Mediterranean coastline encloses a landscape of fertile plains, forest-covered mountains and arid rocks. From the hot, dry south to the cool Alpine foothills, the climate varies markedly. So do the local specialities: rice, maize and ham are northern staples, while olives, durum wheat and tomatoes thrive in the southern heat.

Italy's many kingdoms, states and duchies were unified as a nation in 1861. Each region had distinct linguistic and cultural differences, still present in the culinary practices today. Despite the advent of industrialization and mass-marketing, traditional foods are still central to the cultural identity of each region. This is partly due to the way in which recipes are learned: orally passed from generation to generation, and rarely written down in cookbooks, they survive in families for years with little or no change made to them.

A great deal of Italian food comes from this "contadino", or peasant, heritage. The best combines fresh ingredients with simple cooking techniques. Meats, fish and vegetables are flavoured with herbs and olive oil, and often grilled (broiled) or baked. Aromatic sauces can often be assembled in the time it takes pasta to boil. Many of these recipes can be prepared quickly and economically.

The southern Italian diet, which is high in vegetables and carbohydrates and low in animal fat, is a healthy one. It also tastes exceptionally good. Italian cooking is based on the creative use of fresh, seasonal ingredients. Vegetables and herbs play central roles in almost every aspect of the menu. In the markets, there is a sense of anticipation at the beginning of each new season, heralded by the arrival, on the beautifully displayed stalls, of the year's first artichokes, olives, chestnuts or wild mushrooms. Seasonal recipes come to the fore and make the most of available

produce. Many of the vegetables once considered exotically Mediterranean are now readily available in the markets and supermarkets of most countries. Fennel and aubergine (eggplant), peppers, courgettes (zucchini) and radicchio are used in pasta sauces, soups and pizzas, as well as wonderful accents to meat and fish.

Wherever you shop, look for the freshest possible fruits and vegetables. Choose unblemished, firm, sun-ripened produce, preferably locally or organically grown. Fresh herbs like oregano, basil, parsley and sage are easy to cultivate in window boxes and gardens and have an infinitely finer flavour than their dried counterparts. Italian cuisine is not a complicated or sophisticated style of cooking, but your recipes will benefit immeasurably by starting with the best quality ingredients you can find.

Antipasti are quintessential Italian foods. Salamis, pancetta, air-dried bresaola, and mortadella sausages are some of the most commonly used in Italy. Prosciutto is the most prized of all meats. Perhaps the single most important ingredient in a modern Italian kitchen is olive oil. The fruity flavour of a fine extra virgin olive oil perfumes any dish it is used in, from pesto sauce to the simplest salad dressing. Buy the best olive oil you can afford: one bottle goes a long way and makes a huge difference to any recipe. Balsamic vinegar has now become widely available outside of Italy. Made by the slow wood-aging process of wine vinegar, the finest varieties are deliciously mellow and fragrant. The taste is quite sweet and concentrated, so only a little is needed.

A typical Italian store cupboard also contains a supply of dried, natural ingredients. Dried beans, lentils and grains are stored in air-tight dispensers for use in soups and stews. Polenta, the coarsely ground yellow maize, is a staple of the northern Italian diet, as is the rice used to make risotto. The best known types of rice are Arborio, Vialone Nano and Carnaroli. Dried pasta shapes, capers, pine nuts, sun-dried tomatoes, dried chillies, fennel seeds and dried porcini mushrooms (soaked in water) are some of the other ingredients commonly used to give Italian dishes their characteristic flavours and are excellent basics to keep in the store cupboard.

Making Fresh Egg Pasta

In Italy, there has long been a tradition of making fresh pasta, and now the custom has caught on in other countries, too. The choices of different shapes, flavours and fillings are continually increasing by popular demand. It seems that everybody loves fresh pasta as the quality is excellent and it takes less time to cook than dried pasta.

About Pasta

Most pasta is made from durum wheat flour and water – durum is a special kind of wheat with a very high protein content. Egg pasta, pasta all'uova, contains flour and eggs, and is used for flat noodles such as tagliatelle, or for lasagne. Very little wholewheat pasta is eaten in Italy, but it is quite popular in other countries. All these types of pasta are available dried in packets, and will keep almost indefinitely. Fresh pasta is now more widely available and can be bought in most supermarkets. It can be very good, but can never compare to home-made egg pasta.

Pasta Shapes

There are countless shapes and sizes of both fresh and dried pasta. It is difficult to give a definitive list, as the names for the shapes vary from country to country. In some cases, just within Italy, the same shape can appear with several different names, depending upon which region it is in. Most of the recipes in this book specify the pasta shape most appropriate for a particular sauce. They can, of course, be replaced with another kind. A general rule is that long pasta goes better with tomato or thin, rich sauces, while short pasta and pasta shapes are best for chunkier, meatier sauces. But this rule should not be followed too rigidly. Part of the fun of cooking and eating pasta is in the endless combinations of sauce and pasta shapes. There are also hundreds of varieties of pastina for soups.

How to Make Egg Pasta

This classic recipe for egg noodles from Emilia-Romagna, northern Italy, calls for just three ingredients: flour and eggs, with a little salt. In other regions of Italy water, milk or oil are sometimes added. Use plain unbleached or strong white flour, and large eggs. As a general guide, use 70g/2½oz/½ cup of flour to each egg. Quantities will vary with the size of the eggs.

To serve 3–4

2 eggs, salt
140g/5oz/1 cup flour

To serve 4–6

3 eggs, salt
210g/7½oz/1½ cups flour

To serve 6–8

4 eggs, salt
280g/10oz/2 cups flour

1 Place the flour in the centre of a clean smooth work surface. Make a well in the middle. Break the eggs into the well. Add a pinch of salt.

2 Start beating the eggs with a fork, gradually drawing the flour from the inside walls of the well. As the paste begins to thicken, continue mixing with your hands. Incorporate as much flour as possible, until the mixture forms a mass. It should still be lumpy at this stage. If the dough still sticks to your hands, add a little more plain flour. Set the dough aside. Scrape off all traces of the dough from the work surface until it is perfectly smooth and clean. Wash and dry your hands.

3 Lightly flour the work surface. Knead the dough by pressing it away from you with the heel of your hands, and then folding it over towards you. Repeat this action over and over, turning the dough as you knead. Work for about 10 minutes, or until the dough is smooth and elastic. Do not skimp on the kneading time or the finished pasta will not be light and silky.

4 If you are using more than 2 eggs, divide the dough in half. Flour the rolling pin and the work surface. Pat the dough into a disc and begin rolling it out into a flat circle, rotating it one quarter turn after each roll to keep its shape round. Continue rolling until the disc is about 3mm/⅛in thick.

5 Roll out the dough until it is paper-thin by rolling up on to the rolling pin and simultaneously giving a sideways stretching with the hands. Wrap the near edge of the dough around the centre of the rolling pin, and begin rolling the dough up away from you. As you roll back and forth, slide your hands from the centre towards the outer edges of the pin, carefully stretching and thinning out the pasta.

6 Quickly repeat these movements until about two-thirds of the sheet of pasta is wrapped around the pin. Lift and turn the wrapped pasta sheet about 45° before unrolling it. Repeat the rolling and stretching process, starting from a new point of the sheet each time to keep it evenly thin. By the end (this process should not last more than 8 to 10 minutes or the dough will lose its elasticity) the whole sheet should be smooth, almost transparent and even all over or the shapes will not cook in the sames length of time. If the dough is still sticky, lightly flour your hands as you continue rolling and stretching.

7 If you are making noodles (tagliatelle, fettuccine etc.) lay a clean dish towel on a table and unroll the pasta sheet on it, letting about a third of the sheet hang over the edge. Rotate the dough every 10 minutes. Roll out the second sheet of dough if you are using more than 2 eggs. After 25–30 minutes the pasta will have dried enough to cut. Do not overdry or the pasta will crack as it is cut.

8 To cut tagliatelle, fettuccine or tagliolini, fold the sheet of pasta into a flat roll about 10cm/4in wide. Cut across the roll to form noodles of the desired width. Tagliolini is 3mm/⅛in; Fettuccine is 4mm/⅙in; Tagliatelle is 6mm/¼in. After cutting, open out the noodles, and let them dry for about 5 minutes before cooking. These noodles may be stored for some weeks without refrigeration. Allow them to dry completely before storing them, uncovered, in a dry cupboard.

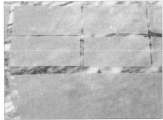

9 To cut the pasta for lasagne or pappardelle, do not fold or dry the rolled out dough. Lasagne is made by cutting rectangles approximately 13cm/5in by 9cm/3½in. Pappardelle are large noodles cut with a fluted pastry wheel. They are about 2cm/¾ in wide. Try to keep the strips the same width or they will not cook evenly.

Pasta Verde

Follow the same recipe, adding ¼ cup cooked, very finely chopped spinach (after having been squeezed very dry) to the eggs and flour. The pasta dough will be much stickier than usual, so you need to add a little extra flour during kneading and when rolling and cutting the dough to absorb the moisture from the spinach. This pasta is very suitable for stuffed recipes such as cannelloni, as it seals better than plain egg pasta.

Basic Tomato Sauce for Pasta

Tomato sauce is without doubt the most popular dressing for pasta in Italy. This sauce is best made with fresh tomatoes, but works well with canned tomatoes. You can enhance the sauce by adding in extra vegetables as desired. It is good served with all types of pasta or could be served as an accompaniment to stuffed vegetables.

Serves 4

*60ml/4 tbsp olive oil
1 medium onion, very finely chopped
1 garlic clove, finely chopped
450g/1lb tomatoes, fresh or canned, chopped, with their juice
salt and freshly ground black pepper
a few fresh basil sprigs or parsley*

1 Heat the oil in a medium pan. Add the onion, and cook over moderate heat until it is tranluscent, 5–8 minutes.

2 Stir in the garlic and the tomatoes with their juice (add 45ml/3 tbsp of water if you are using fresh tomatoes). Season with salt and pepper. Add the herbs. Cook for 20–30 minutes.

3 Pass the sauce through a food mill or purée in a food processor. To serve, reheat gently, correct the seasoning and pour over the drained pasta of your choice.

Using Pasta Machines & Cooking Pasta

Rolling Out Pasta

Making pasta with a machine is quick and easy. The results are perhaps not quite as fine as with handmade pasta, but they are certainly better than store-bought pastas. You will need a pasta-making machine, either hand-cranked or electric. Use the same proportions of eggs, flours and salt as for Egg Pasta.

1 Place the flour in the centre of a clean smooth work surface. Make a well in the middle. Break the eggs into the well. Add a pinch of salt. Start beating the eggs with a fork, gradually drawing the flour from the inside walls of the well. As the paste thickens, continue mixing with your hands. Incorporate as much flour as possible, until the mixture forms a mass. It will still be lumpy. If it sticks to your hands, add a little more flour. Set the dough aside and scrape the work surface clean.

2 Set the machine rollers at their widest (kneading) setting. Pull off a piece of dough the size of a small orange. Place the remaining dough between two soup plates. Feed the dough through the rollers. Fold it in half, end to end, and feed it through again 7 or 8 times, turning it and folding it over after each kneading. The dough should be smooth and fairly evenly rectangular. If it sticks to the machine, brush with flour. Lay it out on a lightly floured work surface

or on a clean dish towel, and repeat with the remaining dough, broken into pieces the same size.

3 Adjust the machine to the next line setting. Feed each strip through once and replace on the drying surface. Keep them in the order in which they were kneaded.

4 Reset the machine to the next setting. Repeat, passing each strip through once. Repeat for each remaining roller setting until the pasta is the right thickness – for most purposes this is given by the next to last setting, except for delicate strips such as tagliolini. If the pasta strips get too long, cut them in half.

5 When all the strips are the desired thickness they may be machine-cut into noodles, or hand-cut for lasagne or pappardelle, as described for Handmade Egg Pasta earlier. When making noodles, be sure the pasta is fairly dry, but not brittle, or the noodles may stick together when cut. Select the desired width of cutter, and feed the strips through.

6 Separate the noodles, and leave to dry for at least 15 minutes before using. They may be stored for some weeks without refrigeration. Allow them to dry before storing them, uncovered, in a dry cupboard. They may also be frozen, first loose on trays and then packed together. If you are making stuffed pasta do not let the pasta dry out before filling them.

Classic Bolognese Sauce

This is a versatile meat sauce. You can toss it with fresh pasta – the quantity here is enough for 450g/1lb tagliatelle, spaghetti or a short pasta shape such as penne – or alternatively you can layer it in a baked dish like lasagne.

Serves 4–6

1 onion
1 small carrot
1 celery stick
2 garlic cloves
45ml/3 tbsp olive oil
400g/14oz/1¾ cups minced
　(ground) beef
120ml/4fl oz/½ cup red wine
200ml/7fl oz/scant 1 cup passata
15ml/1 tbsp tomato purée (paste)
5ml/1 tsp dried oregano
15ml/1 tbsp chopped fresh parsley
350ml/12fl oz/1½ cups beef stock
8 baby Italian tomatoes (optional)
salt and ground black pepper

1 Chop all the vegetables finely. Heat the oil in a large pan, add the chopped vegetable mixture and cook over low heat, stirring frequently, for 5–7 minutes.

2 Add the minced beef and cook for 5 minutes, stirring and breaking up any lumps in the meat with a wooden spoon. Stir in the wine and mix well.

3 Cook for 1–2 minutes, then add the passata, tomato purée, herbs and 60ml/4 tbsp of the stock. Season to taste. Stir well and bring to the boil.

4 Cover the pan, and cook over gentle heat for 30 minutes, stirring occasionally. Add the tomatoes, if using, and simmer for 5–10 minutes more. Taste for seasoning.

How to Cook Egg Pasta

Fresh egg pasta, especially home-made, cooks very much faster than dried pasta. Make sure everything is ready (the sauce, serving dishes etc) before you start boiling egg pasta, as there will not be time once the cooking starts, and egg pasta becomes soft very quickly.

Stuffed shapes require more gentle handling or they may break open and release their filling into the water, so stir them gently during cooking. The best method of draining stuffed shapes after cooking is to lift them carefully out of the water using a large pasta scoop or slotted spoon.

I Always cook pasta in a large pot with a generous amount of rapidly boiling water. Use at least 5 cups of water to a quantity of pasta made with 1 cup of flour. Add a little salt to the water.

2 Drop the pasta into the boiling water all at once. Stir gently to prevent the pasta sticking to itself or to the pan. Cook the pasta at a fast boil.

3 Freshly made pasta can be done as little as 15 seconds after the cooking water comes back to a boil. Stuffed pasta takes a few minutes longer to cook the filling. When done, turn the pasta into the colander and proceed as for dried pasta.

How to Cook Dried Pasta

The cooking time for dried pasta will vary from 8–20 minutes depending on the type and the manufacturer. Always check the time on the label. Start timing the pasta from the moment the water returns to the boil after adding the pasta.

I Always cook pasta in a large pot with a generous amount of rapidly boiling water. Use at least 5 cups of water to each ½ cup pasta.

2 The water should be salted at least 2 minutes before the pasta is added, to give the salt time to dissolve. Add about 1½ tbsp salt per 2 cups of pasta. You may want to vary the saltiness of the cooking water.

3 Drop the pasta into the boiling water all at once. Use a wooden spoon to help ease long pasta in as it softens, to prevent it from breaking. Stir frequently to prevent the pasta sticking to itself or to the pan. Cook the pasta at a fast boil, but be prepared to lower the heat if it boils over.

4 Timing is critical in pasta cooking. Follow package indications for store-bought pasta, but it is best in all cases to test for doneness by tasting, several times if necessary. In Italy pasta is always eaten al dente, which means firm to the bite. Cooked this way it is just tender, but its "soul" (the innermost part) is still firm.

5 Place a colander in the sink before the pasta has finished cooking. As soon as the pasta tastes done, tip it all into the colander (you may first want to reserve a cupful of the hot cooking water to add to the sauce if it needs thinning). Shake the colander lightly to remove most but not all of the cooking water. Pasta should never be over-drained.

6 Quickly turn the pasta into a warmed serving dish, and immediately toss it with a little butter or oil, or the prepared sauce. Alternatively, turn it into the cooking pan with the sauce, where it will be cooked for 1–2 minutes more as it is mixed into the sauce. Never allow pasta to sit undressed, as it will stick together and become unpalatable.

Watchpoint

It is best not to cook more than 675g/1½lb pasta at a time, even if you have a very large saucepan, because of the danger in handling such a large amount of boiling hot water. If you are using the microwave to cook pasta it is best not to cook more than 225g/8oz pasta at a time. Use a large heatproof bowl suitable for a microwave, don't overfill the bowl and transfer it carefully to and from the microwave using heatproof gloves. When the pasta is cooked, always have the colander ready in the sink to drain the pasta.

Making Pizza Dough

Pizzas originate from the south of Italy where they have developed into a universally popular main meal for the whole family. They are fun and quick to make at home and can be personalized with combinations of your favourite ingredients. Making fresh dough takes a little practice but will give you a much tastier base than a supermarket pizza.

Basic Pizza Dough

Pizza dough is leavened with yeast. It usually rises once before being rolled out and filled. The dough can be baked in pizza pans or on a flat baking sheet or cookie sheet.

Serves 4 as a main course or 8 as an appetizer

25g/1oz/2½ tbsp fresh bread yeast or
* 15g/½oz/1½ tbsp active dried yeast*
250ml/8fl oz/1 cup lukewarm water
pinch of sugar
5ml/1 tsp salt
350–400g/12–14oz/3–3½ cups
* unbleached white bread flour,*
* preferably strong*

1 Warm a medium mixing bowl by swirling some hot water in it. Drain. Place the yeast in the bowl, and pour on the warm water. Stir in the sugar, mix with a fork, and allow to stand until the yeast has dispersed and starts to foam, 5–10 minutes.

2 Use a wooden spoon to mix in the salt and about one-third of the flour. Mix in another third of the flour, stirring with the spoon until the dough forms a mass and begins to pull away from the sides of the bowl.

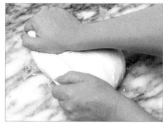

3 Sprinkle some of the remaining flour onto a smooth work surface. Remove the dough from the bowl and begin to knead it, working in the remaining flour a little at a time. Knead for 8–10 minutes. By the end the dough should be elastic and smooth. Form it into a ball.

4 Lightly oil a large mixing bowl. Place the dough in the bowl. Stretch a moistened and wrung-out dish towel across the top of the bowl, and leave it to stand in a warm place, until the dough has doubled in volume, about 40–50 minutes or more, depending on the type of yeast used. (If you do not have a warm enough place, turn the oven on to medium heat for 10 minutes before you knead the dough. Turn it off. Place the bowl with the dough in it in the turned-off oven with the door closed and let it rise there.) To test whether the dough has risen enough, poke two fingers into the dough. If the indentations remain, the dough is ready.

5 Punch the dough firmly down with your fist to release the air. Knead for 1–2 minutes. Divide the dough, if you wish: for 2 medium pizzas, divide into 2 balls, and for 4 individual pizzas, divide into 4 balls.

6 Pat the ball of dough out into a flat circle on a lightly floured surface. With a rolling pin, roll it out to a thickness of about 5mm/¼in . If you are using a pizza pan, roll the dough out about 5mm/¼in larger than the size of the pan to allow for the rim of the crust.

7 Place in the lightly oiled pan, folding the extra dough under to make a thicker rim around the edge. If you are baking the pizza without a round pan, press some of the dough from the center of the circle towards the edge, to make a thicker rim. Place it on a lightly oiled flat cookie sheet. The dough is now ready for filling.

Cook's Tips

• *This basic dough can be used for other recipes in this book, such as Focaccia, Breadsticks (Grissini), Calzone and Sicilian Closed Pizza. The dough may be frozen at the end of step 7, and thawed before filling. To freeze cooked dough, such as Foccaccia, allow to cool to room temperature after baking. Wrap in foil and freeze. Thaw and place in a warm oven before serving.*

• *If you are really pressed for time, try a packaged pizza dough mix. For best results roll out the dough to a 25–30 cm (10–12in) circle; this is slightly larger than stated on the package, but it does produce a perfect thin, crispy base. For a deep-dish version use two packets.*

• *To add variety to wholemeal (whole-wheat) pizza dough, you could try adding flavoured oils, such as chilli or rosemary, basil or thyme herb oil.*

Wholewheat Pizza Dough

Pizza dough can also be made with wholewheat flour, although it is easier to handle and more elastic if a proportion of white flour is used. This dough can be used in any recipe calling for Basic Pizza Dough.

Serves 4 as a main course or 8 as an appetizer

25g/1oz/2½ tbsp fresh bread yeast or 15g/½oz/1½ tbsp active dried yeast
250ml/8fl oz/1 cup lukewarm water
pinch of sugar
30ml/2 tbsp olive oil
5ml/1 tsp salt
150g/5oz/1¼ cups white bread flour
250g/9oz/2 cups stoneground wholemeal (whole-wheat) bread flour

1 Warm a medium mixing bowl by swirling some hot water in it. Drain. Place the yeast in the bowl, and pour on the warm water. Stir in the sugar, mix with a fork, and allow to stand until the yeast has dispersed and starts to foam, 5–10 minutes.

2 Use a wooden spoon to mix in the olive oil and the salt, and the white flour. Mix in about half of the whole-wheat flour, stirring with the spoon until the dough forms a mass and begins to pull away from the sides of the bowl.

3 Proceed with steps 3–7 as for Basic Pizza Dough, punching down the risen dough, and kneading until ready to roll out and place in a pan.

Cook's Tip

It is now possible to buy fresh, frozen or long-life pizza bases from most supermarkets. Although they do not taste as good as home-made pizza they can be useful for quick meals.

To Make the Dough in a Food Processor

1 Have all the ingredients ready and measured out. In a small jug (pitcher) or bowl add the yeast to the warm water. Stir in the sugar, and allow to stand until the yeast has dissolved, 5–10 minutes.

2 Fit the food processor with the metal blades. Place the salt and three-quarters of the flour in the bowl of the food processor. Turn it on, and pour in the yeast mixture and olive oil through the opening at the top. Continue processing until the dough forms one or two balls. Turn the machine off, open it, and touch the dough. If it still feels sticky, add a little more flour, and process again until it is incorporated.

3 Remove the dough from the processor. Knead it for 2–3 minutes on a surface dusted with the remaining flour. Form the dough into a ball, and proceed with Step 4 of Basic Pizza Dough.

Basic Tomato Sauce for Pizza

Tomato sauce forms the basis of the topping in many pizza recipes. Make sure it is well seasoned and thick before spreading it over the crust. You can then add your own fresh toppings. It will keep fresh in a covered container in the refrigerator for up to 3 days.

Covers one 22.5–25cm/10–12-inch round or 25 x 15cm/12 x 7-inch oblong pizza crust

15ml/1 tbsp olive oil
1 medium onion, finely chopped
1 garlic clove, finely chopped
400g/14oz can chopped tomatoes
15ml/1 tbsp tomato purée (paste)
15ml/1 tbsp chopped fresh mixed herbs, such as parsley, thyme, basil or oregano
pinch of sugar
salt and ground black pepper

1 Heat the oil in a medium pan, add the onion and garlic and gently fry for about 5 minutes, or until softened.

2 Add the tomatoes, tomato purée, herbs, sugar and seasoning.

3 Simmer, uncovered, stirring occasionally, for about 15–20 minutes, or until the tomatoes have reduced to a thick pulp. Let cool. Pass through a food mill or food processor.

Raw Vegetables with Olive Oil Dip

Use a combination of any fresh seasonal vegetables for this colourful antipasto from Rome, where the dip usually consists only of olive oil and salt. The vegetables should be raw or lightly blanched.

Serves 6–8

3 large carrots, peeled
2 fennel bulbs
6 tender celery sticks
1 red (bell) pepper
12 radishes, trimmed of roots
2 large tomatoes or
  12 cherry tomatoes
8 spring onions (scallions)
12 small cauliflower florets

For the dip
120ml/4fl oz/¹/₂ cup olive oil
45ml/3 tbsp fresh lemon juice
  (optional)
4 leaves fresh basil, torn into
  small pieces (optional)
salt and ground black pepper

1 Prepare the vegetables: trim the carrots, fennel bulbs and celery sticks, then slice neatly into small sticks. Seed the pepper and cut into small sticks.

2 If using large tomatoes, cut them into sections. Trim the roots and dark green leaves from the spring onions.

3 Arrange the prepared vegetables on a large platter, leaving a space in the centre for the bowl of dip.

4 To make the dip, pour the olive oil into a small bowl. Add salt and pepper. Stir in the lemon juice and basil, if using. Place the bowl in the centre of the vegetable platter.

Cook's Tips
• Lightly cooked asparagus tips would also make a delicious addition to the platter.
• For the dip, it is essential to use a good-quality olive oil. The best is extra virgin olive oil, which is made simply by pressing the olives to extract the oil, with no further processing. The distinctive fruity flavour of this oil makes it ideal for dressings and using raw. The best comes from Lucca in Tuscany.

Celery Stuffed with Gorgonzola

These stuffed celery stalks are very easy to assemble. A delicious combination of creamy cheese and crisp celery, they go beautifully with salamis and and other cured meat but also make a tasty addition to a picnic.

Serves 4–6
12 crisp celery sticks, with
  leaves attached
75g/3oz/¹/₂ cup Gorgonzola
75g/3oz/¹/₂ cup cream cheese
fresh chives, to garnish

1 Wash and dry the celery sticks, then trim the root ends. Leave on the leaves for an attractive finish.

2 Place the Gorgonzola in a small bowl with the cream cheese and mash together until smooth.

3 Fill the celery sticks with the cheese mixture, using a spatula to smooth the top of the filling. Chill in the refrigerator for at least an hour.

4 To serve, arrange the chilled sticks decoratively on a serving platter and garnish the surface of the fillings with finely chopped chives. Serve immediately.

Cook's Tip
These crunchy sticks are also ideal to serve as nibbles with drinks, but guests will find them more manageable if they are sliced into bite-size pieces rather than served whole. Use the trimmed leaves as a garnish.

Variation
If you prefer a less tangy flavour for the filling, try using Dolcelatte, which is a mild version of Gorgonzola. Exceptionally creamy, Dolcelatte will blend easily with the cream cheese and still add enough flavour to the finished dish.

Energy 127Kcal/526kJ; Fat 10.1g; Saturated Fat 1.5g; Carbohydrate 7.3g; Fibre 3.4g

Energy 154Kcal/636kJ; Fat 14.8g; Saturated Fat 9.4g; Carbohydrate 0.5g; Fibre 0.7g

Roasted Pepper Antipasto

Jars of delicious Italian mixed peppers in olive oil are now a common sight in many supermarkets and delicatessens. None, however, can compete with this colourful, freshly made version, perfect as an appetizer on its own or served with tasty Italian salamis and a selection of Italian cold meats.

Serves 6
3 red (bell) peppers
2 yellow or orange (bell) peppers
2 green (bell) peppers
50g/2oz/¹/₂ cup sun-dried
   tomatoes in oil, drained
1 garlic clove
30ml/2 tbsp balsamic vinegar
75ml/5 tbsp olive oil
few drops of chilli sauce
4 canned artichoke hearts,
   drained and sliced
salt and ground black pepper
basil leaves, to garnish

1 Preheat the oven to 200°C/400°F/Gas 6. Lightly oil a foil-lined baking sheet and place the whole peppers on the foil. Bake for about 45 minutes, until beginning to char. Cover with a dish towel and leave to cool for 5 minutes.

2 Slice the sun-dried tomatoes into thin strips. Thinly slice the garlic. Set the tomatoes and garlic aside.

3 Beat together the vinegar, oil and chilli sauce, then season with a little salt and pepper.

4 Remove the skins, cores and seeds from the peppers, then slice the flesh into strips. Mix the peppers with the artichoke hearts, tomatoes and garlic. Pour over the dressing and scatter with the basil leaves.

> **Cook's Tip**
> *Baking the peppers brings out their sweet flavour and makes them meltingly soft. Once the peppers have cooled slightly, you'll find the skins will have loosened from the flesh, making them easy to remove with your fingers.*

Marinated Baby Aubergines with Raisins & Pine Nuts

Bursting with southern Italian flavours, this dish conjures up all the warmth of the sunny Mediterranean shores. Glossy aubergines (eggplants) are a classic Italian ingredient from the south and prepared in this way they make a delicious antipasto. Assemble the dish a day in advance, to allow the sour and sweet flavours of the lemon and vinegar to develop properly.

Serves 4
12 baby aubergines (eggplants),
   halved lengthways
250ml/8fl oz/1 cup extra virgin
   olive oil
juice of 1 lemon
30ml/2 tbsp balsamic vinegar
3 cloves
25g/1oz/¹/₃ cup pine nuts
25g/1oz/2 tbsp raisins
15ml/1 tbsp sugar
1 bay leaf
large pinch of dried chilli flakes
salt and ground black pepper

1 Preheat the grill (broiler) to high. Place the aubergines, cut side up, in the grill pan and brush with a little of the olive oil. Grill (broil) for 10 minutes, until slightly blackened, turning them over half way through cooking.

2 To make the marinade, put the remaining olive oil, the lemon juice, vinegar, cloves, pine nuts, raisins, sugar and bay leaf in a jug. Add the chilli flakes and salt and pepper and mix well.

3 Place the hot aubergines in an earthenware or glass bowl, and pour over the marinade. Leave to cool, turning the aubergines once or twice. Serve cold.

> **Cook's Tip**
> *Baby aubergines are now available from larger supermarkets, but if you have difficulty finding them, you could buy 3 medium to large aubergines and slice them thickly. Grilling gives the aubergines an appetizing finish and flavour, but they also taste good roasted in the oven, with a good drizzle of olive oil.*

Little Onions with Coriander, Wine & Olive Oil

Chillies and aromatic toasted coriander seeds add piquancy to the small onions used here. Bay leaves, garlic, thyme, oregano, lemon, wine and parsley provide an unmistakably Mediterranean kick.

Serves 6

105ml/7 tbsp olive oil
675g/1½lb small onions, peeled
150ml/¼ pint/⅔ cup dry
    white wine
2 bay leaves
2 garlic cloves, bruised
1–2 small dried red chillies
15ml/1 tbsp coriander seeds,
    toasted and lightly crushed
2.5ml/½ tsp sugar
a few fresh thyme sprigs
30ml/2 tbsp currants
10ml/2 tsp chopped fresh
    oregano or marjoram
5ml/1 tsp grated lemon rind
15ml/1 tbsp chopped fresh flat
    leaf parsley
30–45ml/2–3 tbsp pine
    nuts, toasted
salt and ground black pepper

1 Place 30ml/2 tbsp of the olive oil in a wide pan. Add the onions, place over medium heat and cook gently for about 5 minutes, or until the onions begin to colour. Use a slotted spoon to remove from the pan and set aside.

2 Add the remaining oil, the wine, bay leaves, garlic, chillies, coriander seeds, sugar and thyme to the pan. Bring to the boil and cook briskly for 5 minutes.

3 Return the onions to the pan. Add the currants, reduce the heat and cook gently for 15–20 minutes, or until the onions are tender but not falling apart.

4 Using a slotted spoon, transfer the onions to a serving dish, then boil the liquid vigorously until it reduces considerably. Taste and adjust the seasoning, then pour the liquid over the onions.

5 Scatter the onions with the oregano or marjoram, then cool and chill. Just before you are ready to serve, stir the lemon rind, chopped flat leaf parsley and pine nuts into the onions.

Aubergine Fritters

A classic antipasto, these simply delicious fritters also make a superb starter or a vegetarian supper dish.

Serves 4

1 large aubergine (eggplant),
    weighing about 675g/1½lb, cut
    into 1cm/½in thick slices
30ml/2 tbsp olive oil
1 egg, lightly beaten
2 garlic cloves, crushed
60ml/4 tbsp chopped fresh
    parsley
130g/4½oz/2¼ cups fresh
    white breadcrumbs
90g/3½oz/generous 1 cup grated
    Parmesan cheese
90g/3½oz/generous 1 cup feta
    cheese, crumbled
45ml/3 tbsp plain
    (all-purpose) flour
sunflower oil, for shallow frying
salt and ground black pepper

To serve

natural (plain) yogurt, flavoured
    with fried red chillies and
    cumin seeds
lime wedges

1 Preheat the oven to 190°C/375°F/Gas 5. Brush the aubergine slices with the olive oil, then place them on a baking sheet and bake for about 20 minutes, until golden and tender.

2 Chop the aubergine slices finely and place them in a bowl with the egg, garlic, parsley, breadcrumbs, Parmesan and feta. Add salt and pepper to taste, and mix well.

3 Leave the mixture to rest for about 20 minutes. If the mixture looks very sloppy, add more breadcrumbs.

4 Divide the mixture into eight balls and flatten them slightly. Place the flour on a plate and season with salt and pepper. Coat the fritters in the flour, shaking off any excess.

5 Shallow fry the fritters in batches for 1 minute on each side, until golden brown. Remove with a slotted spoon and drain on kitchen paper.

6 Serve the fritters warm, accompanied with the flavoured yogurt and lime wedges.

Roasted Tomatoes & Mozzarella

Roasting the tomatoes in olive oil adds a new dimension to this delicious dish and a superb sweetness to the tomatoes. Make the basil oil just before serving to retain its fresh flavour and vivid green colour.

Serves 4

olive oil, for brushing
6 large plum tomatoes
350g/12oz fresh mozzarella
* cheese, cut into 8–12 slices*
fresh basil leaves, to garnish

For the basil oil
25 fresh basil leaves
60ml/4 tbsp extra virgin olive oil
1 garlic clove, crushed

For the salad
90g/3½oz/4 cups salad leaves
50g/2oz/2 cups fresh salad herbs,
* such as coriander (cilantro),*
* basil and rocket (arugula)*
25g/1oz/3 tbsp pumpkin seeds
25g/1oz/3 tbsp sunflower seeds
60ml/4tbsp extra virgin olive oil
15ml/1 tbsp balsamic vinegar
2.5 ml/½ tsp Dijon mustard

1 Preheat the oven to 200°C/400°F/Gas 6 and oil a baking sheet. Cut the tomatoes in half lengthways and remove the seeds. Place skin-side down on the baking sheet and roast for 20 minutes, or until the tomatoes are tender.

2 Meanwhile, make the basil oil. Place the basil leaves, olive oil and garlic in a food processor and process until smooth. Transfer to a bowl and chill.

3 To make the salad, place the salad leaves in a large bowl. Add the mixed salad herbs and toss lightly to mix.

4 Toast the pumpkin and sunflower seeds in a dry frying pan over medium heat for 2 minutes, until golden, tossing frequently. Allow to cool, then sprinkle over the salad.

5 Whisk together the olive oil, vinegar and mustard and pour over the salad. Toss until the leaves are well coated.

6 To serve, place the tomato halves on top of 2 or 3 slices of mozzarella and drizzle over the basil oil. Season well. Garnish with basil leaves and serve with the salad.

Toasted Ciabatta with Tomatoes, Cheese & Marjoram Flowers

In this very simple but tasty antipasto dish, marjoram flowers are used to give a distinctive flavour. The combination of cheese, tomato and marjoram is great, but lots of extras can be added, such as capers, olives, anchovies or slices of roasted peppers.

Serves 2

1 ciabatta loaf
4 tomatoes
115g/4oz mozzarella or
* Cheddar cheese*
15ml/1 tbsp olive oil
15ml/1 tbsp marjoram flowers
salt and ground black pepper

1 Preheat the grill (broiler) to high. Cut the loaf in half lengthways and toast very lightly under the grill until it has turned a pale golden brown.

2 Meanwhile, skin the tomatoes: to loosen the skins, first plunge the tomatoes in boiling water for 30 seconds, then refresh them in cold water. Peel and cut the flesh into thick slices.

3 Slice or grate the mozzarella or Cheddar cheese. Lightly drizzle the olive oil over the toasted bread and top with the tomato slices and cheese. Season with salt and pepper and scatter the marjoram flowers over the top. Drizzle with a little more olive oil.

4 Place under the hot grill until the cheese bubbles and is just starting to brown. Serve immediately.

Cook's Tip
Add marjoram flowers to your favourite pizza topping. Sprinkle over 7.5–15ml/½–1 tbsp flowers or flowering tops and add a few of the leaves. The flavours are strong, so marjoram flowers should be used with care, especially if you haven't tried them before. The amount you use will depend on your own taste.

Energy 526Kcal/2180kJ; Fat 46.3g; Saturated Fat 15.9g; Carbohydrate 7.6g; Fibre 2.6g

Energy 502Kcal/2113kJ; Fat 21.7g; Saturated Fat 9.5g; Carbohydrate 58.2g; Fibre 4.3g

Marinated Vegetable Antipasto

Offer these three easy-to-make vegetable dishes as a classic antipasto course.

Serves 4

For the peppers
3 red (bell) peppers
3 yellow (bell) peppers
4 garlic cloves, sliced
handful fresh basil, plus extra to garnish
extra virgin olive oil
salt and ground black pepper

For the mushrooms
450g/1lb open cap mushrooms
60ml/4 tbsp extra virgin olive oil
1 large garlic clove, crushed
15ml/1 tbsp chopped fresh rosemary
250ml/8fl oz/1 cup dry white wine
fresh rosemary sprigs, to garnish

For the olives
1 dried red chilli, crushed
grated rind of 1 lemon
120ml/4fl oz/½ cup extra virgin olive oil
225g/8oz/1⅓ cups Italian black olives
30ml/2 tbsp chopped fresh flat leaf parsley
1 lemon wedge, to serve

1 Place the peppers under a hot grill (broiler). Turn occasionally until they are blackened and blistered all over. Remove from the heat and place in a large plastic bag. When cool, remove the skin, halve the peppers and seed. Cut the flesh into strips lengthways and place them in a bowl with the garlic and basil. Add salt to taste, cover with oil and marinate for 3–4 hours, tossing occasionally. Serve garnished with more basil leaves.

2 Thickly slice the mushrooms and place in a large bowl. Heat the oil in a small pan and add the garlic and rosemary. Add the wine, bring to the boil, then lower the heat and simmer for 3 minutes. Add salt and pepper to taste. Pour on to the mushrooms. Mix well and leave to cool, stirring occasionally. Cover and marinate overnight. Serve garnished with rosemary.

3 Prepare the olives. Place the chilli and lemon rind in a small pan with the oil. Heat gently for about 3 minutes. Add the olives and heat for 1 minute more. Tip into a bowl and leave to cool. Marinate overnight. Sprinkle the parsley over just before serving with the lemon wedge.

Peperonata

Richly flavoured and spicy, this tomato and sweet red (bell) pepper dish provides a colourful and fresh-tasting start to an Italian meal. Wonderful served as a chunky dip with crisp Italian-style bread sticks, it is also the perfect foil to salami and other cold meats on a buffet. But you needn't stop there: why not try it as a tasty accompaniment to grilled chicken, turkey and fish dishes. It is delicious served hot, cold or at room temperature.

Serves 4
2 large red (bell) peppers, halved, seeded and sliced
pinch of dried chilli flakes
400g/14oz can pomodorino tomatoes
60ml/4 tbsp garlic-infused olive oil
salt and ground black pepper

1 Heat the oil in a large pan over low heat and add the sliced peppers. Cook very gently, stirring occasionally for 3–4 minutes.

2 Add the chilli flakes to the pan and cook for 1 minute, then pour in the tomatoes and season. Cook gently for 50 minutes to 1 hour, stirring occasionally.

Cook's Tips
• Long, slow cooking helps to bring out the sweetness of the peppers and tomatoes, so don't be tempted to cheat on the cooking time by cooking over a higher heat.
• This dish can be stored in the refrigerator for several days, making it a useful dish to have on stand-by as an instant starter. Cover the dish before chilling.

Variation
For a less spicy flavour, leave out the chilli and add a good handful of torn basil leaves for a truly Italian taste.

Cannellini Bean Pâté

Serve this simple pâté with crunchy melba toast, garlicky olives and roasted (bell) peppers steeped in a tasty olive oil marinade to make a lovely antipasto course.

Serves 4

2 x 400g/14oz cans cannellini
  beans, drained and rinsed
45ml/3 tbsp olive oil
50g/2oz mature Cheddar cheese,
  finely grated
30ml/2 tbsp chopped fresh
  parsley
salt and ground black pepper
a little paprika, to garnish
  (optional)

1 Put the cannellini beans in a food processor with the olive oil, and process to a chunky paste.

2 Transfer the mixture to a bowl and stir in the cheese, parsley and some salt and pepper. Spoon into a serving dish and sprinkle a little paprika on top, if you like.

Cook's Tips
• Canned beans are usually in a sugar, salt and water solution so always drain and rinse them thoroughly before use – otherwise the finished pâté may be too salty.
• To make crisp Melba toast to serve with the pâté, grill (broil) slices of white bread on both sides until golden. Allow to cool slightly, then cut off and discard the crusts. Using a long, thin very sharp knife, carefully slice the bread in half horizontally to make two thinner slices. Toast the cut sides under the grill until golden. Allow the toast to cool, then store in an airtight container until needed.

Variation
To ring the changes, you can use other types of canned beans instead of the cannellini. Try using kidney beans and add a pinch of chilli powder to give an added kick.

Stuffed Roast Peppers with Pesto

Serve these sensational scallop- and pesto-filled red (bell) peppers with chunks of Italian bread, such as ciabatta or focaccia, to mop up the garlicky juices.

Serves 4

4 squat red (bell) peppers
60ml/4 tbsp olive oil
2 large garlic cloves, cut into
  thin slivers
4 shelled scallops
45ml/3 tbsp pesto
salt and ground black pepper
salad leaves and fresh basil
  sprigs, to garnish
freshly grated Parmesan cheese,
  to serve

1 Preheat the oven to 180°C/350°F/Gas 4. Cut the peppers in half lengthways, through their stalks. Scrape out and discard the cores and seeds. Wash the pepper shells and pat dry with kitchen paper.

2 Put the peppers, cut-side up, in an oiled roasting pan. Divide the slivers of garlic equally among them and sprinkle with salt and pepper to taste. Spoon the oil into the peppers, then roast for 40 minutes.

3 Cut each of the shelled scallops in half to make two flat discs. Remove the peppers from the oven and place a scallop half in each pepper half. Top with pesto.

4 Return the pan to the oven and roast for 10 minutes more. Transfer the peppers to individual serving plates, sprinkle with grated Parmesan and garnish each plate with a few salad leaves and fresh basil sprigs. Serve warm.

Cook's Tip
Shelled scallops are available from most fishmongers and supermarkets with fresh fish counters. Remember, never cook scallops for longer than the time stated in the recipe or they will become tough and rubbery.

Mozzarella & Tomato Skewers

Stacks of flavour – layers of oven-baked mozzarella, tangy tomatoes, herby basil and bread. These colourful kebabs will be popular with adults and children alike.

Serves 4
12 slices white country bread, each about 1cm/½in thick
45ml/3 tbsp olive oil

225g/8oz mozzarella cheese, cut into 5mm/¼in slices
3 ripe plum tomatoes, cut into 5mm/¼in slices
15g/½oz/½ cup fresh basil leaves, plus extra to garnish
salt and ground black pepper
30ml/2 tbsp chopped fresh flat leaf parsley, to garnish

1 Preheat the oven to 220°C/425°F/ Gas 7. Trim the crusts from the bread and cut each slice into four equal squares. Arrange on a baking sheet and brush with half the olive oil. Bake for 3–5 minutes, until the squares are a pale golden colour.

2 Remove the bread squares from the oven and place them on a chopping board with the sliced mozzarella and tomatoes and the fresh basil leaves.

3 Make 16 stacks, each starting with a square of bread, then a slice of mozzarella topped with a slice of tomato and a basil leaf. Sprinkle with salt and pepper, then repeat, ending with a piece of bread. Push a skewer through each stack and place on the baking sheet.

4 Drizzle the kebabs with the remaining oil and bake for 10–15 minutes, until the cheese begins to melt. Garnish with basil and flat leaf parsley.

> **Cook's Tips**
> • If you use wooden skewers, soak them in water first, to prevent them from scorching during the cooking time.
> • The bread for these skewers needs to be quite robust, so don't be tempted to use slices from a soft white sandwich loaf.

Vegetable Wraps with Mozzarella

A barbecue with an adjustable grill is ideal for this recipe, as the wraps need to be seared at the end.

Serves 6
2 large yellow courgettes (zucchini), each about 19cm/7½in long
45ml/3 tbsp olive oil

250g/9oz baby leaf spinach
250g/9oz mini mozzarella balls

For the dressing
2 whole, unpeeled garlic cloves
30ml/2 tbsp white wine vinegar
30ml/2 tbsp olive oil
15ml/1 tbsp extra virgin olive oil
45ml/3 tbsp walnut oil
salt and ground black pepper

1 Prepare the barbecue or preheat the grill (broiler). To make the dressing, place the garlic in a small pan with water to cover. Bring to the boil, lower the heat and simmer for 5 minutes. Drain. When cool, pop the garlic cloves out of their skins and crush to a smooth paste with a little salt. Scrape into a bowl and add the vinegar. Whisk in the oils and season to taste.

2 Slice each courgette lengthways into six or more broad strips, about 3mm/⅛in thick. Lay them on a tray. Set aside 5ml/ 1 tsp of the oil and brush the rest over the courgettes to coat.

3 Place a wok over a high heat. When it starts to smoke, add the reserved oil and stir-fry the spinach for 30 seconds, or until just wilted. Strain well, then pat the leaves dry with kitchen paper. Tear or slice the mozzarella balls in half and drain.

4 Lay the courgettes on a heated, lightly oiled rack. Cook on one side only for 2–3 minutes, or until striped golden. As each strip cooks, return it to the tray, cooked-side up.

5 Place small heaps of spinach toward one end of each courgette strip. Lay two pieces of mozzarella on each pile of spinach. Season well. Transfer back to the barbecue rack and cook for about 2 minutes, or until the underside of each has golden stripes. When the cheese starts to melt, fold the courgette over the filling to make a wrap. Lift off carefully and drain on kitchen paper. Serve drizzled with the dressing.

Energy 1692Kcal/7107kJ; Fat 85.9g; Saturated Fat 36g; Carbohydrate 169.4g; Fibre 8.6g

Energy 275Kcal/1133kJ; Fat 24g; Saturated Fat 7.8g; Carbohydrate 2.9g; Fibre 2.1g

Polenta Chips

Here polenta, the popular grain of northern Italy, is flavoured with fresh Parmesan and transformed into tasty little nibbles. The batons are delicious teamed up with a fresh-tasting tomato dip such as Peperonata.

Makes about 80
375g/13oz/3¼ cups quick cook polenta
10ml/2 tsp salt, plus extra
150g/5oz/1½ cups freshly grated Parmesan cheese
90g/3½oz/7 tbsp butter
10ml/2 tsp cracked black pepper
olive oil, for brushing

1 Put 1.5 litres/2½ pints/6¼ cups water into a large heavy pan and bring to the boil. Reduce the heat, add the salt and pour in the polenta in a steady stream, stirring constantly with a wooden spoon. Cook over low heat for about 5 minutes, stirring, until the mixture thickens and comes away from the sides of the pan.

2 Remove the pan from the heat and add the Parmesan cheese and butter. Season to taste. Stir well, until the mixture is smooth. Pour on to a smooth surface, such as a marble slab or a baking sheet.

3 Using a metal spatula, spread out the polenta to a thickness of 2cm/¾in and shape into a rectangle. Leave to stand for at least 30 minutes until cold. Meanwhile, preheat the oven to 200°C/400°F/Gas 6 and lightly oil two or three baking sheets.

4 Cut the polenta slab in half, then carefully cut into even-size strips. Bake for 40–50 minutes, or until dark golden brown and crunchy, turning from time to time. Serve warm.

Cook's Tip
For an easy tomato dip, skin, seed and chop 4 ripe tomatoes. Place in a bowl with a handful of chopped fresh parsley, then stir in 5ml/1 tsp balsamic vinegar and 15ml/1 tbsp extra virgin olive oil. Season well with salt and pepper.

Suppli al Telefono

Bite into these fritters and the cheese inside is drawn out in strings, like telephone wires – hence the name.

Makes 20
45ml/3 tbsp finely chopped fresh parsley

675g/1½lb/6 cups cooked risotto
200g/7oz mozzarella cheese, cut into 20 cubes
2 eggs, beaten
150g/5oz/1¼ cups dried breadcrumbs
oil, for deep-frying
fresh herbs, to garnish

1 Stir the parsley into the risotto, cool, then chill until firm. Divide into 20 portions and shape each into a ball. Press a cube of cheese in each ball and reshape neatly. Coat the rice balls in the beaten egg, then the breadcrumbs, and chill again for 30 minutes to set the coating.

2 Heat the oil for deep-frying to 180°C/350°F. Cook about 5 fritters at a time, for 3–5 minutes, until golden brown and crisp. Drain on kitchen paper and keep warm on an uncovered plate to keep the coating crisp. Serve garnished with fresh herbs.

Crostini with Cheese

These cheese-topped treats will disappear in a flash!

Serves 6
4–6 slices day-old white or brown bread

75g/3oz thinly sliced cheese (Fontina or Gruyère)
anchovy fillets
strips of red (bell) pepper
ground black pepper
butter, for greasing

1 Cut the bread into small squares, triangles or circles. Preheat the oven to 190°C/375°/Gas 5. Butter a baking sheet.

2 Place a slice of cheese on each piece of bread, cutting it to fit. Cut the anchovies and pepper strips into small shapes and place on top. Grind a little pepper over each. Transfer to the baking sheet and bake for 10 minutes, until the cheese has melted.

For 80 Energy 2728Kcal/11348kJ; Fat 135.4g; Saturated Fat 77.6g; Carbohydrate 275g; Fibre 8.3g

Top Energy 138Kcal/578kJ; Fat 7g; Saturated Fat 1.9g; Carbohydrate 14.8g; Fibre 0.8g
Above Energy 151Kcal/632kJ; Fat 9g; Saturated Fat 5.6g; Carbohydrate 8.5g; Fibre 0.7g

Cherry Tomatoes with Pesto

Little tomatoes stuffed with a delicious basil and pine nut filling make a colourful antipasto or a delicious bite to accompany drinks. Serve with crisp grissini for a good contrast in textures.

Serves 8–10
450g/1lb cherry tomatoes (about 36 in total)

For the pesto
90g/3½oz/1 cup fresh basil
3–4 garlic cloves
60ml/4 tbsp pine nuts
5ml/1 tsp salt, plus extra to taste
105ml/7 tbsp olive oil
*45ml/3 tbsp freshly grated
    Parmesan cheese*
*90ml/6 tbsp freshly grated
    Pecorino cheese*
ground black pepper

1 Wash the tomatoes. Using a sharp knife, slice off the top from each tomato and carefully scoop out the seeds with a small spoon or melon baller.

2 Place the basil, garlic, pine nuts, salt and olive oil in a blender or food processor and process until smooth. Transfer the contents to a bowl with a rubber spatula.

3 Fold in the grated cheeses. Season with pepper, and more salt if necessary.

4 Use a small spoon to fill each tomato with a little pesto. This dish is at its best if chilled for about an hour before serving.

Cook's Tip
When fresh basil is plentiful, it is a good idea to make lots of pesto and freeze it in batches. Transfer the mixture to a freezerproof container at the end of step 2 and freeze. To use from frozen, allow the pesto to thaw, then proceed from step 3.

Variation
If Pecorino cheese is not available, you can replace it with more Parmesan instead. The flavour will be just as good.

Aubergine, Garlic & Pepper Pâté

Serve this Italian-style chunky, garlicky pâté of smoky baked aubergine and red peppers on a bed of herby salad, accompanied by crispbreads.

Serves 4
3 aubergines (eggplants)
2 red (bell) peppers
5 garlic cloves
*7.5ml/1½ tsp pink peppercorns
    in brine, drained and crushed*
*30ml/2 tbsp chopped
    fresh coriander (cilantro)*

1 Preheat the oven to 200°C/400°F/Gas 6. Arrange the whole aubergines, peppers and garlic cloves on a baking sheet and place in the oven. After 10 minutes remove the garlic cloves. Turn over the aubergines and peppers and return to the oven.

2 Carefully remove the garlic cloves from their skins and place them in the bowl of a blender or food processor.

3 After a further 20 minutes remove the blistered and charred peppers from the oven and place in a plastic bag. Leave to cool.

4 After a further 10 minutes remove the aubergines from the oven. Split in half and scoop the flesh into a sieve placed over a bowl. Discard the skin. Press the flesh with a spoon to remove the bitter juices. Discard the juices.

5 Add the aubergine flesh to the garlic in the blender or food processor and blend until smooth. Place in a large bowl.

6 Peel and chop the red peppers and stir into the aubergine mixture. Mix in the peppercorns and fresh coriander, spoon into a serving dish and serve at once.

Cook's Tip
Baking the garlic in its skin gives the cloves a mellower flavour, and ensures that they do not overpower the other ingredients in the dish and make the pâté too pungent.

Cannellini Bean Purée with Grilled Chicory

Cannellini beans are often used in the cooking of Tuscany and here they are used to create a lightweight antipasto dish. The slightly bitter flavours of the salad leaves make a wonderful marriage with the creamy bean purée, creating a dish that is healthy and low in fat.

Serves 4

400g/14oz can cannellini beans
45ml/3 tbsp low-fat fromage frais
finely grated rind and juice of 1
    large orange
15ml/1 tbsp finely chopped fresh
    rosemary
4 heads chicory (Belgian endive)
2 heads radicchio
10ml/2 tsp walnut oil
longer shreds of orange rind, to
    garnish (optional)

1 Drain the cannellini beans, then rinse well, and drain them again. Purée the beans in a blender or food processor with the fromage frais, orange rind and juice and chopped rosemary. Set aside.

2 Using a sharp knife, cut the heads of chicory in half along the length. Cut each radicchio head lengthways into eight wedges. Preheat the grill (broiler).

3 Lay out the chicory and radicchio on a baking tray and brush lightly with the walnut oil. Grill (broil) for 2–3 minutes. Arrange on individual plates with the bean purée and scatter over the orange shreds to garnish, if using.

Cook's Tip
To bring out the flavour of the walnut oil, sprinkle the dish with chopped, shelled walnuts as well as orange rind.

Variation
Other suitable pulses to use are haricot, mung or broad beans.

Energy 109Kcal/460kJ; Fat 2.5g; Saturated Fat 0.3g; Carbohydrate 15.8g; Fibre 5.6g

Red & Yellow Pepper Dips with Crudités

Make one or both of these colourful Italian vegetable dips – if you have time to make both, they look spectacular together and are both low-fat too!

Serves 6

2 red (bell) peppers, halved
    and seeded
2 yellow (bell) peppers, halved
    and seeded
2 garlic cloves
30ml/2 tbsp lemon juice
20ml/4 tsp olive oil
50g/2oz/1 cup fresh white
    breadcrumbs
salt and ground black pepper
prepared fresh vegetables, such
    as celery, cucumber and carrot
    sticks, whole cherry tomatoes
    and button mushrooms,
    to serve

1 Place the peppers in two separate pans with a peeled clove of garlic. Add just enough water to cover.

2 Bring to the boil, then cover and simmer for 15 minutes until tender. Drain, cool, then purée the peppers separately in a blender or food processor, adding half the lemon juice and olive oil to each purée.

3 Stir half the breadcrumbs into each purée and season to taste with salt and pepper. Spoon the dips into serving dishes.

4 Garnish with a grinding of black pepper and serve with a selection of fresh vegetables for dipping.

Aubergine Sunflower Pâté

This delicious grilled aubergine (eggplant) pâté, flavoured with sunflower seeds and fresh herbs, makes a lovely summery dish.

Serves 4

1 large aubergine (eggplant)
1 garlic clove, crushed
15ml/1 tbsp lemon juice
30ml/2 tbsp sunflower seeds
45ml/3 tbsp low-fat natural
    (plain) yogurt
handful of fresh coriander
    (cilantro) or parsley, plus extra
    to garnish
ground black pepper
prepared fresh vegetable sticks,
    such as celery, cucumber and
    carrot, to serve

1 Cut the aubergine in half and place, cut-side down, on a baking sheet. Place under a hot grill (broiler) for 15–20 minutes, until the skin is blackened and the flesh is soft.

2 Leave for a few minutes to cool slightly, then scoop the flesh into a blender or food processor. Discard the skin. Add the garlic, lemon juice, sunflower seeds and yogurt to the processor. Blend together until smooth.

3 Roughly chop the fresh coriander or parsley and mix into the aubergine mixture. Season with black pepper, then spoon into a serving dish. Garnish with coriander or parsley and serve with vegetable sticks.

Top Energy 152Kcal/634kJ; Fat 8g; Saturated Fat 1.2g; Carbohydrate 18.6g; Fibre 4.4g
Above Energy 66Kcal/273kJ; Fat 4g; Saturated Fat 0.5g; Carbohydrate 4g; Fibre 2.6g

Ricotta & Herb Fritters

These melt-in-the-mouth herby fritters are particularly good served with a tangy tomato sauce.

Serves 4

250g/9oz/generous I cup ricotta cheese
I large (US extra large) egg, beaten
90ml/6 tbsp self-raising (self-rising) flour
90ml/6 tbsp milk
I bunch spring onions (scallions), finely sliced
30ml/2 tbsp chopped fresh coriander (cilantro)
sunflower oil, for shallow frying
salt and ground black pepper
200ml/7fl oz/scant I cup crème fraîche, to serve
fresh coriander (cilantro) sprigs and lemon or lime wedges, to garnish

I Beat the ricotta until smooth, then beat in the egg and flour, followed by the milk to make a thick batter. Beat in the spring onions and coriander. Season well with pepper and a little salt.

2 Heat a little oil in a non-stick frying pan over medium heat. Add spoonfuls of the mixture to make fritters about 7.5cm/3in across and fry for about 4–5 minutes each side, or until set and browned. The mixture makes 12 fritters.

3 Serve the fritters immediately, with a dollop of crème fraîche. Garnish with coriander sprigs and lime wedges.

Cook's Tip

For an easy tomato sauce accompaniment, heat 30ml/2 tbsp in a pan and fry a finely chopped onion until softened. Add I crushed garlic clove, cook for I minute, stirring, then stir in a large can of chopped tomatoes. Add a handful of chopped basil, season with salt and pepper and cook for 20 minutes.

Variation

The fritters are also good with thinly sliced smoked salmon.

Roast Pepper Terrine

This terrine is perfect for a dinner party because it tastes better if made ahead. Prepare the salsa on the day of serving. Serve with hot Italian bread.

Serves 8

8 (bell) peppers (red, yellow and orange)
675 g/1½ lb/3 cups mascarpone cheese
3 eggs, separated
30 ml/2 tbsp roughly chopped fresh flat leaf parsley
30 ml/2 tbsp shredded fresh basil
I large garlic clove, roughly chopped
salt and ground black pepper

For the salsa

2 red, yellow or orange (bell) peppers, seeded and roughly chopped
I large garlic clove, chopped
30 ml/2 tbsp extra virgin olive oil
10 ml/2 tsp balsamic vinegar
a few basil sprigs
pinch of sugar

I Place the peppers under a hot grill (broiler) for 8–10 minutes, turning them frequently, until the skins are charred and blistered on all sides. Put the hot peppers in plastic bags, seal and leave until cold.

2 Rub off the pepper skins under cold running water. Break open the flesh and rub out the cores and seeds. Drain the peppers, dry them on kitchen paper, then cut seven of them lengthways into thin, even-size strips. Reserve the remaining pepper for the salsa.

3 Put the mascarpone cheese in a bowl with the egg yolks, herbs and half the garlic. Add salt and pepper to taste. Beat well. In a separate bowl, whisk the egg whites to a soft peak, then fold into the cheese mixture until evenly incorporated.

4 Preheat the oven to 180°C/350°F/Gas 4. Line the base of a lightly oiled 900g/2lb loaf tin (pan). Put one-third of the cheese mixture in the tin and spread level. Arrange half the pepper strips on top in an even layer. Repeat until all the cheese and peppers are used.

5 Cover the tin with foil and place in a roasting pan. Pour in boiling water to come halfway up the sides of the pan. Bake for I hour. Leave the terrine to cool in the water bath, then lift out and chill overnight.

6 A few hours before serving, make the salsa. Place the remaining roast pepper and fresh peppers in a food processor. Add the garlic, oil and vinegar. Set aside a few basil leaves for garnishing and add the rest to the processor. Process until finely chopped. Turn into a bowl, then add the sugar and salt and pepper to taste, and mix. Cover and chill until ready to serve.

7 Turn out the terrine, peel off the paper and slice thickly. Garnish with the basil leaves and serve cold, with the salsa.

Variation

For a low-fat version, use ricotta cheese instead of mascarpone.

Roast Garlic with Goat's Cheese Pâté

This pâté is particularly good made with the new season's walnuts, sometimes known as "wet" walnuts, which are available in the early autumn.

Serves 4
4 large garlic bulbs
4 fresh rosemary sprigs
8 fresh thyme sprigs
60ml/4 tbsp olive oil
4–8 slices sourdough bread

sea salt and ground black pepper
shelled walnuts and fresh thyme
  sprigs, to garnish

For the pâté
200g/7oz/scant 1 cup soft
  goat's cheese
5ml/1 tsp finely chopped fresh
  thyme
15ml/1 tbsp chopped fresh
  parsley
50g/2oz/¹/₃ cup chopped walnuts
15ml/1 tbsp walnut oil (optional)

1 Preheat the oven to 180°C/350°F/Gas 4. Strip the papery skin from the garlic bulbs and place in an ovenproof dish large enough to hold them snugly. Tuck in the rosemary and thyme sprigs, drizzle the olive oil over and season with a little sea salt and plenty of ground black pepper.

2 Cover the garlic tightly with foil and bake in the oven for 50–60 minutes, opening the parcel and basting once halfway through the cooking time. Set aside and leave to cool.

3 Preheat the grill (broiler). To make the pâté, cream the cheese with the thyme, parsley and walnuts. Beat in 15ml/1 tbsp of the cooking oil from the garlic and season to taste with black pepper. Transfer to a serving bowl and chill until ready to serve.

4 Brush the bread slices on one side with the remaining cooking oil from the garlic, then grill (broil) until lightly toasted.

5 Divide the pâté among four individual plates, drizzle with walnut oil, if using, and sprinkle with black pepper. Add some garlic to each plate, garnish with shelled walnuts and thyme sprigs, then serve with toasted bread.

Mozzarella in Carozza with Fresh Tomato Dip

The name of this delectable Italian snack translates as cheese "in a carriage". It contains mozzarella and is dipped in beaten egg and fried like French toast.

Serves 4
200g/7oz mozzarella cheese,
  finely sliced
8 thin slices of bread, crusts
  removed
a little dried oregano
30ml/2 tbsp freshly grated
  Parmesan cheese

3 eggs, beaten
olive oil, for frying
salt and ground black pepper
fresh herbs, to garnish

For the dip
4 ripe plum tomatoes, peeled,
  seeded and finely chopped
15ml/1 tbsp chopped fresh
  parsley
5ml/1 tsp balsamic vinegar
15ml/1 tbsp extra virgin olive oil

1 Arrange the mozzarella on 4 slices of the bread. Season with salt and pepper and sprinkle with a little oregano and Parmesan. Top with the other bread slices and press them firmly together.

2 Pour the beaten eggs into a large shallow dish and season with salt and pepper.

3 Add the cheese sandwiches, two at a time, pressing them into the egg with a spatula until they are well coated. Repeat with the remaining sandwiches, then leave them to stand for 10 minutes.

4 To make the dip, put the chopped tomatoes in a bowl and add the parsley. Stir in the vinegar and the extra virgin olive oil. Season well with salt and pepper and set aside.

5 Heat oil for frying to a depth of 5mm/¼in in a large frying pan. Carefully add the sandwiches in batches and cook for about 2 minutes on each side, until golden and crisp. Drain well. Cut in half, garnish with herbs and serve with the dip.

Energy 371Kcal/1534kJ; Fat 32.7g; Saturated Fat 11.3g; Carbohydrate 5.1g; Fibre 1.7g

Energy 472Kcal/1968kJ; Fat 31.7g; Saturated Fat 11.6g; Carbohydrate 27g; Fibre 1.5g

Gratin of Mussels with Pesto

This is the perfect starter for serving when time is short, as both the pesto and the mussels can be prepared in advance, and the dish assembled and cooked at the last minute.

Serves 4
36 large fresh mussels, scrubbed
   and bearded
105ml/7 tbsp dry white wine
60ml/4 tbsp finely chopped fresh
   flat leaf parsley
1 garlic clove, finely chopped

30ml/2 tbsp fresh white
   breadcrumbs
60ml/4 tbsp olive oil
chopped fresh basil, to garnish

For the pesto
2 fat garlic cloves, chopped
2.5ml/½ tsp coarse salt
100g/3¾ oz/3 cups basil leaves
25g/1oz/⅓ cup pine nuts,
   chopped
50g/2oz/⅔ cup freshly grated
   Parmesan cheese
120ml/4fl oz/½ cup extra virgin
   olive oil

1 Put the mussels in a pan with the wine, clamp on the lid and shake over high heat for 3–4 minutes, until the mussels have opened. Discard any which remain closed.

2 As soon as the mussels are cool enough to handle, strain the cooking liquid and keep it for another recipe. Discard the empty half-shells. Arrange the mussels in their half-shells in a single layer in four individual gratin dishes. Cover and set aside.

3 To make the pesto, put the garlic and salt in a mortar and pound to a purée with a pestle. Add the basil leaves and pine nuts and crush to a thick paste. Work in the Parmesan, then beat in enough olive oil, a drop at a time, to make a smooth and creamy paste. This can also be made in a food processor.

4 Spoon the pesto over the mussels in the gratin dishes. Mix together the parsley, garlic and breadcrumbs, then sprinkle over the mussels. Drizzle with the oil.

5 Preheat the grill (broiler) to high. Stand the dishes on a baking sheet and grill (broil) for 3 minutes. Garnish with chopped basil.

Energy 454Kcal/1876kJ; Fat 40.4g; Saturated Fat 7.4g; Carbohydrate 7.2g; Fibre 2g

Prawn & Vegetable Crostini

Use bottled carciofini (tiny artichoke hearts preserved in olive oil) available from delicatessens for this starter.

Serves 4
450g/1lb whole cooked prawns,
   in the shell
4 thick slices of ciabatta, cut
   diagonally across

3 garlic cloves, peeled and
   2 halved lengthways
60ml/4 tbsp olive oil
200g/7oz/2 cups small button
   mushrooms, trimmed
12 bottled carciofin, drained
60ml/4 tbsp chopped flat
   leaf parsley
salt and ground black pepper

1 Peel the prawns and remove the heads. Rub the ciabatta slices on both sides with the cut sides of the halved garlic cloves, drizzle with a little of the olive oil and toast in the oven or grill (broil) until lightly browned. Keep hot.

2 Finely chop the remaining peeled garlic. Heat the remaining olive oil in a pan and gently fry the garlic until golden, but do not allow it to brown.

3 Add the mushrooms and stir to coat with oil. Season with salt and pepper and sauté for about 2–3 minutes. Gently stir in the drained carciofini, then add the chopped flat leaf parsley.

4 Season again with salt and pepper, then stir in the prawns and sauté briefly to warm through. Pile the prawn mixture on to the ciabatta, pour over any remaining cooking juices from the pan and serve immediately.

> **Cook's Tips**
> • Don't be tempted to use thawed frozen prawns, especially those that have been peeled; freshly cooked prawns in their shells are infinitely nicer.
> • For a vegetarian version, simply leave out the prawns, reduce the chopped garlic to 2 cloves and add some freshly grated Parmesan cheese when stirring in the carciofini.

Energy 223Kcal/933kJ; Fat 12.8g; Saturated Fat 1.9g; Carbohydrate 14g; Fibre 2.3g

Crostini with Two Toppings

This popular Italian antipasto was originally a way of using up leftovers and the overabundance of tomatoes from the harvest. Plum tomatoes are traditionally used, but cherry tomatoes make a good alternative.

Serves 4
1 ciabatta loaf or French bread

For the tomato and anchovy topping
400g/14oz can or bottled Italian roasted red (bell) peppers and whole tomatoes
50g/2oz can anchovy fillets
extra virgin olive oil, for drizzling

15–30ml/1–2 tbsp balsamic vinegar
1 garlic clove, peeled and halved
red pesto, for brushing
30ml/2 tbsp chopped fresh chives, oregano or sage, to garnish
15ml/1 tbsp capers, to garnish

For the pesto and mozzarella topping
green pesto sauce, for brushing
120ml/4fl oz/½ cup thick home-made or bottled tomato sauce or pizza topping
115g/4oz good quality mozzarella cheese, cut into thin slices
2–3 ripe plum tomatoes, seeded and cut into strips
fresh basil leaves, to garnish

1 Cut the ciabatta or French bread into 16 slices. Toast until crisp and golden on both sides. Cool on a wire rack.

2 For the tomato and anchovy topping, drain the tomatoes and peppers and dry with kitchen paper. Cut into 1cm/½in strips and place in a shallow dish.

3 Rinse and dry the anchovy fillets and add to the peppers and tomatoes. Drizzle with olive oil and sprinkle with the vinegar.

4 Rub 8 pieces of toast with the cut edge of the clove and brush with a little red pesto. Arrange the tomato mixture decoratively on the toast and sprinkle with herbs and capers.

5 For the pesto and mozzarella topping, brush the remaining toast with the green pesto and spoon on some tomato sauce. Arrange a slice of mozzarella on each and cover with the tomato strips. Garnish with basil leaves.

Energy 110Kcal/464kJ; Fat 3.3g; Saturated Fat 1.4g; Carbohydrate 15.8g; Fibre 1.3g

Marinated Anchovies

These tiny fish tend to lose their freshness very quickly so marinating them in garlic and lemon juice is the perfect way to enjoy them. This is probably the simplest way of preparing these fish as it requires no cooking.

Serves 4
225g/8oz fresh anchovies, heads and tails removed, and split open along the belly
juice of 3 lemons
30ml/2 tbsp extra virgin olive oil
2 garlic cloves, finely chopped
flaked sea salt

1 Turn the anchovies on to their bellies, and press down along their spine with your thumb. Using the tip of a small knife, carefully remove the backbones from the fish, and arrange the anchovies skin-side down in a single layer on a large plate.

2 Squeeze two-thirds of the lemon juice over the fish and sprinkle them with the salt. Cover and leave to stand for at least 1 hour, up to 24 hours, basting occasionally with the juices, until the flesh is white and no longer translucent.

3 Transfer the anchovies to a serving plate and drizzle with the olive oil and the remaining lemon juice. Scatter the fish with the chopped garlic, then cover with clear film (plastic wrap) and chill until ready to serve.

Crostini with Mussels or Clams

To make the most of this recipe from Genoa, use the freshest possible seafood.

Makes 16
16 large fresh mussels or clams, in their shells

4 large slices bread, 2.5cm/1in thick
40g/1½ oz/3 tbsp butter
30ml/2 tbsp chopped fresh parsley
1 shallot, very finely chopped
olive oil, for brushing
lemon sections, to serve

1 Wash the mussels or clams well in several changes of water. Cut the beards off the mussels. Place the shellfish in a pan with a cupful of water and heat until the shells open. (Discard any that do not open.) As soon as they open, lift the molluscs out of the pan. Spoon out of their shells, and set aside. Preheat the oven to 190°C/375°F/Gas 5.

2 Cut the crusts off the bread. Cut each slice into quarters. Scoop out a hollow from the top of each piece, large enough to hold a mussel or clam. Do not cut through to the bottom.

3 Break the scooped-out bread into crumbs, and reserve. In a small frying pan, heat the butter. Cook the parsley with the shallot and the breadcrumbs until the shallot softens.

4 Brush each piece of bread with olive oil. Place one mussel or clam in each hollow. Spoon a small amount of the parsley and shallot mixture on to each mollusc. Place on an oiled baking sheet. Bake for 10 minutes. Serve at once, while still hot, with the lemon sections.

Top Energy 108Kcal/449kJ; Fat 5.6g; Saturated Fat 0.9g; Carbohydrate 0g; Fibre 0g
Above Energy 49Kcal/207kJ; Fat 2.7g; Saturated Fat 1.5g; Carbohydrate 4.6g; Fibre 0.3g

Tuna in Rolled Red Peppers

This savoury combination originated in southern Italy. Grilled red peppers have a sweet, smoky taste that goes particularly well with fish.

Serves 4–6
3 large red (bell) peppers
200g/7oz can tuna fish, drained

30ml/2 tbsp fresh lemon juice
45ml/3 tbsp olive oil
6 green or black olives, pitted and chopped
30ml/2 tbsp chopped fresh parsley
1 garlic clove, finely chopped
1 medium celery stick, very finely chopped
salt and ground black pepper

1 Place the peppers under a hot grill (broiler), turning occasionally, until they are black and blistered on all sides. Remove from the heat and place in a plastic bag. Leave for 5 minutes, and then remove the skins. Cut the peppers into quarters, and remove the core and seeds.

2 Meanwhile, flake the tuna and combine with the lemon juice and oil. Stir in the remaining ingredients. Season to taste.

3 Lay the pepper segments out flat, skin-side down. Spread the tuna mixture evenly over them, then roll the peppers up. Place the pepper rolls in the refrigerator for at least 1 hour. Just before serving, cut each roll in half with a sharp knife.

Fried Whitebait with Tomato Sauce

Fresh, crispy whitebait is served with a slightly spicy tomato sauce for a sensational combination of flavours and textures.

Serves 4
225g/8oz whitebait, thawed if frozen
30ml/2 tbsp seasoned flour
60ml/4 tbsp olive oil
60ml/4 tbsp vegetable oil

For the sauce
1 shallot, finely chopped
2 garlic cloves, finely chopped
4 ripe tomatoes, roughly chopped
1 small red chilli, seeded and finely chopped
30ml/2 tbsp olive oil
60ml/4 tbsp sweet sherry
30–45ml/2–3 tbsp chopped fresh herbs, such as basil, parsley or coriander (cilantro)
25g/1oz/1/2 cup fresh white breadcrumbs
salt and ground black pepper

1 To make the sauce, place the shallot, garlic, tomatoes, chilli and oil in a pan. Cover and cook gently for 10 minutes.

2 Pour in the sherry and add salt and pepper to taste. Stir in the herbs, then add the breadcrumbs. Stir to mix, then cover and keep hot while the whitebait is being prepared.

3 Wash the whitebait, drain, then dust in the seasoned flour. Heat both oils together in a frying pan and cook the fish in batches until crisp and golden. Drain on kitchen paper and keep warm in a low oven.

4 Serve the whitebait with the tomato sauce in a separate bowl.

Stuffed Mussels

Simple Italian cooking at its best, this tasty appetizer is a speciality of southern Italy. Always use the freshest seafood available for the maximum flavour.

Serves 4
675g/1½lb large fresh mussels in their shells

75g/3oz/1/3 cup unsalted butter, at room temperature
25g/1oz/1/2 cup dry breadcrumbs
2 garlic cloves, finely chopped
45ml/3 tbsp chopped fresh parsley
25g/1oz/1/4 cup freshly grated Parmesan cheese
salt and ground black pepper

1 Scrub the mussels well under cold running water, cutting off the beard with a small knife. Preheat the oven to 230°C/450°F/Gas 8.

2 Place the mussels with a cupful of water in a large pan over medium heat. As soon as they open, lift them out one by one. Remove and discard the empty half shells, leaving the meat in the other half. (Discard any mussels that do not open.)

3 Combine all the remaining ingredients in a small bowl. Blend well. Place in a small pan and heat gently until the stuffing mixture begins to soften.

4 Arrange the mussel halves on a baking sheet. Spoon a small amount of the stuffing over each mussel. Bake for about 7 minutes, until golden. Serve hot or at room temperature.

Cook's Tip
When cleaning the mussels, make sure you discard any with cracked shells and any open ones that do not close after a tap.

Variation
This dish can be made equally well with fresh clams.

Top Energy 130Kcal/541kJ; Fat 8.3g; Saturated Fat 1.3g; Carbohydrate 6.3g; Fibre 1.8g
Above Energy 1630Kcal/6767kJ; Fat 131g; Saturated Fat 13.3g; Carbohydrate 50g; Fibre 6.1g

Energy 287Kcal/1203kJ; Fat 16g; Saturated Fat 9.3g; Carbohydrate 19.5g; Fibre 0.6g

Crispy Fish Balls

You can use any white fish such as cod or haddock to make these divine, crispy balls. Cod, haddock and monkfish fillets all work extremely well.

Serves 4
I egg
a pinch of saffron threads
2 garlic cloves, roughly chopped
45ml/3 tbsp fresh parsley leaves
225g/8oz white fish, skinned, boned and cubed
75g/3oz white bread, crusts removed
60ml/4 tbsp seasoned flour
vegetable oil, for frying
salt and ground black pepper
lemon wedges, to serve

I Beat together the egg and saffron threads in a cup, then set aside for 5 minutes.

2 In a food processor, whizz together the garlic and parsley until finely chopped. Add the fish and bread and whizz until well blended. Scrape the fish mixture into a bowl and stir in the egg and saffron. Season with plenty of salt and pepper.

3 Shape the mixture into 24 small balls with your hands. Spread out the seasoned flour in a shallow dish and add the fish balls. Gently shake the dish to coat the fish balls evenly.

4 Heat the oil in a deep frying pan. Fry the fish balls, in batches if necessary, until crisp and golden, shaking the pan to keep them moving and prevent them from sticking. Remove with a slotted spoon and drain thoroughly on kitchen paper. Serve immediately with lemon wedges.

Cook's Tip
These fish balls are delicious as a light appetizer, served with a refreshing tomato and basil sauce. They're also good as an canapé with drinks – serve them with a small bowl of plain or garlic-flavoured mayonnaise, such as aioli and offer cocktail sticks for spearing the fish balls, to make dipping them easier.

Hard-boiled Eggs with Tuna Sauce

The combination of hard-boiled eggs with a tasty tuna mayonnaise makes a nourishing first course that is quick and easy to prepare.

Serves 6
6 large (US extra large) eggs
200g/7oz can tuna in olive oil
3 anchovy fillets
15ml/1 tbsp capers, drained
30ml/2 tbsp fresh lemon juice
60ml/4 tbsp olive oil
salt and ground black pepper
capers and anchovy fillets, to garnish (optional)

For the mayonnaise
I egg yolk, at room temperature
5ml/1 tsp Dijon mustard
5ml/1 tsp white wine vinegar or fresh lemon juice
150ml/¼ pint/⅔ cup extra virgin olive oil

I Boil the eggs for 12–14 minutes. Drain under cold water. Peel carefully and set aside.

2 To make the mayonnaise, whisk the egg yolk, mustard and vinegar or lemon juice together in a small bowl. Whisk in the oil a few drops at a time, until 3 or 4 tbsps of oil have been incorporated. Pour in the remaining oil in a slow stream, whisking constantly.

3 Place the tuna with its oil, the anchovies, capers, lemon juice and olive oil in the bowl of a blender or food processor. Process until smooth.

4 Fold the tuna sauce into the mayonnaise. Season with black pepper, and extra salt if necessary. Chill for at least 1 hour.

5 To serve, cut the eggs in half lengthways. Arrange on a serving platter. Spoon on the sauce, and garnish with capers and anchovy fillets, if using. Serve chilled.

Variation
As an alternative finish to the eggs, try using steamed green asparagus tips instead of the anchovy fillets.

Prosciutto with Figs

The famous Italian cured ham, prosciutto, makes an excellent appetizer sliced thinly and served with fresh figs or melon.

Serves 4
12 paper-thin slices prosciutto
8 ripe green or black figs
crusty bread and unsalted butter,
*   to serve*

1 Arrange the slices of prosciutto on a serving plate.

2 Wipe the figs with a damp cloth. Cut them almost into quarters but do not cut all the way through the base. If the skins are tender, they may be eaten along with the inner fruit. If you prefer, you may peel each quarter carefully by pulling the peel gently away from the pulp.

3 Arrange the figs on top of the prosciutto. Serve with bread and unsalted butter.

Parmesan Tuiles

These lacy tuiles look very impressive and make splendid nibbles with drinks.

Makes 8–10
115g/4oz Parmesan cheese

1 Preheat the oven to 200°C/400°F/Gas 6. Line two baking sheets with baking parchment. Grate the cheese using a fine grater, pulling it down slowly to make long strands.

2 Spread the grated cheese in 7.5–9cm/3–3½in rounds on the baking parchment, forking it into shape. Do not spread the cheese too thickly; it should just cover the parchment. Bake for 5–7 minutes, or until bubbling and golden brown.

3 Leave the tuiles on the baking sheet for about 30 seconds and then, using a metal spatula, carefully transfer to a wire rack to cool completely. Alternatively, drape over a rolling pin to make a curved shape.

Top Energy 241Kcal/1024kJ; Fat 2.5g; Saturated Fat 0.3g; Carbohydrate 48.9g; Fibre 6.9g
Above Energy 48Kcal/199kJ; Fat 3g; Saturated Fat 2g; Carbohydrate 0g; Fibre 0g

Carpaccio with Rocket

A favourite antipasto, carpaccio is a fine dish of thinly sliced raw beef in lemon juice and olive oil. It is traditionally served with flakes of fresh Parmesan cheese. The key to success with this dish is to use very fresh meat of the best possible quality.

Serves 4
1 garlic clove, peeled and cut
*   in half*
1½ lemons
50ml/2fl oz/¼ cup extra virgin
*   olive oil*
2 bunches rocket (arugula)
4 very thin slices beef fillet or
*   top round*
115g/4oz/1 cup Parmesan
*   cheese, thinly shaved*
salt and ground black pepper

1 Rub a small bowl all over with the cut side of the garlic. Squeeze the lemons into the bowl. Whisk in the olive oil. Season with salt and pepper. Allow the sauce to stand for at least 15 minutes before using.

2 Carefully wash the rocket and tear off any thick stalks. Spin or pat dry. Arrange the rocket around the edge of a serving platter, or divide between 4 individual plates.

3 Place the beef in the centre of the platter, and pour on the sauce, spreading it evenly over the meat. Arrange the shaved Parmesan on top of the meat slices. Serve at once.

> **Cook's Tip**
> *Make sure you buy the meat from a reputable butcher. If you are cutting the meat yourself, cut it as thinly as possible.*

> **Variation**
> *If you are feeding a crowd, buy a whole piece of fillet, season it well and sear it on a hot ridged pan or a barbecue for a few minutes to give the meat a lovely smoky flavour.*

Energy 197Kcal/814kJ; Fat 16.8g; Saturated Fat 4.9g; Carbohydrate 0.4g; Fibre 0.5g

Roast Asparagus with Crispy Prosciutto

A marvellous combination of meltingly soft asparagus spears and crisply cooked Italian ham, this dish makes a simple yet delicious appetizer. Serve with chunks of Italian bread, such as ciabatta or foccacia.

Serves 4
350g/12oz fine asparagus
  spears, trimmed
30ml/2 tbsp olive oil
1 small handful fresh
  basil leaves
4 prosciutto slices
salt and ground black pepper

1 Preheat the oven to 190°C/375°F/Gas 5. Put the asparagus in a roasting pan and drizzle with olive oil.

2 Sprinkle over the basil and season with salt and ground black pepper. Gently stir to coat in the oil, then spread the asparagus in a single layer.

3 Lay the slices of prosciutto on top of the asparagus and cook for 10–15 minutes, or until the prosciutto is crisp and the asparagus is just tender. Serve immediately.

Cook's Tips
• *Choose tender, fine asparagus for this recipe, as it cooks through quickly in the oven without losing its flavour or texture.*
• *For the best flavour, it is probably best to get the prosciutto specially sliced for you at a delicatessen or at the cold meat counter of a supermarket. The ham needs to be cut thinly. If you buy more than you need, remember that it will dry out quite quickly – only keep for a few days in the refrigerator.*

Variation
Instead of roasting, steam the asparagus, drizzle with an olive oil and balsamic dressing and serve warm with cold prosciutto.

Chicken livers are heightened with a touch of Tuscan sweet wine in this classic starter from Florence.

Serves 4
75g/3oz fresh baby spinach
  leaves
75g/3oz lollo rosso leaves

75ml/5 tbsp olive oil
15ml/1 tbsp butter
225g/8 oz chicken livers, trimmed
  and thinly sliced
45ml/3 tbsp vin santo or sweet
  dessert wine
50–75 g/2–3 oz fresh Parmesan
  cheese, shaved into curls
salt and ground black pepper

1 Wash and dry the spinach and lollo rosso. Tear the leaves into a large bowl, season with salt and pepper to taste and toss gently to mix.

2 Heat 30 ml/2 tbsp of the oil with the butter in a large heavy frying pan. When foaming, add the chicken livers and toss over medium to high heat for 5 minutes, or until the livers are browned on the outside but still pink in the centre. Remove from the heat.

3 Remove the livers from the pan with a slotted spoon, drain them on kitchen paper, then place on top of the spinach.

4 Return the pan to medium heat, add the remaining oil and the vin santo and stir until sizzling.

5 Pour the hot dressing over the spinach and livers and toss to coat. Put the salad in a serving bowl and sprinkle over the Parmesan shavings. Serve at once.

Cook's Tips
• *This Florentine recipe uses vino santo, a sweet dessert wine from Tuscany, but this is not essential for the dish – any dessert wine will do, or a sweet or cream sherry.*
• *For speedy preparation, use a ready-prepared bag of mixed baby spinach, rocket (arugula) and watercress for the salad.*

Cannellini Bean & Cavolo Nero Soup

Bursting with authentic Italian flavour, this chunky soup from Tuscany is very quick and easy to make. Offer it as a substantial starter or a nourishing lunch dish, served with warmed ciabatta bread.

Serves 4
2 x 400g/14oz cans chopped
  tomatoes with herbs
250g/9oz cavolo nero leaves
400g/14oz can cannellini beans
60ml/4 tbsp extra virgin olive oil
salt and ground black pepper

1 Pour the tomatoes into a large pan and add a can of cold water. Season with salt and pepper and bring to the boil, then reduce the heat to a simmer.

2 Roughly shred the cavolo nero leaves and add them to the pan. Partially cover the pan and simmer gently for about 15 minutes, or until the cabbage is tender.

3 Drain the cannellini beans through a strainer, then rinse under cold running water. Add the beans to the pan and warm through for a few minutes. Check and adjust the seasoning, then ladle the soup into bowls, drizzle each one with a little olive oil and serve immediately.

Cook's Tips
• Cavolo nero is a very dark green cabbage from Tuscany and southern Italy. It has a delicious nutty flavour and adds an authentic taste to this traditional recipe. Cavolo nero is available in most large supermarkets, but if you can't find it, Savoy cabbage is a perfectly good substitute.
• Olive oil is traditionally drizzled into the soup to add flavour, but instead you could spoon a little green pesto into each bowl and add a sprinkling of Parmesan shavings.
• Toasted Italian bread, rubbed with garlic and drizzled with olive oil, makes a classic accompaniment.

Energy 225Kcal/941kJ; Fat 12.2g; Saturated Fat 1.9g; Carbohydrate 22.7g; Fibre 8g

Onion Soup

This warming winter soup comes from Umbria, central Italy, where it is sometimes thickened with beaten eggs and lots of grated Parmesan cheese. It is then served on top of hot toasted croûtes – rather like savoury scrambled eggs.

Serves 4
115g/4oz pancetta rashers, any
  rinds removed, roughly chopped
30ml/2 tbsp olive oil
15g/½oz/1 tbsp butter
675g/1½lb onions, thinly sliced
10ml/2 tsp sugar
about 1.2 litres/2 pints/5 cups
  chicken stock
350g/12oz ripe Italian plum
  tomatoes, peeled and
  roughly chopped
a few basil leaves, shredded
salt and ground black pepper
freshly grated Parmesan cheese,
  to serve

1 Put the chopped pancetta in a large pan and heat gently, stirring constantly, until the fat runs. Increase the heat to medium, add the oil, butter, onions and sugar and stir well to mix.

2 Half cover the pan and cook the onions gently for about 20 minutes, until golden. Stir frequently and lower the heat if necessary, to prevent sticking.

3 Add the stock, tomatoes and salt and pepper and bring to the boil, stirring. Lower the heat, half cover the pan and simmer, stirring occasionally, for about 30 minutes. Regularly check the consistency of the soup and add a little more stock or water if it is too thick.

4 Just before serving, stir in most of the basil and adjust the seasoning. Serve hot, garnished with the remaining shredded basil. Hand round the freshly grated Parmesan separately.

Cook's Tip
Look for Vidalia onions to make this soup. They are available at large supermarkets, and have a very sweet flavour and attractive yellowish flesh.

Energy 233Kcal/965kJ; Fat 16g; Saturated Fat 5.2g; Carbohydrate 16.2g; Fibre 3.3g

Tiny Pasta in Broth

This simple soup is ideal for a light supper served with ciabatta bread and also makes a delicious first course for an al fresco supper. Soup pasta is called pastini in Italian and is now widely available. Choose one shape or use a mixture of different types for an interesting result.

Serves 4
1.2 litres/2 pints/5 cups well-flavoured beef stock
75g/3oz/³⁄₄ cup dried tiny soup pasta
2 pieces bottled roasted red (bell) pepper, about 50g/2oz
coarsely shaved Parmesan cheese, to serve

1 Bring the beef stock to the boil in a large pan. Add seasoning to taste, then drop in the dried soup pasta. Stir well and bring the stock back to the boil.

2 Reduce the heat so that the soup simmers and cook for 7–8 minutes, until the pasta shapes are *al dente*, or tender but still firm to the bite.

3 Drain the pieces of roasted pepper and dice them finely. Place them in the base of four warmed soup plates. Taste the soup for seasoning before ladling it into the soup plates. Serve immediately, topped with shavings of Parmesan.

> **Cook's Tip**
> *There are many different pastini to choose from, including stellette (stars), anellini (tiny thin rounds), risoni (rice-shaped) and farfalline (little butterflies). You could also use the fine "angel hair" pasta, capellini, broken into smaller pieces.*

> **Variation**
> *Use fresh (bell) peppers instead of bottled: first roast them until charred, then remove the skins and seeds and dice.*

Cappelletti in Broth

This soup is traditionally served in northern Italy on Santo Stefano (St Stephen's Day, the day after Christmas) and on New Year's Day as a welcome light change from all the special celebration food. Cappelletti are little stuffed pasta shapes that resemble hats.

Serves 4
1.2 litres/2 pints/5 cups home-made chicken stock
90–115g/3¹⁄₂–4oz/1 cup fresh or dried cappelletti
about 45ml/3 tbsp finely chopped fresh flat leaf parsley (optional)
about 30ml/2 tbsp freshly grated Parmesan cheese
salt and ground black pepper

1 Pour the chicken stock into a large pan and bring to the boil. Add a little seasoning to taste, then drop in the pasta.

2 Stir well and bring back to the boil. Lower the heat to a simmer and cook until the pasta is *al dente*, or tender but still firm to the bite.

3 Swirl in the finely chopped fresh flat leaf parsley, if using, then taste and adjust the seasoning, if necessary.

4 Ladle into four warmed soup plates, then sprinkle with the freshly grated Parmesan cheese and serve immediately.

> **Cook's Tip**
> *This soup needs a well-flavoured stock as a base. If you don't have home-made stock use two 300g/11oz cans of condensed beef consommé, adding water as instructed. Alternatively, buy chilled commercial chicken stock.*

> **Variation**
> *Use other small filled pasta shapes such as tortellini, or for a very lightweight soup, simply use small, dried soup pasta. Use a meat stock if you prefer.*

Cream of Courgette Soup

The beauty of this soup is its delicate colour, rich and creamy texture and subtle taste. If you prefer a more pronounced cheese flavour, use Gorgonzola instead of Dolcelatte.

Serves 4–6

30ml/2 tbsp olive oil
15g/½oz/1 tbsp butter
1 onion, roughly chopped

900g/2lb courgettes (zucchini), trimmed and sliced
5ml/1 tsp dried oregano
about 600ml/1 pint/2½ cups vegetable or chicken stock
115g/4oz Dolcelatte cheese, rind removed, diced
300ml/½ pint/1¼ cups single (light) cream
salt and ground black pepper
fresh oregano and extra Dolcelatte, to garnish

1 Heat the oil and butter in a large pan until foaming. Add the onion and cook gently for about 5 minutes, stirring frequently, until softened but not brown.

2 Add the courgettes and oregano to the pan, with salt and pepper to taste. Cook over medium heat for 10 minutes, stirring frequently.

3 Pour in the stock and bring to the boil, stirring. Lower the heat, half cover the pan and simmer gently, stirring occasionally, for about 30 minutes. Stir in the diced Dolcelatte until melted.

4 Process the soup in a blender or food processor until smooth, then press through a sieve (strainer) into a clean pan.

5 Add two-thirds of the cream and stir over low heat until hot, but not boiling. Check the consistency and add more stock if the soup is too thick. Adjust the seasoning, then pour into heated bowls. Swirl in the remaining cream. Garnish with oregano and extra cheese and serve.

Variation
Replace half the cream with milk for a less rich soup.

Wild Mushroom Soup

The Italian dried wild porcini mushrooms are quite expensive, but they have an intense flavour, so only a small amount is needed for this recipe. Beef stock may seem unusual for a vegetable soup, but it helps strengthen the earthy flavour of the mushrooms.

Serves 4

25g/1oz/½ cup dried porcini mushrooms
30ml/2 tbsp olive oil

15g/½oz/1 tbsp butter
2 leeks, thinly sliced
2 shallots, roughly chopped
1 garlic clove, roughly chopped
225g/8oz/3 cups fresh wild mushrooms, such as ceps or chanterelles
about 1.2 litres/2 pints/5 cups beef stock
2.5ml/½ tsp dried thyme
150ml/¼ pint/⅔ cup double (heavy) cream
salt and ground black pepper
fresh thyme sprigs, to garnish

1 Put the dried porcini in a bowl, add 250 ml/8 fl oz/1 cup warm water and leave to soak for 20–30 minutes. Lift out of the liquid and squeeze over the bowl to remove as much of the soaking liquid as possible. Strain all the liquid and reserve to use later. Finely chop the porcini.

2 Heat the oil and butter in a large pan until foaming. Add the leeks, shallots and garlic and cook gently for about 5 minutes, stirring frequently, until softened but not coloured.

3 Chop or slice the fresh mushrooms and add to the pan. Stir over medium heat for a few minutes until the mushrooms begin to soften. Add the stock and bring to the boil. Add the porcini, soaking liquid, thyme and salt and pepper. Lower the heat, half cover the pan and simmer gently for 30 minutes, stirring occasionally.

4 Pour about three-quarters of the soup into a blender or food processor and process until smooth. Return to the soup remaining in the pan, stir in the cream and heat through. Check the consistency and add more stock if the soup is too thick. Taste for seasoning. Serve hot, garnished with thyme sprigs.

Tomato & Fresh Basil Soup

A soup for late summer when fresh tomatoes are at their most plentiful and flavoursome. You can use canned tomatoes out of season.

Serves 4–6

15ml/1 tbsp olive oil
25g/1oz/2 tbsp butter
1 onion, finely chopped
900g/2lb ripe Italian plum
   tomatoes, roughly chopped
1 garlic clove, roughly chopped
about 750ml/1¼ pints/3 cups
   chicken or vegetable stock
120ml/4 fl oz/½ cup dry
   white wine
30ml/2 tbsp sun-dried
   tomato paste
30ml/2 tbsp shredded fresh basil,
150ml/¼ pint/⅔ cup double
   (heavy) cream
salt and ground black pepper
a few whole basil leaves,
   to garnish

1 Heat the oil and butter in a large pan until foaming. Add the onion and cook gently for about 5 minutes, stirring frequently, until softened but not brown.

2 Stir in the chopped tomatoes and garlic, then add the stock, white wine and sun-dried tomato paste, with salt and pepper to taste. Bring to the boil, then lower the heat, half cover the pan and simmer gently for 20 minutes, stirring occasionally to stop the tomatoes sticking to the base of the pan.

3 Process the soup with the shredded basil in a blender or food processor, then press through a sieve (strainer) into a clean pan.

4 Add the double cream and heat through, stirring. Do not allow the soup to approach boiling point. Add more stock if necessary and then taste for seasoning. Pour into heated bowls and garnish with basil. Serve at once.

> **Variation**
> *The soup can also be served chilled. Transfer to a bowl at the end of step 3 and chill for at least 4 hours.*

Lentil Soup with Tomatoes

A classic rustic Italian soup flavoured with rosemary, delicious served with chunks of garlic bread.

Serves 4

225g/8oz/1 cup dried green or
   brown lentils
45ml/3 tbsp extra virgin olive oil
3 rindless streaky (fatty) bacon
   slices, cut into small dice
1 onion, finely chopped
2 celery sticks, finely chopped
2 carrots, finely diced
2 fresh rosemary sprigs,
   finely chopped
2 bay leaves
400g/14oz can chopped
   plum tomatoes
1.75 litres/3 pints/7½ cups
   vegetable stock
salt and ground black pepper
bay leaves and rosemary sprigs,
   to garnish

1 Place the lentils in a bowl and cover with cold water. Leave to soak for 2 hours. Rinse and drain well.

2 Heat the oil in a large pan. Add the bacon and cook for about 3 minutes, then stir in the onion and cook for 5 minutes, until softened.

3 Stir in the celery, carrots, rosemary, bay leaves and lentils. Toss over the heat for 1 minute, until thoroughly coated in the oil.

4 Add the tomatoes and stock and bring to the boil. Lower the heat, half cover the pan, and simmer for about 1 hour, or until the lentils are perfectly tender.

5 Remove the bay leaves from the soup and add salt and pepper to taste. Serve garnished with fresh bay leaves and rosemary sprigs.

> **Cook's Tip**
> *Look out for the small brown Italian lentils that are grown in the area around Umbria – they do not break up during cooking and, in Italian cuisine, they are often mixed with small pasta shapes or rice for a contrast of flavours and textures.*

Minestrone with Pasta & Beans

This classic minestrone from Lombardy includes pancetta for a pleasant touch of saltiness. Milanese cooks vary the recipe according to what is on hand, and you can do the same.

Serves 4
45ml/3 tbsp olive oil
115g/4oz pancetta, any rinds
  removed, roughly chopped
2–3 celery sticks, finely chopped
3 medium carrots, finely chopped
1 medium onion, finely chopped
1–2 garlic cloves, crushed
2 x 400g/14oz cans chopped
  Italian plum tomatoes
about 1 litre/1¾ pints/4 cups
  chicken stock
400g/14oz can cannellini beans,
  drained and rinsed
50g/2oz/½ cup short–cut
  macaroni
30–60ml/2–4tbsp chopped flat
  leaf parsley, to taste
salt and ground black pepper

1 Heat the oil in a large pan. Add the pancetta, celery, carrots and onion and cook over low heat for 5 minutes, stirring constantly, until the vegetables are softened.

2 Add the garlic and tomatoes, breaking them up well with a wooden spoon. Pour in the chicken stock. Add salt and pepper to taste and bring to the boil. Half cover the pan, lower the heat and simmer gently for about 20 minutes, until the vegetables are soft.

3 Drain the beans and add them to the pan with the macaroni. Bring to the boil again. Cover, lower the heat and continue to simmer for about 20 minutes more.

4 Check the consistency and add more stock if necessary. Stir in the parsley and adjust the seasoning. Serve hot, sprinkled with plenty of Parmesan cheese.

> **Variation**
> Use long-grain rice instead of the pasta, and borlotti beans
> instead of cannellini beans.

Energy 324Kcal/1356kJ; Fat 16.6g; Saturated Fat 3.9g; Carbohydrate 32.3g; Fibre 8.5g

Summer Minestrone

This brightly coloured, fresh-tasting soup makes the most of summer vegetables. Serve with a selection of Italian cheeses and warm chunks of crusty bread for a lunch full of sunny flavours.

Serves 4
45ml/3 tbsp olive oil
1 large onion, finely chopped
15ml/1tbsp sun-dried tomato
  paste
450g/1lb ripe Italian plum
  tomatoes, peeled and
finely chopped
225g/8oz green courgettes
  (zucchini), trimmed and
  roughly chopped
225g/8oz yellow courgettes
  (zucchini), trimmed and
  roughly chopped
3 waxy new potatoes, diced
2 garlic cloves, crushed
about 1.2 litres/2 pints/5 cups
  chicken stock or water
60ml/4 tbsp shredded fresh basil
50g/2oz/⅔ cup grated
  Parmesan cheese
salt and ground black pepper

1 Heat the oil in a large pan, add the onion and cook gently for about 5 minutes, stirring constantly, until softened.

2 Stir in the sun-dried tomato paste, chopped tomatoes, courgettes, diced potatoes and garlic. Mix well and cook gently for 10 minutes, uncovered, shaking the pan frequently to stop the vegetables sticking to the base.

3 Pour in the stock. Bring to the boil, lower the heat, half cover the pan and simmer gently for 15 minutes, or until the vegetables are just tender. Add more stock if necessary.

4 Remove the pan from the heat, stir in the basil and half the cheese. Season and serve hot, sprinkled with the remaining cheese.

> **Cook's Tip**
> The Italian cook understands that vegetables in season provide
> by far the best flavour – and they are cheaper!

Energy 228Kcal/951kJ; Fat 13.4g; Saturated Fat 4.1g; Carbohydrate 18.8g; Fibre 3.1g

Clam & Pasta Soup

This soup is a version of the famous pasta dish, spaghetti alle vongole, using store-cupboard ingredients. It's the perfect dish for a last-minute, informal gathering.

Serves 4
30ml/2 tbsp olive oil
1 large onion, finely chopped
2 garlic cloves, crushed
400g/14oz can chopped Italian plum tomatoes
15ml/1 tbsp sun-dried tomato paste

5ml/1 tsp sugar
5ml/1 tsp dried mixed herbs
about 750ml/1¼ pints/3 cups fish or vegetable stock
150ml/¼ pint/⅔ cup red wine
50g/2oz/½ cup small pasta shapes
150g/5oz jar or can clams in natural juice
30ml/2 tbsp finely chopped fresh flat leaf parsley
salt and ground black pepper
a few fresh flat leaf parsley sprigs, to garnish

1 Heat the oil in a large pan. Add the onion and cook gently for 5 minutes, stirring frequently, until softened.

2 Add the garlic, tomatoes, tomato paste, sugar, herbs, stock and red wine, with salt and pepper to taste. Bring to the boil. Lower the heat, half cover the pan and simmer for 10 minutes, stirring occasionally.

3 Add the pasta and continue simmering, uncovered, for about 10 minutes, or until *al dente*. Stir occasionally, to prevent the pasta shapes from sticking together.

4 Add the clams and their juice to the soup and heat through gently for 3–4 minutes, adding more stock if required. Do not let it boil or the clams will be tough. Remove from the heat, stir in the parsley and adjust the seasoning. Serve hot, sprinkled with coarsely ground black pepper and parsley leaves.

> **Cook's Tip**
> *This soup has a fuller flavour if it is made the day before.*

Energy 190Kcal/796kJ; Fat 6.5g; Saturated Fat 1g; Carbohydrate 18.5g; Fibre 2.7g

Tuscan Bean Soup

There are lots of versions of this wonderful soup. This one uses cannellini beans, leeks, cabbage and good olive oil – and tastes even better reheated. The Tuscans are renowned for their fondness for beans and they really know how to make the most of them!

Serves 4
45ml/3 tbsp extra virgin olive oil
1 onion, roughly chopped
2 leeks, roughly chopped
1 large potato, diced
2 garlic cloves, finely chopped
1.2 litres/2 pints/5 cups vegetable stock

400g/14oz can cannellini beans, drained, liquid reserved
175g/6oz Savoy cabbage, shredded
45ml/3 tbsp chopped fresh flat leaf parsley
30ml/2 tbsp chopped fresh oregano
75g/3oz/1 cup shaved Parmesan cheese
salt and ground black pepper

For the garlic toasts
30–45ml/2–3 tbsp extra virgin olive oil
6 thick slices country bread
1 garlic clove, peeled and bruised

1 Heat the oil in a large pan, add the onion, leeks, potato and garlic and cook gently for 4–5 minutes. Pour on the stock and the liquid from the beans (reserving the beans). Cover and simmer for 15 minutes.

2 Stir in the cabbage and beans, with half the herbs. Season and cook for 10 minutes more. Spoon about one-third of the soup into a food processor or blender and process until fairly smooth. Return to the soup in the pan, taste for seasoning and heat through for 5 minutes.

3 Meanwhile make the garlic toasts. Drizzle a little oil over the slices of bread, then rub both sides of each slice with the garlic. Toast until browned on both sides.

4 Ladle the soup into bowls. Sprinkle with the remaining herbs and the Parmesan shavings. Add a drizzle of olive oil and serve immediately with the garlic toasts.

Energy 445Kcal/1863kJ; Fat 21.8g; Saturated Fat 6g; Carbohydrate 45.8g; Fibre 9.1g

Broccoli Soup

Broccoli grows abundantly around Rome and this delicate-tasting soup really brings out its flavour. A simple dish, it is typical of the Romans' preference for uncomplicated cooking. You could try purple-sprouting broccoli for an unusual coloured soup.

Serves 6
675g/1½lb broccoli spears
1.75 litres/3 pints/7½ cups fresh chicken or vegetable stock
15ml/1 tbsp fresh lemon juice
salt and ground black pepper

To serve
6 slices white bread
1 large garlic clove, cut in half
freshly grated Parmesan cheese (optional)

1 Using a small sharp knife, peel the broccoli stems, starting from the base of the stalks and pulling gently up towards the florets. (The peel comes off very easily.) Chop the broccoli into small chunks.

2 Bring the stock to a boil in a large pan. Add the broccoli and simmer for 30 minutes, or until soft.

3 Transfer about half of the broccoli soup to a blender or food processor and process until smooth. Return the purée to the soup in the pan and stir well together. Season with salt, pepper and lemon juice, to taste.

4 Just before serving, reheat the soup to just below boiling point. Toast the bread, rub with garlic and cut into quarters. Place 3 or 4 pieces of toast in the bottom of each soup plate. Ladle on the soup. Serve at once, with Parmesan if desired.

> **Cook's Tip**
> The Italian idea of placing garlic-flavoured toast in the bowl before adding the soup is quite delicious. The toast soaks up the liquid and adds not only a wonderful texture to the soup, but also a subtle touch of garlic.

Tomato & Bread Soup

This colourful Florentine recipe was created to use up stale, leftover bread. It can be made with very ripe fresh or canned Italian plum tomatoes.

Serves 4
90ml/6 tbsp olive oil
small piece of dried chilli, crumbled (optional)
175g/6oz/1½ cups stale coarse white bread, cut into 2.5cm/1in cubes
1 onion, finely chopped
2 garlic cloves, finely chopped
675g/1½lb ripe tomatoes, peeled and chopped, or 2 x 400g/14oz cans peeled plum tomatoes, chopped
45ml/3 tbsp chopped fresh basil
1.5 litres/2½ pints/6¼ cups home-made or ready-prepared stock or water, or a combination of both
salt and ground black pepper
extra virgin olive oil, to serve (optional)

1 Heat 4 tbsp of the oil in a large pan. Add the chilli, if using, and stir for 1–2 minutes. Add the bread cubes and cook until golden. Transfer to a plate and drain on paper towels.

2 Add the remaining oil to the pan with the onion and garlic, and cook until the onion softens. Stir in the tomatoes, bread and basil. Season with salt. Cook over medium heat, stirring occasionally, for about 15 minutes.

3 Meanwhile, heat the stock or water to simmering. Add to the pan of tomato mixture and mix well. Bring to the boil. Lower the heat slightly and simmer for 20 minutes.

4 Remove the soup from the heat. Use a fork to mash the tomatoes and the bread together. Season with pepper, and more salt if necessary. Allow to stand for 10 minutes.

5 Just before serving the soup, swirl in a little olive oil, if wished.

> **Variation**
> Mix in grated Pecorino or other hard Italian cheese at step 4.

White Bean Soup

A thick purée of cooked dried beans is at the heart of this substantial country soup from Tuscany. It makes a warming winter lunch or supper dish.

Serves 6

350g/12oz/scant 2 cups dried cannellini or other white beans
1 bay leaf
75ml/5 tbsp olive oil
1 onion, finely chopped
1 carrot, finely chopped
1 celery stick, finely chopped
3 tomatoes, peeled and finely chopped
2 garlic cloves, finely chopped
5ml/1 tsp fresh thyme leaves, or 2.5ml/½ tsp dried thyme
750ml/1¼ pints/3½ cups boiling water
salt and ground black pepper
extra virgin olive oil, to serve

1 Pick over the beans carefully, discarding any stones or other particles. Leave the beans to soak in a large bowl of cold water overnight.

2 Drain the beans and place them in a large pan of water. Bring to the boil and cook for 20 minutes. Drain. Return the beans to the pan, cover with cold water and bring to the boil again. Add the bay leaf and cook for 1–2 hours, until the beans are tender. Drain again. Remove the bay leaf.

3 Process about three-quarters of the beans in a blender or food processor, or pass through a food mill, adding a little water if necessary.

4 Heat the oil in a large pan. Add the onion and cook, stirring, until it softens. Add the carrot and celery and cook for 5 minutes more.

5 Stir in the tomatoes, garlic and thyme. Cook for a further 6–8 minutes, stirring frequently.

6 Pour in the boiling water. Stir in the beans and the bean purée. Season with salt and pepper. Simmer for 10–15 minutes, then transfer to individual soup bowls and serve, drizzled with a little extra virgin olive oil.

Fish Soup

Liguria is famous for its fish soups. In this one, the fish is cooked in a vegetable-flavoured broth and then puréed. The soup can also be used as a dressing for pasta when cooked down to the consistency of a sauce.

Serves 6

900g/2lb mixed fish or fish pieces (such as cod, haddock, whiting and monkfish)
90ml/6 tbsp olive oil, plus extra to serve
1 onion, finely chopped
1 celery stick, chopped
1 carrot, chopped
60ml/4 tbsp chopped fresh parsley
175ml/6fl oz/¾ cup dry white wine
3 tomatoes, peeled and chopped
2 garlic cloves, finely chopped
1.5 litres/2½ pints/6¼ cups boiling water
salt and ground black pepper
rounds of French bread, to serve

1 Scale and clean the fish, discarding all innards, but leaving the heads on. Cut into large pieces. Rinse well in cool water.

2 Heat the oil in a large pan and add the onion. Cook over low to medium heat until it begins to soften. Stir in the celery and carrot and cook for 5 minutes more. Add the parsley.

3 Pour in the wine, increase the heat and cook until it reduces by about half. Stir in the tomatoes and garlic. Cook for 3–4 minutes, stirring occasionally. Pour in the boiling water and bring back to the boil. Cook over medium heat for 15 minutes.

4 Stir in the fish, and simmer for 10–15 minutes, or until the fish are tender. Season with salt and pepper.

5 Remove the fish from the soup with a slotted spoon. Discard any bones. Purée the soup in a food processor, reheat and adjust seasoning. If the soup is too thick, add a little more water.

6 To serve, bring the soup to a simmer. Toast the rounds of bread and drizzle one side with olive oil. Place two or three in each soup bowl before pouring over the soup.

Energy 188Kcal/788kJ; Fat 9.8g; Saturated Fat 1.4g; Carbohydrate 18.1g; Fibre 6.2g

Energy 239Kcal/995kJ; Fat 12.4g; Saturated Fat 1.8g; Carbohydrate 3.6g; Fibre 1.4g

Pumpkin Soup

Pumpkins often feature in northern Italian cooking, their sweet, orange flesh producing a beautifully coloured soup.

Serves 4

450g/1lb piece of peeled and
  seeded pumpkin
50g/2oz/¼ cup butter
1 onion, finely chopped
750ml/1¼ pints/3½ cups
  chicken stock or water
475ml/16fl oz/2 cups milk
pinch of freshly grated nutmeg
40g/1½oz spaghetti, broken into
  small pieces
90ml/6 tbsp freshly grated
  Parmesan cheese
salt and ground black pepper

1 Chop the piece of pumpkin into 2.5cm/1in cubes.

2 Heat the butter in a large pan. Add the onion and cook over medium heat for 6–8 minutes, until it softens. Stir in the pumpkin and cook for a further 2–3 minutes.

3 Add the stock or water and cook for about 15 minutes, until the pumpkin is soft. Remove from the heat.

4 Process the soup in a blender or food processor. Return it to the pan and stir in the milk and nutmeg. Season with salt and pepper. Bring the soup back to the boil.

5 Stir the broken spaghetti into the soup. Cook until the pasta is al dente. Stir in the Parmesan and serve immediately.

Cook's Tip

For cooking purposes, do not be tempted to buy enormous pumpkins, as their flesh tends to be stringy and flavourless.

Variation

Other squashes are also popular in northern Italian cooking. In this recipe, try using butternut squash instead of pumpkin.

Minestrone with Pesto

Minestrone is a thick mixed vegetable soup using almost any combination of seasonal vegetables. Here pesto has been added for extra flavour.

Serves 6

1.5 litres/2½ pints/6¼ cups
  stock or water, or combination
45ml/3 tbsp olive oil
1 large onion, finely chopped
1 leek, sliced
2 carrots, finely chopped
1 celery stick, finely chopped
2 garlic cloves, finely chopped
2 potatoes, diced
1 bay leaf
1 sprig fresh thyme, or 1.5ml/
  ¼ tsp dried thyme leaves
115g/4oz/¾ cup peas, fresh
  or frozen
2–3 courgettes (zucchini),
  finely chopped
3 tomatoes, peeled and
  finely chopped
425g/15oz/3 cups cooked
  or canned beans such
  as cannellini
45ml/3 tbsp pesto sauce
salt and ground black pepper
freshly grated Parmesan cheese,
  to serve

1 In a medium pan, heat the stock or water until simmering.

2 Heat the olive oil in a large pan. Stir in the onion and leek, and cook for 5–6 minutes, or until the onion softens. Add the carrots, celery and garlic and cook over moderate heat, stirring frequently, for another 5 minutes. Add the potatoes and cook for 2–3 minutes more.

3 Pour in the hot stock or water and stir well. Add the herbs and season with salt and pepper. Bring to the boil, reduce the heat slightly and cook for 10–12 minutes.

4 Stir in the peas, if fresh, and the courgettes. Simmer for 5 minutes more. Add the frozen peas, if using, and the tomatoes. Cover the pan, and boil for 5–8 minutes.

5 About 10 minutes before serving the soup, uncover and stir in the beans. Simmer for 10 minutes. Stir in the pesto sauce and adjust the seasoning. Simmer for a further 5 minutes, then remove from the heat. Allow the soup to stand for a few minutes before serving with the grated Parmesan.

Energy 257Kcal/1072kJ; Fat 13.7g, Saturated Fat 2.6g; Carbohydrate 24.3g; Fibre 6.5g

Energy 240Kcal/997kJ; Fat 16.9g; Saturated Fat 10.5g; Carbohydrate 12.6g; Fibre 1.6g

Barley & Vegetable Soup

This soup comes from the Alto Adige region, in Italy's mountainous north. A thick, nourishing soup, it is the perfect warming food for cold winter days. Serve with chunks of warm crusty bread.

Serves 6–8

225g/8oz/1 cup pearl barley, preferably organic
2 litres/3½ pints/9 cups beef stock or water
45ml/3 tbsp olive oil
2 carrots, finely chopped
1 large onion, finely chopped
2 celery sticks, finely chopped
1 leek, thinly sliced
1 large potato, finely chopped
115g/4oz/½ cup diced ham
1 bay leaf
45ml/3 tbsp chopped fresh parsley
1 small sprig fresh rosemary
salt and ground black pepper
freshly grated Parmesan cheese, to serve (optional)

1 Pick over the barley and discard any stones or other particles. Rinse in cold water. Leave the barley to soak in cold water for at least 3 hours.

2 Drain the barley and place in a large pan with the stock or water. Bring to the boil, lower the heat and simmer for 1 hour. Skim off any scum.

3 Stir in the oil, all the vegetables and the ham. Add the herbs. If necessary add more water: the ingredients should be covered by at least 2.5cm/1in. Simmer for 1–1½ hours, or until the vegetables and barley are very tender.

4 Season to taste with salt and pepper. Serve hot with grated Parmesan, if wished.

Cook's Tip
The cooking of the German-speaking region of Alto Adige is very much influenced by its neighbouring country, Austria. Pork is a main feature of the cuisine, particularly sausages and speck, a smoked ham, but fish from the Adige river is also important.

Rice & Bean Soup

This thick soup makes the most of fresh broad (fava) beans while they are in season. It also works well with frozen beans for the rest of the year.

Serves 4

1kg/2lb broad (fava) beans in their pods, or 400g/14oz shelled frozen beans, thawed
90ml/6 tbsp olive oil
1 onion, finely chopped
2 tomatoes, peeled and finely chopped
200g/7oz/1 cup risotto or other uncooked rice
25g/1oz/2 tbsp butter
1 litre/1¾ pints/4 cups boiling water
salt and ground black pepper
freshly grated Parmesan cheese, to serve (optional)

1 Shell the beans if they are fresh. Bring a large pan of water to the boil and blanch the beans, fresh or frozen, for 3–4 minutes. Rinse under cold water, then peel off the skins.

2 Heat the oil in a large pan. Add the chopped onion and cook over low to medium heat, until it softens. Stir in the broad beans, and cook for about 5 minutes, stirring often to coat them with the oil. Season with salt and pepper. Add the tomatoes, and cook for a further 5 minutes, stirring often.

3 Stir in the rice and cook for 1–2 minutes. Add the butter and stir until it melts. Pour in the water, a little at a time, until the whole amount has been added. Taste for seasoning.

4 Continue cooking the soup until the rice is tender. Serve hot, with grated Parmesan if wished.

Cook's Tip
Risotto rice, such as Arborio, is particularly good for this soup. A short grain rice, it has rounder grains than the long grain variety. This type of rice has the ability to absorb water and cook to a creamy smoothness yet still retain its shape.

Pasta & Dried Bean Soup

This peasant soup is very thick. In Italy it is made with dried, soaked, or fresh beans, never canned, and served hot or at room temperature.

Serves 4–6

300g/11oz/1½ cups dried borlotti or cannellini beans
400g/14oz can plum tomatoes, chopped, with their juice
3 garlic cloves, crushed
2 bay leaves
pinch coarsely ground black pepper
90ml/6 tbsp olive oil
10ml/2 tsp salt
200g/7oz/2¼ cups ditalini or other small soup pasta
45ml/3 tbsp chopped fresh parsley

To Serve

extra virgin olive oil (optional)
freshly grated Parmesan cheese

1 Place the beans in a bowl, cover with cold water and leave to soak overnight. Rinse and drain well.

2 Place the beans in a large pan and cover with water. Bring to the boil and cook for 10 minutes. Rinse and drain again.

3 Return the beans to the pan. Add enough water to cover them by 2.5cm/1in. Stir in the coarsely chopped tomatoes with their juice, the garlic, bay leaves, black pepper and the oil.

4 Simmer for 1½–2 hours, or until the beans are tender. If necessary, add more water.

5 Remove the bay leaves. Pass about half of the bean mixture through a food mill or process in a food processor. Stir into the pan with the remaining bean mixture. Add 750ml/1¼ pints/3½ cups water and bring the soup to the boil.

6 Add the salt and the pasta. Stir well, and cook until the pasta is al dente. Stir in the parsley.

7 Allow the soup to stand for at least 10 minutes before serving. To serve, drizzle with a little olive oil, if using, and serve with grated Parmesan passed separately.

Pasta & Lentil Soup

The small brown lentils which are grown in central Italy are traditionally used in this wholesome soup, but green lentils may be substituted, if preferred.

Serves 4–6

225g/8oz/1 cup dried green or brown lentils
90ml/6 tbsp olive oil
50g/2oz/¼ cup ham or salt pork, cut into small dice
1 onion, finely chopped
1 celery stick, finely chopped
1 carrot, finely chopped
2 litres/3½ pints/9 cups chicken stock or water, or a combination of both
1 fresh sage leaf or large pinch of dried
1 sprig fresh thyme or 1.5ml/¼ tsp dried
175g/6oz/2½ cups ditalini or other small soup pasta
salt and ground black pepper

1 Carefully check the lentils for small stones. Place them in a bowl, cover with cold water and soak for 2–3 hours. Rinse and drain well.

2 In a large pan, heat the oil and cook the ham or salt pork for 2–3 minutes. Add the onion, and cook gently until it softens.

3 Stir in the celery and carrot, and cook for a further 5 minutes, stirring frequently. Add the lentils and stir to coat them in the fat.

4 Pour in the stock or water, add the herbs and bring the soup to the boil. Cook over medium heat for about 1 hour, or until the lentils are tender. Add salt and pepper to taste.

5 Stir in the pasta and cook it until al dente or tender but still firm to the bite. Allow the soup to stand for a few minutes before serving.

Variation
Add 1 crushed garlic clove with the onion at step 2.

Energy 284Kcal/1191kJ; Fat 12.1g; Saturated Fat 1.8g; Carbohydrate 34g; Fibre 2.7g

Energy 270Kcal/1135kJ; Fat 12.1g; Saturated Fat 1.8g; Carbohydrate 31.2g; Fibre 7.5g

Spinach & Rice Soup

Use very young spinach leaves to prepare this light and fresh-tasting soup.

Serves 4
675g/1½lb fresh spinach leaves, washed
45ml/3 tbsp extra virgin olive oil
1 small onion, finely chopped
2 garlic cloves, finely chopped
1 small fresh red chilli, seeded and finely chopped
225g/8oz/generous 1 cup risotto rice, such as Arborio
1.2 litres/2 pints/5 cups vegetable stock
salt and ground black pepper
Parmesan or Pecorino cheese shavings, to serve

1 Place the spinach in a large pan with just the water that clings to its leaves after washing. Add a large pinch of salt. Heat gently until the spinach has wilted, then remove from the heat and drain, reserving any liquid.

2 Either chop the spinach finely using a large kitchen knife or place in a food processor and process the leaves to a fairly coarse purée.

3 Heat the oil in a large pan and gently cook the onion, garlic and chilli for 4–5 minutes, until softened. Stir in the rice until well coated with the oil, then pour in the stock and reserved spinach liquid. Bring to the boil, lower the heat and simmer for 10 minutes.

4 Add the spinach, with salt and pepper to taste. Cook for 5–7 minutes, until the rice is tender. Check the seasoning. Serve in heated bowls, topped with the shavings of cheese.

Cook's Tip
Buy Parmesan or Pecorino cheese in the piece from a reputable supplier, as it will be full of flavour and easy to grate or shave with a vegetable peeler.

Ribollita

Ribollita is rather like minestrone, but includes beans and not pasta. In Italy, it is traditionally served ladled over bread and a rich green vegetable, although you could omit this for a lighter and speedier version.

Serves 6–8
45ml/3 tbsp olive oil
2 onions, chopped
2 carrots, sliced
4 garlic cloves, crushed
2 celery sticks, thinly sliced
1 fennel bulb, trimmed and chopped
2 large courgettes (zucchini), thinly sliced
400g/14oz can chopped tomatoes
30ml/2 tbsp home-made or ready-made pesto
900ml/1½ pints/3¾ cups vegetable stock
400g/14oz can haricot or borlotti beans, drained
salt and ground black pepper

To finish
450g/1lb young spinach
15ml/1 tbsp extra virgin olive oil, plus extra for drizzling
6–8 slices white bread
Parmesan cheese shavings

1 Heat the oil in a large pan. Add the onions, carrots, garlic, celery and fennel and fry gently for 10 minutes. Add the courgettes and fry for a further 2 minutes.

2 Add the chopped tomatoes, pesto, stock and beans and bring to the boil. Reduce the heat, cover and simmer gently for 25–30 minutes, until the vegetables are completely tender. Season with salt and pepper to taste.

3 To serve, fry the spinach in the oil for 2 minutes, or until wilted. Place the bread in the base of the soup bowls and spoon the wilted spinach on top. Ladle the soup over the top. Serve with extra virgin olive oil for drizzling on to the soup and Parmesan cheese to sprinkle on top.

Variation
Use other dark greens, such as chard or cabbage, instead of the spinach; shred and cook until tender.

Energy 225Kcal/943kJ; Fat 8.5g; Saturatd Fat 1.8g; Carbohydrate 28.8g; Fibre 6.6g

Energy 324Kcal/1346kJ; Fat 9.9g; Saturated Fat 1.4g; Carbohydrate 48.8g; Fibre 3.8g

Parmesan & Cauliflower Soup

A silky smooth, mildly cheesy soup which isn't overpowered by the cauliflower. It makes an elegant dinner-party soup served with crisp, home-made Melba toast.

150ml/¼ pint/⅔ cup single (light) cream or milk
freshly grated nutmeg
pinch of cayenne pepper
60ml/4 tbsp freshly grated Parmesan cheese
salt and ground black pepper

Serves 6
1 large cauliflower
1.2 litres/2 pints/5 cups chicken or vegetable stock
175g/6oz/1½ cups dried farfalle

For the Melba toast
3–4 slices day-old white bread
freshly grated Parmesan cheese, for sprinkling
1.5ml/¼ tsp paprika

1 Cut the leaves and central stalk away from the cauliflower and discard. Divide the cauliflower into even-size florets.

2 Bring the stock to the boil and add the cauliflower. Simmer for about 10 minutes, or until very soft. Remove the cauliflower with a slotted spoon and place in a blender or food processor.

3 Add the pasta to the stock and simmer for 10 minutes, until al dente. Drain, reserving the liquid. Set the pasta aside and pour the reserved liquid over the cauliflower. Add the cream or milk, nutmeg and cayenne to the cauliflower. Blend until smooth, then press through a sieve (strainer).

4 Stir in the cooked pasta. Reheat the soup and then stir in the Parmesan. Taste and adjust the seasoning if necessary.

5 Meanwhile make the Melba toast. Preheat the oven to 180°C/350°F/Gas 4. Toast the bread lightly on both sides. Quickly cut off the crusts and split each slice in half horizontally. Scrape off any doughy bits and sprinkle with Parmesan cheese and paprika.

6 Place on a baking sheet and bake in the oven for about 10–15 minutes, or until uniformly golden. Serve with the soup.

Red Onion & Beetroot Soup

This beautiful, vivid ruby-red soup will look stunning at any dinner-party table.

1.2 litres/2 pints/5 cups vegetable stock or water
30ml/2 tbsp raspberry vinegar or red wine vinegar
salt and ground black pepper
low-fat yogurt or crème fraîche, to garnish
snipped chives, to garnish

Serves 4–6
15ml/1 tbsp olive oil
350g/12oz red onions, sliced
2 garlic cloves, crushed
50g/2oz/½ cup dried small pasta shapes
275g/10oz cooked beetroot (beets), cut into sticks

1 Heat the olive oil in a flameproof casserole and add the red onions and garlic.

2 Cook gently for 20 minutes, or until soft and tender.

3 Cook the pasta in salted boiling water according to the instructions on the packet. Drain.

4 Add the beetroot (beets), stock or water, cooked pasta and vinegar, and heat through. Season to taste with salt and pepper.

5 Ladle into warmed soup bowls. Top each one with a spoonful of low-fat yogurt or crème fraîche and sprinkle with chives.

> **Cook's Tip**
> Red onions are widely available. They have a milder taste than white onions and help to add colour to the soup.

> **Variation**
> For extra texture, add with the onions one celery stick and two carrots, trimmed and cut into sticks.

Energy 83Kcal/347kJ; Fat 2.2g; Saturated Fat 0.3g; Carbohydrate 14.3g; Fibre 1.9g

Energy 263Kcal/1105kJ; Fat 10g; Saturated Fat 5.6g; Carbohydrate 32.4g; Fibre 2.3g

Consommé with Agnolotti

Dainty seafood-filled pasta shapes floating in a clear consommé broth make an elegant and satisfying dish.

Serves 4–6

75g/3oz cooked, peeled prawns
  (shrimp)
75g/3oz canned crab meat,
  drained
5ml/1 tsp fresh root ginger, peeled
  and finely grated
15ml/1 tbsp fresh white
  breadcrumbs

5ml/1 tsp light soy sauce
1 spring onion (scallion), chopped
1 garlic clove, crushed
1 quantity handmade Egg Pasta
  (see page 8)
flour, for dusting
egg white, beaten
400g/14oz can chicken or fish
  consommé
30ml/2 tbsp sherry or vermouth
salt and ground black pepper
50g/2oz cooked, peeled prawns
  (shrimp) and fresh coriander
  leaves, to garnish

1 To make the filling, put the prawns, crab meat, ginger, breadcrumbs, soy sauce, onion, garlic and seasoning into a food processor or blender and process until smooth.

2 Roll the pasta into thin sheets and dust lightly with flour. Stamp out 32 rounds with a 5cm/2in fluted pastry cutter.

3 Place a small teaspoon of the filling in the centre of half the pasta rounds. Brush the edges of each round with egg white and sandwich together with a second round on top. Pinch the edges together firmly to stop the filling seeping out.

4 Cook the pasta, in batches, in a large pan of boiling salted water for 5 minutes. Remove and drop into a bowl of cold water for 5 seconds before placing on a tray.

5 Heat the chicken or fish consommé in a pan with the sherry or vermouth. When piping hot, add the pasta shapes and simmer for 1–2 minutes.

6 Serve in a shallow soup bowl covered with hot consommé. Garnish with extra peeled prawns and fresh coriander leaves.

Courgette Soup with Conchigliette

This pretty, fresh-tasting soup combines a popular Italian summer vegetable with attractive little shell-shaped pasta.

Serves 4–6

60ml/4 tbsp olive or sunflower oil
2 onions, finely chopped
1.5 litres/2½ pints/6¼ cups
  chicken stock

900g/2lb courgettes (zucchini)
115g/4oz/1 cup dried
  conchigliette
freshly squeezed lemon juice
30ml/2 tbsp chopped fresh
  chervil
salt and ground black pepper
soured cream, to serve

1 Heat the oil in a large pan and add the finely chopped onions. Cover and cook gently for about 20 minutes, until very soft but not coloured, stirring occasionally.

2 Add the chicken stock to the pan and bring the mixture to the boil.

3 Meanwhile grate the courgettes and stir into the boiling stock with the pasta. Reduce the heat and simmer for 15 minutes, until the pasta is *al dente*. Season to taste with lemon juice, salt and pepper.

4 Stir in the chopped fresh chervil and add a swirl of soured cream before serving.

Cook's Tip
Courgettes are now available almost all the year round, but they are at their best in spring and summer. Choose smaller ones.

Variation
To ring the changes, try replacing the courgettes with cucumber and use any of the little soup pasta available.

Energy 189Kcal/790kJ; Fat 8.5g; Saturated Fat 1.1g; Carbohydrate 23.6g; Fibre 3.2g

Energy 269Kcal/1144kJ; Fat 1.6g; Saturated Fat 0.2g; Carbohydrate 51.5g; Fibre 2g

Egg & Cheese Soup

In this classic Roman soup, eggs and cheese are beaten into hot broth, producing a slightly "stringy" texture characteristic of the dish.

Serves 6
3 eggs
45ml/3 tbsp fine semolina
90ml/6 tbsp freshly grated Parmesan cheese
pinch of freshly grated nutmeg
1.5 litres/2½ pints/6¼ cups beef or chicken stock
salt and ground black pepper
12 rounds of ciabatta or rustic bread, to serve

1 Beat the eggs in a bowl with the semolina and the cheese. Add the nutmeg. Beat in 250ml/8fl oz/1 cup of the cool stock.

2 Meanwhile, heat the remaining stock to simmering point in a large pan.

3 When the stock is hot, and a few minutes before you are ready to serve the soup, whisk the egg mixture into the broth.

4 Increase the heat slightly and bring it barely to the boil. Season with salt and pepper. Cook for 3–4 minutes. As the egg cooks, the soup will not be completely smooth.

5 To serve, toast the rounds of bread and place 2 in the bottom of each soup bowl.

6 Ladle on the hot soup and serve immediately.

Cook's Tip
Semolina is made from coarsely milled durum wheat, the wheat used for making pasta. The grains of semolina are very tough and when cooked they do not turn into a paste, but add an attractive, light texture to a dish. For the best results, use Italian semolina, which is available from Italian groceries. In Italy semolina is often used for making gnocchi, the little Italian dumplings, as it helps to give them a lightweight texture.

Mediterranean Fish Soup

Packed with fish and shellfish, the fresh flavours of this soup will transport you to the warm, sunny Mediterranean shores of Italy.

Serves 4
30ml/2 tbsp olive oil
1 onion, sliced
1 garlic clove, crushed
1 leek, sliced
225g/8oz can chopped tomatoes
pinch of Mediterranean herbs
1.5ml/¼ tsp saffron strands (optional)

115g/4oz/1 cup dried small pasta shapes
about 8 fresh mussels in the shell
450g/1lb filleted and skinned white fish, such as cod, plaice or monkfish
salt and ground black pepper

To finish
2 garlic cloves, crushed
1 canned pimiento, drained and chopped
15ml/1 tbsp fresh white breadcrumbs
60ml/4 tbsp mayonnaise
toasted bread, to serve

1 Heat the oil in a large pan and add the onion, garlic and leek. Cover and cook gently for 5 minutes, stirring until the vegetables are soft.

2 Pour in 1 litre/1¾ pints/4 cups water, the tomatoes, herbs, saffron, if using, and pasta. Season with salt and ground black pepper and cook for 15–20 minutes.

3 Scrub the mussels and pull off the beards. Discard any that will not close when sharply tapped.

4 Cut the fish into bite-size chunks and add to the soup in the pan, placing the mussels on top. Then simmer with the lid on for 5–10 minutes, until the mussels open and the fish is just cooked. Discard any unopened mussels.

5 To finish, pound the garlic, canned pimiento and breadcrumbs together in a pestle and mortar or process in a food processor. Then stir in the mayonnaise and season well.

6 Spread the pimiento paste on the toast; serve with the soup.

Chickpea & Parsley Soup

Chickpeas are a popular ingredient in Italian country cooking and this thick and tasty soup is a classic example of good, comforting rustic food. If short of time, use canned chickpeas.

Serves 6
225g/8oz/1¾ cups chickpeas, soaked overnight
1 small onion, halved
1 bunch fresh parsley, about 40g/1½oz
30ml/2 tbsp olive oil and sunflower oil, mixed
1.2 litres/2 pints/5 cups chicken stock
juice of ½ lemon
salt and ground black pepper
lemon wedges and finely pared strips of rind, to garnish
crusty bread, to serve

1 Drain the chickpeas and rinse them under cold running water. Cook in rapidly boiling water for 10 minutes, then simmer for 1–1½ hours until just tender. Drain.

2 Place the onion and parsley in a food processor or blender and process until finely chopped.

3 Heat the olive and sunflower oils in a pan or flameproof casserole dish and fry the onion mixture for 5 minutes over low heat, until the onion is slightly softened.

4 Add the chickpeas, cook gently for 1–2 minutes and add the chicken stock. Season well with salt and pepper. Bring the soup to the boil, then cover and simmer for 20 minutes, until the chickpeas are soft.

5 Allow the soup to cool a little. Part-purée the soup in a food processor or blender, or by mashing the chickpeas fairly roughly with a fork, so that the soup is thick but still has plenty of texture to it.

6 Return the soup to a clean pan, add the lemon juice and adjust the seasoning if necessary. Heat gently and then serve, garnished with lemon wedges and finely pared lemon rind, and accompanied by crusty bread.

Pea & Ham Soup

Peas feature in the cooking of northern Italy and are combined here with pasta to make an attractive-looking soup. The soup works well with frozen peas, which provide fresh flavour and a bright colour.

Serves 4
115g/4oz/1 cup dried small pasta shapes, such as tubetti
30ml/2 tbsp vegetable oil
1 small bunch spring onions (scallions), chopped
350g/12oz/3 cups frozen peas
1.2 litres/2 pints/5 cups chicken stock
225g/8oz raw unsmoked ham or gammon
60ml/4 tbsp double (heavy) cream
salt and ground black pepper
warm crusty bread, to serve

1 Bring a pan of lightly salted water to the boil, add the small pasta shapes and cook until al dente or just tender. Drain thoroughly, then return to the pan again, cover with cold water and set aside until required.

2 Heat the vegetable oil in a large heavy pan and cook the spring onions gently, stirring, until soft but not browned. Add the frozen peas and chicken stock to the pan, then simmer gently over a low heat for about 10 minutes.

3 Process the soup in a blender or food processor then return to the pan. Cut the ham or gammon into short fingers and add, with the pasta, to the pan. Simmer for 2–3 minutes and season with salt and pepper to taste.

4 Stir in the double cream and serve the soup immediately with the warm crusty bread.

> **Cook's Tip**
> Use petits pois for a more delicate taste. The pea and ham combination also goes well with cheese – try sprinkling the soup with freshly grated Parmesan cheese.

Fennel & Orange Salad

In seventeenth-century Italy, fennel was often served at the end of the meal, sprinkled with course salt, as an aid to digestion. In this recipe from Sicily, the fennel is deliciously teamed with zesty orange to make a refreshing salad, perfect on its own or as part of a cold buffet spread.

Serves 4
2 large fennel bulbs (about 700g1 ½lb)
2 sweet oranges
2 spring onions (scallions), to garnish

For the dressing
60ml/4 tbsp extra virgin olive oil
30ml/2 tbsp fresh lemon juice
salt and ground black pepper

1 Wash the fennel bulbs and remove any brown or stringy outer leaves. Slice the bulbs and stems into thin pieces. Place in a shallow serving bowl.

2 Peel the oranges with a sharp knife, cutting away the white pith. Slice thinly. Cut each slice into thirds. Arrange over the fennel, adding any juice from the oranges.

3 To make the dressing, mix the oil and lemon juice together. Season with salt and pepper. Pour the dressing over the salad and toss well together.

4 Slice the white and green sections of the spring onions thinly. Sprinkle over the salad and serve.

> **Cook's Tip**
> *Fennel bulb (not to be confused with the feathery green herb) resembles a fat white celery root and has a delicate but distinctive flavour of aniseed and a crisp texture.*

> **Variation**
> *Add a sprinkling of lightly toasted pine nuts or almonds.*

Artichoke Salad with Eggs

Artichoke bottoms are best when cut from fresh artichokes, but can also be bought frozen. This salad is easily assembled for a light lunch or even a starter.

For the mayonnaise
1 egg yolk
10ml/2 tsp Dijon mustard
15ml/1 tbsp white wine vinegar
250ml/8fl oz/1 cup olive or vegetable oil
2 tbsp chopped fresh parsley
salt and ground black pepper

Serves 4
4 large artichokes, or 4 frozen artichoke bottoms, thawed
½ lemon
4 eggs, hard-boiled and shelled

1 If using fresh artichokes, wash them. Squeeze the lemon, and put the juice and the squeezed half in a bowl of cold water. Prepare the artichokes one at a time. Cut off only the tip from the stem, then peel the stem with a small knife, pulling upwards towards the leaves. Pull off the small leaves around the stem and continue snapping off the upper part of the dark outer leaves until you reach the taller inner leaves. Cut the tops off the leaves with a sharp knife. Place in the acidulated water. Repeat with the other artichokes.

2 Boil or steam fresh artichokes until just tender (when a leaf comes away quite easily when pulled). Cook frozen artichoke bottoms according to the package instructions. Allow to cool.

3 To make the mayonnaise, combine the egg yolk, mustard and vinegar in a mixing bowl. Add salt and pepper to taste, then add the oil in a thin stream while beating vigorously with a wire whisk. When the mixture is thick and smooth, stir in the parsley. Blend well. Cover and refrigerate until needed.

4 Pull the leaves off the fresh artichokes. Cut the stems off level with the base and scrape the hairy "choke" off with a knife

5 Cut the eggs and artichokes into wedges. Arrange on a serving plate and serve garnished with the mayonnaise.

Tricolore Salad

A popular salad, this dish depends for its success on the quality of its ingredients. Mozzarella di bufala is the best cheese to serve uncooked. Whole ripe plum tomatoes give up their juices to blend with extra virgin olive oil to form a natural dressing – delicious mopped up with chunks of ciabatta bread.

Serves 2

150g/5oz mozzarella di bufala cheese, thinly sliced
4 large plum tomatoes, sliced
1 large avocado
about 12 basil leaves or a small handful of flat leaf parsley leaves
45–60ml/3–4 tbsp extra virgin olive oil
sea salt flakes and ground black pepper

1 Arrange the sliced mozzarella cheese and tomatoes in a random pattern on two individual plates. Crush over a few good pinches of sea salt flakes. This will help to draw out some of the juices from the tomatoes. Set aside in a cool place to marinate for 30 minutes.

2 Just before serving, cut the avocado in half using a large sharp knife and twist to separate. Carefully lift out the stone and remove the skin.

3 Slice the avocado flesh crossways into half-moons, or cut it into large chunks or cubes if that is easier.

4 Place the avocado on the salad, then sprinkle with the basil or parsley.

5 Drizzle over the olive oil, add a little more salt, if liked, and some black pepper. Serve the salad at room temperature.

> **Variation**
> A light sprinkling of balsamic vinegar added just before serving will give this salad a refreshing tang, while a few thinly sliced red onion rings will add extra colour and flavour.

Roasted Peppers with Tomatoes & Anchovies

This is a Sicilian-style salad, using some typical ingredients from the Italian island. The flavour improves if the salad is made and dressed an hour or two before serving.

Serves 4

1 red (bell) pepper
1 yellow (bell) pepper
4 sun-dried tomatoes in oil, drained
4 ripe plum tomatoes, sliced
2 canned anchovies, drained and chopped
15ml/1 tbsp capers, drained
15ml/1 tbsp pine nuts
1 garlic clove, very thinly sliced

For the dressing
75ml/5 tbsp extra virgin olive oil
15ml/1 tbsp balsamic vinegar
5ml/1 tsp lemon juice
chopped fresh mixed herbs
salt and ground black pepper

1 Cut the peppers in half, then remove the cores and seeds. Cut into quarters and cook, skin-side up, under a hot grill (broiler), until the skin chars. Transfer to a bowl and cover with a plate. Leave to cool. Peel the peppers and cut into strips.

2 Thinly slice the sun-dried tomatoes. Arrange the peppers and fresh tomatoes on a serving dish. Scatter over the anchovies, sun-dried tomatoes, capers, pine nuts and garlic.

3 To make the dressing, mix together the olive oil, vinegar, lemon juice and chopped herbs and season with salt and pepper. Pour over the salad and serve one or two hours later.

> **Cook's Tip**
> To bring out the flavour of the pine nuts, lightly toast them before adding to the salad: place them in a heated frying pan over medium heat and toss frequently until lightly browned.

Energy 235Kcal/973kJ; Fat 20.1g; Saturated Fat 2.8g; Carbohydrate 11.2g; Fibre 3.2g

Energy 526Kcal/2180kJ; Fat 47.1g; Saturated Fat 16g; Carbohydrate 8.3g; Fibre 5.8g

Bocconcini with Fennel & Basil

These tiny balls of mozzarella, each one hand-stretched and rolled, then preserved in brine, are best when they are perfectly fresh. If you can't find bocconcini, use ordinary buffalo mozzarella cut into bitesize pieces.

Serves 6
450g/1lb bocconcini mozzarella
45ml/3 tbsp extra virgin olive oil
5ml/1 tsp fennel seeds, lightly
* crushed*
a small bunch of fresh basil
* leaves, roughly torn*
salt and ground black pepper

1 Drain the bocconcini well and place in a bowl. Stir in the olive oil, fennel seeds and basil, and season with salt and pepper. Cover and chill for 1 hour.

2 Remove the bowl from the refrigerator and leave to stand for about 30 minutes for the cheese to return to room temperature before serving.

Potato Salad

The potatoes are dressed while still warm so that they fully absorb the flavours.

Serves 6
1kg/2lb waxy potatoes
90ml/6 tbsp extra virgin olive oil

juice of 1 lemon
1 garlic clove, very finely chopped
30ml/2 tbsp chopped fresh herbs,
* such as parsley, basil or thyme*
salt and ground black pepper

1 Wash the potatoes, but do not peel them. Boil or steam the potatoes until tender. When they are cool enough to handle, peel them. Dice the potatoes and place in a serving bowl.

2 While the potatoes are cooking, mix together the olive oil, lemon juice, garlic and herbs. Season with salt and pepper, then pour over the potatoes while they are still warm. Mix well. Serve at room temperature or cold.

Chickpea Salad

This salad makes a good light meal and is very quick to assemble if you use canned chickpeas.

Serves 4–6
2 x 400g/14oz cans chickpeas,
* or 450g/1lb/3 cups cooked*
* chickpeas*
6 spring onions (scallions),
* trimmed and chopped*
2 tomatoes, cut into cubes
1 small red onion, finely chopped

12 black olives, pitted and
* cut in half*
15ml/1 tbsp capers, drained
30ml/2 tbsp finely chopped fresh
* parsley or mint leaves*
4 hard-boiled eggs, cut into
* quarters, to garnish*

For the dressing
75ml/5 tbsp olive oil
45ml/3 tbsp wine vinegar
salt and ground black pepper

1 Rinse the chickpeas under cold water. Drain. Place in a serving bowl.

2 Add the spring onions, tomatoes, red onion, olives, capers and parsley or mint. Mix well.

3 To make the dressing, whisk the olive oil with the vinegar in a small bowl, then season with salt and pepper.

4 Pour the dressing over the salad and toss well. Adjust the seasoning. Allow to stand for at least 1 hour. Just before serving decorate the salad with the egg wedges.

Cook's Tip
If using dried chickpeas, soak them for at least 12 hours, then cook them in plenty of boiling water for 2 hours.

Variation
Other types of canned cooked beans may be substituted in this salad, such as cannellini or borlotti.

Top Energy 243Kcal/1008kJ; Fat 21g; Saturated Fat 11g; Carbohydrate 0g; Fibre 0g
Above Energy 206Kcal/863kJ; Fat 11.5g; Saturated Fat 1.7g; Carbohydrate 24g; Fibre 1.8g

Energy 268Kcal/1118kJ; Fat 16.4g; Saturated Fat 2.8g; Carbohydrate 19.4g; Fibre 5.1g

Tomato & Bread Salad

This salad is a traditional peasant dish from Tuscany and was created to use up bread that was several days old. The success of the dish depends on the quality of the tomatoes – they must be ripe and well flavoured. Serve with a green salad for a good contrast in colour and texture.

Serves 4
225g/8oz stale white or brown
   bread or rolls
4 large tomatoes
1 large red onion or 6 spring
   onions (scallions)
a few leaves fresh basil, to garnish

For the dressing
60ml/4 tbsp extra virgin olive oil
30ml/2 tbsp white wine vinegar
salt and ground black pepper

1 Cut the bread or rolls into thick slices. Place in a shallow bowl and add enough cold water to soak the bread. Leave for at least 30 minutes.

2 Cut the tomatoes into chunks and place in a serving bowl. Finely slice the onion or spring onions and add them to the tomatoes. Squeeze as much water out of the bread as possible, and add it to the vegetables.

3 To make the dressing, whisk the olive oil with the vinegar, then season with salt and pepper.

4 Pour the dressing over the salad and mix well. Decorate with the basil leaves. Allow to stand in a cool place for a least 2 hours before serving.

> **Cook's Tip**
> Tomatoes left to ripen on the vine will have the best flavour so try to buy "vine-ripened" varieties. If you can only find unripened tomatoes, you can help them along by putting them in a brown paper bag with a ripe tomato or leaving them in a fruit bowl with a banana; the gases the ripe fruits give off will ripen them, but, unfortunately, this process cannot improve the flavour.

Grilled Pepper Salad

This colourful salad hails from southern Italy; all the ingredients – peppers, capers and olives – are sun-lovers which thrive in the hot, dry Mezzogiorno, as the area is sometimes called.

Serves 6
4 large (bell) peppers, red or
   yellow or a combination of both
30ml/2 tbsp capers in salt,
   vinegar or brine, rinsed
18–20 black or green olives

For the dressing
90ml/6 tbsp extra virgin olive oil
2 garlic cloves, finely chopped
30ml/2 tbsp balsamic or
   wine vinegar
salt and ground black pepper

1 Place the peppers under a hot grill (broiler), turning occasionally until they are black and blistered on all sides.

2 Remove from the heat and place in a plastic bag. Leave for 5 minutes.

3 Peel the peppers, then cut into quarters. Remove the cores and seeds.

4 Cut the peppers into strips and arrange them in a serving dish. Distribute the capers and olives evenly over the peppers.

5 To make the dressing, mix the oil and garlic together in a small bowl, crushing the garlic with a spoon to release as much flavour as possible. Mix in the vinegar and season with salt and pepper.

6 Pour the dressing over the salad, mix well and allow to stand for at least 30 minutes before serving.

> **Cook's Tip**
> Peppers come in a range of colours – red, yellow, orange and green – but they all have much the same sweetish flavour. Choose firm specimens that have shiny skins.

Energy 238Kcal/998kJ; Fat 12.5g; Saturated Fat 1.9g; Carbohydrate 28g; Fibre 3.2g

Energy 145Kcal/598kJ; Fat 12.4g; Saturated Fat 1.8g; Carbohydrate 7.5g; Fibre 2.1g

Tuna Carpaccio

Fillet of beef is most often used for carpaccio, but meaty fish like tuna makes an unusual change. The secret is to slice the fish wafer thin, made possible by freezing the fish first, a technique used by Japanese chefs for making sashimi. Serve with a green salad.

Serves 4
2 fresh tuna steaks, about
   450g/1lb total weight
60ml/4 tbsp extra virgin olive oil
15ml/1 tbsp balsamic vinegar
5ml/1 tsp caster (superfine) sugar
30ml/2 tbsp drained bottled
   green peppercorns or capers
salt and ground black pepper
lemon wedges, to serve

1 Remove the skin from each tuna steak and place each steak between two sheets of clear film (plastic wrap) or non-stick baking paper. Pound with a rolling pin until flattened slightly.

2 Roll up the tuna as tightly as possible, then wrap tightly in clear film and place in the freezer for 4 hours or until firm.

3 Unwrap the tuna and cut crossways into the thinnest possible slices. Arrange on individual plates.

4 Whisk together the remaining ingredients, season with salt and pepper and pour over the tuna. Cover and allow to come to room temperature for 30 minutes before serving with lemon wedges.

> **Cook's Tip**
> Raw fish is safe to eat as long as it is very fresh, so check with your fishmonger before purchasing, and make sure to serve the carpaccio on the same day. Do not buy fish that has been frozen and thawed.

> **Variation**
> Use another fish with a meaty texture, such as swordfish.

Genoese Squid Salad

Squid is immensely popular in Italy where it is often served cut into rings as part of delicious salads.

Serves 4–6
450g/1lb prepared squid, cut
   into rings
4 garlic cloves, roughly chopped
300ml/½ pint/1¼ cups red wine
450g/1lb waxy new potatoes,
   scrubbed clean
225g/8 oz green beans, trimmed
   and cut into short lengths
2–3 drained sun-dried tomatoes
   in oil, thinly sliced lengthways
60ml/4 tbsp extra virgin olive oil
15ml/1 tbsp red wine vinegar
salt and ground black pepper

1 Preheat the oven to 180°C/350°F/Gas 4. Put the squid rings in an earthenware dish with half the garlic, the wine and pepper to taste. Cover and cook for 45 minutes, or until the squid is tender.

2 Put the potatoes in a pan, cover with cold water and add a good pinch of salt. Bring to the boil, cover and simmer for 15–20 minutes, or until tender. Using a slotted spoon, lift out the potatoes and set aside. Add the beans to the boiling water and cook for 3 minutes. Drain.

3 When the potatoes are cool enough to handle, slice them thickly on the diagonal and place them in a bowl with the warm beans and sun-dried tomatoes. Whisk the oil, wine vinegar and the remaining garlic in a jug and add salt and pepper to taste. Pour over the potato mixture.

4 Drain the squid and discard the wine and garlic. Add the squid to the potato mixture and fold very gently to mix. Arrange the salad on individual plates and grind pepper liberally all over. Serve warm.

> **Cook's Tip**
> Prepared squid can be bought from supermarkets with fresh fish counters, as well as from fishmongers.

Energy 256Kcal/1068kJ; Fat 16.2g; Saturated Fat 2.9g; Carbohydrate 1.1g; Fibre 0g

Energy 227Kcal/950kJ; Fat 9.2g; Saturated Fat 1.5g; Carbohydrate 14.8g; Fibre 1.7g

Pasta Salade Niçoise

Along the Mediterranean coast, where Italy meets France, the cuisines of both countries have many similarities. Here a classic French salade niçoise is given a modern Italian twist.

Serves 4

115g/4oz green beans, topped
  and tailed and cut into
  5cm/2in lengths
250g/9oz/2¼ cups dried
  penne rigate
105ml/7 tbsp extra virgin olive oil

2 fresh tuna steaks, total weight
  350–450g/12oz–1lb
6 baby Italian plum tomatoes,
  quartered lengthways
50g/2oz/½ cup pitted black
  olives, halved lengthways
6 bottled or canned anchovies in
  olive oil, drained and chopped
30–45ml/2–3 tbsp chopped fresh
  flat leaf parsley, to taste
juice of ½–1 lemon, to taste
2 heads chicory (Belgian endive),
  leaves separated
salt and ground black pepper
lemon wedges, to serve

1 Cook the beans in a large pan of salted boiling water for 5–6 minutes. Remove the beans with a large slotted spoon and refresh under the cold tap.

2 Add the pasta to the pan of bean cooking water, bring back to the boil and cook until the pasta is *al dente*.

3 Meanwhile, heat a ridged cast-iron pan over a low heat. Dip a wad of kitchen paper in the oil, wipe it over the surface of the pan and heat gently. Brush the tuna steaks on both sides with oil and sprinkle liberally with pepper. Cook over a medium to high heat for 1–2 minutes on each side. Remove and set aside.

4 Drain the cooked pasta well and tip into a large bowl. Add the remaining oil, the beans, tomato quarters, black olives, anchovies, parsley, lemon juice and salt and pepper to taste. Toss well to mix, then leave to cool.

5 Flake or slice the tuna into large pieces, discarding the skin, then fold it into the salad. Taste the salad for seasoning. Arrange the chicory leaves in a large shallow bowl. Spoon the pasta salad into the centre and serve with lemon wedges.

Energy 563Kcal/2364kJ; Fat 26.9g; Saturated Fat 4.4g; Carbohydrate 52.2g; Fibre 4.8g

Salad Leaves with Gorgonzola

Crispy fried pancetta makes tasty "croûtons", which contrast well in texture and flavour with the softness of mixed salad leaves and the sharp taste of Gorgonzola.

Serves 4

225g/8oz pancetta rashers,
  any rinds removed, coarsely
  chopped

2 large garlic cloves, roughly
  chopped
75g/3oz rocket (arugula) leaves
75g/3oz radicchio leaves
50g/2oz/½ cup walnuts,
  roughly chopped
115g/4oz Gorgonzola cheese
60ml/4 tbsp olive oil
15ml/1 tbsp balsamic vinegar
salt and ground black pepper

1 Put the chopped pancetta and garlic in a non-stick or heavy frying pan and heat gently, stirring constantly, until the pancetta fat runs. Increase the heat and fry until the pancetta and garlic are crisp. Remove with a slotted spoon and drain on kitchen paper. Leave the pancetta fat in the pan, off the heat.

2 Tear the rocket and radicchio leaves into a salad bowl. Sprinkle over the walnuts, pancetta and garlic. Add salt and pepper and toss to mix. Crumble the Gorgonzola on top.

3 Return the frying pan to medium heat and add the oil and balsamic vinegar to the pancetta fat. Stir until sizzling, then pour over the salad. Serve at once, to be tossed at the table.

Cook's Tip
Pancetta is made from pork belly and is cured in salt and spices to give it a mild flavour. It resembles bacon and is also sold in a smoked form.

Variation
Use walnut oil instead of olive oil, or hazelnuts and hazelnut oil instead of walnuts and olive oil.

Energy 448Kcal/1850kJ; Fat 41.4g; Saturated Fat 12.4g; Carbohydrate 1g; Fibre 1.2g

Chicken & Broccoli Salad

Gorgonzola makes a tangy dressing that goes well with both chicken and broccoli. Serve for a lunch or supper dish with lots of crusty Italian bread.

Serves 4

175g/6oz broccoli florets, divided into small sprigs
225g/8oz/2 cups dried farfalle
2 large cooked chicken breasts

For the dressing
90g/3¹/₂oz Gorgonzola cheese
15ml/1 tbsp white wine vinegar
60ml/4 tbsp extra virgin olive oil
2.5–5ml/¹/₂–1 tsp finely chopped fresh sage, plus extra sage sprigs to garnish
salt and ground black pepper

1 Cook the broccoli florets in a large pan of salted boiling water for 3 minutes. Remove with a slotted spoon and rinse under cold running water, then spread out on kitchen towels to drain and dry.

2 Add the pasta to the broccoli cooking water, then bring back to the boil and cook until al dente, or tender but still firm to the bite. When cooked, drain the pasta into a colander, rinse under cold running water until cold, then leave to drain and dry, shaking the colander occasionally.

3 Remove the skin from the cooked chicken breasts and cut the meat into bite-size pieces.

4 To make the dressing, put the cheese in a serving bowl and mash with a fork, then whisk in the wine vinegar followed by the oil and sage and salt and pepper to taste.

5 Add the pasta, chicken and broccoli. Toss well, then season to taste and serve, garnished with sage.

Variation
Scatter with pieces of crisply cooked pancetta or cubes of ham.

Pasta Salad with Salami & Olives

Tasty salami and olives tossed with pasta in a tangy dressing is an easy way to make the most of flavourful Italian ingredients. Simply serve with a crisp green salad and ciabatta for a satisfying supper.

Serves 4

225g/8oz/2 cups dried gnocchi or conchiglie
50g/2oz/¹/₂ cup pitted black olives, quartered lengthways

75g/3oz thinly sliced salami, any skin removed, diced
¹/₂ small red onion, finely chopped
1 large handful fresh basil leaves, shredded

For the dressing
60ml/4 tbsp extra virgin olive oil
good pinch of sugar, to taste
juice of ¹/₂ lemon
5ml/1 tsp Dijon mustard
10ml/2 tsp dried oregano
1 garlic clove, crushed
salt and ground black pepper

1 Bring a large pan of lightly salted water to the boil and cook the pasta until al dente.

2 Meanwhile, make the dressing for the pasta. Put the extra virgin olive oil in a large serving bowl with the sugar, lemon juice, mustard, oregano, garlic and a little salt and pepper to taste. Whisk well to mix.

3 Drain the pasta thoroughly, add it to the bowl of dressing and toss well to mix. Leave the dressed pasta to cool, stirring occasionally.

4 When the pasta is cold, add the black olives, diced salami, chopped onion and shredded basil and toss well to mix again. Adjust the seasoning, then serve immediately.

Cook's Tip
There are many different types of Italian salami that can be used for this salad. Salame napoletano is coarse cut and peppery, while salame milanese is fine cut and mild in flavour. It's a matter of individual taste!

Energy 467Kcal/1959kJ; Fat 19.9g; Saturated Fat 6.3g; Carbohydrate 42.8g; Fibre 3.4g

Energy 392Kcal/1641kJ; Fat 20.8g; Saturated Fat 4.6g; Carbohydrate 43g; Fibre 2.2g

Tuna & Sweetcorn Salad

This is an excellent main course salad for a summer lunch al fresco. The dish travels very well, so it is good for picnics, too.

Serves 4

175g/6oz/1½ cups dried
  conchiglie
175g/6oz canned tuna in olive oil,
  drained and flaked
175g/6oz canned sweetcorn,
  drained
75g/3oz bottled roasted red (bell)
  pepper, rinsed, dried and
  chopped
1 handful fresh basil leaves,
  roughly chopped
salt and ground black pepper

For the dressing

60ml/4 tbsp extra virgin olive oil
15ml/1 tbsp balsamic vinegar
5ml/1 tsp red wine vinegar
5ml/1 tsp Dijon mustard
5–10ml/1–2 tsp honey, to taste

1 Cook the pasta in boiling water until *al dente* or just tender. Drain it thoroughly, then rinse well under cold running water. Leave to drain until cold and dry, shaking the colander occasionally.

2 To make the salad dressing, put the olive oil in a large serving bowl, add the balsamic and red wine vinegar and whisk well together until emulsified. Add the Dijon mustard, honey and salt and pepper to taste and whisk again until thick.

3 Add the cooked pasta to the dressing and toss well to mix, then add the tuna, sweetcorn and roasted pepper and toss again. Mix in about half the fresh basil leaves and taste for seasoning. Serve at room temperature or chill for 2 hours. Sprinkle with the remaining basil just before serving.

Variation

If you have a little more time on your hands, try chargrilling or pan-frying fresh tuna steak, then break up and add to the salad. Also use two fresh red (bell) peppers instead of the bottled ones: simply roast, cool slightly, then remove the skin and chop.

Pink & Green Salad

Spiked with a little fresh chilli, this pretty salad makes a delicious light lunch served with hot ciabatta rolls and a bottle of sparkling dry Italian white wine. Prawns (shrimp) and avocado are a winning combination, so it's also a good choice for a buffet party spread.

Serves 4

225g/8oz/2 cups dried farfalle
juice of ½ lemon
1 small fresh red chilli, seeded
  and very finely chopped
60ml/4 tbsp chopped fresh basil
30ml/2 tbsp chopped fresh
  coriander
60ml/4 tbsp extra virgin olive oil
15ml/1 tbsp mayonnaise
250g/9oz/1½ cups peeled
  cooked prawns (shrimp)
1 avocado
salt and ground black pepper

1 Bring a pan of lightly salted water to the boil, add the pasta and cook until *al dente*.

2 Meanwhile, put the lemon juice and chilli in a serving bowl with half the basil and coriander and salt and pepper to taste. Whisk well to mix, then whisk in the oil and mayonnaise until thick. Add the prawns and gently stir to coat in the dressing.

3 Drain the pasta into a colander and rinse under cold running water until cold. Leave to drain and dry, shaking occasionally.

4 Halve, stone and peel the avocado, then cut the flesh into neat dice. Add to the prawns and dressing with the pasta, toss well to mix and taste for seasoning. Serve immediately, sprinkled with the remaining basil and coriander.

Cook's Tip

This pasta salad can be made several hours ahead of time, without the avocado. Cover the bowl with clear film (plastic wrap) and chill in the refrigerator. Prepare the avocado and add it to the salad just before serving or it will discolour.

Energy 398Kcal/1674kJ; Fat 16.3g; Saturated Fat 2.4g; Carbohydrate 47.2g; Fibre 2.2g

Energy 417Kcal/1750kJ; Fat 20.2g; Saturated Fat 3.2g; Carbohydrate 42.6g; Fibre 3.2g

Chargrilled Pepper Salad

This is a good dish to serve with plain barbecued chicken or grilled fish. The ingredients are simple, inexpensive and few, but the overall flavour is mouthwatering.

Serves 4

2 large (bell) peppers (red and green)

250g/9oz/2¼ cups dried fusilli tricolore
1 handful fresh basil leaves
1 handful fresh coriander leaves
1 garlic clove
salt and ground black pepper

For the dressing
30ml/2 tbsp pesto sauce
juice of ½ lemon
60ml/4 tbsp extra virgin olive oil

1 Put the peppers under a hot grill (broiler) and grill (broil) them for about 10 minutes, turning them frequently, until they are charred on all sides. Put the hot peppers in a plastic bag, seal the bag and set aside until the peppers are cool.

2 Meanwhile, cook the pasta according to the packet instructions. Whisk all the dressing ingredients together in a large serving bowl. Drain the cooked pasta well and add to the bowl of dressing. Toss well to mix and set aside to cool.

3 Remove the peppers from the bag and hold them one at a time under cold running water. Peel off the charred skins with your fingers, split the peppers open and pull out the cores. Rub off all the seeds under the running water, then pat the peppers dry on kitchen paper.

4 Chop the peppers and add them to the pasta. Put the basil, coriander and garlic on a board and chop them all together. Add to the pasta and toss to mix, then add salt and pepper to taste and serve.

> **Cook's Tip**
> Good-quality bottled pesto sauce is widely available and is a quick way of adding delicious flavour to pasta dishes.

Roasted Cherry Tomato & Rocket Salad

Roasted tomatoes are very juicy, with an intense, smoky-sweet flavour. Toss them with pasta to make a mouthwatering Italian-style salad, perfect to serve with plainly cooked meat.

Serves 4
225g/8oz/2 cups dried chifferini or pipe
450g/1lb ripe baby Italian plum tomatoes, halved lengthways

75ml/5 tbsp extra virgin olive oil
2 garlic cloves, cut into thin slivers
30ml/2 tbsp balsamic vinegar
2 pieces sun-dried tomato in olive oil, drained and chopped
large pinch of sugar, to taste
1 handful rocket (arugula), weighing about 65g/2½oz
salt and ground black pepper

1 Preheat the oven to 190°C/375°F/Gas 5. Meanwhile, bring a pan of lightly salted water to the boil, add the pasta and cook until al dente, or tender but still firm to the bite.

2 Arrange the halved tomatoes cut-side up in a roasting pan, drizzle 30ml/2tbsp of the oil over them and sprinkle with the slivers of garlic and salt and pepper to taste. Roast in the oven for 20 minutes, turning once.

3 Put the remaining oil in a large serving bowl with the vinegar, sun-dried tomatoes, sugar and a little salt and pepper to taste. Stir well to mix. Drain the pasta, add it to the bowl of dressing and toss to mix. Add the roasted tomatoes and mix gently.

4 Before serving, add the chopped rocket, toss lightly and taste for seasoning. Serve either at room temperature or chilled.

> **Variation**
> To make the salad a little more substantial, add 150g/5oz mozzarella cheese, drained and diced, with the rocket in Step 5.

Warm Tagliatelle Salad with Asparagus

A lovely pasta salad for spring days, warm tagliatelle is coated in a wonderful asparagus sauce and topped with eggs and ham.

Serves 4
450g/1lb asparagus
400g/14oz dried tagliatelle
225g/8oz cooked ham, in
  5mm/¼in thick slices, cut
  into fingers

2 eggs, hard-boiled and sliced
salt and ground black pepper
50g/2oz Parmesan cheese,
  shaved, to garnish

For the dressing
50g/2oz cooked potato
75ml/5 tbsp olive oil
15ml/1 tbsp lemon juice
10ml/2 tsp Dijon mustard
120ml/4fl oz/½ cup vegetable
  stock

1 Trim and discard the tough woody part of the asparagus. Cut the spears in half and cook the stem halves in salted boiling water for 12 minutes. After 6 minutes add the tips. Drain, then refresh under cold water until warm.

2 Finely chop 150g/5oz of the stem asparagus pieces. Place in a food processor with the dressing ingredients and process until smooth. Season with salt and pepper.

3 Bring a large pan of lightly salted water to the boil and cook the pasta until al dente. Drain, refresh under cold water until warm, then drain again.

4 To serve, toss the pasta with the asparagus sauce and divide among four pasta plates. Top with the ham, hard-boiled eggs and asparagus tips. Serve with a sprinkling of Parmesan shavings and black pepper.

> **Cook's Tip**
> When buying asparagus, look for spears with firm, tight tips. If they are drooping and open, the asparagus is past its best.

Seafood Salad

An Italian favourite, this salad can be served as a substantial first course or light main meal.

Serves 4–6
450g/1lb fresh mussels
250ml/8fl oz/1 cup dry
  white wine
2 garlic cloves, roughly chopped
1 handful fresh flat leaf parsley
175g/6oz/1 cup prepared squid
  rings

175g/6oz/1½ cups small dried
  pasta shapes
175g/6oz/1 cup cooked peeled
  prawns (shrimp)

For the dressing
90ml/6 tbsp extra virgin olive oil
juice of 1 lemon
5–10ml/1–2 tsp capers, to taste,
  roughly chopped
1 garlic clove, crushed
1 small handful fresh flat leaf
  parsley, finely chopped
salt and ground black pepper

1 Scrub the mussels under cold running water to remove the beards. Discard any that are open or that do not close when sharply tapped against the work surface.

2 Pour half the wine into a large pan, add the garlic, parsley and mussels. Cover the pan tightly and bring to the boil over high heat. Cook for about 5 minutes, shaking, until the mussels open. Turn the mussels and their liquid into a colander over a bowl. When cool enough to handle, remove the mussels from their shells, tipping any liquid into the bowl. Discard any closed ones.

3 Return the mussel cooking liquid to the pan and add the remaining wine and the squid. Bring to the boil, cover and simmer gently, stirring occasionally, for 30 minutes, or until the squid is tender. Leave the squid to cool in the cooking liquid.

4 Meanwhile, cook the pasta in boiling water until al dente and whisk all the dressing ingredients together in a large bowl. Drain the pasta, add to the dressing and toss well to mix. Cool.

5 Turn the cooled squid into a colander and rinse under cold water. Add the squid, mussels and prawns to the dressed pasta and toss. Cover the bowl tightly and chill well before serving.

Avocado, Tomato & Mozzarella Salad

This salad is made from ingredients representing the colours of the Italian flag – a sunny, cheerful dish!

Serves 4
175g/6oz/1½ cups dried farfalle
6 ripe red tomatoes
225g/8oz mozzarella cheese
1 large ripe avocado
30ml/2 tbsp chopped fresh basil
30ml/2 tbsp pine nuts, toasted
fresh basil sprig, to garnish

For the dressing
90ml/6 tbsp olive oil
30ml/2 tbsp wine vinegar
5ml/1 tsp balsamic vinegar
  (optional)
5ml/1 tsp wholegrain mustard
pinch of sugar
salt and ground black pepper

1 Cook the pasta in plenty of salted boiling water according to the instructions on the packet. Drain well and cool.

2 Using a sharp knife, slice the tomatoes thinly. Repeat for the mozzarella cheese, slicing it into thin, even rounds.

3 Halve the avocado, remove the stone and peel off the skin. Slice the flesh lengthways.

4 To make the dressing, place all the dressing ingredients together in a small bowl and whisk until well blended.

5 Arrange the sliced tomato, mozzarella cheese and avocado overlapping one another around the edge of a flat platter.

6 Toss the pasta with half the dressing and the chopped basil. Pile into the centre of the plate. Pour the remaining dressing over, scatter the pine nuts over the top and garnish with a sprig of fresh basil. Serve immediately.

> **Variation**
> For a starter, omit the pasta and top with half the dressing.

Cheese & Walnut Pasta Salad

The classic combination of blue cheese and walnuts gives this pasta salad lovely texture and taste.

Serves 4
225g/8oz/2 cups dried pasta
  shapes
mixed salad leaves, such as rocket
  (arugula), curly endive (US
  chicory), lamb's lettuce, baby
spinach, radicchio etc
225g/8oz Gorgonzola cheese,
  roughly crumbled
115g/4oz/1 cup walnut halves

For the dressing
30ml/2 tbsp walnut oil
60ml/4 tbsp sunflower oil
30ml/2 tbsp red wine vinegar or
  sherry vinegar
salt and ground black pepper

1 Bring a pan of lightly salted water to the boil, add the pasta and cook until al dente. Drain well and set aside to cool.

2 Wash the salad leaves, pat dry on kitchen paper and transfer to a large serving bowl.

3 To make the dressing, whisk together the walnut oil, sunflower oil, vinegar and salt and pepper to taste.

4 Pile the pasta in the centre of the leaves, scatter the cheese over the top and pour the dressing on top.

5 Scatter the walnuts over the salad. Toss just before serving.

> **Cook's Tip**
> Try toasting the walnuts under the grill (broiler) for a couple of minutes to release the flavour before adding to the salad.

> **Variation**
> Replace the Gorgonzola with Parmesan cheese shavings or crumbled goat's cheese.

Energy 520Kcal/2170kJ; Fat 34.3g; Saturated Fat 10.7g; Carbohydrate 37.4g; Fibre 2.9g

Energy 537Kcal/2241kJ; Fat 33.9g; Saturated Fat 12.7g; Carbohydrate 42.1g; Fibre 1.9g

Artichoke Pasta Salad

The exquisite taste of the artichokes adds a sweetness to this colourful vegetable pasta salad. Serve with salami and ciabatta for a tasty lunch dish.

Serves 4

150g/5oz broccoli
105ml/7 tbsp olive oil
1 red (bell) pepper, quartered, seeded and thinly sliced
1 onion, halved and thinly sliced
5ml/1 tsp dried thyme
45ml/3 tbsp sherry vinegar
450g/1lb/4 cups dried pasta shapes, such as penne or fusilli
2 x 175g/6oz jars marinated artichoke hearts, drained and thinly sliced
20–25 salt-cured black olives, pitted and chopped
30ml/2 tbsp chopped fresh parsley
salt and ground black pepper

1 Bring a pan of water to the boil, add the broccoli and cook for 5 minutes until tender. Drain and immediately refresh under cold running water. Drain again, then chop roughly and set aside until required.

2 Heat 30ml/2 tbsp of the olive oil in a non-stick frying pan. Add the red pepper and onion and cook over low heat for about 10 minutes, until just softened, stirring from time to time.

3 Stir in the thyme, 1.5ml/¼ tsp salt and the vinegar. Cook, stirring, for a further 30 seconds, then set aside until required.

4 Bring a pan of lightly salted water to the boil, add the pasta and cook until al dente. Drain, rinse with hot water, then drain again. Transfer to a large bowl. Add 30ml/2 tbsp of the oil and toss to coat thoroughly.

5 Add the artichokes, broccoli, olives, parsley, onion mixture and remaining oil to the pasta. Season with salt and pepper. Stir gently to mix well.

6 Leave the salad to stand for at least 1 hour before serving or chill overnight. Serve at room temperature.

Pasta Salad with Olives

This delicious salad combines all the flavours of the Mediterranean. A light and fresh-tasting way to serve pasta, this salad is particularly suitable for a picnic or barbecue on a hot summer's day.

Serves 6

450g/1lb/4 cups dried pasta shapes, such as farfalle or penne
60ml/4 tbsp extra virgin olive oil
10 sun-dried tomatoes, thinly sliced
30ml/2 tbsp capers, in brine or salted
115g/4oz/1 cup pitted black olives
2 garlic cloves, finely chopped
45ml/3 tbsp balsamic vinegar
45ml/3 tbsp chopped fresh parsley
salt and ground black pepper

1 Bring a pan of lightly salted water to the boil, add the pasta and cook until al dente. Drain and refresh under cold water until warm. Drain well and turn into a large serving bowl. Toss with the olive oil and set aside until required.

2 Soak the tomatoes in a bowl of hot water for 10 minutes, then drain, reserving the soaking water. Rinse the capers well. If they have been preserved in salt, soak them in a little hot water for 10 minutes. Rinse again.

3 Combine the olives, tomatoes, capers, garlic and vinegar in a small bowl. Season with salt and pepper.

4 Stir the olive mixture into the cooked pasta and toss well. Add 30–45ml/2–3 tbsp of the tomato soaking water if the salad seems too dry. Toss with the parsley and allow to stand for 15 minutes before serving.

> **Cook's Tip**
> This recipe uses sun-dried tomatoes that are sold dry in packets. The tomatoes are softened by soaking in hot water, then the soaking liquid, which has a great tomato flavour, can be used to moisten the pasta.

Energy 614Kcal/2583kJ; Fat 23.5g; Saturated Fat 3.3g; Carbohydrate 89.2g; Fibre 7.2g

Energy 353Kcal/1491kJ; Fat 11g; Saturated Fat 1.6g; Carbohydrate 57.3g; Fibre 3.6g

Roasted Mediterranean Vegetables with Pecorino

Shavings of tangy Pecorino cheese give this delicious dish of roasted vegetables a wonderful piquant flavour.

Serves 4–6

1 aubergine (eggplant), sliced
2 courgettes (zucchini), sliced
2 red or yellow (bell) peppers, quartered and seeded
1 large onion, thickly sliced
2 large carrots, cut in batons
4 firm plum tomatoes, halved
extra virgin olive oil, for brushing and sprinkling
45ml/3 tbsp chopped fresh parsley
45ml/3 tbsp pine nuts, lightly toasted
115g/4oz piece of Pecorino cheese
salt and ground black pepper

1 Layer the aubergine slices in a colander, sprinkling each layer with a little salt. Leave to drain over a sink for about 20 minutes, then rinse thoroughly under cold running water. Drain well and pat dry with kitchen paper. Preheat the oven to 220°C/425°F/Gas 7.

2 Spread out the aubergine slices, courgettes, peppers, onion, carrots and tomatoes in one or two large roasting pans. Brush the vegetables lightly with olive oil and roast for 20–30 minutes, or until they are lightly browned and the skins on the peppers have begun to blister.

3 Transfer the vegetables to a large serving platter. If you like, peel the peppers and discard the skins. Drizzle over any vegetable juices from the roasting pan and season to taste with salt and pepper.

4 As the vegetables cool, sprinkle them with more olive oil. When they are at room temperature, mix in the fresh parsley and toasted pine nuts.

5 Using a swivel vegetable peeler, shave the Pecorino and sprinkle the shavings over the vegetables.

Sweet & Sour Aubergine

In this delicious Sicilian dish, deep-fried aubergine (eggplant) is enhanced with a piquant celery, olive and tomato sauce. It is fantastic mopped up with chunks of rustic bread.

Serves 4

700g/1½lb aubergines (eggplants)
30ml/2 tbsp olive oil
1 onion, finely sliced
1 garlic clove, finely chopped
225g/8oz can plum tomatoes, peeled and finely chopped
120ml/4fl oz/½ cup white wine vinegar
30ml/2 tbsp sugar
tender central sticks of a head of celery (about 175g/6oz)
30ml/2 tbsp capers, rinsed
75g/3oz/½ cup green olives, pitted
oil, for deep-frying
30ml/2 tbsp chopped fresh parsley
salt and ground black pepper

1 Wash the aubergines and cut into small cubes. Sprinkle with salt and leave to drain in a colander for 1 hour.

2 Heat the oil in a large pan. Stir in the onion and cook until soft. Add the garlic and tomatoes and cook over a medium heat for 10 minutes, stirring occasionally.

3 Stir in the vinegar, sugar and black pepper. Simmer for a further 10 minutes until the sauce reduces.

4 Blanch the celery sticks in boiling water until tender. Drain, and chop into 2.5cm/1in pieces. Add to the sauce with the capers and olives.

5 Rinse the aubergine and pat dry with kitchen paper. Heat the oil to 185°C/360°F in a deep-fat frying pan and fry the aubergine in batches until golden. Drain on kitchen paper.

6 Add the aubergine to the sauce. Stir gently and season with salt and pepper. Stir in the parsley.

7 Allow the aubergine salad to stand for 30 minutes. Serve at room temperature.

Energy 223Kcal/928kJ; Fat 18g; Saturated Fat 2.7g; Carbohydrate 14.1g; Fibre 4.8g

Energy 225kcal/936kJ; Fat 14.3g; Saturated Fat 4.8g; Carbohydrate 13.2g; Fibre 4.5g

Aubergine Parmigiana

A classic Italian dish, this features blissfully tender sliced aubergines (eggplant) layered with melting creamy mozzarella, fresh Parmesan and a good home-made tomato sauce.

Serves 4–6
3 aubergines (eggplants), thinly sliced
olive oil, for brushing
300g/11oz mozzarella cheese, sliced
115g/4oz/1¼ cups freshly grated Parmesan cheese
30–45ml/2–3 tbsp dried breadcrumbs
salt and ground black pepper
basil sprigs, to garnish

For the sauce
30ml/2 tbsp olive oil
1 onion, finely chopped
2 garlic cloves, crushed
400g/14oz can chopped tomatoes
5ml/1 tsp sugar
about 6 basil leaves

1 Layer the aubergine slices in a colander, sprinkling each layer with a little salt. Leave to drain over a sink for about 20 minutes, then rinse the slices thoroughly under cold running water and pat dry with kitchen paper.

2 Preheat the oven to 200°C/400°F/Gas 6. Spread out the aubergine slices on non-stick baking sheets, brush the tops with olive oil and bake for 10–15 minutes, until softened.

3 To make the sauce, heat the oil in a pan and sauté the onion and garlic for 5 minutes. Add the canned tomatoes and sugar, with salt and pepper to taste. Bring to the boil, then lower the heat and simmer for about 10 minutes, until reduced and thickened. Tear the basil leaves into small pieces and add them to the tomato sauce.

4 Layer the aubergines in a greased baking dish with the mozzarella, the tomato sauce and the Parmesan, ending with Parmesan mixed with breadcrumbs. Bake for 20–25 minutes, until golden brown and bubbling. Stand for 5 minutes before serving, garnished with basil.

Potatoes Baked with Tomatoes

This simple, hearty dish from the south of Italy is best when tomatoes are in season and bursting with flavour, but it can also be made with canned plum tomatoes very successfully.

Serves 6
90ml/6 tbsp olive oil, plus extra for greasing
2 large red or yellow onions, thinly sliced
1kg/2¼lb baking potatoes, thinly sliced
450g/1lb tomatoes, fresh or canned, sliced
115g/4oz/1–1¼ cups freshly grated Cheddar or Parmesan cheese
a few fresh basil leaves
salt and ground black pepper

1 Preheat the oven to 180°C/350°F/Gas 4. Brush a large ovenproof dish generously with oil. Arrange some onions in a layer on the base of the dish, followed by a layer of potato and tomato slices.

2 Pour a little of the oil over the surface of the layered ingredients and sprinkle with some of the cheese. Season with salt and add a generous grinding of black pepper.

3 Continue to layer the ingredients in the dish until they are used up, adding oil, cheese and seasoning as before, and ending with an overlapping layer of potatoes and tomatoes.

4 Tear the basil leaves into small pieces, and add them here and there among the top layer, saving a few for garnish. Sprinkle the top with the remaining grated cheese and oil.

5 Pour 60ml/4 tbsp water over the dish. Bake in the oven for 1 hour, until the ingredients are tender.

6 Check the potatoes towards the end of cooking and if they are browning too much, place a sheet of foil or a flat baking sheet on top of the dish. Garnish the dish with the remaining fresh basil and serve hot.

Carrots with Marsala

The sweet flavour of Marsala is used to heighten the sweetness of the carrots in this Sicilian dish.

Serves 4
50g/2oz/4 tbsp butter
450g/1lb carrots, cut into sticks
5ml/1 tsp sugar
2.5ml/½ tsp salt
50ml/2fl oz/¼ cup Marsala

1 Melt the butter in a medium pan and add the carrots. Stir well to coat with the butter. Add the sugar and salt and mix well. Stir in the Marsala and simmer for 4–5 minutes.

2 Pour in enough water to barely cover the carrots. Cover the pan and cook until the carrots are tender. Remove the cover and cook until the liquid reduces almost completely. Serve hot.

Courgettes with Sun-dried Tomatoes

One way to preserve tomatoes for winter is to dry them in the sun, as they do all over southern Italy. These tomatoes have a concentrated, sweet flavour that goes well with courgettes (zucchini).

Serves 6
10 sun-dried tomatoes
175g/6fl oz/¾ cup warm water
75ml/5 tbsp olive oil
1 large onion, finely sliced
2 garlic cloves, finely chopped
1kg/2lb courgettes (zucchini), cut into thin strips
salt and ground black pepper

1 Slice the tomatoes into thin strips. Place in a bowl with the warm water. Allow to stand for 20 minutes.

2 Heat the oil in a large frying pan and stir in the onion. Cook gently to soften but do not allow to brown. Stir in the garlic and the courgettes. Cook for about 5 minutes, stirring.

3 Stir in the tomatoes and their liquid. Season with salt and pepper. Increase the heat; cook until the courgettes are tender.

Broccoli with Oil & Garlic

This is a very simple way of transforming steamed or blanched broccoli into a succulent Mediterranean dish. Peeling the broccoli stalks is easy and allows for even cooking.

Serves 6
1kg/2lb fresh broccoli
90ml/6 tbsp olive oil
2–3 garlic cloves, finely chopped
salt and ground black pepper

1 Wash the broccoli. Cut off any woody parts at the base of the stems. Using a small sharp knife, peel the broccoli stems. Cut any very long or wide stalks in half.

2 If steaming the broccoli, place water in the bottom of a pan equipped with a steamer and bring to the boil. Put the broccoli in the steamer, cover tightly and cook for 8–12 minutes, or until the stems are just tender when pierced with the point of a knife. Remove from the heat.

3 If blanching the broccoli, bring a large pan of water to the boil, drop the broccoli into the pan of boiling water and blanch for 5–6 minutes, until just tender. Drain.

4 In a frying pan large enough to hold all the broccoli pieces, gently heat the oil with the garlic. When the garlic is light golden (do not let it brown or it will be bitter) add the broccoli and cook over medium heat for 3–4 minutes, turning carefully to coat it with the hot oil. Season with salt and pepper. Serve hot or cold.

Variation
To turn the dish into a vegetarian topping for pasta, add about 25g/1oz each fresh breadcrumbs and pine nuts to the garlic at the beginning of step 4 and cook until golden. Then add the broccoli with 25g/1oz sultanas (golden raisins) and some chopped fresh parsley. Toss into cooked pasta and serve with roasted tomatoes.

Top Energy 189Kcal/782kJ; Fat 12.7g; Saturated Fat 7.9g; Carbohydrate 11.8g; Fibre 2.7g
Above Energy 136Kcal/561kJ; Fat 10g; Saturated Fat 1.5g; Carbohydrate 8.2g; Fibre 2.6g

Energy 159Kcal/657kJ; Fat 12.5g; Saturated Fat 1.9g; Carbohydrate 3.8g; Fibre 4.5g

Stewed Artichokes

Artichokes are eaten in many ways in Italy, sometimes sliced paper-thin and eaten raw as a salad, sometimes cut up and stewed lightly with garlic, parsley and wine, as in this delectable recipe.

Serves 6
1 lemon
4 large or 6 small globe
   artichokes
25g/1oz/2 tbsp butter
60ml/4 tbsp olive oil
2 garlic cloves, finely chopped
60ml/4 tbsp chopped fresh
   parsley
90ml/6 tbsp milk
90ml/6 tbsp white wine
salt and ground black pepper

1 Squeeze the lemon and put the juice and the squeezed halves in a large bowl of cold water. Wash the artichokes and prepare them one at a time. Cut off only the tip from the stem. Peel the stem with a small knife, pulling upwards towards the leaves. Pull off the small leaves around the stem, and continue snapping off the upper part of the dark outer leaves until you reach the taller inner leaves.

2 Slice the topmost part of the leaves off. Cut the artichoke into 4 or 6 segments.

3 Cut out the bristly "choke" from each segment. Place in the acidulated water to prevent the artichokes from darkening while you prepare the rest.

4 Blanch the artichokes in a large pan of rapidly boiling water for 4–5 minutes. Drain.

5 Heat the butter and olive oil in a large pan. Add the garlic and parsley and cook for 2–3 minutes. Stir in the artichokes. Season with salt and pepper.

6 Add 45ml/3 tbsp water and the milk, then cook for about 10 minutes or until the liquid has evaporated. Stir in the wine, cover and cook until the artichokes are tender.

Stuffed Onions

These savoury onions, stuffed with ham, cheese and herbs, are very versatile – either serve them as a snack or as an accompaniment to a meat dish.

Serves 6
6 large onions
115g/4oz/scant ¹/₂ cup ham, cut
   into small dice
1 egg
25g/1oz/¹/₂ cup fresh white
   breadcrumbs
45ml/3 tbsp finely chopped fresh
   parsley
1 garlic clove, finely chopped
pinch of freshly grated nutmeg
175g/6oz/³/₄ cup grated cheese,
   such as Parmesan or Romano
90ml/6 tbsp olive oil
salt and ground black pepper

1 Peel the onions without cutting through the base. Cook them in a large pan of boiling water for about 20 minutes. Drain and refresh in plenty of cold water.

2 Using a small sharp knife, cut around and scoop out the central section. Remove about half the inside (save it for soup). Lightly salt the empty cavities, then leave the onions to drain upside down.

3 Preheat the oven to 200°C/400°F/Gas 6. In a small bowl, beat the ham into the egg. Stir in the breadcrumbs, parsley, garlic, nutmeg and all but 45ml/3 tbsp of the grated cheese. Add 45ml/3 tbsp of the oil and season with salt and pepper.

4 Pat the insides of the onions dry with kitchen paper. Spoon the filling into each onion. Arrange the onions in one layer in an oiled baking dish.

5 Sprinkle the tops with the remaining cheese, then drizzle with oil. Bake for 45 minutes, or until the onions are tender and golden on top.

Green Beans with Tomatoes

A good dish for slightly over-ripe tomatoes.

Serves 4–6
45ml/3 tbsp olive oil
1 onion, preferably red, finely sliced
350g/12oz plum tomatoes, fresh
   or canned, peeled and chopped
5–6 leaves fresh basil, torn into
   pieces
450g/1lb fresh green beans,
   trimmed
salt and ground black pepper

1 Heat the oil in a large frying pan with a cover. Add the onion and cook for 5–6 minutes, until just soft. Add the tomatoes and cook over medium heat for about 6–8 minutes until softened. Stir in 120ml/4fl oz/¹/₂ cup water. Season and add the basil.

2 Stir in the green beans, turning them in the pan to coat with the sauce. Cover the pan and cook over medium heat for about 15–20 minutes, until the beans are tender. Stir occasionally and add a little more water if the sauce seems to be drying out too much. Serve hot or cold.

Energy 126Kcal/521kJ; Fat 11.9g; Saturated Fat 3.8g; Carbohydrate 1.5g; Fibre 1g

Top Energy 324Kcal/1350kJ; Fat 18.5g; Saturated Fat 5.4g; Carbohydrate 29g; Fibre 3.6g
Above Energy 82Kcal/341kJ; Fat 6.1g; Saturated Fat 0.9g; Carbohydrate 5.3g; Fibre 2.5g

Broad Bean Purée

Peeling broad (fava) beans leaves them tender and sweet, producing a tasty, colourful purée, perfect for serving alongside a selection of Italian meats.

Serves 4
1kg/2lb fresh broad (fava) beans in their pods, or 400g/14oz shelled broad (fava) beans, thawed if frozen
1 onion, finely chopped
2 small potatoes, peeled and diced
50g/2oz/¼ cup prosciutto crudo
15ml/1 tbsp extra virgin olive oil
salt and ground black pepper

1 Remove the beans from their pods, if using fresh beans. Place the shelled beans in a pan and cover with water. Bring to the boil and cook for 5 minutes. Drain thoroughly. When they are cool enough to handle, remove the skins from the beans.

2 Place the peeled beans in a pan with the onion and potatoes. Add enough water just to cover the vegetables. Bring to the boil. Lower the heat slightly, cover and simmer for 15–20 minutes, until the vegetables are very soft. Check occasionally that all the water has not evaporated: if necessary add a few tablespoons more.

3 Chop the prosciutto ham into very small dice. Heat the oil and sauté until the ham is golden.

4 Mash or purée the bean mixture. Return to the pan. If the mixture is very moist, cook it over medium heat until it reduces slightly. Stir in the oil with the ham. Season to taste and cook for 2 minutes. Serve immediately.

> **Cook's Tip**
> When skinning the broad (fava) beans, hold the hot beans under cold running water for a while; you'll find the skins will slip off quite easily.

Energy 246Kcal/1032kJ; Fat 9.8g; Saturated Fat 1.6g; Carbohydrate 27.9g; Fibre 8g

Grilled Radicchio & Courgettes

Radicchio is often grilled or barbecued in Italian cooking to give it a special flavour. Combined with courgettes (zucchini), it makes a quick and tasty side dish.

Serves 4
2–3 firm heads radicchio, round or long type, rinsed
4 courgettes (zucchini)
90ml/6 tbsp olive oil
salt and ground black pepper

1 Preheat the grill (broiler) or prepare a barbecue. Using a sharp knife, cut the radicchio in half through the root section or base. Cut the courgettes into 1cm/½in diagonal slices.

2 When ready to cook, brush the vegetables with the olive oil and add salt and pepper. Cook for 4–5 minutes on each side.

Deep-fried Cauliflower

Deep-frying is a popular form of cooking in Italy and it is used for everything, from cheese to fruit. These cauliflower florets, with their crisp coating, make a good antipasto or side dish.

Serves 4
1 large cauliflower
1 egg
100g/3½oz/scant 1 cup flour
175ml/6fl oz/¾ cup white wine
oil, for deep-frying
salt and ground black pepper

1 Soak the cauliflower in a bowl of salted water. Beat the egg in a mixing bowl, then season and beat in the flour to make a thick paste. Add the wine, and, if necessary, add more to make a fairly runny batter. Cover and allow to rest for 30 minutes.

2 Steam or boil the cauliflower until just tender – do not overcook. Cut it into small florets when cool.

3 Heat the oil to about 185°C/360°F, or until a small bread cube sizzles as soon as it is dropped in. Dip each floret into the batter before deep-frying until golden. Remove with a slotted spoon and drain on kitchen paper. Serve sprinkled with salt.

Top Energy 311Kcal/1294kJ; Fat 19g; Saturated Fat 2.6g; Carbohydrate 22.7g; Fibre 2.6g
Above Energy 189Kcal/780kJ; Fat 17.6g; Saturated Fat 2.6g; Carbohydrate 4.4g; Fibre 2g

Roast Mushroom Caps

Hunting for edible wild mushrooms is one of the Italians' great passions. The most prized are porcini, which grow in forests and are sometimes available here fresh in the autumn.

Serves 4

4 large mushroom caps
2 garlic cloves, chopped
45ml/3 tbsp chopped fresh
  parsley
extra virgin olive oil, for drizzling
salt and ground black pepper

1 Preheat the oven to 190C°/375°F/Gas 5. Carefully wipe the mushrooms clean with a damp cloth or kitchen paper. Cut off the stems. (Save them for soup if they are not too woody). Oil a baking dish large enough to hold the mushrooms in one layer.

2 Place the mushroom caps in the dish, smooth-side down. Mix together the chopped garlic and parsley and sprinkle the mixture over the mushroom caps.

3 Season the mushrooms with salt and pepper, then sprinkle with oil. Bake for 20–25 minutes until cooked through.

Baked Fennel with Parmesan

Fennel is widely eaten in Italy, both raw and cooked. It is delicious married with the sharpness of Parmesan cheese in this quick and simple dish.

Serves 4–6

1kg/2lb fennel bulbs, washed and
  cut in half
50g/2oz/2 tbsp butter
40g/1½oz/½ cup freshly grated
  Parmesan cheese

1 Cook the fennel in a large pan of boiling water until just tender and not at all mushy. Drain well. Preheat the oven to 200°C/400°F/Gas 6.

2 Cut the fennel bulbs lengthways into 4 or 6 pieces. Place them in a buttered baking dish. Dot with butter, sprinkle with Parmesan and bake for about 20 minutes, until golden.

Piedmontese Aromatic Stewed Mushrooms

The people of Piedmont are very partial to garlic and use it to great effect in their cuisine. In this traditional recipe, the garlic is used to transform a simple dish of mushrooms into something quite memorable.

Serves 6

750g/1½lb fresh mushrooms, a
  mixture of wild and cultivated
90ml/6 tbsp olive oil
2 garlic cloves, finely chopped
45ml/3 tbsp chopped fresh
  parsley
salt and ground black pepper

1 Clean the mushrooms carefully by wiping them with a damp cloth or kitchen paper.

2 Cut off the woody tips of the stems and discard. Slice the stems and caps fairly thickly.

3 Heat the oil in a large frying pan. Stir in the garlic and cook for about 1 minute. Add the mushrooms and cook for 8–10 minutes, stirring occasionally.

4 Season with salt and pepper and stir in the parsley. Cook for a further 5 minutes, then transfer to a warmed serving dish and serve immediately.

Cook's Tip
Ideally you should use a combination of both wild and cultivated mushrooms for this dish to give a nicely balanced flavour. A good mixture of mushroom varieties would be chanterelles and chestnut mushrooms: both are now sold in good supermarkets.

Variation
For a tasty snack, use the mushrooms to fill an omelette or stir them into scrambled eggs and serve on buttered toast.

Top Energy 149Kcal/616kJ; Fat 12.6g; Saturated Fat 7.8g; Carbohydrate 2.8g; Fibre 3.6g
Above Energy 189Kcal/780kJ; Fat 17.6g; Saturated Fat 2.6g; Carbohydrate 4.4g; Fibre 2g

Energy 122Kcal/502kJ; Fat 11.7g; Saturated Fat 1.7g; Carbohydrate 1.5g; Fibre 1.9g

Fresh Tomato Sauce

This is the famous Neapolitan sauce that is made in summer when tomatoes are very ripe and sweet. It is very simple, so that nothing detracts from the flavour of the tomatoes themselves. It is served here with spaghetti, which is the traditional choice of pasta.

Serves 4
675g/1½lb ripe Italian plum tomatoes
60ml/4 tbsp olive oil
1 onion, finely chopped
350g/12oz fresh or dried spaghetti
1 small handful fresh basil leaves
salt and ground black pepper
shaved Parmesan cheese, to serve

1 With a sharp knife, cut a cross in the base of each tomato. Bring a medium pan of water to the boil and remove from the heat. Plunge a few of the tomatoes into the water, leave for 30 seconds or so, then lift them out with a slotted spoon. Repeat with the remaining tomatoes, then peel off the skins and roughly chop the flesh.

2 Heat the oil in a large pan, add the chopped onion and cook over low heat, stirring frequently, for about 5 minutes, until softened and lightly coloured. Add the tomatoes, with salt and pepper to taste, bring to a simmer, then turn the heat down to low and cover. Cook, stirring occasionally, for 30–40 minutes, until thick.

3 Meanwhile, bring a pan of lightly salted water to the boil, add the pasta and cook until al dente. Shred the basil leaves finely.

4 Remove the sauce from the heat, stir in the basil and taste for seasoning. Drain the pasta, turn it into a warmed serving bowl, pour the sauce over and toss well. Serve immediately, with coarsely shaved Parmesan handed separately.

> **Cook's Tip**
> The Italian plum tomatoes called San Marzano are the best variety to use. When fully ripe, their thin skins peel off easily.

Rigatoni with Winter Tomato Sauce

In winter, when fresh tomatoes are not at their best, this is the sauce the Italians make. Canned tomatoes combined with soffritto (the sautéed mixture of chopped onion, carrot, celery and garlic) and herbs give a better flavour than winter tomatoes.

Serves 6–8
60ml/4 tbsp olive oil
1 garlic clove, thinly sliced
1 onion, finely chopped
1 carrot, finely chopped
1 celery stick, finely chopped

a few leaves each fresh basil, thyme and oregano or marjoram
2 x 400g/14oz cans chopped Italian plum tomatoes
15ml/1 tbsp sun-dried tomato paste
5ml/1 tsp sugar
about 90ml/6 tbsp dry red or white wine (optional)
350g/12oz/3 cups dried rigatoni
salt and ground black pepper
coarsely shaved Parmesan cheese, to serve
chopped fresh mixed herbs, to garnish (optional)

1 Heat the olive oil in a medium pan, add the garlic slices and stir over very low heat for 1–2 minutes.

2 Add the chopped onion, carrot and celery and the fresh herbs. Cook over a low heat, stirring frequently, for 5–7 minutes, until the vegetables have softened and are lightly coloured.

3 Add the canned tomatoes, tomato paste and sugar, then stir in the wine, if using. Add salt and pepper to taste. Bring to the boil, stirring, then lower the heat to a gentle simmer. Cook, uncovered, for about 45 minutes, stirring occasionally to prevent sticking on the bottom of the pan.

4 Bring a pan of lightly salted water to the boil and cook the pasta until al dente. Drain and turn into a warmed serving bowl.

5 Taste the sauce for seasoning, pour the sauce over the pasta and toss well. Garnish with chopped mixed fresh herbs, if you like. Serve immediately, with shavings of Parmesan handed separately in a bowl.

Energy 431Kcal/1821kJ; Fat 13.2g; Saturated Fat 1.9g; Carbohydrate 70.4g; Fibre 4.9g

Energy 226Kcal/956kJ; Fat 6.6g; Saturated Fat 1g; Carbohydrate 37.8g; Fibre 2.7g

Cappelletti with Tomatoes & Cream

Tomatoes, cream and fresh basil are a winning combination. In this very quick and easy recipe, the sauce coats little pasta purses filled with soft cheeses to make a substantial supper dish for vegetarians. If you prefer a lighter dish, you can use the sauce to coat plain, unstuffed pasta. Small shapes such as penne, farfalle or conchiglie are best.

Serves 4
400ml/14fl oz/1²/₃ cups passata
90ml/6 tbsp dry white wine
150ml/¼ pint/²/₃ cup double (heavy) cream
225g/8oz/2½ cups fresh cappelletti
1 small handful fresh basil leaves
60ml/4 tbsp freshly grated Parmesan cheese
salt and ground black pepper

1 Pour the passata and wine into a medium pan and stir to mix. Bring to the boil over medium heat, then add the cream and stir until evenly mixed and bubbling. Turn the heat down to low and leave to simmer.

2 Cook the cappelletti until *al dente*: 5–7 minutes or according to the instructions on the packet. Meanwhile, finely shred most of the basil leaves.

3 Drain the pasta well, return it to the pan and toss it with the grated Parmesan. Taste the sauce for seasoning, pour it over the pasta and toss well. Serve immediately, sprinkled with shredded basil and whole basil leaves.

Cook's Tips

• *Cappelletti with a variety of fillings are available at supermarkets and Italian delicatessens. Other stuffed pasta shapes, such as tortelloni and ravioli can be used with this sauce.*
• *The tomato sauce can be made up to a day ahead, then chilled until ready to use. Reheat gently in a heavy pan while the pasta is cooking.*

Pasta with Uncooked Tomato Sauce

This is a wonderfully simple uncooked tomato sauce that goes well with many different kinds of pasta, both long strands and short shapes. It is always made in summer when plum tomatoes have ripened on the vine in the sun and have their fullest flavour. The ricotta salata gives it extra texture and flavour.

Serves 4
500g/1¼lb ripe Italian plum tomatoes
1 large handful fresh basil leaves
75ml/5 tbsp extra virgin olive oil
115g/4oz ricotta salata cheese, diced
1 garlic clove, crushed
350g/12oz/3 cups dried pasta
salt and ground black pepper
coarsely shaved Pecorino cheese, to serve

1 Roughly chop the plum tomatoes, removing the cores and as many of the seeds as you can. Tear the basil leaves into shreds with your fingers.

2 Put the tomatoes in a bowl with the basil, olive oil, diced ricotta and garlic. Add salt and pepper to taste and stir well. Cover and leave at room temperature for 1–2 hours to allow the flavours to mingle.

3 Meanwhile, bring a pan of lightly salted water to the boil, add the pasta and cook until *al dente*.

4 Drain the pasta and turn into a large serving dish. Taste the tomato sauce to check the seasoning, then pour it over the hot pasta. Serve immediately with shavings of Pecorino handed separately in a small bowl.

Cook's Tip

Ricotta salata is a salted and dried version of ricotta cheese. It is firmer than the traditional soft white ricotta, and can be easily diced, crumbled and even grated. It is available from specialist delicatessens. If you have a problem finding it, try using feta cheese instead.

Energy 479Kcal/2004kJ; Fat 26.2g; Saturated Fat 15.7g; Carbohydrate 45.7g; Fibre 2.7g

Energy 196Kcal/813kJ; Fat 18.3g; Saturated 4.7g; Carbohydrate 4.8g; Fibre 1.3g

Tagliatelle with Italian Mushrooms

Porcini mushrooms give this sauce a wonderful depth.

Serves 2–4

25g/1oz dried porcini mushrooms
175ml/6fl oz/³⁄₄ cup warm water
900g/2lb tomatoes, peeled,
  seeded and chopped or drained
  canned tomatoes, crushed
1.5ml/¼ tsp dried hot chilli flakes

45ml/3 tbsp olive oil
4 slices pancetta or rashers
  unsmoked back bacon, cut into
  thin strips
1 large garlic clove, finely chopped
350g/12oz fresh or dried
  tagliatelle or fettuccine
salt and ground black pepper
freshly grated Parmesan cheese,
  to serve

1 Put the mushrooms in a bowl and cover with the warm water. Leave to soak for 20 minutes.

2 Meanwhile, put the tomatoes in a pan with the chilli flakes and seasoning. Bring to the boil, reduce the heat and simmer for about 30–40 minutes, until reduced to 750ml/1¼ pints/ 3 cups. Stir from time to time to prevent sticking.

3 Lift the mushrooms out of the soaking liquid and squeeze the remaining liquid into the bowl. Set the mushrooms aside. Pour the soaking liquid into the tomatoes through a muslin-lined sieve (strainer). Simmer the tomatoes for a further 15 minutes.

4 Meanwhile, heat 30ml/2 tbsp of the oil in a frying pan. Add the pancetta and fry until golden but not crisp. Add the garlic and mushrooms and fry for 3 minutes, stirring. Set aside.

5 Bring a pan of lightly salted water to the boil, add the pasta and cook until *al dente*.

6 Add the bacon and mushroom mixture to the tomato sauce and mix well. Season with salt and ground black pepper.

7 Drain the pasta and return to the pan. Add the remaining oil and toss to coat. Divide the pasta among hot plates, spoon the sauce on top and serve with grated Parmesan cheese.

Fusilli with Tomato & Vegetable Sauce

The tomatoes in this sauce are enhanced by the addition of extra vegetables. Tasty and easy to make, the sauce is good with all types of pasta, from spiral-shaped fusilli to tubular penne.

Serves 4

500g/1¼ lb tomatoes, fresh or
  canned, chopped

1 carrot chopped
1 celery stick, chopped
1 onion, chopped
1 garlic clove, crushed
75ml/5 tbsp olive oil
a few leaves fresh basil or a small
  pinch dried oregano
350g/12oz/3 cups dried fusilli
salt and ground black pepper

1 Place the tomatoes in a heavy pan with the carrot, celery, onion, garlic, oil and herbs. Season with salt and pepper and simmer for 30 minutes.

2 Process the tomato sauce in a food processor or press through a sieve (strainer) to purée.

3 Return the sauce to the pan, correct the seasoning and simmer again for about 15 minutes. Meanwhile, bring a pan of lightly salted water to the boil and cook the pasta until *al dente*.

4 Remove the sauce from the heat and taste for seasoning. Drain the pasta, turn into a warmed serving dish, pour the sauce over and toss well. Serve immediately.

Spaghetti with Garlic & Oil

Popular throughout Italy, this is one of the simplest and most satisfying pasta dishes of all. For the best flavour, it is essential to use a top quality olive oil.

Serves 4

400g/14oz spaghetti
90ml/6 tbsp extra virgin olive oil
3 garlic cloves, chopped
60ml/4 tbsp chopped fresh
  parsley
salt and ground black pepper
freshly grated Parmesan cheese,
  to serve (optional)

1 Bring a large pan of lightly salted water to the boil and drop in the spaghetti.

2 Heat the oil in a large frying pan and gently sauté the garlic until it is barely golden. Do not let it brown or it will taste bitter. Stir in the parsley. Season with salt and pepper. Remove from the heat until the pasta is ready.

3 Drain the pasta when it is barely *al dente*. Add it to the pan with the oil and garlic and cook together for 2–3 minutes, stirring well to coat the spaghetti with the sauce. Serve immediately in a warmed serving bowl, with freshly grated Parmesan handed separately, if liked.

Energy 464Kcal/1961kJ; Fat 15g; Saturated Fat 3.1g; Carbohydrate 71.8g; Fibre 4.9g

Top Energy 108Kcal/447kJ; Fat 9.5g, Saturated Fat 1.4g; Carbohydrate 4.9g; Fibre 1.5g
Above Energy 545Kcal/2296kJ; Fat 19g; Saturated Fat 2.6g; Carbohydrate 85g; Fibre 4.2g

Spaghetti with Walnut Sauce

Like pesto, this sauce is traditionally ground in a mortar and pestle, but works just as well made in a food processor. It is also very good on tagliatelle and other noodles.

Serves 4
115g/4oz/1 cup walnut pieces or
  halves
45ml/3 tbsp fresh breadcrumbs

45ml/3 tbsp olive or walnut oil
45ml/3 tbsp chopped fresh
  parsley
1–2 garlic cloves (optional)
50g/2oz/¼ cup butter, at room
  temperature
30ml/2 tbsp cream
salt and ground black pepper
400g/14oz wholewheat spaghetti
  freshly grated Parmesan cheese,
  to serve

1 Drop the nuts into a small pan of boiling water and cook for 1–2 minutes. Drain. Slip off the skins and pat dry on kitchen paper. Coarsely chop and set aside about a quarter of the nuts.

2 Place the remaining nuts, the breadcrumbs, oil, parsley and garlic, if using, in a food processor or blender. Process to a paste. Transfer to a bowl and stir in the softened butter and the cream. Season with salt and pepper.

3 Bring a pan of lightly salted water to the boil and cook the pasta until *al dente*. Drain, then toss with the sauce. Sprinkle with the reserved nuts and serve with the Parmesan cheese.

> **Cook's Tip**
> When cooking long shapes like spaghetti, drop one end of the pasta into the water and, as it softens, push it down gently until it bends in the middle and is completely immersed. Refer to the packet instructions for cooking times as these can vary from type to type. As a general rule, dried pasta needs 8–10 minutes. Do not be tempted to overcook pasta; it should be cooked until al dente, that is until it is tender but still firm to the bite. Always test pasta for doneness just before you think it should be ready to avoid overcooking.

Linguine with Pesto Sauce

Pesto, the famous Italian basil sauce, originates in Liguria, where the sea breezes are said to give the local basil a particularly fine flavour. It is traditionally made with a mortar and pestle, but it is easier to make in a food processor or blender.

Serves 5–6
65g/2½oz/¾ cup fresh basil
  leaves
3–4 garlic cloves, peeled
45ml/3 tbsp pine nuts
2.5ml/½ tsp salt
75ml/5 tbsp olive oil
50g/2oz/½ cup freshly grated
  Parmesan cheese
60ml/4 tbsp freshly grated
  Pecorino cheese
ground black pepper
500g/1¼lb linguine

1 Place the basil in a mortar with the garlic, pine nuts, salt and olive oil and crush to a paste with a pestle. Alternatively, place the ingredients in a blender or food processor and process until smooth. Transfer to a bowl.

2 Stir in the Parmesan and Pecorino cheeses, then season with salt and pepper to taste.

3 Bring a large pan of lightly salted water to the boil, add the pasta and cook until *al dente*. Just before draining the pasta, remove about 60ml/4 tbsp of the cooking water and stir it into the pesto sauce.

4 Drain the pasta thoroughly, transfer to a serving bowl, add the sauce and toss together. Serve immediately.

> **Cook's Tip**
> Hard Pecorino can be grated and used exactly like Parmesan. It has a more pungent flavour, which is well suited to spicy pasta dishes, such as penne all'arrabiata, but it is too strong for more delicate dishes like risotto. Well-matured (sharp) Pecorino will keep in the refrigerator for several weeks wrapped in foil.

Energy 607Kcal/2553kJ; Fat 25g; Saturated Fat 7.3g; Carbohydrate 75.9g; Fibre 3.8g

Energy 736Kcal/3080kJ; Fat 42.5g; Saturated Fat 12g; Carbohydrate 74.6g; Fibre 9.9g

Tagliatelle with Sun-dried Tomatoes

Sun-dried tomatoes, with their intense flavour, are combined with fresh plum tomatoes to make a tasty sauce that is perfect with any type of pasta.

Serves 4
1 garlic clove, crushed
1 celery stick, finely sliced
115g/4oz/1 cup sun-dried
  tomatoes, finely chopped
90ml/3½fl oz/scant ½ cup red
  wine
8 plum tomatoes
350g/12oz dried tagliatelle
salt and ground black pepper

1 Put the garlic, celery, sun-dried tomatoes and wine into a large pan. Gently cook for about 15 minutes.

2 Slash the bottoms of the plum tomatoes and plunge into a pan of boiling water for 1 minute, then transfer them to a pan of cold water. Slip off their skins. Cut in half, remove the seeds and cores and roughly chop the flesh.

3 Add the plum tomatoes to the pan and simmer for a further 5 minutes. Season to taste.

4 Meanwhile, bring a pan of lightly salted water to the boil, add the pasta and cook until *al dente*. Drain well. Toss with half the sauce and serve on warmed plates, with the remaining sauce spooned over each serving.

Cook's Tip

Sun-drying tomatoes intensifies their flavour and is a way of savouring the full taste of tomatoes in winter. In Italy, it is still possible to find tomatoes that have been literally dried in the sun, but the commercially produced "sun-dried" varieties are usually air-dried by machine. A wrinkled, dark red colour, they are sold dry in packets or preserved in olive oil. Both types are suitable for this recipe. Usually it is best to soak the dry type in hot water until soft before using in a recipe.

Fusilli with Peppers & Onions

Peppers are characteristic of southern Italy. When grilled and peeled they have a delicious smoky flavour, and are easier to digest. Simply team them up with red onion and garlic that has been lightly cooked in olive oil, to make an easy pasta sauce bursting with authentic Italian flavours.

Serves 4
450g/1lb red and yellow (bell)
  peppers
90ml/6 tbsp olive oil
1 large red onion, thinly sliced
2 garlic cloves, minced
400g/14oz/3½ cups fusilli
45ml/3 tbsp finely chopped
  fresh parsley
salt and ground black pepper
freshly grated Parmesan cheese,
  to serve

1 Place the peppers under a hot grill (broiler) and turn occasionally until they are black and blistered on all sides. Remove from the heat, place in a plastic bag and leave for 5 minutes.

2 Peel the skin from the peppers. Cut them into quarters, remove the cores and seeds and slice into thin strips.

3 Heat the oil in a large frying pan. Add the onion and cook over medium heat for 5–8 minutes, until it is translucent. Stir in the garlic and cook for a further 2 minutes.

4 Bring a pan of lightly salted water to the boil, add the pasta and cook until *al dente*.

5 Meanwhile, add the pepper strips to the onion and mix together gently. Stir in about 45ml/3 tbsp of the pasta cooking water. Season with salt and pepper to taste, then stir in the chopped parsley.

6 Drain the pasta thoroughly. Add the pasta to the frying pan containing the vegetables and cook over medium heat for 1–2 minutes, stirring constantly to coat the pasta with the vegetable sauce. Serve with the freshly grated Parmesan handed round separately.

Energy 369Kcal/1570kJ; Fat 2.3g; Saturated Fat 0.4g; Carbohydrate 74.9g; Fibre 5.3g

Energy 536kcal/2255kJ; Fat 18.9g; Saturated Fat 2.7g; Carbohydrate 82.8g.; Fibre 5.5g

Orecchiette with Broccoli

Puglia, in southern Italy, specializes in imaginative pasta and vegetable combinations. Here the famous ear-shaped pasta from the region is tossed with fresh-tasting broccoli florets and a tangy garlic dressing.

Serves 6
800g/1¾lb broccoli
450g/1lb/4 cups orecchiette
or penne
90ml/6 tbsp olive oil
3 garlic cloves, finely chopped
salt and ground black pepper

1 Using a small sharp knife, peel the stems of the broccoli, starting from the base and pulling up towards the florets. Discard the woody parts of the stem. Cut the florets and stems into 5cm/2in pieces.

2 Bring a large pan of water to the boil. Drop in the broccoli, and boil for about 5–8 minutes, until barely tender. Using a slotted spoon, transfer the broccoli pieces from the pan to a serving bowl. Do not discard the cooking water.

3 Add salt to the broccoli cooking water. Bring it back to the boil. Drop in the pasta, stir well and cook until *al dente*.

4 Meanwhile, heat the oil in a small pan. Add the garlic and cook for 2–3 minutes. Using a fork, mash the garlic to a paste. Cook gently for a further 3–4 minutes.

5 Before draining the pasta, ladle 1–2 cupfuls of the cooking water over the broccoli. Add the drained pasta and the hot oil mixture. Toss well and season with salt and pepper, if necessary. Serve immediately.

Cook's Tip
The pasta is cooked in the broccoli cooking water to help it absorb more of the vegetable's flavour and to keep the nutrients in the water.

Short Pasta with Cauliflower

This is an Italian pasta version of cauliflower cheese. Serve with a fresh green salad for a well-balanced supper dish.

Serves 6
1 cauliflower
475ml/16fl oz/2 cups milk
1 bay leaf

50g/2oz/¼ cup butter
50g/2oz/½ cup flour
75g/3oz/¾ cup freshly grated
Parmesan or Romano cheese
500g/1¼lb/5 cups pennoni rigati,
tortiglioni, or other short pasta
salt and ground black pepper

1 Bring a large pan of water to the boil. Wash the cauliflower well and divide into florets. Boil the florets for 8–10 minutes until they are just tender. Remove them from the pan with a slotted spoon. Chop the cauliflower into bite-size pieces and set aside. Do not discard the cooking water.

2 Make a béchamel sauce by gently heating the milk with the bay leaf in a small pan, without allowing it to boil. Melt the butter in a heavy pan. Add the flour and mix to a paste with a wire whisk, making sure that there are no lumps. Cook gently for 2–3 minutes, whisking constantly: do not allow the mixture to turn brown.

3 Strain the hot milk into the flour and butter mixture and mix with the whisk until smooth.

4 Bring the sauce to the boil, stirring constantly, and cook for 4–5 minutes more. Season with salt and pepper. Add the cheese and stir over low heat until it melts. Stir in the cauliflower pieces.

5 Bring the cauliflower cooking water back to the boil. Add salt, stir in the pasta and cook until *al dente*. Drain the pasta and transfer to a warm serving bowl.

6 Pour the cauliflower sauce over the pasta. Stir gently together and serve immediately.

Short Pasta with Spring Vegetables

In spring, the Italian markets are overflowing with an astonishing range of seasonal vegetables, all bursting with flavour. Local cooks take great delight in turning this abundant produce into fresh-tasting sauces for pasta.

Serves 6

1 or 2 small young carrots
2 spring onions (scallions)
175g/6oz courgettes (zucchini)
2 tomatoes
75g/3oz green beans
1 yellow (bell) pepper
60ml/4 tbsp olive oil
25g/1oz/2 tbsp butter
75g/3oz/³⁄₄ cup shelled peas,
    fresh or frozen
1 garlic clove, finely chopped
5–6 leaves fresh basil, torn
    into pieces
salt and ground black pepper
500g/1¼lb/5 cups short coloured
    or plain pasta such as fusilli,
    penne or farfalle
freshly grated Parmesan cheese,
    to serve

1 Cut the carrots, spring onions, courgettes, tomatoes and beans into small, bite-size pieces. Cut the pepper in half, remove the core and seeds, then cut into similar size pieces.

2 Heat the oil and butter in a large frying pan. Add the chopped vegetables and peas and cook over medium heat for 5–6 minutes, stirring occasionally.

3 Add the garlic and the basil to the vegetables in the pan and season with salt and pepper. Cover the pan and cook for 5–8 minutes more, or until the vegetables are just tender.

4 Meanwhile, bring a pan of lightly salted water to the boil. Add the pasta and cook until *al dente*. Reserve a cupful of the cooking water, then drain the pasta.

5 Turn the pasta into the pan of sauce and mix well to distribute the vegetables evenly. If the sauce seems too dry, add a few tablespoons of the reserved pasta water.

6 Transfer to a warmed serving dish and serve with the Parmesan handed separately.

Energy 429Kcal/1810kJ; Fat 13.6g; Saturated Fat 4g; Carbohydrate 68.7g; Fibre 4.9g

Fusilli with Mascarpone & Spinach

This creamy, green sauce tossed in lightly cooked pasta is best served with plenty of sun-dried tomato ciabatta bread and sprigs of fresh thyme.

Serves 4

350g/12oz/3 cups fresh or dried
    fusilli
50g/2oz/¼ cup butter
1 onion, chopped
1 garlic clove, chopped
30ml/2 tbsp fresh thyme leaves
225g/8oz frozen spinach leaves,
    thawed
225g/8oz/1 cup mascarpone
    cheese
salt and ground black pepper
fresh thyme sprigs, to garnish

1 Cook the pasta in plenty of boiling salted water according to the instructions on the packet.

2 Melt the butter in a large pan and fry the onion for 10 minutes, until softened.

3 Stir in the garlic, thyme leaves, spinach and seasoning and heat gently for about 5 minutes, stirring occasionally, until completely heated through.

4 Stir in the mascarpone cheese and cook gently, until heated through. Do not boil.

5 Drain the pasta thoroughly and stir into the sauce. Toss until well coated. Serve immediately, garnished with thyme sprigs.

> **Cook's Tip**
> *Mascarpone is a rich Italian cream cheese. If you cannot find any, use ordinary full-fat cream cheese instead.*

> **Variation**
> *Add one or two spoonfuls of pesto sauce and/or pine nuts into the sauce just before draining the pasta to enhance the herby flavour.*

Energy 513kcal/2155kJ; Fat 20.5g; Saturated Fat 11.9g; Carbohydrate 68.8g; Fibre 3.9g

Linguine with Sun-dried Tomato Pesto

Tomato pesto was once a rarity, but is becoming increasingly popular. It is made using sun-dried tomatoes instead of basil.

Serves 4
25g/1oz/⅓ cup pine nuts
25g/1oz/⅓ cup freshly grated
  Parmesan cheese
50g/2oz/½ cup sun-dried
  tomatoes in olive oil
1 garlic clove, roughly chopped
60ml/4 tbsp olive oil
350g/12oz fresh or dried linguine
ground black pepper
basil leaves, to garnish
coarsely shaved Parmesan cheese,
  to serve

1 Put the pine nuts in a small non-stick frying pan and toss over low to medium heat for 1–2 minutes, or until the nuts are lightly toasted and golden.

2 Turn the nuts into a food processor. Add the Parmesan, sun-dried tomatoes and garlic, with pepper to taste. Process until finely chopped.

3 Gradually add the olive oil to the mixture in the food processor through the feeder tube, with the machine running, until it has all been incorporated evenly and all the ingredients have formed a smooth-looking paste.

4 Bring a pan of lightly salted water to the boil and cook the pasta until al dente. Reserve a little of the cooking water, then drain the pasta. Turn the pasta into a warmed bowl, add the pesto and a few spoonfuls of the hot water and toss well. Serve garnished with basil leaves. Serve Parmesan separately.

Cook's Tip
You can make this pesto up to 2 days in advance and keep it in the refrigerator until ready to use. Place in a bowl, pour a thin film of olive oil over the pesto, then cover the bowl tightly.

Fusilli with Tomato & Balsamic Vinegar Sauce

This is a modern Cal-Ital recipe (Californian/Italian). The intense, sweet-sour flavour of balsamic vinegar gives a pleasant kick to a sauce made with canned tomatoes.

Serves 6–8
2 x 400g/14oz cans chopped
  Italian plum tomatoes
2 pieces of sun-dried tomato in
  olive oil, drained and sliced
2 garlic cloves, crushed
45ml/3 tbsp olive oil
5ml/1 tsp sugar
350g/12oz/3 cups fresh or
  dried fusilli
45ml/3 tbsp balsamic vinegar
salt and ground black pepper
coarsely shaved Pecorino cheese
  and rocket (arugula) salad,
  to serve

1 Put the canned and sun-dried tomatoes in a medium pan with the garlic, olive oil and sugar. Add salt and pepper to taste. Bring to the boil, stirring. Lower the heat and simmer for about 30 minutes until reduced.

2 Meanwhile, bring a pan of lightly salted water to the boil, add the pasta and cook until al dente.

3 Add the balsamic vinegar to the sauce and stir to mix evenly. Cook for 1–2 minutes, then remove from the heat and taste for seasoning.

4 Drain the pasta and turn it into a warmed bowl. Pour the sauce over the pasta and toss well. Serve immediately, with rocket salad and the shaved Pecorino handed separately.

Cook's Tip
Balsamic vinegar is made in the area around Modena from local trebbiano grapes. The best is aged in a series of barrels, giving it a slightly syrupy texture and a rich, dark colour.

Energy 210Kcal/891kJ; Fat 5.2g; Saturated Fat 0.8g; Carbohydrate 36.9g; Fibre 2.5g

Energy 498Kcal/2096kJ; Fat 21.7g; Saturated Fat 3.7g; Carbohydrate 65.9g; Fibre 2.9g

Farfalle with Gorgonzola Cream

Sweet and simple, this sauce has a nutty tang from the blue cheese. It is also good with long pasta, such as spaghetti or trenette.

Serves 4
350g/12oz/3 cups dried farfalle
175g/6oz Gorgonzola cheese, any
  rind removed, diced

150ml/¼ pint/⅔ cup panna da
  cucina or double (heavy) cream
pinch of sugar
10ml/2 tsp finely chopped fresh
  sage, plus fresh sage leaves, to
  garnish
salt and ground black pepper

1 Bring a large pan of lightly salted water to the boil, add the pasta and cook until *al dente*.

2 Meanwhile, put the Gorgonzola and cream in a medium pan. Add the sugar and plenty of ground black pepper and heat gently, stirring frequently, until the cheese has melted. Remove the pan from the heat.

3 Drain the cooked pasta well and return it to the pan in which it was cooked. Pour the Gorgonzola sauce into the pan with the drained pasta.

4 Add the chopped sage to the pasta and toss over a medium heat until the pasta is evenly coated. Taste for seasoning, adding salt if necessary, then divide among four warmed bowls. Garnish each portion with sage and serve immediately.

Cook's Tip
Gorgonzola, Italy's famous creamy, blue-veined cheese, is made from the curds of stracchino cheese. The curds are layered to encourage the blue mould to grow. Originally Gorgonzola was made only in the town of that name, but nowadays it is made all over Lombardy. Its flavour can range from very mild (dolce) to extremely powerful (piccante). The cheeses are matured from 3–5 months; the longer the ageing, the stronger the flavour.

Trenette with Pesto, French Beans & Potatoes

In Liguria, it is traditional to serve pesto with trenette, French beans and diced potatoes. The ingredients for making fresh pesto are quite expensive, so the French beans and potatoes are added to help make the pesto go further.

Serves 4
about 40 fresh basil leaves
2 garlic cloves, thinly sliced

25ml/1½ tbsp pine nuts
45ml/3 tbsp freshly grated
  Parmesan cheese, plus extra
  to serve
30ml/2 tbsp freshly grated
  Pecorino cheese, plus extra
  to serve
60ml/4 tbsp extra virgin olive oil
2 potatoes, total weight about
  250g/9oz
100g/3½oz French beans
350g/12oz dried trenette
salt and ground black pepper

1 Put the basil leaves, garlic, pine nuts and cheeses in a blender or food processor and process for about 5 seconds. Add half the olive oil and a pinch of salt and process for 5 seconds more. Stop the machine, remove the lid and scrape down the side of the bowl. Add the remaining olive oil and process for 5–10 seconds.

2 Cut the potatoes in half lengthways. Slice each half crossways into 5mm/¼in thick slices. Top and tail the beans, then cut them into 2cm/¾in pieces. Plunge the potatoes and beans into a large saucepan of salted boiling water and boil, uncovered, for 5 minutes.

3 Add the pasta, bring the water back to the boil, stir well, then cook for 5–7 minutes, or until the pasta is *al dente*.

4 Meanwhile, put the pesto in a large bowl and add 45–60ml/ 3–4 tbsp of the water used for cooking the pasta. Mix well.

5 Drain the pasta and vegetables, add them to the pesto and toss well. Serve immediately on warmed plates, with extra grated Parmesan and Pecorino handed separately.

Energy 639Kcal/2677kJ; Fat 34.4g; Saturated Fat 21.1g; Carbohydrate 66.5g; Fibre 2.6g

Energy 579Kcal/2436kJ; Fat 23.4g; Saturated Fat 6g; Carbohydrate 76.2g; Fibre 4.3g

Spaghetti with Tomatoes & Herbs

This sauce comes from Spoleto in Umbria. It is a fresh, light sauce in which the tomatoes are cooked for a short time, so it should only be made in summer when tomatoes have a good flavour.

Serves 4

350g/12oz ripe Italian plum tomatoes

30ml/2 tbsp olive oil
1 onion, finely chopped
350g/12oz/3 cups fresh or dried spaghetti
2–3 fresh marjoram sprigs, leaves stripped
salt and ground black pepper
shredded fresh basil, to garnish
freshly grated Pecorino cheese, to serve

1 With a sharp knife, cut a cross in the bottom end of each plum tomato. Bring a medium pan of water to the boil and remove from the heat. Plunge a few of the tomatoes into the water, leave for 30 seconds or so, then lift them out with a slotted spoon and set aside. Repeat with the remaining tomatoes, then peel off the skin when cool and finely chop the flesh.

2 Put the chopped onion in a medium pan with the oil. Stir over low heat. Cook gently for about 10 minutes, stirring frequently, until the onion has softened.

3 Add the tomatoes, with salt and pepper to taste. Stir well and cook, uncovered, for about 10 minutes. Meanwhile, cook the pasta in a pan of lightly salted water until *al dente*.

4 Remove the sauce from the heat, stir in the marjoram sprigs and taste for seasoning. Drain the pasta and turn into a warmed bowl. Pour the sauce over the pasta and toss well.

5 Divide among four warmed bowls and serve immediately, sprinkled with shredded basil. Hand the grated Pecorino separately.

Paglia e Fieno with Sun-dried Tomatoes & Radicchio

This is a light, modern pasta dish of the kind served in fashionable restaurants. It is the presentation that sets it apart, not the preparation, which is actually very quick and easy.

Serves 4

45ml/3 tbsp pine nuts
350g/12oz dried paglia e fieno

45ml/3 tbsp extra virgin olive oil
30ml/2 tbsp sun-dried tomato paste
2 pieces sun-dried tomatoes in olive oil, drained and cut into very thin slivers
40g/1½oz radicchio leaves, finely shredded
4–6 spring onions (scallions), thinly sliced into rings
salt and ground black pepper

1 Put the pine nuts in a non-stick frying pan and toss over low to medium heat for 1–2 minutes, or until they are lightly toasted and golden. Remove and set aside.

2 Cook the pasta according to the packet instructions, keeping the colours separate by using two pans.

3 While the pasta is cooking, heat 15ml/1 tbsp of the oil in a medium skillet or saucepan. Add the sun-dried tomato paste and the sun-dried tomatoes, then stir in 2 ladlefuls of the water used for cooking the pasta. Simmer until the sauce is slightly reduced, stirring constantly.

4 Mix in the radicchio, then taste and season if necessary. Keep on low heat. Drain the paglia e fieno, keeping the colours separate, and return the noodles to the pans in which they were cooked. Add about 15ml/1 tbsp oil to each pan and toss over medium to high heat, until the pasta is glistening.

5 Arrange a portion of green and white pasta in each of four warmed bowls, then spoon the sun-dried tomato and radicchio mixture in the centre. Sprinkle the spring onions and pine nuts over the top and serve immediately. Before eating, each diner should toss the sauce ingredients with the pasta to mix well.

Energy 369Kcal/1564kJ; Fat 7.4g; Saturated Fat 1.1g; Carbohydrate 68.7g; Fibre 3.6g

Energy 474Kcal/1995kJ; Fat 17.7g; Saturated Fat 1.9g; Carbohydrate 69.3g; Fibre 3.7g

Alfredo's Fettuccine

This simple recipe was invented by a Roman restaurateur called Alfredo, who became famous for serving it with a gold fork and spoon. It tastes wonderful, regardless of how it is served!

Serves 4
50g/2oz/¹/₄ cup butter
200ml/7fl oz/scant 1 cup
   panna da cucina or double
   (heavy) cream
50g/2oz/²/₃ cup freshly grated
   Parmesan cheese, plus extra
   to garnish
350g/12oz fresh fettuccine
salt and ground black pepper

1 Melt the butter in a large pan or frying pan. Add the cream and bring it to the boil. Simmer for 5 minutes, stirring, then add the Parmesan, with salt and pepper to taste, and turn off the heat under the pan.

2 Bring a large pan of lightly salted water to the boil. Drop in the pasta all at once and quickly bring back to the boil, stirring occasionally. Cook for 2–3 minutes until the pasta is al dente. Drain thoroughly.

3 Turn the heat under the pan of cream to low, add the pasta all at once and toss until it is coated in the sauce. Taste for seasoning. Serve immediately, with extra grated Parmesan handed around separately.

Cook's Tips
• With so few ingredients, it is particularly important to use only the best-quality ones for this dish to be a success. Use good unsalted butter and top-quality Parmesan cheese. The best is Parmigiano-Reggiano – available from Italian delicatessens – which has its name stamped on the rind. Grate it only just before using.
• Fresh fettuccine is traditional, so either make it yourself or buy it from an Italian delicatessen. If you cannot get fettuccine, you can use tagliatelle instead.

Vermicelli with Lemon

Fresh and tangy, this makes an excellent first course for a dinner party. It doesn't rely on fresh seasonal ingredients, so it is good at any time of year.

Serves 4
350g/12oz dried vermicelli
juice of 2 large lemons

50g/2oz/¹/₄ cup butter
200ml/7fl oz/scant 1 cup
   panna da cucina or double
   (heavy) cream
115g/4oz/1¹/₄ cups freshly grated
   Parmesan cheese
salt and ground black pepper

1 Bring a pan of lightly salted water to the boil, add the pasta and cook until al dente.

2 Meanwhile, pour the lemon juice into a medium pan. Stir in the butter and cream, then add salt and pepper to taste.

3 Bring to the boil, then lower the heat and simmer for about 4 minutes, stirring occasionally, until the cream reduces slightly.

4 Drain the pasta and return it to the pan it was cooked in. Add the grated Parmesan, then taste the sauce for seasoning and pour it over the pasta. Toss quickly over medium heat until the pasta is evenly coated with the sauce, then divide among four warmed bowls and serve immediately.

Cook's Tip
Lemons vary in the amount of juice they yield. On average, a large fresh lemon will yield 60–90ml/4–6 tbsp. The lemony flavour of this dish is supposed to be quite sharp – but you can use less juice if you prefer.

Variation
For an even tangier taste, add a little grated lemon rind to the sauce when you add the butter and the cream in Step 2.

Pasta with Roast Tomatoes & Goat's Cheese

Roasting tomatoes brings out their flavour and sweetness, which contrasts perfectly with the sharp taste and creamy texture of goat's cheese. Serve with a crisp green salad flavoured with herbs.

Serves 4
8 large ripe tomatoes
60ml/4 tbsp garlic-infused olive oil
450g/1lb any dried
  pasta shapes
200g/7oz firm goat's
  cheese, crumbled
salt and ground black pepper

1 Preheat the oven to 190°C/375°F/Gas 5. Place the tomatoes in a roasting pan and drizzle over 30ml/2 tbsp of the oil. Season well with salt and pepper and roast for 20–25 minutes, or until soft and slightly charred.

2 Meanwhile, cook the pasta in plenty of salted, boiling water, according to the instructions on the packet. Drain well and return to the pan.

3 Roughly mash the tomatoes with a fork, and stir the contents of the roasting pan into the pasta. Gently stir in the goat's cheese and the remaining oil and serve.

Cook's Tips
• Goat's cheese is not a traditional Italian ingredient but some contemporary recipes use this particular type of cheese. Good ones to try are Chèvre Log or Bucheron from France, but available throughout Europe; Crottin de Chavignol (AOC) and Selles-sur-Cher (AOC), both from the Loire region in France, which are traditional, farmhouse creamery, unpasteurized, natural-rind cheeses.
• Irish goat's cheese is superb. Try Blue Rathgore, Boilie, Corleggy, Croghan, Mine-Gabhar, Oisin (Ireland's only blue goat's milk cheese) or St Tola (made with organic milk, and very popular).

Fusilli with Wild Mushrooms

A very rich dish with an earthy flavour and lots of garlic, this makes an ideal main course for vegetarians, especially if it is followed by a crisp green salad.

Serves 4
150g/5oz bottled wild mushrooms
  in olive oil
25g/1oz/2 tbsp butter
225g/8oz/2 cups fresh wild
  mushrooms, thinly sliced
5ml/1 tsp finely chopped fresh
  thyme
5ml/1 tsp finely chopped fresh
  marjoram or oregano, plus
  extra to garnish
4 garlic cloves, crushed
350g/12oz/3 cups fresh or
  dried fusilli
200ml/7fl oz/scant 1 cup
  panna da cucina or double
  (heavy) cream
salt and ground black pepper

1 Drain about 15ml/1 tbsp of the oil from the mushrooms into a medium pan. Slice or chop the bottled mushrooms into bite-size pieces, if they are large.

2 Add the butter to the oil in the pan and place over low heat until sizzling. Add the bottled and the fresh mushrooms. Stir in the chopped fresh herbs and the garlic, then add salt and pepper to taste.

3 Simmer the mushrooms over medium heat, stirring frequently, for about 10 minutes or until the fresh mushrooms are soft and tender.

4 Meanwhile, bring a pan of lightly salted water to the boil, add the pasta and cook until al dente.

5 As soon as the mushrooms are cooked, increase the heat to high and toss the mixture with a wooden spoon to drive off any excess liquid. Pour in the cream and bring to the boil, stirring, then taste and add more salt and pepper if needed.

6 Drain the pasta and turn it into a warmed serving bowl. Pour the sauce over the pasta and toss well. Serve immediately, sprinkled with finely chopped fresh herbs.

Spaghetti with Olives & Capers

This spicy sauce originated in the Naples area. It is a good dish for a midweek meal as it can be quickly assembled using a few storecupboard ingredients.

Serves 4
60ml/4 tbsp olive oil
2 garlic cloves, finely chopped
small piece dried chilli, crumbled
450g/12oz tomatoes, fresh or canned, chopped
115g/4oz/²/₃ cup pitted black olives
30ml/2 tbsp capers, rinsed
15ml/1 tbsp tomato purée (paste)
400g/14oz spaghetti
30ml/2 tbsp chopped fresh parsley, to serve

1 Heat the olive oil in a large frying pan. Add the chopped garlic and the dried chilli and cook for 2–3 minutes, until the garlic is just golden.

2 Stir in the tomatoes, olives, capers and tomato purée (paste). Stir well and cook over moderate heat.

3 Bring a large pan of lightly salted water to the boil, add the spaghetti and cook until al dente. Drain well.

4 Turn the spaghetti into the sauce. Increase the heat and cook for 1–2 minutes, turning the pasta constantly. Sprinkle with parsley if liked and serve immediately.

Cook's Tips
• *Traditionally, this dish is not served with an accompaniment of grated cheese.*
• *Capers are widely available in jars, pickled in brine, and it is a matter of taste whether you rinse them or not. In Italy they are often preserved in salt and sold loose. If you can find them, they are excellent for adding tangy flavour to pasta sauces, but must be rinsed well before use.*
• *Anchovies are a delicious addition to this recipe. Mash them with the golden garlic at the beginning of step 2.*

Fusilli with Walnuts

A classic Italian dish with a strong, nutty flavour, this should be served with a delicately flavoured salad.

Serves 4
350g/12oz/3 cups dried fusilli
50g/2oz/½ cup walnut pieces
25g/1oz/2 tbsp butter
300ml/½ pint/1¼ cups milk
50g/2½oz/1 cup fresh breadcrumbs
25g/1oz/⅓ cup freshly grated Parmesan cheese
pinch of freshly grated nutmeg
salt and ground black pepper
fresh rosemary sprigs, to garnish

1 Bring a pan of lightly salted water to the boil, add the pasta and cook until al dente. Meanwhile, preheat the grill (broiler).

2 Spread the walnuts evenly over the grill pan. Grill (broil) for about 5 minutes, turning occasionally, until evenly toasted.

3 Remove the walnuts from the heat, place in a clean dish towel and rub away the skins. Roughly chop the nuts.

4 Heat the butter and milk in a pan until the butter has completely melted. Stir in the breadcrumbs and chopped nuts and heat gently for 2 minutes, stirring constantly until the mixture has thickened.

5 Add the Parmesan cheese and a pinch of nutmeg, then season to taste with salt and pepper.

6 Drain the pasta thoroughly and turn into a warmed serving dish. Pour the sauce over the top and combine thoroughly. Serve immediately, garnished with fresh sprigs of rosemary.

Variation
This sauce works well with any other shaped pasta, such as conchiglie (shells), lumache (snails), rotelle (wheels) or farfalle (bow-ties). For a texture contrast, serve with a simple salad of spinach and young salad leaves, tossed in a balsamic dressing.

Curly Lasagne with Tomato & Herb Sauce

A classic sauce that teams up well with large ribbons.

Serves 4
30ml/2 tbsp olive oil
1 onion, chopped
30ml/2 tbsp tomato purée (paste)
5ml/1 tsp paprika
2 x 400g/14oz cans chopped
  tomatoes, drained
pinch of dried oregano
300ml/½ pint/1¼ cups dry
  red wine
large pinch of sugar
350g/12oz fresh or dried curly
  lasagne sheets
salt and ground black pepper
chopped fresh flat leaf parsley,
  to garnish
Parmesan cheese shavings,
  to serve

1 Heat the oil in a large frying pan and fry the onion for 10 minutes, stirring occasionally, until softened but not brown. Add the tomato purée (paste) and paprika and cook for a further 3 minutes, stirring frequently.

2 Add the tomatoes, oregano, wine and sugar to the pan. Season the mixture to taste with salt and black pepper, then bring to the boil.

3 Simmer for 20 minutes, until the sauce has reduced and thickened, stirring occasionally.

4 Meanwhile, bring a pan of lightly salted water to the boil, add the pasta and cook until al dente. Drain thoroughly and turn into a large serving dish.

5 Pour the sauce over the pasta and toss to coat. Serve sprinkled with chopped parsley and Parmesan cheese shavings.

Cook's Tip
If you cannot find curly lasagne in the supermarket use plain lasagne snipped in half lengthways.

Fusilli with Asparagus & Potato

A meal in itself, this is a real treat when made with fresh asparagus just in season. Delicious served with a chilled white wine, such as pinot grigio.

Serves 4
225g/8oz/2 cups wholewheat
  fusilli or other pasta shapes
60ml/4 tbsp extra virgin olive oil
350g/12oz new potatoes
225g/8oz fresh asparagus
115g/4oz Parmesan cheese
salt and ground black pepper

1 Bring a pan of lightly salted water to the boil, add the pasta and cook until al dente. Drain well and toss with the olive oil and salt and pepper while still warm.

2 Wash the potatoes and cook in salted boiling water for about 12–15 minutes, or until just tender. Drain the potatoes and gently toss with the pasta.

3 Trim any woody ends off the asparagus and halve the stalks if very long. Blanch in salted boiling water for 6 minutes, until bright green and still crunchy. Drain, refresh in cold water and allow to cool. Drain well and pat dry with kitchen paper.

4 Toss the asparagus with the potatoes and pasta, season with salt and pepper and transfer to a shallow bowl. Using a rotary vegetable peeler, shave the Parmesan over. Serve immediately or chill until required.

Cook's Tips
• Wholewheat pasta has more fibre in it than ordinary pasta. This gives it a slightly chewier texture, which makes the dish seem more satisfying. Wholewheat pasta may be the healthier option, but in fact any type of pasta is a nutritious carbohydrate food that can play an important role in a healthy diet.
• The olive oil is added to the warm pasta to help prevent the shapes sticking together, as well as to help permeate the pasta with a tasty olive flavour. Use a good-quality extra virgin oil.

Energy 445Kcal/1882kJ; Fat 7.7g; Saturated Fat 1.2g; Carbohydrate 73.5g; Fibre 5g

Energy 487Kcal/2042kJ; Fat 22.4g; Saturated Fat 7.8g; Carbohydrate 52.5g; Fibre 6.6g

Penne with Artichokes

Artichokes are a very popular vegetable in Italy, and are often used in sauces for pasta. This sauce is garlicky and richly flavoured, the perfect dinner party first course during the globe artichoke season.

Serves 6

juice of ¹/₂–1 lemon
2 globe artichokes
30ml/2 tbsp olive oil
1 small fennel bulb, thinly sliced,
with feathery tops reserved
1 onion, finely chopped
4 garlic cloves, finely chopped
1 handful fresh flat leaf parsley, roughly chopped
400g/14oz can chopped Italian plum tomatoes
150ml/¹/₄ pint/²/₃ cup dry white wine
350g/12oz/3 cups dried penne
10ml/2 tsp capers, chopped
salt and ground black pepper
freshly grated Parmesan cheese, to serve

1 Have ready a bowl of cold water to which you have added the juice of half a lemon. Cut off the artichoke stalks, then discard the outer leaves until the pale inner leaves that are almost white at the base remain.

2 Cut off the tops of these leaves so that the base remains. Cut the base in half lengthways, then prise the hairy "choke" out of the centre with the tip of the knife and discard. Cut the artichokes lengthways into 5mm/¹/₄in slices, adding them immediately to the bowl of acidulated water.

3 Bring a large pan of water to the boil. Add a good pinch of salt, then drain the artichokes and add them immediately to the water. Boil for 5 minutes, drain and set aside.

4 Heat the oil in a large skillet or pan and add the fennel, onion, garlic and parsley. Cook over low to medium heat, stirring frequently, for about 10 minutes, until the fennel has softened and is lightly coloured.

5 Add the tomatoes and wine, with salt and pepper to taste. Bring to the boil, stirring, then lower the heat, cover the pan and simmer for 10–15 minutes. Stir in the artichokes, replace the lid and simmer for 10 minutes more. Meanwhile, cook the pasta in salted boiling water according to the instructions on the packet.

6 Drain the pasta, reserving a little of the cooking water. Stir the capers into the sauce, then taste for seasoning and add the remaining lemon juice if you like.

7 Tip the pasta into a warmed large bowl, pour the sauce over and toss well to mix, adding a little of the reserved cooking water if you like a runnier sauce. Serve immediately, garnished with the reserved fennel fronds. Hand around a bowl of grated Parmesan separately.

> **Cook's Tip**
> When in season, use fresh Italian plum tomatoes instead of canned tomatoes, for a really flavourful dish.

Garganelli with Asparagus & Cream

A lovely recipe for late spring when bunches of fresh young asparagus are found on sale in shops and markets everywhere.

Serves 4

1 bunch fresh young asparagus, weighing 250–300g/9–11oz
350g/12oz/3 cups dried garganelli
25g/1oz/2 tbsp butter
200ml/7fl oz/scant 1 cup panna da cucina or double (heavy) cream
30ml/2 tbsp dry white wine
90–115g/3¹/₂–4oz/1–1¹/₄ cups freshly grated Parmesan cheese
30ml/2 tbsp chopped fresh mixed herbs, such as basil, flat leaf parsley, chervil, marjoram and oregano
salt and ground black pepper

1 Trim off and throw away the woody ends of the asparagus – after trimming, you should have about 200g/7oz asparagus spears. Cut the spears diagonally into pieces that are roughly the same length and shape as the garganelli.

2 Blanch the asparagus stems in salted boiling water for 2 minutes, the tips for 1 minute. Immediately after blanching, drain the asparagus stems and tips, rinse in cold water and set aside.

3 Bring a pan of lightly salted water to the boil and cook the pasta until *al dente*. Meanwhile, put the butter and cream in a medium pan, add salt and pepper to taste and bring to the boil. Simmer for a few minutes until the cream reduces and thickens, then add the asparagus, wine and about half the grated Parmesan. Taste for seasoning and keep on low heat.

4 Drain the pasta when cooked and turn into a warmed bowl. Pour the sauce over the pasta, sprinkle with the fresh herbs and toss well. Serve topped with the remaining Parmesan.

> **Cook's Tip**
> Garganelli all'uovo (with egg) are just perfect for this dish. You can buy packets of this pasta in Italian delicatessens. Penne (quills) or penne rigate (ridged quills) can also be used.

Energy 716Kcal/2994kJ; Fat 41.3g; Saturated Fat 24.8g; Carbohydrate 67g; Fibre 3.6g

Energy 268Kcal/1133kJ; Fat 5g; Saturated Fat 0.7g; Carbohydrate 46.7g; Fibre 3.2g

Farfalle with Mushrooms & Cheese

Fresh wild mushrooms are very good in this sauce, but they are expensive. To cut the cost, use half wild and half cultivated, or as many wild as you can afford – even a small handful will intensify the mushroom flavour of the sauce.

Serves 4

15g/¹⁄₂oz/¹⁄₄ cup dried porcini
  mushrooms
250ml/8fl oz/1 cup warm water
25g/1oz/2 tbsp butter
1 small onion, finely chopped
1 garlic clove, crushed
225g/8oz/3 cups fresh
  mushrooms, thinly sliced
a few fresh sage leaves, very finely
  chopped, plus a few whole
  leaves to garnish
150ml/¹⁄₄ pint/²⁄₃ cup dry
  white wine
225g/8oz/2 cups dried farfalle
115g/4oz/¹⁄₂ cup mascarpone
  cheese
115g/4oz Gorgonzola or torta di
  Gorgonzola cheese, crumbled
salt and ground black pepper

1 Put the dried porcini in a small bowl with the warm water and soak for 20–30 minutes. Remove the porcini with a slotted spoon and squeeze over the bowl to extract as much liquid as possible. Strain the liquid and set aside. Finely chop the porcini.

2 Melt the butter in a large pan, add the onion and porcini and cook gently, stirring for about 3 minutes, until the onion is soft. Add the garlic and fresh mushrooms, sage, salt and plenty of black pepper. Cook over medium heat, stirring frequently, for about 5 minutes, or until the mushrooms are soft and juicy. Stir in the soaking liquid and the wine and simmer gently.

3 Bring a pan of lightly salted water to the boil and cook the pasta for about 10 minutes, or until al dente.

4 Meanwhile, stir the mascarpone and Gorgonzola into the mushroom sauce. Heat through, stirring, until melted. Taste for seasoning and adjust if necessary.

5 Drain the pasta, add to the sauce and toss to mix. Serve, sprinkled with black pepper and garnished with sage leaves.

Sardinian Ravioli

These tasty ravioli, with their unusual potato and mint filling, are from northern Sardinia. When baked with cheese and butter, they are irresistible.

Serves 4–6

1 quantity handmade Egg Pasta
  (see page 8)
50g/2oz/¹⁄₄ cup butter, melted
50g/2oz/²⁄₃ cup freshly grated
  hard Pecorino cheese

For the filling

2 potatoes, each about 200g/7oz,
  diced
65g/2¹⁄₂oz/generous ²⁄₃ cup
  freshly grated hard salty
  Pecorino cheese
75g/3oz soft fresh Pecorino cheese
1 egg yolk
1 large bunch fresh mint, leaves
  removed and chopped
good pinch of saffron powder
flour, for dusting
salt and ground black pepper

1 To make the filling, cook the potatoes in salted boiling water for 15–20 minutes, until soft. Drain the potatoes, then mash until smooth. Leave until cold. Add the cheeses, egg yolk, mint, saffron and salt and pepper to taste and stir well to mix.

2 Using a pasta machine, roll out one-quarter of the pasta into a 90cm–1m/36in–3ft strip. Cut the strip with a sharp knife into two 45–50cm/18–20in lengths.

3 With a fluted 10cm/4in cutter, cut out 4–5 discs from one of the pasta strips. Put a heaped teaspoon of filling on to one side of each disc. Brush a little water around the edge of each disc, then fold the plain side of the disc over the filling to make a half-moon shape. Pleat the curved edge to seal.

4 Put the ravioli on floured dish towels, sprinkle with flour and leave to dry. Repeat the process with the remaining dough to make 32–40 ravioli altogether. Preheat the oven to 190°C/375°F/Gas 5. Cook the ravioli in a large pan of boiling water for 4–5 minutes.

5 Drain the ravioli, turn them into a baking dish and pour the melted butter over them. Sprinkle with the Pecorino and bake for 10–15 minutes, until golden. Serve after 5 minutes.

Energy 393Kcal/1655kJ; Fat 15.3g; Saturated Fat 8.7g; Carbohydrate 50.9g; Fibre 2.6g

Energy 375Kcal/1575kJ; Fat 14.8g; Saturated Fat 8.9g; Carbohydrate 43.4g; Fibre 2.5g

Farfalle with Prawns & Peas

A small amount of saffron in the sauce gives this dish a lovely golden colour.

Serves 4
45ml/3 tbsp olive oil
25g/1oz/2 tbsp butter
2 spring onions (scallions), chopped
225g/8oz/1 cup frozen petits pois or peas, thawed
400g/14oz/3½ cups farfalle
350g/12oz peeled prawns (shrimp)
250ml/8fl oz/1 cup dry white wine
a few whole strands saffron or 1ml/⅛ tsp powdered saffron
salt and ground black pepper
30ml/2 tbsp chopped fresh fennel or dill, to serve

1 Heat the oil and butter in a large frying pan and sauté the spring onions lightly. Add the peas and cook for 2–3 minutes.

2 Bring a pan of lightly salted water to the boil, add the pasta and cook until al dente.

3 Meanwhile, add the prawns, wine and saffron to the pan of peas. Increase the heat and cook until the wine is reduced by about half. Add salt and pepper to taste. Cover the pan and reduce the heat to low.

4 Drain the pasta and add to the pan of sauce. Stir over high heat for 1–2 minutes, coating the pasta with the sauce. Sprinkle with the fresh herbs and serve immediately.

Cook's Tip
The Italian coastal waters boast a wide variety of prawns and shrimp, ranging from the small gamberetti, usually served as part of an antipasto, to the larger gamberi rossi, which turn bright red when cooked, and the even bigger gamberoni, large succulent prawns from the Adriatic which have a superb flavour. In Italy they are usually sold raw. Look for medium prawns for this recipe: choose ones that feel firm and have bright shells and a fresh smell. Pre-cooked prawns could also be used.

Spaghetti with Mussels

Mussels are popular in all the coastal regions of Italy, and are delicious with pasta. This simple dish is greatly improved by using the freshest mussels available.

75ml/5 tbsp olive oil
3 garlic cloves, finely chopped
60ml/4 tbsp finely chopped fresh parsley
60ml/4 tbsp white wine
400g/14oz spaghetti
salt and ground black pepper

Serves 4
1kg/2lb fresh mussels, in their shells

1 Scrub the mussels well under cold running water, cutting off the beard with a small sharp knife.

2 Place the mussels with a cupful of water in a large pan over moderate heat. As soon as they open, lift them out one by one. When all the mussels have opened (discard any that do not), strain the liquid in the pan through a layer of kitchen paper and reserve until needed.

3 Bring a pan of lightly salted water to the boil, add the pasta and cook until al dente.

4 Meanwhile, heat the oil in a large frying pan. Add the garlic and parsley and cook for 2–3 minutes. Add the mussels, their strained juices and the wine. Cook over medium heat. Add a generous amount of freshly ground black pepper to the sauce. Taste for seasoning, adding salt as necessary.

5 Drain the pasta and add to the pan of sauce. Stir well over medium heat for 1–2 minutes more. Serve immediately.

Cook's Tip
Mussels should be firmly closed when fresh. If a mussel is slightly open, pinch it closed or tap it on a table. If it remains closed on its own, it is alive. If it remains open, discard it.

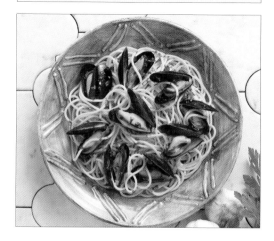

Linguine with Clam & Tomato Sauce

There are two types of traditional Italian clam sauce for pasta: one with tomatoes and one without. This is the tomato version.

Serves 4

1kg/2lb fresh clams in their shells, or 350g/12oz canned clams, with their liquid

90ml/6 tbsp olive oil
1 garlic clove, crushed
400g/14oz tomatoes, fresh or canned, very finely chopped
400g/14oz linguine
60ml/4 tbsp chopped fresh parsley
salt and ground black pepper

1 Scrub and rinse the clams well under cold running water. Place them in a large pan with a cupful of water and heat until the clams begin to open. Lift each clam out as soon as it opens and scoop it out of its shell using a small spoon. Place in a bowl.

2 If the clams are large, chop them into 2 or 3 pieces. Reserve any liquids from the shells in a separate bowl. When all the clams have opened (discard any that do not open) pour the cooking liquid into the juices from the clams, then strain through a piece of kitchen paper to remove any sand. If using canned clams, use the liquid from the can and the cooking liquid.

3 Bring a pan of lightly salted water to the boil and cook the pasta until al dente.

4 Meanwhile, place the olive oil in a medium pan with the crushed garlic. Cook over medium heat, until the garlic is just golden. Remove the garlic and discard. Add the chopped tomatoes to the oil and pour in the clam liquid. Mix well and cook until the sauce begins to dry out and thicken slightly.

5 Stir the parsley and the clams into the tomato sauce, and increase the heat. Add salt and pepper to taste. Drain the pasta and turn it into a serving bowl. Pour on the hot sauce and mix well before serving.

Linguine with Scallops & Tomatoes

Garlic-flavoured scallops combine beautifully with tomatoes, pasta and basil to create a simple yet flavourful dish, capturing the very essence of Italian cooking.

Serves 4

450g/1lb fresh or dried linguine
30ml/2 tbsp olive oil
2 garlic cloves, crushed
450g/1lb sea scallops, shelled and halved horizontally

2.5ml/½ tsp salt
30ml/2 tbsp chopped fresh basil
ground black pepper

For the sauce

30ml/2 tbsp olive oil
½ onion, finely chopped
1 garlic clove, crushed
2 x 400g/14oz cans Italian plum tomatoes

1 To make the tomato sauce, heat the oil in a non-stick frying pan. Add the onion, garlic and a little salt, and cook over medium heat for about 5 minutes, until just softened, stirring occasionally.

2 Add the tomatoes to the pan, with their juice, and crush with a fork. Bring the mixture to the boil, then reduce the heat and simmer gently for 15 minutes, stirring occasionally. Remove from the heat and set aside.

3 Bring a pan of lightly salted water to the boil, add the pasta and cook until al dente.

4 Meanwhile, heat the oil in another non-stick frying pan and cook the garlic for about 30 seconds, until just sizzling. Add the scallops and the salt and cook over high heat, for about 3 minutes, tossing the pan, until the scallops are cooked through.

5 Add the scallops to the tomato sauce. Season with salt and pepper, stir and keep warm.

6 Drain the pasta, rinse under hot water and drain again. Place in a large serving dish. Add the sauce and the basil and toss together thoroughly. Serve the pasta immediately.

Energy 656Kcal/2777kJ; Fat 15.2g; Saturated Fat 2.5g; Carbohydrate 94.6g; Fibre 5.5g

Energy 579Kcal/2441kJ; Fat 19.3g; Saturated Fat 2.8g; Carbohydrate 79.2g; Fibre 4.5g

Macaroni with King Prawns & Ham

Radicchio makes a novel addition to this sauce. The bitter flavour of the leaves mellows on cooking and perfectly complements the richness of the shellfish.

Serves 4

350g/12oz/3 cups dried short macaroni
45ml/3 tbsp olive oil
12 raw king prawns (jumbo shrimp), peeled
1 garlic clove, chopped
175g/6oz/generous 1 cup diced smoked ham
150ml/¼ pint/⅔ cup red wine
½ small radicchio lettuce, shredded
2 egg yolks, beaten
30ml/2 tbsp chopped fresh flat leaf parsley
150ml/¼ pint/⅔ cup double (heavy) cream
salt and ground black pepper
shredded fresh basil, to garnish

1 Bring a pan of lightly salted water to the boil, add the pasta and cook until *al dente*.

2 Meanwhile, heat the oil in a frying pan and cook the prawns, garlic and ham for about 5 minutes, stirring occasionally, until the prawns are just opaque and tender. Be careful not to overcook the prawns.

3 Add the wine and radicchio, bring to the boil and boil rapidly until the juices are reduced by about half. Remove from the heat, add the egg yolks to the sauce and stir well to blend.

4 Stir in the parsley and cream and bring almost to the boil, stirring constantly, then simmer until the sauce thickens slightly. Check the seasoning and adjust if necessary.

5 Drain the pasta thoroughly and toss in the sauce to coat. Serve immediately, garnished with some shredded fresh basil.

> **Cook's Tip**
> *To peel prawns, pull off the heads, peel off the body shell and legs, then pick out the black vein running down the back.*

Energy 707Kcal/2963kJ; Fat 34.7g; Saturated Fat 15.2g; Carbohydrate 66.7g; Fibre 3.3g

Black Tagliatelle with Scallops

A stunning pasta dish using black tagliatelle with a contrasting white fish sauce.

Serves 4

120ml/4fl oz/½ cup low-fat crème fraîche
10ml/2 tsp wholegrain mustard
2 garlic cloves, crushed
30–45ml/2–3 tbsp freshly squeezed lime juice
60ml/4 tbsp chopped fresh parsley
30ml/2 tbsp snipped chives
350g/12oz fresh or dried black tagliatelle
12 large fresh scallops, shelled
60ml/4 tbsp white wine
150ml/¼ pint/⅔ cup fish stock
salt and ground black pepper
lime wedges and parsley sprigs, to garnish

1 To make the tartare sauce, mix the crème fraîche, mustard, garlic, lime juice, herbs and seasoning together in a bowl.

2 Bring a pan of lightly salted water to the boil, add the pasta and cook until *al dente*. Drain the pasta thoroughly.

3 Slice each of the scallops in half horizontally. Keep any coral whole. Put the white wine and fish stock into a medium pan and heat until the mixture reaches simmering point. Add the scallops to the pan and cook very gently for 3–4 minutes (do not be tempted to cook them for any longer or they will become tough).

4 Remove the scallops from the pan with a slotted spoon. Boil the wine and stock to reduce by half and add the tartare sauce to the pan.

5 Heat the combined mixture gently to warm, replace the scallops and cook gently for 1 minute. Spoon over the pasta and garnish with lime wedges and sprigs of parsley.

> **Cook's Tip**
> *Dramatic-looking black tagliatelle is flavoured and coloured with squid ink. It is suitable for seafood pasta dishes.*

Energy 417Kcal/1767kJ; Fat 6.8g; Saturated Fat 3.4g; Carbohydrate 68g; Fibre 2.6g

Fusilli with Vegetable & Prawn Sauce

You will need to start this recipe the day before because the prawns (shrimp) should be left to marinate overnight.

Serves 4

450g/1lb peeled prawns (shrimp)
60ml/4 tbsp soy sauce
45ml/3 tbsp olive oil
350g/12oz/3 cups fusilli col buco
1 yellow (bell) pepper, cored, seeded and cut into strips
225g/8oz broccoli florets
1 bunch spring onions (scallions), shredded
2.5cm/1in piece fresh root ginger, peeled and shredded
15ml/1 tbsp chopped fresh oregano
30ml/2 tbsp dry sherry
15ml/1 tbsp cornflour (cornstarch)
300ml/½ pint/1¼ cups fish stock
salt and ground black pepper

1 Place the prawns in a mixing bowl. Stir in half the soy sauce and 30ml/2 tbsp of the olive oil. Cover and marinate overnight in the refrigerator.

2 Bring a pan of lightly salted water to the boil, add the pasta and cook until *al dente*.

3 Meanwhile, heat the remaining oil in a wok or frying pan and fry the prawns for 1 minute, stirring.

4 Add the pepper, broccoli, spring onions, ginger and oregano and fry, stirring, for about 1–2 minutes.

5 Drain the pasta thoroughly, set aside and keep warm. Meanwhile, in a bowl, blend together the sherry and cornflour until smooth. Stir in the fish stock and remaining soy sauce until well blended.

6 Pour the stock mixture into the wok or pan, bring to the boil and fry, stirring constantly, for 2 minutes, until the liquid has thickened. Pour the prawn mixture over the pasta, toss lightly together and serve immediately.

Tagliatelle with Saffron Mussels

Mussels in a delicate saffron and cream sauce are served with tagliatelle in this recipe, but you can use any other pasta if you prefer.

Serves 4

1.75kg/4lb fresh mussels, in their shells
2 shallots, chopped
150ml/¼ pint/⅔ cup dry white wine
350g/12oz dried tagliatelle
25g/1oz/2 tbsp butter
2 garlic cloves, crushed
250ml/8fl oz/1 cup double (heavy) cream
generous pinch saffron threads
1 egg yolk
salt and ground black pepper
30ml/2 tbsp chopped fresh parsley, to garnish

1 Scrub the mussels well under cold running water. Remove the beards and discard any mussels that are open.

2 Place the mussels in a large pan with the shallots and pour over the wine. Cover and cook over high heat, shaking the pan occasionally, for 5–8 minutes, until the mussels have opened. Drain the mussels, reserving the liquid. Discard any that remain closed. Shell all but a few of the mussels and keep warm.

3 Bring the reserved cooking liquid to the boil in the pan, then reduce by half. Strain the liquid into a jug to remove any grit.

4 Bring a pan of lightly salted water to the boil, add the tagliatelle and cook until *al dente*.

5 Meanwhile, melt the butter in a large frying pan and fry the garlic for 1 minute. Pour in the mussel liquid, cream and saffron threads. Heat gently until the sauce thickens slightly.

6 Remove the pan from the heat, stir in the egg yolk and shelled mussels and season the sauce to taste.

7 Drain the tagliatelle and transfer to warmed serving dishes. Spoon the sauce over and sprinkle with chopped parsley. Garnish with the mussels in shells and serve at once.

Energy 477Kcal/2022kJ; Fat 5.9g; Saturated Fat 0.9g; Carbohydrate 74.3g; Fibre 5.2g

Energy 815Kcal/3415kJ; Fat 44.3g; Saturated Fat 25.1g; Carbohydrate 67.4g; Fibre 2.8g

Pink & Green Farfalle

In this modern recipe, pink prawns and green courgettes combine prettily with cream and pasta bows to make a substantial main course. Serve with crusty Italian rolls or chunks of warm ciabatta bread.

Serves 4
50g/2oz/¼ cup butter
2–3 spring onions (scallions), very thinly sliced on the diagonal
350g/12oz courgettes (zucchini), thinly sliced on the diagonal
60ml/4 tbsp dry white wine
300g/11oz/2⅔ cups dried farfalle
75ml/5 tbsp crème fraîche
225g/8oz/1⅓ cups peeled cooked prawns (shrimp), thawed and thoroughly dried if frozen
15ml/1 tbsp finely chopped fresh marjoram or flat leaf parsley, or a mixture
salt and ground black pepper

1 Melt the butter in a large pan, add the sliced spring onions and cook over low heat, stirring frequently, for about 5 minutes, until softened. Add the sliced courgettes, with salt and pepper to taste, and cook, stirring frequently, for 5 minutes. Pour over the wine and let it bubble, then cover and simmer for 10 minutes.

2 Bring a pan of lightly salted water to the boil, add the pasta and cook until *al dente*.

3 Meanwhile, add the crème fraîche to the courgette mixture in the pan and simmer for about 10 minutes until the sauce is well reduced.

4 Add the prawns to the courgette mixture, heat through gently and taste for seasoning. Drain the pasta and turn it into a warmed bowl. Pour the sauce over, add the chopped herbs and toss well. Serve immediately.

> **Variation**
> Use dried penne instead of the farfalle, and try replacing the courgettes with asparagus tips.

Energy 490Kcal/2058kJ; Fat 19.8g; Saturated Fat 11.9g; Carbohydrate 57.9g; Fibre 3g

Penne with Prawns & Pernod

This is a modern recipe, typical of those found on menus in the most innovative Italian restaurants. The Pernod and dill go well together, but you could use white wine and basil.

Serves 4
200ml/7fl oz/scant 1 cup panna
da cucina or double (heavy) cream
250ml/8fl oz/1 cup fish stock
350g/12oz/3 cups dried penne
30–45ml/2–3 tbsp Pernod
225g/8oz/1⅓ cups peeled cooked prawns (shrimp), thawed and thoroughly dried if frozen
30ml/2 tbsp chopped fresh dill, plus extra to garnish
salt and ground black pepper

1 Put the cream and the fish stock in a medium pan and bring to the boil. Lower the heat and simmer, stirring occasionally, for 10–15 minutes, until reduced by about half.

2 Meanwhile, bring a pan of lightly salted water to the boil, add the pasta and cook until *al dente*.

3 Add the Pernod and prawns to the cream sauce, with salt and pepper to taste, if necessary. Heat the prawns through very gently. Drain the pasta and turn it into a warmed bowl. Pour the sauce over the pasta, add the dill and toss well. Serve immediately, sprinkled with chopped dill.

Chilli, Anchovy & Tomato Pasta

The sauce for this tasty pasta dish packs a punch, thanks to the robust flavours of red chillies, anchovies and capers.

Serves 4
45ml/3 tbsp olive oil
2 garlic cloves, crushed
2 fresh red chillies, seeded and chopped
6 canned anchovy fillets, drained
500g/1½lb ripe tomatoes, peeled, seeded and chopped
30ml/2 tbsp sun-dried tomato paste
30ml/2 tbsp drained capers
1 cup black pitted olives, roughly chopped
125g/4oz/1 cup dried penne
salt and freshly ground black pepper
roughly chopped fresh basil, to garnish

1 Heat the oil in a saucepan, and sauté the garlic and chilli over low heat for 2–3 minutes.

2 Add the anchovies, mashing them with a fork, then stir in the tomatoes, sun-dried tomato paste, capers and olives. Add salt and pepper to taste. Simmer gently, uncovered, for 20 minutes, stirring occasionally.

3 Meanwhile, bring a large pan of lightly salted water to the boil and add the penne. Cook until *al dente*.

4 Drain the pasta, return it to the clean pan and add the sauce. Mix thoroughly, transfer to a heated serving dish, garnish with the basil and serve immediately.

Top Energy 607Kcal/2544kJ; Fat 28.8g; Saturated Fat 16.9g; Carbohydrate 66g; Fibre 2.6g
Above Energy 445Kcal/1850kJ; Fat 34.8g; Saturated Fat 5g; Carbohydrate 28.4g; Fibre 2.9g

Ravioli with Crab

This exciting recipe uses chilli-flavoured pasta, which works well with crab, but you can use plain pasta if you prefer.

Serves 4

1 quantity handmade Egg Pasta
  (see page 8) flavoured with
  chillies (optional)
flour, for dusting
90g/3½oz/7 tbsp butter
juice of 1 lemon

For the filling

175g/6oz/¾ cup mascarpone
  cheese
175g/6oz/¾ cup crab meat
30ml/2 tbsp finely chopped fresh
  flat leaf parsley
finely grated rind of 1 lemon
pinch of crushed dried chillies
  (optional)
salt and ground black pepper

1 To make the filling, put the mascarpone in a bowl and mash it with a fork. Add the crab meat, parsley, lemon rind, crushed dried chillies (if using) and salt and pepper to taste. Stir well.

2 Using a pasta machine, roll out one-quarter of the pasta into a 90cm–1m/36in–3ft strip. Cut the strip with a sharp knife into two 45–50cm/18–20in lengths (you can do this during rolling if the strip gets too long to manage).

3 With a 6cm/2½in fluted cutter, cut out 8 squares from each pasta strip. Using a teaspoon, put a mound of filling in the centre of half the squares. Brush a little water around the edge, then top with the plain squares; press the edges to seal. For a decorative finish, press the edges with the tines of a fork.

4 Put the ravioli on floured dish towels, sprinkle lightly with flour and leave to dry while repeating the process with the rest of the dough to make 32 ravioli. If you have any stuffing left, you can re-roll the pasta trimmings and make more ravioli.

5 Cook the ravioli in a large pan of salted boiling water for 4–5 minutes. Meanwhile, melt the butter and lemon juice in a small pan until sizzling. Drain the ravioli and divide equally among four warmed bowls. Drizzle the lemon butter over and serve immediately.

Penne with Prawns & Artichokes

This is a good dish to make in late spring or early summer, when greeny-purple baby artichokes appear on the scene.

Serves 4

juice of ½ lemon
4 baby artichokes
90ml/6tbsp olive oil
2 garlic cloves, crushed
30ml/2 tbsp chopped fresh mint
30ml/2 tbsp chopped fresh flat
  leaf parsley
350g/12oz/3 cups dried penne
8–12 peeled, cooked large pawns
  (shrimp), each cut into
  2–3 pieces
25g/1oz/2 tbsp butter
salt and ground black pepper

1 Have ready a bowl of cold water to which you have added the lemon juice. To prepare the artichokes, cut off the artichoke stalks, if any, and cut across the tops of the leaves. Peel off and discard any tough or discoloured outer leaves.

2 Cut the artichokes lengthways into quarters and remove any hairy "chokes" from their centres. Finally, cut the pieces of artichoke lengthways into 5mm/¼in slices and put these in the bowl of acidulated water.

3 Drain the slices of artichoke and pat them dry. Heat the olive oil in a non-stick frying pan and add the artichokes, the crushed garlic and half the mint and parsley to the pan.

4 Season with plenty of salt and pepper. Cook over low heat, stirring frequently, for about 10 minutes, or until the artichokes feel tender when pierced with a sharp knife.

5 Meanwhile, bring a pan of lightly salted water to the boil, add the pasta and cook until al dente.

6 Add the prawns to the artichokes, stir well to mix, then heat through gently for 1–2 minutes.

7 Drain the pasta and turn into a warmed bowl. Add the butter and toss until melted. Spoon the artichokes over the pasta and toss together. Serve sprinkled with the remaining herbs.

Vermicelli with Clam Sauce

This recipe comes from the city of Naples, where both fresh tomato sauce and seafood are traditionally served with vermicelli.

Serves 4

1kg/2¼lb fresh clams
250ml/8fl oz/1 cup dry
   white wine
2 garlic cloves, bruised
1 large handful fresh flat leaf
   parsley
30ml/2 tbsp olive oil
1 small onion, finely chopped
8 ripe Italian plum tomatoes,
   peeled, seeded and finely
   chopped
½–1 fresh red chilli, seeded and
   finely chopped
350g/12oz dried vermicelli
salt and ground black pepper

1 Scrub the clams thoroughly under cold running water and discard any that are open or do not close when sharply tapped.

2 Pour the wine into a large pan, add the garlic and half the parsley, then the clams. Cover tightly and bring to the boil over high heat. Cook for 5 minutes, shaking, until the clams open.

3 Tip the clams into a large colander set over a bowl and let the liquid drain through. When cool enough to handle, remove about two-thirds from their shells, tipping the clam liquid into the bowl of cooking liquid. Discard any unopened clams. Set the clams aside; keep the unshelled clams warm in a covered bowl.

4 Heat the oil in a pan, add the onion and cook gently, stirring, for about 5 minutes, until lightly coloured. Add the tomatoes, then strain in the clam cooking liquid. Add the chilli, then season.

5 Bring to the boil, half cover and simmer gently for 15–20 minutes. Meanwhile, cook the pasta in lightly salted boiling water until al dente. Chop the remaining parsley finely.

6 Add the shelled clams to the tomato sauce, stir well and heat through very gently for 2–3 minutes. Drain the pasta well and tip it into a warmed bowl. Taste the sauce for seasoning, then pour the sauce over the pasta and toss everything together well. Garnish with the reserved clams and chopped parsley.

Conchiglie & Scallops

A thoroughly modern dish, this warm salad consists of succulent wine-cooked scallops tossed into pasta with tangy leaves and a chilli-flavoured dressing.

Serves 4

8 large fresh scallops, shelled
300g/11oz/2¾ cups dried
   conchiglie
15ml/1 tbsp olive oil
15g/½oz/1 tbsp butter
120ml/4fl oz/½ cup dry white
   wine
90g/3½oz rocket (arugula)
   leaves, stalks trimmed
salt and ground black pepper

For the vinaigrette
60ml/4 tbsp extra virgin olive oil
15ml/1 tbsp balsamic vinegar
1 piece bottled roasted (bell)
   pepper, drained and finely
   chopped
1–2 fresh red chillies, seeded and
   chopped
1 garlic clove, crushed
5–10ml/1–2 tsp clear honey

1 Cut each scallop into 2–3 pieces. If the corals are attached, pull them off and cut each piece in half. Season the scallops and corals with salt and pepper.

2 To make the vinaigrette, put the oil, vinegar, chopped pepper and chillies in a jug with the garlic and honey and whisk well.

3 Bring a pan of lightly salted water to the boil, add the pasta and cook until al dente.

4 Meanwhile, heat the oil and butter in a non-stick frying pan until sizzling. Add half the scallops and toss over high heat for 2 minutes. Remove with a slotted spoon and keep warm. Cook the remaining scallops in the same way.

5 Add the wine to the liquid remaining in the pan and stir over high heat, until the mixture has reduced to a few tablespoons. Remove from the heat and keep warm.

6 Drain the pasta and turn it into a warmed bowl. Add the rocket, scallops, the reduced cooking juices and the vinaigrette and toss well to combine. Serve immediately.

Tagliatelle with Scallops

Scallops and brandy make this a relatively expensive dish, but it is so delicious that you will find it well worth the cost. Serve it for a dinner party first course.

Serves 4

200g/7oz fresh scallops, shelled and sliced
30ml/2 tbsp plain (all-purpose) flour
275g/10oz fresh spinach-flavoured tagliatelle
40g/1 ½oz/3 tbsp butter
2 spring onions (scallions), cut into thin rings
½–1 small fresh red chilli, seeded and very finely chopped
30ml/2 tbsp finely chopped fresh flat leaf parsley
60ml/4 tbsp brandy
105ml/7 tbsp fish stock
salt and ground black pepper

1 Toss the scallops in the flour, then shake off the excess.

2 Bring a pan of lightly salted water to the boil, add the pasta and cook until *al dente*.

3 Meanwhile, melt the butter in a frying pan or large pan. Add the spring onions, finely chopped chilli and half the parsley and fry, stirring frequently, for 1–2 minutes over medium heat. Add the scallops and toss over the heat for 1–2 minutes.

4 Pour the brandy over the scallops, then set it alight with a match. As soon as the flames have died down, stir in the fish stock and salt and pepper to taste. Mix well. Simmer for 2–3 minutes, then cover the pan and remove it from the heat.

5 Drain the pasta, add to the sauce and toss over medium heat until mixed. Serve at once, in warmed bowls sprinkled with the remaining parsley.

> **Cook's Tip**
> Buy fresh scallops, with their corals if possible. Fresh scallops always have a better texture and flavour than frozen scallops, which tend to be watery.

Spaghetti with Squid & Peas

In Tuscany, squid is often cooked with peas in a tomato sauce. This recipe is a variation on the theme, and it works very well.

Serves 4

450g/1lb prepared squid
30ml/2 tbsp olive oil
1 small onion, finely chopped
400g/14oz can chopped Italian plum tomatoes
1 garlic clove, finely chopped
15ml/1 tbsp red wine vinegar
5ml/1 tsp sugar
10ml/2 tsp finely chopped fresh rosemary
115g/4oz/1 cup frozen peas
350g/12oz fresh or dried spaghetti
15ml/1 tbsp chopped fresh flat leaf parsley
salt and ground black pepper

1 Cut the prepared squid into strips about 5mm/¼in wide. Finely chop any tentacles.

2 Heat the oil in a frying pan or medium pan, add the finely chopped onion and cook gently, stirring, for about 5 minutes, until softened. Add the squid, tomatoes, garlic, red wine vinegar and sugar.

3 Add the rosemary, with salt and pepper to taste. Bring to the boil, stirring, then cover and simmer gently for 20 minutes. Uncover the pan, add the peas and cook for 10 minutes.

4 Meanwhile, bring a pan of lightly salted water to the boil, add the pasta and cook until *al dente*.

5 Drain the pasta thoroughly and turn it into a warmed serving bowl. Pour the sauce over the pasta, add the parsley, then toss well and serve.

> **Cook's Tip**
> Prepared squid consists of the body pouch and tentacles – the head and body contents are removed and discarded. You can usually buy squid ready prepared from fish counters.

Energy 429Kcal/1809kJ; Fat 10.3g; Saturated Fat 5.6g; Carbohydrate 58.7g; Fibre 2.3g

Energy 490Kcal/2076kJ; Fat 9.8g; Saturated Fat 1.6g; Carbohydrate 74.8g; Fibre 5.1g

Tagliolini with Clams & Mussels

Serve on white china to make the most of this dramatic looking dish.

Serves 4

450g/1lb fresh mussels, in their shells
450g/1lb fresh clams, in their shells
60ml/4 tbsp olive oil
1 small onion, finely chopped
2 garlic cloves, finely chopped
1 large handful fresh flat leaf parsley, plus extra to garnish
175ml/6fl oz/³⁄₄ cup dry white wine
250ml/8fl oz/1 cup fish stock
1 small fresh red chilli, seeded and chopped
350g/12oz black tagliolini or tagliatelle
salt and ground black pepper

1 Scrub the mussels and clams under cold running water and discard any that are open or damaged, or that do not close when sharply tapped against the work surface.

2 Heat half the oil in a large pan, add the onion and cook gently for about 5 minutes until softened. Sprinkle in the garlic, then add about half the parsley sprigs and season with salt and pepper to taste.

3 Add the cleaned mussels and clams and pour in the wine. Cover with a lid and bring to the boil over high heat. Cook for about 5 minutes, shaking the pan frequently, until the shellfish have opened.

4 Turn the mussels and clams into a fine sieve (strainer) set over a bowl and let the liquid drain through. Discard the flavourings in the strainer, together with any mussels or clams that have failed to open. Return the liquid to the cleaned out pan and add the fish stock.

5 Chop the remaining parsley finely and add it to the liquid with the chopped chilli. Bring to the boil, then lower the heat and simmer, stirring, for a few minutes, until slightly reduced. Turn off the heat.

6 Remove and discard the top shells from about half the mussels and clams. Put all the mussels and clams in the pan of liquid and seasonings, then cover the pan tightly and set aside.

7 Bring a pan of lightly salted water to the boil, add the pasta and cook until al dente.

8 Drain the pasta well, then return to the clean pan; toss with the remaining olive oil. Put the pan of shellfish over high heat and toss to heat the shellfish through quickly, combine with the liquid and seasonings.

9 Divide the pasta among four warmed plates, spoon the shellfish mixture over, then serve, garnished with parsley.

Spaghetti with Salmon & Prawns

This is a lovely fresh-tasting pasta dish, perfect for an al fresco meal in summer.

Serves 4

300g/11oz salmon fillet
200ml/7fl oz/scant 1 cup dry white wine
a few fresh basil sprigs, plus extra basil leaves to garnish
6 ripe Italian plum tomatoes, peeled and finely chopped
150ml/¼ pint/²⁄₃ cup double (heavy) cream
350g/12oz fresh or dried spaghetti
115g/4oz/²⁄₃ cup peeled cooked prawns (shrimp), thawed and thoroughly dried if frozen
salt and ground black pepper

1 Put the salmon skin-side up in a shallow pan. Pour the wine over, then add the basil to the pan and sprinkle the fish with salt and pepper. Bring the wine to the boil, cover the pan and simmer gently for no more than 5 minutes. Using a metal spatula, lift the fish out of the pan and leave to cool a little.

2 Add the tomatoes and cream to the liquid remaining in the pan and bring to the boil. Stir well, then lower the heat and simmer, uncovered, for 10–15 minutes. Meanwhile, cook the pasta in plenty of boiling water until al dente.

3 When cool enough to handle, flake the fish into large chunks, discarding the skin and any bones. Add the fish to the sauce with the prawns, shaking the pan until the fish and shellfish are well coated. Taste for seasoning.

4 Drain the pasta and turn into a warmed bowl. Pour the sauce over the pasta and toss to combine. Serve immediately, garnished with fresh basil leaves.

> **Cook's Tip**
> Check the salmon fillet carefully for small bones when you are flaking the flesh. Although the salmon is already filleted, you will always find a few stray "pin" bones. Pick them out carefully using tweezers or your fingertips.

> **Variation**
> If clams are not available, use double the amount of fresh mussels. The chilli can be omitted, if preferred.

Linguine with Crab

Serve this glorious dish from Rome with crusty bread, as a foil to the richness.

Serves 4

about 250g/9oz fresh crabmeat
45ml/3 tbsp olive oil
I small handful fresh flat leaf
  parsley, roughly chopped, plus
  extra to garnish
I garlic clove, crushed
350g/12oz ripe Italian plum
  tomatoes, peeled and chopped
60–90ml/4–6 tbsp dry white
  wine
350g/12oz fresh or dried linguine
salt and ground black pepper

I Put the crabmeat in a mortar and pound to a rough pulp with a pestle. If you do not have a pestle and mortar, use a sturdy bowl and the end of a rolling pin. Set aside.

2 Heat 30ml/2 tbsp of the oil in a large pan. Add the parsley and garlic, with salt and pepper to taste, and fry for a few minutes until the garlic begins to brown.

3 Add the tomatoes, pounded crabmeat and wine, cover the pan and simmer gently for 15 minutes, stirring occasionally.

4 Meanwhile, cook the pasta until al dente. Drain well, reserving a few spoonfuls of the cooking water.

5 Return the pasta to the clean pan, add the remaining oil and toss quickly over medium heat to coat in oil. Add the crab mixture to the pasta and toss again, adding a little of the reserved cooking water if you think it necessary. Adjust the seasoning. Serve in warmed bowls, sprinkled with parsley.

Cook's Tip
The best way to obtain crabmeat is to ask a fishmonger to remove it from the shell for you, or buy dressed crab from the supermarket. For this recipe you will need one large crab, and you should use both the white and dark meat.

Capelli d'Angelo with Lobster

This is a sophisticated dish for a special occasion.

Serves 4

meat from the body, tail and
  claws of I cooked lobster
juice of ½ lemon
40g/1½oz/3 tbsp butter
4 fresh tarragon sprigs, leaves
  stripped and chopped
60ml/4 tbsp double (heavy)
  cream
90ml/6 tbsp sparkling dry
  white wine
60ml/4 tbsp fish stock
300g/11oz fresh capelli d'angelo
salt and ground black pepper
about 10ml/2 tsp lumpfish roe, to
  garnish (optional)

I Cut the lobster meat into small pieces and put it in a bowl. Sprinkle with the lemon juice. Melt the butter in a large pan, add the lobster meat and tarragon and stir over the heat for a few seconds. Add the cream and stir for a few seconds more, then pour in the wine and stock, with salt and pepper to taste. Simmer for 2 minutes, then remove from the heat and cover.

2 Cook the pasta in lightly salted boiling water until al dente. Drain well, reserving a few spoonfuls of the cooking water.

3 Place the lobster sauce over medium to high heat, add the pasta and toss just long enough to combine and heat through; moisten with a little of the reserved water from the pasta. Serve in warmed bowls, sprinkled with lumpfish roe if you like.

Cook's Tip
To remove the meat from a lobster, place the lobster on a board with its underbelly facing uppermost. With a large sharp knife, cut the lobster in half lengthways. Spoon out the liver and any pink roe and reserve these, then remove and discard the gills and stomach sac near the head. Pull the white tail meat out from the shell and discard the black intestinal vein. Crack the claws with a nutcracker and remove the meat from the base. Pull away the small pincer and remove the meat from this part of the shell. Pull the meat from the large pincer shell.

Trenette with Shellfish

Colourful and delicious, this typical Genoese dish is ideal for a dinner party. The sauce is quite runny, so serve it with crusty bread and spoons as well as forks, so that nothing is missed.

Serves 4
45ml/3 tbsp olive oil
1 small onion, finely chopped
1 garlic clove, crushed
1/2 fresh red chilli, seeded and chopped
200g/7oz canned chopped Italian plum tomatoes
30ml/2 tbsp chopped fresh flat leaf parsley
400g/14oz fresh clams, in their shells
400g/14oz fresh mussels, in their shells
60ml/4 tbsp dry white wine
400g/14oz/3 1/2 cups dried trenette
a few fresh basil leaves
90g/3 1/2oz/2/3 cup peeled cooked prawns, (shrimp) thawed and thoroughly dried if frozen
salt and ground black pepper
chopped fresh herbs, to garnish

1 Heat 30ml/2 tbsp of the oil in a frying pan or medium pan. Add the onion, garlic and chilli and cook over medium heat for 1–2 minutes, stirring constantly. Stir in the tomatoes, half the parsley and pepper to taste. Bring to the boil, lower the heat, cover and simmer for 15 minutes.

2 Meanwhile, scrub the clams and mussels under cold running water. Discard any that are open or that do not close when sharply tapped against the work surface.

3 In a large pan, heat the remaining oil. Add the clams and mussels, with the rest of the parsley and toss over high heat for a few seconds. Pour in the wine, then cover tightly. Cook for about 5 minutes, shaking the pan frequently, until the clams and mussels have opened.

4 Remove the pan from the heat and transfer the clams and mussels to a bowl with a slotted spoon, discarding any shellfish that have failed to open.

5 Strain the cooking liquid into a measuring jug and set aside. Reserve eight clams and four mussels in their shells for the garnish, then remove the rest of the clams and mussels from their shells, adding any juices to the cooking liquid in the jug.

6 Bring a pan of lightly salted water to the boil, add the pasta and cook until *al dente*.

7 Meanwhile, add 120ml/4fl oz/1/2 cup of the reserved shellfish liquid to the tomato sauce. Bring to the boil over high heat, stirring. Lower the heat, tear the basil leaves and add with the prawns, the shelled clams and mussels. Stir well, then taste for seasoning.

8 Drain the pasta and turn it into a warmed bowl. Add the seafood sauce and toss well to combine.

9 Serve in individual bowls, sprinkle with herbs and garnish each portion with the reserved shellfish in their shells: two clams and one mussel per portion.

Paglia e Fieno with Prawns & Vodka

The combination of prawns, vodka and pasta may seem unusual, but it has become something of a modern classic in Italy. Here it is stylishly presented with two-coloured pasta.

Serves 4
30ml/2 tbsp olive oil
1/4 large onion, finely chopped
1 garlic clove, crushed
15–30ml/1–2 tbsp sun-dried tomato paste
200ml/7fl oz/scant 1 cup panna da cucina or double (heavy) cream
350g/12oz fresh or dried paglia e fieno
12 large raw prawns (shrimp), peeled and chopped
30ml/2 tbsp vodka
salt and ground black pepper

1 Heat the oil in a medium pan, add the onion and garlic and cook gently, stirring frequently, for 5 minutes, until softened.

2 Add the tomato paste and stir for 1–2 minutes, then add the cream and bring to the boil, stirring. Season with salt and pepper to taste and let the sauce bubble until it starts to thicken slightly. Remove from the heat.

3 Bring a pan of lightly salted water to the boil and cook the pasta until *al dente*. When it is almost ready, add the prawns and vodka to the sauce; toss quickly over a medium heat for 2–3 minutes, until the prawns turn pink.

4 Drain the pasta well and turn into a warmed bowl. Pour the sauce over and toss to mix. Serve immediately.

> **Cook's Tip**
> The sauce is best served as soon as it is ready, otherwise the prawns will overcook and become tough. Make sure that the pasta has only a minute or two of cooking time left before adding the prawns to the sauce.

Energy 650Kcal/2722kJ; Fat 34.2g; Saturated Fat 17.7g; Carbohydrate 67.4g; Fibre 2.9g

Energy 524Kcal/2218kJ; Fat 11.4g; Saturated Fat 1.7g; Carbohydrate 78.1g; Fibre 4g

Spaghetti with Anchovies & Olives

The strong flavours of this dish are typical of Sicilian cuisine. Serve with a hearty Italian red wine and chunks of rustic bread.

Serves 4

45ml/3 tbsp olive oil
1 large red (bell) pepper, seeded and chopped
1 small aubergine (eggplant), finely chopped
1 onion, finely chopped
8 ripe Italian plum tomatoes, peeled, seeded and finely chopped
2 garlic cloves, finely chopped
120ml/4fl oz/½ cup dry red or white wine
1 handful fresh herbs, such as basil, flat leaf parsley and rosemary
300g/11oz dried spaghetti
50g/2oz canned anchovies, roughly chopped, plus extra whole anchovies to garnish
12 pitted black olives
15–30ml/1–2 tbsp drained capers, to taste
salt and ground black pepper

1 Heat the oil in a pan and add the pepper, aubergine, onion, tomatoes and garlic. Cook gently, stirring frequently, for 10–15 minutes until the vegetables are soft.

2 Pour in the wine and 120ml/4fl oz/½ cup water, add the fresh herbs and pepper to taste and bring to the boil. Lower the heat and simmer, stirring occasionally, for 10–15 minutes.

3 Meanwhile, bring a pan of lightly salted water to the boil, add the pasta and cook until *al dente*.

4 Add the chopped anchovies, olives and capers to the sauce, heat through for a few minutes and taste for seasoning. Drain the pasta and turn it into a warmed bowl. Pour the sauce over the pasta, toss well and serve immediately.

> **Cook's Tip**
> *If the anchovies are omitted, this makes a good sauce for vegetarians. Serve with wholewheat spaghetti for extra fibre.*

Penne with Cream & Smoked Salmon

This modern way of serving pasta is popular all over Italy. The three essential ingredients combine together beautifully, and the dish is very quick and easy to make.

Serves 4

350g/12oz/3 cups dried penne
115g/4oz thinly sliced smoked salmon
2–3 fresh thyme sprigs
25g/1oz/2 tbsp butter
150ml/¼ pint/⅔ cup single (light) cream
salt and ground black pepper

1 Bring a pan of lightly salted water to the boil, add the pasta and cook until *al dente*.

2 Meanwhile, using kitchen scissors, cut the smoked salmon into thin strips, about 5mm/¼in wide. Strip the leaves from the thyme sprigs.

3 Melt the butter in a large pan. Stir in the cream with about a quarter of the salmon and thyme leaves, then season with pepper. Heat gently for 3–4 minutes, stirring all the time. Do not allow the sauce to boil. Taste for seasoning.

4 Drain the pasta, return to the pan, then toss in the cream and salmon sauce. Divide among four warmed bowls and top with the remaining salmon and thyme leaves. Serve hot.

> **Cook's Tip**
> *It is important that the cream mixture does not boil in step 3.*

> **Variation**
> *Although penne is traditional with this sauce, it also goes very well with fresh ravioli stuffed with spinach and ricotta.*

Energy 509Kcal/2146kJ; Fat 15g; Saturated Fat 2.3g; Carbohydrate 76.5g; Fibre 7.8g

Energy 475Kcal/2005kJ; Fat 17g; Saturated Fat 9g; Carbohydrate 67g; Fibre 2.7g

Saffron Pappardelle

Wide ribbon pasta not only looks attractive with this delicious seafood sauce, but it tastes fantastic, too. For an even prettier effect, use the type of pappardelle with a curly edge.

Serves 4
large pinch of saffron threads
4 sun-dried tomatoes, chopped
5ml/1 tsp fresh thyme
60ml/4 tbsp hot water

12 large prawns (shrimp) in their shells
225g/8oz baby squid
225g/8oz monkfish fillet
2–3 garlic cloves
2 small onions, quartered
1 small fennel bulb, trimmed and sliced
150ml/¼ pint/⅔ cup white wine
225g/8oz fresh or dried pappardelle
salt and ground black pepper
chopped fresh parsley, to garnish

1 Put the saffron threads, sun-dried tomatoes and thyme into a bowl and pour over the hot water. Mix together and then leave to soak for at least 30 minutes.

2 Wash the prawns and carefully remove the shells, leaving the heads and tails intact.

3 Pull the body from the squid, remove the quill and cut off the tentacles, then rinse. Pull off the outer skin and cut into 5mm/¼in rings. Cut the monkfish into 2.5cm/1in cubes.

4 Put the garlic, onions and fennel into a pan and pour over the wine. Cover and simmer for 5 minutes until tender.

5 Add the monkfish, with the saffron, tomatoes and thyme in their liquid. Cover and cook for 3 minutes. Then add the prawns and squid. Cover and cook gently for a further 1–2 minutes (do not overcook or the squid will become tough).

6 Meanwhile, bring a pan of lightly salted water to the boil and cook the past until al dente. Drain the pasta thoroughly.

7 Divide the pasta among four dishes and top each one with the seafood sauce. Sprinkle with parsley and serve immediately.

Energy 370Kcal/1566kJ; Fat 2.6g; Saturated Fat 0.4g; Carbohydrate 49.8g; Fibre 4g

Tagliatelle with Smoked Salmon

In Italy smoked salmon is imported, and therefore quite expensive. This elegant creamy sauce makes a little go a long way.

Serves 4–5
175g/6oz/¾ cup smoked salmon slices or ends, fresh or frozen

300ml/½ pint/1¼ cups single (light) cream
pinch of ground mace or nutmeg
350g/12oz dried green and white tagliatelle
salt and ground black pepper
45ml/3 tbsp chopped fresh chives, to garnish

1 Cut the salmon into thin strips about 5cm/2in long. Place in a bowl with the cream and the mace or nutmeg. Stir, cover, and allow to stand for at least 2 hours in a cool place.

2 Bring a pan of lightly salted water to the boil, add the pasta and cook until al dente.

3 Meanwhile, gently warm the cream and salmon mixture in a small pan without allowing it to boil.

4 Drain the cooked pasta and turn into a serving dish. Pour the sauce over the pasta and mix well. Season with salt and pepper and garnish with the chives. Serve immediately.

Cook's Tip
A mix of green and white pasta noodles is known as paglia e fieno, which translates as straw and hay.

Variation
For a quick spinach version, omit the marinating stage and simply stir the smoked salmon strips directly into the drained pasta with handfuls of baby spinach and some spoonfuls of crème fraîche. Stir over gentle heat until the salmon changes colour and the spinach begins to wilt. Add pepper and nutmeg.

Energy 415Kcal/1750kJ; Fat 14.6g; Saturated Fat 7.8g; Carbohydrate 53.4g; Fibre 2.5g

Salmon Rigatoni with Parsley Sauce

This dish is incredibly quick and easy to make and totally irresistible.

Serves 4
450g/1lb salmon fillet, skinned
225g/8oz/2 cups dried rigatoni
175g/6oz cherry tomatoes, halved
150ml/¼ pint/⅔ cup low-fat crème fraîche
45ml/3 tbsp finely chopped parsley
finely grated rind of ½ orange
salt and ground black pepper

1 Cut the salmon into bite-size pieces, arrange on a heatproof plate and cover with foil.

2 Bring a large pan of lightly salted water to the boil, add the pasta and bring back to the boil. Place the plate of salmon on top of the pan and simmer for 10–12 minutes, until the pasta and salmon are cooked.

3 Drain the pasta and toss with the tomatoes and salmon. In a separate bowl mix together the crème fraîche, parsley, orange rind and pepper to taste. Spoon this mixture over the salmon and pasta, toss well and serve hot or cold.

> **Variation**
> *Fillets of fresh trout could be used instead, if salmon is unavailable.*

Spaghetti with Bottarga

Although this may seem an unusual recipe, with bottarga (salted and air-dried mullet or tuna roe) as the principal ingredient, it is very well known in Sardinia and also Sicily and parts of southern Italy. It is simplicity itself to make and tastes very, very good. Bottarga can be bought from Italian delicatessens.

Serves 4
350g/12oz dried spaghetti
about 60ml/4 tbsp olive oil
2–3 garlic cloves, peeled
ground black pepper
60–90ml/4–6 tbsp bottarga

1 Cook the pasta in lightly salted water according to the instructions on the packet.

2 Meanwhile, heat half the olive oil in a large saucepan. Add the garlic and cook gently, stirring, for a few minutes. Remove the pan from the heat, scoop out the garlic with a slotted spoon and discard, leaving the garlic-flavoured oil in the bottom.

3 Drain the pasta very well. Return the pan of oil to the heat and add the pasta. Toss well, season with pepper and moisten with the remaining oil, or more to taste.

4 Divide the pasta among four warmed bowls, sprinkle the grated bottarga over the top and serve immediately.

Penne with Tuna & Mozzarella

This tasty sauce is quickly made from kitchen cupboard staples, with the addition of fresh mozzarella.

Serves 4
400g/14oz/3½ cups dried penne, or other short pasta
15ml/1 tbsp capers, in brine or salt
2 garlic cloves
45ml/3 tbsp chopped fresh parsley
200g/7oz can tuna in olive oil, drained
75ml/5 tbsp olive oil
salt and ground black pepper
115g/4oz/⅔ cup mozzarella cheese, cut into small dice

1 Bring a large pan of lightly salted water to the boil, add the pasta and cook until *al dente*.

2 Meanwhile, rinse the capers well in water. Chop them finely with the garlic. Combine with the parsley and the tuna. Stir in the oil and season with salt and pepper, if necessary.

3 Drain the cooked pasta and turn it into a large frying pan. Add the tuna sauce and the diced mozzarella and cook over medium heat, stirring constantly, until the cheese just begins to melt. Serve immediately.

> **Cook's Tips**
> • *Use tuna canned in olive oil rather than brine, if possible.*
> • *For this dish, cow's milk mozzarella is perfectly adequate, but if you are serving mozzarella uncooked, it is much better, and more traditional, to use the buffalo milk variety. The best is made around Naples and has a moist, springy texture and a deliciously milky flavour.*

> **Variation**
> *Black or green olives could be used instead of capers; chop roughly and mix with the garlic, tuna, parsley and oil.*

Top Energy 467Kcal/1962kJ; Fat 19.3g; Saturated Fat 6g; Carbohydrate 45g; Fibre 2.6g
Above Energy 419Kcal/1769kJ; Fat 13.4g; Saturated Fat 2g; Carbohydrate 66g; Fibre 2.9g

Energy 638kcal/2684kJ; Fat 26g; Saturated Fat 6.9g; Carbohydrate 74.4g; Fibre 3.5g

Spaghetti with Tomatoes, Anchovies, Olives & Capers

This classic sauce from Campania in the south uses strongly flavoured ingredients typical of the region. A few anchovies and olives give the sauce bags of punchy taste.

Serves 4
30ml/2 tbsp olive oil
1 small onion, finely chopped
1 garlic clove, finely chopped
4 canned anchovies, drained
50g/2oz/½ cup pitted black olives, sliced
15ml/1 tbsp capers
400g/14oz can chopped Italian plum tomatoes
15ml/1 tbsp chopped fresh flat leaf parsley
350g/12oz fresh or dried spaghetti
salt and ground black pepper

1 Heat the oil in a medium pan and add the onion, garlic and drained anchovies. Cook over low heat, stirring constantly, for 5–7 minutes, or until the anchovies break down to form a very soft pulp. Add the black olives and capers and stir-fry for a minute or so.

2 Add the tomatoes, 45ml/3tbsp water, half the parsley and salt and pepper to taste. Stir well and bring to the boil, then lower the heat and cover the pan. Simmer gently for 30 minutes, stirring occasionally.

3 Meanwhile, bring a pan of lightly salted water to the boil, add the pasta and cook until al dente.

4 Drain the pasta and turn into a warmed bowl. Taste the sauce for seasoning, pour it over the pasta and toss well. Serve immediately, with the remaining parsley sprinkled on top.

> **Cook's Tip**
> Use good-quality, shiny black olives – the small Gaeta olives from Liguria are among the best of the Italian crop.

Spaghetti with Tuna, Anchovies, Olives & Mozzarella

This recipe from Capri is fresh, light and full of flavour, just like the beautiful island itself. Serve the dish as soon as it is cooked to enjoy it at its best.

Serves 4
300g/11oz dried spaghetti
30ml/2 tbsp olive oil
6 ripe Italian plum tomatoes, chopped
5ml/1 tsp sugar
50g/2oz jar anchovies in olive oil, drained
about 60 ml/4 tbsp dry white wine
200g/7oz can tuna in olive oil, drained
50g/2oz/½ cup pitted black olives, quartered lengthways
125g/4½oz mozzarella cheese, drained and diced
salt and ground black pepper
fresh basil leaves, to garnish

1 Bring a pan of lightly salted water to the boil, add the pasta and cook until al dente.

2 Meanwhile, heat the oil in a medium pan. Add the chopped tomatoes, sugar and pepper to taste, and toss over medium heat for a few minutes, until the tomatoes soften and the juices run. Using kitchen scissors, snip a few anchovies at a time into the pan of tomatoes.

3 Add the wine, tuna and olives and stir once or twice until they are just evenly mixed into the sauce. Add the mozzarella and heat through without stirring. Taste; add salt if necessary.

4 Drain the pasta well and turn into a warmed serving dish. Pour the sauce over, toss gently and sprinkle with basil leaves. Serve immediately.

> **Cook's Tip**
> In Italy, anchovy fillets are preserved in salt as well as oil. The salted fillets have a superior flavour and are worth looking for.

Energy 390Kcal/1650kJ; Fat 9.1g; Saturated Fat 1.3g; Carbohydrate 69.1g; Fibre 4.1g

Energy 557Kcal/2346kJ; Fat 20.8g; Saturated Fat 6.6g; Carbohydrate 61.4g; Fibre 4g

Orecchiette with Anchovies & Broccoli

With its robust flavours, this pasta dish is typical of southern Italian cooking: anchovies, pine nuts, garlic and Pecorino are all popular.

Serves 4

300g/11oz/2 cups broccoli florets
40g/1½oz/½ cup pine nuts
350g/12oz/3 cups dried
  orecchiette
60ml/4 tbsp olive oil
1 small red onion, thinly sliced
50g/2oz jar anchovies in olive oil
1 garlic clove, crushed
50g/2oz/⅔ cup freshly grated
  Pecorino cheese
salt and ground black pepper

1 Break the broccoli florets into small sprigs and cut off the stalks: slice large stalks. Cook the broccoli florets and stalks in a pan of boiling salted water for 2 minutes, then drain and refresh under cold running water. Leave to drain on kitchen paper.

2 Put the pine nuts in a dry non-stick frying pan and toss over low to medium heat for 1–2 minutes, or until the nuts are lightly toasted and golden. Remove and set aside.

3 Cook the pasta in boiling water until *al dente*. Meanwhile, heat the oil in a frying pan, add the onion and fry gently, stirring frequently, for about 5 minutes, until softened. Add the anchovies with their oil, then the garlic and cook, stirring frequently, for 1–2 minutes, until the anchovies break down to a paste. Add the broccoli and plenty of pepper. Toss over heat for 1–2 minutes, until the broccoli is hot. Taste for seasoning.

4 Drain the pasta and turn into a warmed bowl. Add the broccoli mixture and grated Pecorino and toss well to combine. Sprinkle the pine nuts over the top and serve immediately.

Cook's Tip

Orecchiette (little ears) from Puglia are a special type of pasta with a chewy texture. You can use conchiglie instead, if wished.

Farfalle with Tuna

This quick dish makes a good weekday supper if you have canned tomatoes and tuna in the storecupboard.

Serves 4

30ml/2 tbsp olive oil
1 small onion, finely chopped
1 garlic clove, finely chopped
400g/14oz can chopped Italian
  plum tomatoes
45ml/3 tbsp dry white wine
8–10 pitted black olives, cut
  into rings
10ml/2 tsp chopped fresh
  oregano or 5ml/1 tsp
  dried oregano, plus extra
  fresh oregano to garnish
400g/14oz/3½ cups dried
  farfalle
175g/6oz canned tuna in olive oil
salt and ground black pepper

1 Heat the olive oil in a medium frying pan or pan, add the onion and garlic and fry gently for 2–3 minutes, until the onion is soft and golden.

2 Add the plum tomatoes to the pan and bring to the boil, then pour over the white wine and simmer the mixture for a minute or so. Stir in the olives and oregano, with salt and pepper to taste, then cover and cook for 20–25 minutes, stirring from time to time.

3 Meanwhile, bring a pan of lightly salted water to the boil, add the pasta and cook until *al dente*.

4 Drain the canned tuna and flake it with a fork. Add the tuna to the sauce with about 60ml/4 tbsp of the water used for cooking the pasta. Taste and adjust the seasoning.

5 Drain the cooked pasta well and turn into a warmed large serving bowl. Pour the tuna sauce over the top and toss to mix. Serve immediately, garnished with sprigs of oregano.

Variation

If you are cooking for children, try adding some canned corn to give the dish colour and a different texture.

Energy 578Kcal/2425kJ; Fat 25.5g; Saturated Fat 5.1g; Carbohydrate 67.8g; Fibre 4.9g

Energy 514Kcal/2174kJ; Fat 12.4g; Saturated Fat 1.9g; Carbohydrate 78.7g; Fibre 4.8g

Rigatoni with Tuna & Olive Sauce

This baked dish is ideal for using short, thicker pasta, and the colourful tomato sauce marries well with the crumb and cheese topping.

Serves 4
350g/12oz/3 cups dried rigatoni
30ml/2 tbsp olive oil
1 onion, chopped
2 garlic cloves, chopped
400g/14oz can chopped Italian
 plum tomatoes
50g/2oz/4 tbsp tomato purée
 (paste)
50g/2oz/1/2 cup pitted black
 olives, quartered
15ml/1 tbsp chopped fresh
 oregano
225g/8oz canned tuna in olive oil,
 drained and flaked
2.5ml/1/2 tsp anchovy purée
15ml/1 tbsp capers, rinsed
115g/4oz/1 cup grated Cheddar
 cheese
45ml/3 tbsp fresh white
 breadcrumbs
salt and ground black pepper
flat leaf parsley sprigs, to garnish
chunks of hot bread, to serve

1 Bring a pan of lightly salted water to the boil, add the pasta and cook until *al dente*.

2 Meanwhile, heat the oil in a frying pan and fry the onion and garlic for about 10 minutes, until softened.

3 Add the chopped tomatoes, tomato purée and salt and pepper. Bring to the boil, then simmer gently for 5 minutes, stirring occasionally.

4 Stir the olives, oregano, tuna, anchovy purée and capers into the pan. Spoon the mixture into a large mixing bowl.

5 Drain the pasta, turn into the bowl of sauce and toss well to combine. Spoon into four individual flameproof serving dishes or one large dish.

6 Preheat the grill (broiler) and sprinkle the cheese and breadcrumbs evenly over the pasta. Place under the grill for about 10 minutes, until the pasta is heated through and the cheese has melted. Garnish with fresh parsley sprigs and serve immediately with chunks of hot bread.

Spaghettini with Vodka & Caviar

This is an elegant yet easy way to serve spaghettini. In Rome the dish is an after-theatre favourite.

Serves 4
60ml/4 tbsp olive oil
3 spring onions (scallions),
 thinly sliced
1 garlic clove, finely chopped
120ml/4fl oz/1/2 cup vodka
150ml/1/4 pint/2/3 cup double
 (heavy) cream
75g/3oz/1/2 cup black or
 red caviar
salt and ground black pepper
400g/14oz spaghettini

1 Heat the oil in a small pan. Add the spring onions and garlic, and cook gently for 4–5 minutes.

2 Add the vodka and cream, and cook over low heat for about 5–8 minutes more.

3 Remove from the heat and stir in half the caviar. Season with salt and pepper as necessary.

4 Meanwhile, bring a pan of lightly salted water to the boil, add the pasta and cook until *al dente*.

5 Drain the pasta and toss with the caviar sauce. Spoon the remaining caviar on top and serve immediately.

> **Cook's Tips**
> • The finest caviar is salted sturgeon roe. Red "caviar" is salmon roe, cheaper and often saltier than sturgeon roe, as is the black-dyed lump fish roe.
> • Spaghettini is a thinner version of spaghetti and goes particularly well with this delicate sauce, but you could use other long pasta such as vermicelli or thin flat ribbons such as linguine; fresh fettuccine would also team well with the sauce.
> • Serve the dish with a light fresh salad, such as a mix of baby spinach leaves and rocket (arugula), tossed in a balsamic vinegar and olive oil dressing.

Energy 658Kcal/2774kJ; Fat 23.5g; Saturated Fat 8.4g; Carbohydrate 79.2g; Fibre 4.8g

Energy 668Kcal/2798kJ; Fat 33.7g; Saturated Fat 14.4g; Carbohydrate 75g; Fibre 3g

Spaghetti with Hot & Sour Fish

An example of fusion cooking, this lively dish combines classic Italian ingredients with spicy oriental flavourings. The result is an explosion of wonderful tastes.

Serves 4

350g/12oz fresh or dried spaghetti
450g/1lb monkfish, skinned
225g/8oz courgettes (zucchini)
1 green chilli, seeded (optional)
15ml/1 tbsp olive oil
1 large onion, chopped
5ml/1 tsp turmeric
115g/4oz/1 cup shelled peas, thawed if frozen
10ml/2 tsp lemon juice
75ml/5 tbsp hoisin sauce
salt and ground black pepper
fresh dill sprig, to garnish

1 Bring a pan of lightly salted water to the boil, add the pasta and cook until *al dente*.

2 Cut the monkfish into bite-size pieces. Thinly slice the courgettes, then finely chop the chilli, if using.

3 Heat the oil in a large frying pan and fry the onion for 5 minutes, until softened. Add the turmeric.

4 Add the chilli, if using, the courgettes and peas, and fry over medium heat for 5 minutes, until the vegetables have softened.

5 Stir in the fish, lemon juice, hoisin sauce and 150ml/¼ pint/⅔ cup water. Bring the mixture to the boil, then simmer, uncovered, for about 5 minutes, or until the fish is tender. Season with salt and pepper.

6 Drain the pasta thoroughly and turn into a serving dish. Toss in the sauce to coat. Serve at once, garnished with fresh dill.

> **Variation**
> *For a purely Italian version, omit the chilli, turmeric and hoisin sauce and stir in thick cream and parsley at the end of step 5.*

Energy 481Kcal/2038kJ; Fat 5.6g; Saturated Fat 0.8g; Carbohydrate 80.4g; Fibre 5.6g

Fish with Fregola

This Sardinian speciality is a cross between a soup and a stew. If you have difficulty finding the tiny fregola pasta shapes, just use another small soup pasta, such as corallini or ditalini.

Serves 4–6

75ml/5 tbsp olive oil
4 garlic cloves, finely chopped
½ small fresh red chilli, seeded and finely chopped
1 large handful fresh flat leaf parsley, roughly chopped
1 red snapper, about 450g/1lb, cleaned, with head and tail removed
1 red or grey mullet, about 500g/1¼lb, cleaned, with head and tail removed
350–450g/12oz–1lb thick cod fillet
400g/14oz can chopped Italian plum tomatoes
175g/6oz/1½ cups dried fregola
salt and ground black pepper

1 Heat 30ml/2 tbsp of the olive oil in a large flameproof casserole. Add the chopped garlic and chilli, with about half the chopped parsley. Fry over medium heat, stirring occasionally, for about 5 minutes.

2 Cut all of the fish into large chunks – including the skin and the bones in the case of the snapper and mullet – and add the pieces to the casserole as you cut them. Sprinkle the pieces with a further 30ml/2 tbsp of the olive oil and fry for a few minutes more.

3 Add the chopped tomatoes, then fill the empty can with water and pour this into the pan. Bring to the boil. Stir in salt and pepper to taste, lower the heat and cook for 10 minutes, stirring occasionally.

4 Add the fregola and simmer for 5 minutes, then add 250ml/8fl oz/1 cup water and the remaining oil. Simmer for about 15 minutes, until the fregola is *al dente*.

5 If the sauce becomes too thick, add more water, then taste for seasoning. Serve sprinkled with the remaining parsley.

Energy 339Kcal/1426kJ; Fat 13.4g; Saturated Fat 1.7g; Carbohydrate 24g; Fibre 2g

Tagliatelle with Bolognese Sauce

This authentic ragù from the city of Bologna in Emilia-Romagna, central Italy, is traditionally served with tagliatelle.

Serves 6–8

450g/1lb fresh or dried tagliatelle
salt and ground black pepper
freshly grated Parmesan cheese,
   to serve

For the ragù
25g/1oz/2 tbsp butter
15ml/1 tbsp olive oil
1 onion, finely chopped

2 garlic cloves, finely chopped
2 carrots, finely chopped
2 celery sticks, finely chopped
130g/4¹/₂oz pancetta or rindless
   streaky (fatty) bacon, diced
250g/9oz lean minced beef
250g/9oz lean minced pork
120ml/4fl oz/¹/₂ cup dry white
   wine
2 x 400g/14oz cans crushed
   Italian plum tomatoes
475–750ml/16fl oz–1¹/₄
   pints/2–3 cups beef stock
100ml/3¹/₂fl oz/scant ¹/₂ cup
   panna da cucina or double
   (heavy) cream

1 Make the ragù first. Heat the butter and oil in a large pan until sizzling. Add the onion, garlic, vegetables and the pancetta or bacon and cook over medium heat, stirring frequently, for 10 minutes, or until the vegetables have softened.

2 Add the minced beef and pork, lower the heat and cook gently for 10 minutes, stirring frequently and breaking up any lumps in the meat with a wooden spoon. Stir in salt and pepper to taste, then add the wine and stir again. Simmer for about 5 minutes, or until reduced.

3 Add the tomatoes and 250ml/8fl oz/1 cup of the beef stock and bring to the boil. Stir well, then lower the heat. Half cover the pan with a lid and simmer very gently for 2 hours, stirring occasionally and adding more stock as it becomes absorbed.

4 Stir in the cream, then simmer, without a lid, for another 30 minutes, stirring frequently. Meanwhile, cook the pasta in boiling water until *al dente*. Taste for seasoning. Drain the pasta and turn into a warmed bowl. Pour the sauce over the pasta and toss well. Serve immediately, sprinkled with Parmesan.

Energy 491Kcal/2058kJ; Fat 24g; Saturated Fat 10.9g; Carbohydrate 46.8g; Fibre 3.1g

Spaghetti with Meatballs

Tiny mouthwatering meatballs simmered in a delicious piquant tomato sauce are perfect with spaghetti or linguine.

Serves 6–8

350g/12oz minced beef
1 egg
60ml/4 tbsp roughly chopped
   fresh flat leaf parsley
2.5ml/¹/₂ tsp crushed dried
   red chillies

1 thick slice white bread, crusts
   removed and torn into pieces
30ml/2 tbsp milk
about 30ml/2 tbsp olive oil
300ml/¹/₂ pint/1¹/₄ cups passata
400ml/14fl oz/1²/₃ cups
   vegetable stock
5ml/1 tsp sugar
350–450g/12oz–1lb fresh or
   dried spaghetti
salt and ground black pepper
freshly grated Parmesan cheese,
   to serve

1 Put the beef in a large bowl. Add the egg and half the parsley and crushed chillies. Season with plenty of salt and pepper.

2 Place the bread in a small bowl. Moisten with the milk. Leave to soak for a few minutes, then squeeze out the excess milk and crumble the bread over the meat mixture. Mix well with a wooden spoon, then use your hands to squeeze and knead the mixture so that it becomes smooth and quite sticky.

3 Wash your hands, rinse them under the cold tap, then pick up small pieces of the mixture and roll them between your palms to make about 60 very small balls. Place the meatballs on a tray and chill for about 30 minutes.

4 Heat the oil in a large, deep non-stick frying pan. Cook the meatballs in batches until browned all over. Pour the passata and stock into the pan. Heat gently, then add the remaining chillies and the sugar, with salt and pepper to taste. Return all the meatballs to the pan. Bring to the boil, lower the heat and cover. Simmer for 20 minutes.

5 Cook the pasta until *al dente*, then drain and turn into a warm large bowl. Pour the sauce over and toss gently. Sprinkle with the remaining parsley and serve with grated Parmesan.

Energy 324Kcal/1364kJ; Fat 11.6g; Saturated Fat 3.8g; Carbohydrate 40.3g; Fibre 2.7g

Tagliatelle with Red Wine Bolognese Sauce

This is a versatile meat sauce. Here the quantity is also enough for 450g/1lb short shapes, such as penne or fusilli.

Serves 4–6

1 onion
1 small carrot
1 celery stick
2 garlic cloves
45ml/3 tbsp olive oil

400g/14oz minced beef
120ml/4fl oz/½ cup red wine
200ml/7fl oz/scant 1 cup passata
15ml/1 tbsp tomato purée (paste)
5ml/1 tsp dried oregano
15ml/1 tbsp chopped fresh flat
   leaf parsley
350ml/12fl oz/1½ cups beef
   stock
8 baby Italian tomatoes (optional)
450g/1lb/4 cups dried tagliatelle
salt and ground black pepper

1 Chop all the vegetables finely, either in a food processor or by hand. Heat the oil in a large pan, add the finely chopped vegetable mixture and cook over low heat, stirring frequently, for 5–7 minutes.

2 Add the minced beef and cook for 5 minutes, stirring frequently and breaking up any lumps in the meat with a wooden spoon. Stir in the wine and mix well.

3 Cook for 1–2 minutes, then add the passata, tomato purée, herbs and 60ml/4 tbsp of the stock. Season with salt and pepper to taste. Stir well and bring to the boil.

4 Cover the pan and cook over gentle heat for 30 minutes, stirring from time to time and adding more stock as necessary. Add the tomatoes, if using, and simmer for 5–10 minutes more.

5 Meanwhile, bring a pan of lightly salted water to the boil, add the pasta and cook until *al dente*.

6 Drain the pasta thoroughly and turn into a warmed serving bowl. Taste the sauce for seasoning, then add to the pasta and and toss to combine. Serve immediately.

Energy 228Kcal/946kJ; Fat 16.4g; Saturated Fat 5.4g; Carbohydrate 3.2g; Fibre 0.8g

Rigatoni with Bresaola & Peppers

Bresaola – cured raw beef – is usually served thinly sliced as an antipasto. Here its strong, almost gamey, flavour is used to good effect in a sauce for pasta.

Serves 6

30ml/2 tbsp olive oil
1 small onion, finely chopped
150g/5oz bresaola, cut into
   thin strips

1 small handful fresh basil leaves
4 (bell) peppers (red and orange
   or yellow), seeded and diced
120ml/4fl oz/½ cup dry
   white wine
400g/14oz can chopped Italian
   plum tomatoes
450g/1lb/4 cups dried rigatoni
50g/2oz/⅔ cup freshly shaved
   Parmesan cheese
salt and ground black pepper
fresh basil leaves, to garnish

1 Heat the oil in a medium pan, add the onion and bresaola. Cover the pan and cook over low heat for 5–8 minutes, until the onion has softened.

2 Stir in the basil leaves, then add the peppers, wine, 5ml/1 tsp salt and plenty of pepper. Stir well, then simmer gently for 10–15 minutes.

3 Add the canned tomatoes to the pan and increase the heat to high. Bring to the boil, stirring, then lower the heat and replace the lid again. Simmer gently, stirring occasionally, for 20 minutes or until the peppers are very soft and quite creamy.

4 Meanwhile, bring a pan of lightly salted water to the boil, add the pasta and cook until *al dente*.

5 Drain the cooked pasta and turn into a warmed bowl. Taste the sauce for seasoning, then pour it over the pasta and add half the Parmesan. Toss well, garnish with basil leaves and serve immediately, with the remaining Parmesan sprinkled on top.

> **Variation**
> *Use pancetta or streaky (fatty) bacon instead of the bresaola.*

Energy 391Kcal/1651kJ; Fat 9.1g; Saturated Fat 2.8g; Carbohydrate 60.1g; Fibre 4.6g

Fusilli Lunghi with Pepperoni

Long spiral pasta with a tangy sausage sauce makes a warming supper dish.

Serves 4
1 red (bell) pepper
1 green (bell) pepper
30ml/2 tbsp olive oil, plus extra
  for tossing the pasta
1 onion, chopped
2 x 400g/14oz cans chopped
  Italian plum tomatoes
30ml/2 tbsp tomato purée (paste)
10ml/2 tsp paprika
175g/6oz pepperoni or
  chorizo sausage
45ml/3 tbsp chopped fresh
  parsley
400g/14oz dried fusilli lunghi
salt and ground black pepper

1 Halve, core and seed the peppers. Cut the flesh into dice.

2 Heat the oil in a medium pan, add the onion and cook for 2–3 minutes, until beginning to colour and soften; do not allow them to turn brown.

3 Add the peppers, tomatoes, tomato purée and paprika to the pan and bring to the boil. Simmer, uncovered, for about 15–20 minutes, until reduced and thickened.

4 Slice the pepperoni or chorizo and stir into the sauce with 30ml/2 tbsp of the chopped parsley. Season to taste with salt and pepper.

5 While the sauce is simmering, bring a pan of lightly salted water to the boil, add the pasta and cook until *al dente*.

6 Drain the pasta well and turn into a bowl. Add the remaining parsley and toss together with a little extra olive oil. Divide among four warmed bowls and top with the prepared sauce.

> **Cook's Tip**
> *All types of sausage are suitable for this dish, but if using raw Italian sausages, such as Luganega, add them with the onion to cook through or cook separately, then cut into bite-size chunks.*

Tagliatelle with Prosciutto & Parmesan

Consisting of a few prime Italian ingredients, this pasta dish is simplicity itself to make yet tastes wonderful. Serve with a fresh salad and chunks of ciabatta for lunch.

Serves 4
115g/4oz prosciutto
400g/14oz fresh or dried tagliatelle
75g/3oz/6 tbsp butter
50g/2oz/²⁄₃ cup freshly grated
  Parmesan cheese
salt and ground black pepper
a few fresh sage leaves, to garnish

1 Cut the prosciutto into strips the same width as the tagliatelle. Bring a pan of lightly salted water to the boil, add the pasta and cook until *al dente*.

2 Meanwhile, melt the butter gently in a pan, stir in the prosciutto strips and heat through over very gentle heat, being careful not to let them colour.

3 Drain the tagliatelle through a colander and pile into a warmed serving dish.

4 Sprinkle the Parmesan cheese over the pasta and pour the buttery prosciutto on the top. Season well with black pepper and garnish with the sage leaves.

> **Cook's Tip**
> *Both fresh and dried tagliatelle taste good with this sauce. The flat ribbons are usually 1cm/½in wide and the dried version is often sold folded into nests, which then unravel as they cook. For the best flavour, try making your own fresh tagliatelle from egg dough. To ring the changes, try different coloured tagliatelle: green pasta is flavoured and coloured with spinach, while the pink variety has tomato added to it. The pasta can also be flavoured with mushrooms, beetroot (beets) and saffron. Fettuccine, a narrower ribbon, also works well with this recipe.*

Energy 655Kcal/2756kJ; Fat 25.6g; Saturated Fat 7.7g; Carbohydrate 87.5g; Fibre 7.1g

Energy 569Kcal/2394kJ; Fat 22.3g; Saturated Fat 12.9g; Carbohydrate 74.5g; Fibre 2.9g

Rigatoni with Pork

This is an excellent meat sauce using minced pork rather than the more usual minced beef.

Serves 4
1 small onion
$\frac{1}{2}$ carrot
$\frac{1}{2}$ celery stick
2 garlic cloves
25g/1oz/2 tbsp butter
30ml/2 tbsp olive oil

150g/5oz minced pork
60ml/4 tbsp dry white wine
400g/14oz can chopped Italian plum tomatoes
a few fresh basil leaves, plus extra shredded basil leaves to garnish
400g/14oz/3½ cups dried rigatoni
salt and ground black pepper
freshly shaved Parmesan cheese, to serve

1 Chop all the fresh vegetables finely, either in a food processor or by hand. Heat the butter and oil in a large pan until just sizzling, add the chopped vegetables and cook over medium heat, stirring frequently, for 3–4 minutes.

2 Add the minced pork and cook gently for 2–3 minutes, breaking up any lumps in the meat with a wooden spoon.

3 Lower the heat and fry for 2–3 minutes, stirring frequently, then stir in the wine. Mix in the tomatoes, whole basil leaves, salt to taste and plenty of pepper. Bring to the boil, then lower the heat, cover and simmer for 40 minutes, stirring occasionally.

4 Cook the pasta in boiling water until *al dente*. Just before draining the pasta, add a ladleful or two of the cooking water to the sauce. Stir the sauce well, then taste for seasoning. Drain the pasta, toss with the sauce and serve sprinkled with shredded basil and shaved Parmesan.

> **Variation**
> To give the sauce a more intense flavour, soak 15g/½oz dried porcini mushrooms in 175ml/6fl oz/¾ cup warm water for 15–20 minutes, then drain, chop and add with the meat.

Bucatini with Sausage & Pancetta

This rich sauce makes a satisfying main course dish when teamed up with bucatini, a long, hollow pasta that looks like thin drinking straws when raw.

Serves 4
115g/4oz pork sausagemeat, preferably salsiccia a metro
400g/14oz can Italian plum tomatoes

15ml/1 tbsp olive oil
1 garlic clove, crushed
115g/4oz pancetta or rindless streaky (fatty) bacon, roughly chopped
30ml/2 tbsp chopped fresh flat leaf parsley
400g/14oz dried bucatini
60–75ml/4–5 tbsp panna da cucina or double (heavy) cream
2 egg yolks
salt and ground black pepper

1 Remove any skin from the sausagemeat and break the meat up roughly with a knife. Purée the tomatoes in a food processor or blender.

2 Heat the oil in a medium frying pan or pan, add the garlic and fry over low heat for 1–2 minutes. Remove the garlic with a slotted spoon and discard it.

3 Add the pancetta and the sausagemeat and cook over medium heat for 3–4 minutes. Stir constantly to break up the sausagemeat – it will turn brown and look crumbly.

4 Add the puréed tomatoes to the pan with half the parsley and salt and pepper to taste. Stir well and bring to the boil, scraping up any sediment from the sausagemeat that has stuck to the bottom of the pan. Lower the heat, cover and simmer for 30 minutes, stirring occasionally. Taste for seasoning.

5 Meanwhile, bring a pan of lightly salted water to the boil, add the pasta and cook until *al dente*.

6 Put the cream and egg yolks in a warmed bowl and mix. Drain the pasta well, add to the cream mixture and toss to coat. Pour the sausagemeat sauce over the pasta and toss again. Serve sprinkled with the remaining parsley.

Fettuccine with Ham & Peas

This simple dish makes a very good first course for six people, or a main course for three to four. The ingredients are all easy to find, so the recipe makes an ideal impromptu supper.

Serves 3–6

50g/2oz/¼ cup butter
I small onion, finely chopped
200g/7oz/1¾ cups fresh or
  frozen peas
100ml/3½fl oz/scant ½ cup
  chicken stock
2.5ml/½ tsp sugar
175ml/6fl oz/¾ cup dry
  white wine
350g/12oz fresh fettuccine
75g/3oz piece cooked ham, cut
  into bite-size chunks
115g/4oz/1¼ cups freshly grated
  Parmesan cheese
salt and ground black pepper

I Melt the butter in a medium pan, add the onion and cook over low heat for about 5 minutes, until softened but not coloured. Add the peas, stock and sugar, with salt and pepper to taste.

2 Bring to the boil, then lower the heat and simmer for 3–5 minutes, or until the peas are tender. Add the wine, increase the heat and boil until the wine has reduced.

3 Bring a pan of lightly salted water to the boil and add the pasta. When it is almost *al dente*, add the ham to the sauce, with about a third of the grated Parmesan. Heat through, stirring, then taste for seasoning.

4 Drain the pasta and turn into a warmed large bowl. Pour the sauce over the pasta and toss well. Serve immediately, sprinkled with the remaining grated Parmesan.

> **Cook's Tip**
> *If you make home-made pasta often, it may be worth investing in a pasta machine which has rollers that thin out the dough and cutters for producing ribbons of different widths.*

Linguine with Ham & Mascarpone

Mascarpone cheese masquerades as cream in this recipe. Its thick, unctuous consistency makes it perfect for sauces. Have the water boiling, ready for the pasta, before you start making the sauce, because everything cooks so quickly.

Serves 6

25g/1oz/2 tbsp butter
90g/3½ oz cooked ham, cut into
  thin strips
150g/5oz/⅔ cup mascarpone
  cheese
30ml/2 tbsp milk
45ml/3 tbsp freshly grated
  Parmesan cheese, plus extra
  to serve
500g/1¼lb fresh linguine
salt and ground black pepper

I Melt the butter in a medium pan, add the ham, mascarpone and milk and stir well over low heat, until the mascarpone has melted. Add 15ml/1 tbsp of the grated Parmesan and plenty of pepper and stir well.

2 Bring a pan of lightly salted water to the boil, add the pasta and cook until *al dente*.

3 Drain the cooked pasta well and turn into a warmed bowl. Pour the sauce over the pasta, add the remaining Parmesan and toss well until thoroughly combined.

4 Taste for seasoning and serve the pasta immediately, with more ground black pepper sprinkled on top and extra grated Parmesan handed separately.

> **Cook's Tips**
> • *Linguine, meaning "little tongues", is a flat version of spaghetti and is good with a wide range of sauces. You could also use spaghetti very successfully in this recipe.*
> • *Mascarpone is a rich, thick cream cheese from Lombardy, with a texture similar to whipped cream. Made from cow's milk, it has a delicate flavour with a natural sweetness.*

Energy 412Kcal/1731kJ; Fat 15.1g; Saturated Fat 8.6g; Carbohydrate 48.1g; Fibre 3.4g

Energy 413Kcal/1745kJ; Fat 11.6g; Saturated Fat 6.4g; Carbohydrate 62.9g; Fibre 2.4g

Pipe Rigate with Creamy Ham & Peas

Prettily flecked with pink and green, this is a lovely supper dish. The ridged, hollow pasta shapes not only look attractive, but are also ideal for trapping the prosciutto and peas.

Serves 4

25g/1oz/2 tbsp butter
15ml/1 tbsp olive oil
150–175g/5–6oz/1¼–1½ cups frozen peas, thawed
1 garlic clove, crushed
150ml/¼ pint/⅔ cup chicken stock, dry white wine or water
30ml/2 tbsp chopped fresh flat leaf parsley
175ml/6fl oz/¾ cup panna da cucina or double (heavy) cream
115g/4oz prosciutto, shredded
350g/12oz/3 cups dried pipe rigate
salt and ground black pepper
chopped fresh herbs, to garnish

1 Melt half the butter with the olive oil in a medium pan until foaming. Add the thawed frozen peas and the crushed garlic to the pan, followed by the chicken stock, wine or water.

2 Sprinkle in the chopped parsley and add salt and pepper to taste. Cook over medium heat, stirring frequently, for 5–8 minutes, or until most of the liquid has been absorbed.

3 Add about half the cream, increase the heat to high and let the cream bubble, stirring constantly, until it thickens and coats the peas. Remove from the heat, stir in the prosciutto and taste for seasoning.

4 Bring a pan of lightly salted water to the boil, add the pasta and cook until *al dente*.

5 Immediately melt the remaining butter with the rest of the cream in the pan in which the pasta was cooked. Add the pasta and toss over medium heat, until it is evenly coated.

6 Pour in the prosciutto sauce, toss lightly to mix with the pasta and heat through. Serve immediately, sprinkled with fresh herbs.

Tortellini with Ham

Ready-prepared, fresh tortellini, enclosing tasty fillings, are now widely available. Combined with ham and tomato sauce, they make a delicious and instant Italian-style meal.

Serves 4

250g/9oz packet tortellini alla carne (meat-filled tortellini)
30ml/2 tbsp olive oil
¼ large onion, finely chopped
115g/4oz piece cooked ham, cut into bite-size chunks
150ml/¼ pint/⅔ cup passata
100ml/3½fl oz/scant ½ cup panna da cucina or double (heavy) cream
about 90g/3½oz/generous 1 cup freshly grated Parmesan cheese
salt and ground black pepper

1 Cook the tortellini in plenty of boiling water.

2 Meanwhile, heat the oil in a large pan, add the onion and cook over low heat, stirring frequently, for about 5 minutes, until softened. Add the ham and cook, stirring occasionally, until it darkens.

3 Add the tomato passata. Fill the empty carton with water and pour it into the pan. Stir well, then add salt and pepper to taste. Bring to the boil, lower the heat and simmer the sauce for a few minutes, stirring occasionally, until it has reduced slightly. Stir the cream into the sauce.

4 Drain the pasta well and add to the sauce. Add a handful of grated Parmesan to the pan. Stir, then toss well and taste for seasoning. Serve in warmed individual bowls, topped with the remaining grated Parmesan.

> **Cook's Tips**
> • *Passata is simply strained crushed tomatoes. Often sold in cartons, it is a handy shortcut for making quick sauces.*
> • *Tortellini are small stuffed shapes, each made from a round of filled dough, folded in half and wrapped round into a ring.*

Energy 350Kcal/1452kJ; Fat 28.6g; Saturated Fat 14.6g; Carbohydrate 7.2g; Fibre 0.6g

Energy 643Kcal/2693kJ; Fat 33.8g; Saturated Fat 18.5g; Carbohydrate 70.1g; Fibre 4.3g

Fettuccine with Ham & Cream

Lightly fried prosciutto combines beautifully with shallots and cream to make a delicate tasting sauce that is set off perfectly by the fettuccine ribbons.

Serves 4

115g/4oz slice prosciutto or other cured ham
50g/2oz/¼ cup butter
2 shallots, very finely chopped
salt and ground black pepper
150ml/¼ pint/⅔ cup double (heavy) cream
350g/12oz fettuccine
50g/2oz/⅔ cup grated Parmesan cheese
1 sprig fresh parsley, to garnish

1 Cut the fat from the prosciutto, then cut both lean and fat parts separately into small squares.

2 Melt the butter in a medium frying pan, add the shallots and the squares of prosciutto fat. Cook until golden. Add the lean pieces of meat and cook for a further 2 minutes. Season with black pepper. Stir in the cream and keep warm over low heat while the pasta is cooking.

3 Bring a pan of lightly salted water to the boil, add the pasta and cook until *al dente*. Drain the pasta, then turn into a warmed serving bowl. Add the sauce and toss well together. Stir in the grated Parmesan cheese and serve at once, garnished with a sprig of parsley.

Variations

• For an added touch of luxury, add 115g/4oz lightly cooked asparagus tips in step 3, with the cheese.
• For fettuccine primavera, a creamy vegetable dish, omit the prosciutto. Finely chop 1 carrot, 2 small courgettes (zucchini), ½ red (bell) pepper and 1 tender celery stalk, then add to the shallots and cook until softened. Stir in the cream with a handful of chopped parsley and season with black pepper. Toss with the sauce and use half the amount of Parmesan.

Fusilli with Tomato & Smoky Bacon

Prepare this sauce using tomatoes that are perfectly ripe and sweet.

Serves 4

900g/2lb ripe tomatoes
6 rashers (strips) smoked streaky (fatty) bacon
50g/2oz/¼ cup butter
1 onion, chopped
15ml/1 tbsp chopped fresh oregano or 5ml/1 tsp dried
450g/1lb fresh or dried fusilli col buco or other short shape
salt and ground black pepper
freshly grated Parmesan cheese, to serve

1 Plunge the tomatoes into a bowl of boiling water for 45 seconds, then plunge into a bowl of cold water for 30 seconds. Slip off the skins. Halve the tomatoes, remove the seeds and cores and roughly chop the flesh.

2 Remove and discard the rind from the streaky bacon, then roughly chop the rashers.

3 Melt the butter in a pan and add the chopped bacon. Fry until lightly browned on all sides, then add the onion and cook gently, stirring, for 5 minutes, until softened.

4 Add the tomatoes and oregano to the pan and season with salt and pepper to taste. Simmer gently for 10 minutes.

5 Bring a pan of lightly salted water to the boil, add the pasta and cook until *al dente*. Drain well and toss with the tomato sauce. Serve with plenty of freshly grated Parmesan cheese.

Cook's Tip

Fusilli col buco – short pasta spirals with a hole running through them – are ideal for trapping chunky pieces of the sauce. Ordinary short fusilli would also be fine for this dish, or try the long strands of fusilli lunghi, which resemble curly wires.

Energy 667Kcal/2792kJ; Fat 36.9g; Saturated Fat 22.1g; Carbohydrate 67g; Fibre 2.8g

Energy 608Kcal/2564kJ; Fat 20.4g; Saturated Fat 9.5g; Carbohydrate 91.6g; Fibre 5.7g

Rigatoni with Garlic Crumbs

If you like spicy dishes, then this is the pasta dish for you. The bacon is an optional addition; you can leave it out if you are cooking for vegetarians.

Serves 4–6
45ml/3 tbsp olive oil
2 shallots, chopped
8 rashers (strips) streaky (fatty) bacon, chopped (optional)

10ml/2 tsp crushed dried red chillies
400g/14oz can chopped tomatoes with garlic and herbs
6 slices white bread
115g/4oz/½ cup butter
2 garlic cloves, chopped
450g/1lb/4 cups fresh or dried rigatoni
salt and ground black pepper

1 Heat the oil in a medium pan and fry the shallots and bacon, if using, gently for about 6–8 minutes, stirring constantly until golden. Add the dried chillies and chopped tomatoes, half-cover the pan and simmer for 20 minutes.

2 Meanwhile, cut the crusts off the bread and discard them. Reduce the bread to crumbs in a blender or food processor.

3 Heat the butter in a frying pan, add the garlic and breadcrumbs and stir-fry until golden and crisp. (Keep stirring and don't let the crumbs catch and burn or the final result will be ruined.)

4 Bring a pan of lightly salted water to the boil, add the pasta and cook until *al dente*. Drain well.

5 Toss the pasta with the tomato sauce and divide among four or six warmed serving plates. Sprinkle the pasta with the golden breadcrumbs and serve immediately.

> **Cook's Tip**
> To keep the breadcrumbs crisp and dry after frying, drain them on kitchen paper and place in a low oven until ready to use.

Spaghetti with Bacon & Onion

The great thing about pasta is that it can be turned into an instant, tasty meal, using ingredients that are almost always at hand.

Serves 6
30ml/2 tbsp olive oil
115g/4oz/½ cup unsmoked lean bacon, cut into matchsticks

1 small onion, finely chopped
120ml/4fl oz/½ cup dry white wine
450g/1lb fresh or canned tomatoes, chopped
2.5ml/½ tsp thyme leaves
salt and ground black pepper
500g/1¼lb spaghetti
freshly grated Parmesan, to serve

1 In a medium frying pan, heat the oil. Add the bacon and onion, and cook over low to medium heat for about 8–10 minutes, until the onion is golden and the bacon has released its fat and is beginning to brown.

2 Add the wine to the bacon and onion, increase the heat, and cook rapidly until the liquid boils off. Add the tomatoes and thyme, then season with salt and pepper. Cover and cook over medium heat for 10–15 minutes.

3 Meanwhile, bring a pan of lightly salted water to the boil, add the pasta and cook until *al dente*.

4 Drain the pasta and turn into a warmed serving bowl. Add the sauce and toss together. Serve with the grated Parmesan.

> **Cook's Tip**
> If using fresh tomatoes, peel them first: cover in boiling water for 45 seconds, then plunge into cold water and remove the skins.

> **Variation**
> Add 115g/4oz sliced mushrooms to the pan in step 1, after the onion and bacon have been cooking for 5 minutes.

Energy 619Kcal/2597kJ; Fat 31.2g; Saturated Fat 13.7g; Carbohydrate 71.9g; Fibre 3.4g

Energy 438Kcal/1856kJ; Fat 8.5g; Saturated Fat 1.8g; Carbohydrate 77.3g; Fibre 3.8g

Tagliatelle with Prosciutto & Asparagus

Prosciutto and asparagus harmoniously blend with a creamy cheese sauce and pasta in this elegant dish.

Serves 4

350g/12oz fresh tagliatelle
25g/1oz/2 tbsp butter
15ml/1 tbsp olive oil
225g/8oz asparagus tips
1 garlic clove, chopped
115g/4oz prosciutto, sliced
   into strips
30ml/2 tbsp chopped fresh sage
150ml/¼ pint/⅔ cup single
   (light) cream
115g/4oz/1 cup grated chive-and-
   onion double Gloucester cheese
115g/4oz/1 cup grated Gruyère
   cheese
salt and ground black pepper
fresh sage sprigs, to garnish

1 Bring a pan of lightly salted water to the boil, add the pasta and cook until *al dente*.

2 Melt the butter and oil in a frying pan and gently fry the asparagus tips for about 5 minutes, stirring occasionally, until they are almost tender.

3 Stir the garlic and prosciutto into the pan of asparagus and cook for 1 minute, stirring gently.

4 Stir in the chopped sage and cook for a further 1 minute. Pour in the cream and bring the mixture to the boil.

5 Add the cheeses and simmer gently, stirring occasionally, until thoroughly melted. Season with salt and pepper to taste.

6 Drain the pasta thoroughly and toss with the sauce to coat. Serve immediately in four warmed plates, garnished with fresh sage sprigs.

> **Variation**
> Use plain double Gloucester and add snipped chives in step 5.

Penne with Sausage & Parmesan Sauce

Spicy sausage tossed in a cheesy tomato sauce is delicious served on a bed of tubular pasta.

Serves 4

350g/12oz/3 cups dried penne
450g/1lb ripe tomatoes
30ml/2 tbsp olive oil
225g/8oz pepperoni or chorizo
   sausage, diagonally sliced
1 garlic clove, chopped
30ml/2 tbsp chopped fresh flat
   leaf parsley
grated rind of 1 lemon
50g/2oz/⅔ cup freshly grated
   Parmesan cheese
salt and ground black pepper
finely chopped fresh flat leaf
   parsley, to garnish

1 Bring a pan of lightly salted water to the boil, add the pasta and cook until *al dente*.

2 Meanwhile, slash the bottoms of the tomatoes with a knife, making a cross. Place in a large bowl, cover with boiling water and leave to stand for 45 seconds. Plunge into cold water for 30 seconds, then peel off the skins and roughly chop the flesh.

3 Heat the oil in a frying pan and fry the sliced sausage for 5 minutes, stirring from time to time, until browned.

4 Add the chopped tomatoes, garlic, parsley and grated lemon rind. Heat through gently, stirring, for 1 minute.

5 Finally, add the grated Parmesan cheese to the sauce, stir to combine and season to taste with salt and pepper.

6 Drain the pasta well, turn into a serving bowl and toss with the sauce to coat. Serve immediately, garnished with parsley.

> **Cook's Tip**
> Use other pasta with hollows, such as lumache or rigatoni.

Energy 542Kcal/2282kJ; Fat 18.6g; Saturated Fat 8.9g; Carbohydrate 67.1g; Fibre 3.5g

Energy 675Kcal/2833kJ; Fat 33.7g; Saturated Fat 11.9g; Carbohydrate 69g; Fibre 4.4g

Tagliatelle with Devilled Kidneys

Kidneys are popular in northern Italy where they are often simply sautéed to make the most of their texture and flavour. In this recipe, they are enhanced by a tangy paprika and mustard sauce and served up with fresh tagliatelle as a foil to the rich, strong flavours.

Serves 4
8–10 lamb's kidneys
15ml/1 tbsp sunflower oil
25g/1oz/2 tbsp butter
10ml/2 tsp paprika
5–10ml/1–2 tsp mild grainy
    mustard
salt
225g/8oz fresh tagliatelle
chopped fresh parsley, to garnish

1 Cut the kidneys in half and neatly cut out the white cores with scissors. Cut the kidneys in half again if very large.

2 Heat the sunflower oil and butter together. Add the lamb's kidneys and cook, turning frequently, for about 2 minutes. Blend the paprika and mustard together with a little salt and stir into the pan.

3 Continue cooking the kidneys, basting frequently, for a further 3–4 minutes.

4 Meanwhile, bring a pan of lightly salted water to the boil, add the pasta and cook until *al dente*.

5 Drain the pasta and turn into a serving dish. Top with the kidneys and their sauce, sprinkle with the chopped fresh parsley and serve immediately.

> **Cook's Tips**
> • *Ask your butcher to prepare the kidneys for you, if you prefer.*
> • *Try serving with tomato and mozzarella toasts: toast thin slices of ciabatta, then spread with sun-dried tomato paste on one side and arrange small pieces of mozzarella over the top. Put on a baking sheet, sprinkle with herbs and olive oil and bake in a hot oven until the mozzarella is bubbling.*

Golden-topped Eliche

Relaxed food for friends, Italian-style. This recipe is ideal for a last-minute get-together as it is very flexible and can be easily stretched to feed eight instead of four people. It's also a great way to use up left-over cooked meat. Children will love it.

Serves 4–6
225g/8oz/2 cups dried eliche
115g/4oz/¾ cup chopped cooked
    ham, beef or turkey
350g/12oz par-cooked mixed
    vegetables, such as carrots,
    cauliflower, beans, etc
5–10ml/1–2 tsp oil

For the cheese sauce
25g/1oz/2 tbsp butter
25g/1oz/2 tbsp plain (all-purpose)
    flour
300ml/½ pint/1¼ cups milk
175g/6oz/1½ cups grated
    Cheddar cheese
5–10ml/1–2 tsp mustard
salt and ground black pepper

1 Bring a pan of lightly salted water to the boil, add the pasta and cook until *al dente*. Drain and place in a flameproof dish with the chopped meat, the mixed vegetables and oil.

2 To make the sauce, melt the butter in a pan, stir in the flour and cook for 1 minute, stirring. Remove from the heat and gradually stir in the milk.

3 Return to the heat, bring to the boil and cook for 2 minutes, stirring frequently. Add half the cheese and the mustard and season with salt and pepper to taste.

4 Spoon the sauce over the meat and vegetables. Sprinkle with the rest of the cheese, place under a hot grill (broiler) and grill (broil) quickly until golden and bubbling. Allow to stand for a few minutes before serving.

> **Variation**
> *Any mature hard cheese is suitable for the topping. Red Leicester will give the sauce a deep golden colour and is always a favourite with hungry children.*

Tagliatelle with Radicchio & Cream

This is a modern recipe that is very quick and easy to make. It is deliciously rich, and makes a good dinner party first course.

Serves 4

225g/8oz dried tagliatelle
75–90g/3–3½oz pancetta or streaky (fatty) bacon, diced
25g/1oz/2 tbsp butter
1 onion, finely chopped
1 garlic clove, crushed
1 head of radicchio, about 115–175g/4–6oz, finely shredded
150ml/¼ pint/⅔ cup panna da cucina or double (heavy) cream
50g/2oz/⅔ cup freshly grated Parmesan cheese
salt and ground black pepper

1 Bring a pan of lightly salted water to the boil, add the pasta and cook until *al dente*.

2 Meanwhile, put the pancetta or bacon in a medium pan and heat gently until the fat begins to run. Increase the heat slightly and fry the pancetta or bacon for a further 5 minutes, stirring frequently, until crisp and golden.

3 Add the butter, onion and garlic to the pan and cook for 5 minutes more, stirring. Add the radicchio and toss for 1–2 minutes until wilted.

4 Pour in the cream and add the grated Parmesan, with salt and pepper to taste. Stir for 1–2 minutes, until the cream is bubbling and well mixed in. Taste for seasoning.

5 Drain the pasta and turn into a warmed bowl. Pour the sauce over and toss well. Serve immediately.

> **Cook's Tip**
> In Italy, cooks use a type of radicchio called radicchio di Treviso. It is very striking to look at, having long leaves that are dramatically striped in dark red and white. If you cannot get it, use the round radicchio instead, which is very easy to obtain.

Bucatini with Tomato & Chilli Sauce

This classic tomato sauce is called "Amatriciana" after the town of Amatrice in the Sabine hills, Lazio. If you visit Rome, you will see it on many menus served with either bucatini or spaghetti.

Serves 4

15ml/1 tbsp olive oil
1 small onion, finely sliced
115g/4oz smoked pancetta or rindless smoked streaky (fatty) bacon, diced
1 fresh red chilli, seeded and cut into thin strips
400g/14oz can chopped Italian plum tomatoes
30–45ml/2–3 tbsp dry white wine or water
350g/12oz/3 cups dried bucatini
30–45ml/2–3 tbsp freshly grated Pecorino cheese, plus extra to serve (optional)
salt and ground black pepper

1 Heat the oil in a medium pan and cook the onion, pancetta and chilli over low heat for 5–7 minutes, stirring. Add the tomatoes and wine or water, with salt and pepper to taste. Bring to the boil, stirring, then cover and simmer for 15–20 minutes, stirring occasionally. If the sauce becomes too dry, stir in a little of the pasta water.

2 Meanwhile, bring a pan of lightly salted water to the boil, add the pasta and cook until al *dente*. Drain the pasta and turn it into a warmed bowl.

3 Taste the sauce for seasoning, pour it over the pasta and add the grated Pecorino. Toss well. Serve immediately, with more grated Pecorino handed separately, if liked.

> **Cook's Tip**
> Always take care when dealing with chillies. They contain a substance called capsaicin, which will irritate delicate skin, so it's a good idea to wear rubber gloves when handling them.

Energy 543Kcal/2264kJ; Fat 35g; Saturated Fat 20g; Carbohydrate 44g; Fibre 2.1g

Energy 467Kcal/1972kJ; Fat 13.9g; Saturated Fat 4.6g; Carbohydrate 69.2g; Fibre 3.8g

Pork Meatballs with Corn Spaghetti & Tomato Sauce

Serve these meatballs on a bed of freshly cooked gluten-free corn spaghetti.

Serves 6

450g/1lb lean minced pork
1 leek, finely chopped
115g/4oz/1½ cups mushrooms, finely chopped
15ml/1 tbsp chopped fresh thyme
15ml/1 tbsp tomato purée
1 egg, beaten
30ml/2 tbsp potato flour
15ml/1 tbsp sunflower oil
350–500g/12oz–1¼lb fresh or dried corn spaghetti

fresh thyme sprigs, to garnish

For the tomato sauce
1 onion, finely chopped
1 carrot, finely chopped
1 celery stick, finely chopped
1 garlic clove, crushed
675g/1½lb ripe tomatoes, skinned, seeded and chopped
150ml/¼ pint/⅔ cup white wine
150ml/¼ pint/⅔ cup well-flavoured vegetable stock
15ml/1 tbsp tomato purée
15ml/1 tbsp chopped fresh basil
salt and ground black pepper

1 Preheat the oven to 180°C/350°F/Gas 4. Put the pork, leek, mushrooms, chopped thyme, tomato purée, egg and potato flour in a bowl and mix together. Shape into small balls, place on a plate, cover and chill.

2 Place all the sauce ingredients in a saucepan and season, then bring to the boil. Boil, uncovered, for 10 minutes, until thickened.

3 Heat the oil in a frying pan, add the meatballs and cook in batches until lightly browned.

4 Place the meatballs in a shallow, ovenproof dish and pour the sauce over. Cover and bake for 1 hour.

5 Meanwhile, cook the pasta in a pan of lightly salted, boiling water for 8–12 minutes, or according to the packet instructions, until al dente. Rinse under boiling water and drain. Divide the pasta into warmed bowls, spoon the meatballs and sauce over the top and serve garnished with fresh thyme.

Energy 425Kcal/1794kJ; Fat 11.8g; Saturated Fat 3.5g; Carbohydrate 54.2g; Fibre 4.5g

Spaghetti Carbonara

An all-time favourite that needs no introducing. This version has plenty of pancetta or bacon and is not too creamy, but you can vary the amounts as you please. Serve with a green salad and a smooth chianti.

Serves 4

30ml/2 tbsp olive oil
1 small onion, finely chopped
8 pancetta or rindless smoked streaky (fatty) bacon rashers (strips), cut into 1cm/½in strips

350g/12oz fresh or dried spaghetti
4 eggs
60ml/4 tbsp crème fraîche
60ml/4 tbsp freshly grated Parmesan cheese, plus extra to serve
salt and ground black pepper
fresh parsley sprigs, to garnish (optional)

1 Heat the oil in a large pan or frying pan, add the finely chopped onion and cook over low heat, stirring frequently, for about 5 minutes, until softened but not coloured.

2 Add the strips of pancetta or bacon to the onion in the pan and cook for about 10 minutes, stirring almost all of the time.

3 Meanwhile, bring a pan of lightly salted water to the boil, add the pasta and cook until al dente.

3 Put the eggs, crème fraîche and grated Parmesan in a bowl. Grind in plenty of pepper, then beat everything together well.

4 Drain the pasta, turn into the pan with the pancetta or bacon and toss well to mix. Turn the heat off under the pan. Immediately add the egg mixture and toss vigorously so that it cooks lightly and coats the pasta.

5 Quickly taste for seasoning and adjust if necessary, then divide among four warmed individual bowls and garnish with parsley, if using. Serve immediately, with extra grated Parmesan handed separately.

Energy 707Kcal/2964kJ; Fat 36.8g; Saturated Fat 14.3g; Carbohydrate 66.4g; Fibre 2.8g

Sardinian Sausage & Pasta

In Sardinia they call this dish simply "Malloreddus", which is the local name for the type of pasta traditionally used to make it. For authenticity, use sartizzu sardo sausage if you can find it.

Serves 4–6
30ml/2 tbsp olive oil
6 garlic cloves

200g/7oz Italian pure pork
  sausage, diced small
2 small handfuls fresh basil leaves
400g/14oz can chopped Italian
  plum tomatoes
a good pinch of saffron threads
15ml/1 tbsp sugar
350g/12oz/3 cups dried
  malloreddus (gnocchi sardi)
75g/3oz/1 cup freshly grated
  Pecorino sardo cheese
salt and ground black pepper

1 Heat the oil in a medium pan. Add the garlic, sausage and half the basil leaves. Fry, stirring frequently, until the sausage is browned all over.

2 Remove and discard the garlic. Add the tomatoes. Fill the empty can with water, pour into the pan, then stir in the saffron, sugar, 5ml/1 tsp salt and pepper to taste. Bring to the boil, lower the heat and simmer for 20–30 minutes, stirring occasionally.

3 Meanwhile, bring a pan of lightly salted water to the boil, add the pasta and cook until *al dente*.

4 Drain the pasta and turn into a warmed bowl. Taste the sauce for seasoning, pour over the pasta and toss well. Add one-third of the grated Pecorino and the remaining basil and toss well. Sprinkle with the remaining Pecorino and serve.

> **Cook's Tip**
> *In Sardinia, a special type of sausage is used for Malloreddus. It is flavoured with aniseed and black pepper and is called sartizzu sardo. A good alternative to sartizzu sardo would be the piquant salsiccia piccante. If, however, you prefer a slightly milder flavour, try luganega, which is more widely available.*

Eliche with Sausage & Radicchio

Sausage and radicchio may seem odd companions, but their combined flavour is really delicious.

Serves 4
30ml/2 tbsp olive oil
1 onion, finely chopped

200g/7oz Italian pure pork
  sausage
175ml/6fl oz/³⁄₄ cup passata
90ml/6 tbsp dry white wine
300g/11oz/2³⁄₄ cups dried eliche
50g/2oz radicchio leaves, finely
  shredded
salt and ground black pepper

1 Heat the olive oil in a large, pan. Add the finely chopped onion and cook over low heat, stirring frequently, for about 5 minutes, until softened.

2 Snip the end off the sausage skin and squeeze the sausagemeat into the pan. Stir the sausagemeat to mix it with the oil and onion and break it up into small pieces.

3 Continue to fry the mixture, increasing the heat if necessary, until the sausagemeat is brown and looks crumbly. Stir in the passata, then sprinkle in the wine and salt and pepper to taste. Simmer over low heat, stirring occasionally, for 10–12 minutes.

4 Meanwhile, bring a pan of lightly salted water to the boil and cook the pasta until *al dente*. Just before draining the pasta, add a ladleful or two of the cooking water to the sausage sauce and stir it in well. Taste the sauce to check the seasoning.

5 Drain the pasta and add to the sausage sauce. Add the radicchio and toss well to combine. Serve immediately.

> **Cook's Tips**
> • *The best sausage to use is called salsiccia puro suino, available from Italian delicatessens. It is made from 100 per cent pure pork plus flavourings and seasonings.*
> • *If you can get it, use the long, tapering radicchio di Treviso for this dish; otherwise the round radicchio can be used.*

Pasta with Lamb & Peppers

This simple sauce is a speciality of the Abruzzo-Molise region, east of Rome, where it is traditionally served with maccheroni alla chitarra – square-shaped long macaroni.

Serves 4–6
60ml/4 tbsp olive oil
250g/9oz boneless lamb neck
   fillet, diced quite small
2 garlic cloves, finely chopped
2 bay leaves, torn
250ml/8fl oz/1 cup dry white wine
4 ripe Italian plum tomatoes, peeled
   and chopped
2 large red (bell) peppers, seeded
   and diced
400g/14oz/3 cups long pasta or
   maccheroni alla chitarra
salt and ground black pepper

1 Heat half the olive oil in a medium pan, add the lamb and season with a little salt and pepper. Cook over medium to high heat for about 10 minutes, stirring often, until browned.

2 Sprinkle in the garlic and add the bay leaves, then pour in the wine and let it bubble until reduced.

3 Add the remaining oil, the tomatoes and the peppers; stir to mix with the lamb. Season again. Cover with the lid and simmer over low heat for 45–55 minutes, or until the lamb is very tender. Stir occasionally during cooking and moisten with water if the sauce becomes too dry.

4 Meanwhile, cook the pasta until al dente, then drain. Remove the bay leaves from the sauce, then serve with the pasta.

> **Cook's Tips**
> • If you need to add water to the sauce towards the end of cooking, take it from the pan used for cooking the pasta.
> • You can make your own fresh maccheroni alla chitarra or buy the dried pasta from an Italian delicatessen. Alternatively, this sauce is just as good with ordinary long or short macaroni. You will need 350–425g/12–15oz/3–4 cups.

Fusilli with Sausage

Spicy hot sausage and tomato sauce are married with spirals of pasta to make this really tasty dish from southern Italy. Pecorino cheese, with its strong and salty flavour, is the perfect accompaniment, along with a full-bodied red wine and country bread.

Serves 4
400g/14oz spicy pork sausages
30ml/2 tbsp olive oil
1 small onion, finely chopped
2 garlic cloves, crushed
1 large yellow (bell) pepper,
   seeded and cut into strips
5ml/1 tsp paprika
5ml/1 tsp dried mixed herbs
5–10ml/1–2 tsp chilli sauce
400g/14oz can Italian plum
   tomatoes
250–300ml/8–10fl oz/1–1¼
   cups vegetable stock
300g/11oz/2¾ cups fresh or
   dried fusilli
salt and ground black pepper
freshly grated Pecorino cheese,
   to serve

1 Grill (broil) the sausages for 10–12 minutes, until they are browned on all sides, then drain them on kitchen paper.

2 Heat the oil in a large frying pan or pan, add the onion and garlic and cook over low heat, stirring frequently, for 5–7 minutes, until soft. Add the yellow pepper, paprika, herbs and chilli sauce to taste. Cook gently for 5–7 minutes, stirring occasionally.

3 Add the tomatoes, breaking them up with a wooden spoon. Add salt and pepper to taste. Cook over medium heat for 10–12 minutes, adding the stock gradually as the sauce reduces.

4 While the tomato sauce is cooking, cut the grilled sausages diagonally into 1cm/½in pieces.

5 Add the sausage pieces to the sauce, reduce the heat to low and cook for 10 minutes. Meanwhile, cook the pasta in a pan of lightly salted water until al dente.

6 Taste the sauce for seasoning. Drain the pasta and toss into the pan of sauce. Serve with Pecorino handed separately.

Energy 704Kcal/2947kJ; Fat 39.4g; Saturated Fat 13.3g; Carbohydrate 71g; Fibre 4.4g

Energy 423Kcal/1783kJ; Fat 13.6g; Saturated Fat 3.5g; Carbohydrate 54.9g; Fibre 3.4g

Tagliatelle with Chicken & Herb Sauce

Chicken is enhanced with vermouth and herbs in this delicious creamy pasta dish.

Serves 4

30ml/2 tbsp olive oil
1 red onion, cut into wedges
350g/12oz fresh or dried
   tagliatelle
1 garlic clove, chopped

350g/12oz chicken breast fillets,
   skinned and diced
300ml/½ pint/1¼ cups dry
   vermouth
45ml/3 tbsp chopped fresh mixed
   herbs
150ml/¼ pint/⅔ cup fromage
   frais
salt and ground black pepper
shredded fresh mint, to garnish

1 Heat the oil in a large frying pan, add the red onion and fry for 10 minutes, until softened but not coloured and the layers have separated.

2 Bring a pan of lightly salted water to the boil, add the pasta and cook until *al dente*.

3 Add the garlic and chicken to the frying pan and fry for 10 minutes, stirring occasionally, until the chicken is browned all over and cooked through.

4 Pour in the vermouth, bring to boiling point and boil rapidly until reduced by about half. Stir in the herbs, fromage frais and salt and pepper to taste. Heat through gently, without allow the sauce to boil.

5 Drain the pasta thoroughly, turn into a warmed serving dish and spoon the sauce over. Toss the mixture to coat the pasta. Serve immediately, garnished with shredded fresh mint.

> **Variation**
> Use mascarpone cheese, instead of fromage frais, if preferred.

Fusilli with Chicken & Tomato

Just the job for a speedy supper – serve with a mixed bean salad.

Serves 4

15ml/1 tbsp olive oil
1 onion, chopped
1 carrot, chopped
50g/2oz drained sun-dried
   tomatoes in olive oil
1 garlic clove, chopped

400g/14oz can chopped Italian
   plum tomatoes, drained
15ml/1 tbsp tomato purée
   (paste)
150ml/¼ pint/⅔ cup chicken
   stock
350g/12oz/3 cups dried fusilli
225g/8oz chicken breast fillets,
   diagonally sliced
salt and ground black pepper
fresh mint sprigs, to garnish

1 Heat the oil in a large frying pan and fry the chopped onion and carrot for 5 minutes, stirring the vegetables occasionally.

2 Chop the sun-dried tomatoes and set aside until needed.

3 Stir the garlic, canned tomatoes, tomato purée and stock into the onions and carrots in the frying pan and bring to the boil. Simmer for 10 minutes, stirring occasionally.

4 Bring a pan of lightly salted water to the boil, add the pasta and cook until *al dente*.

5 Pour the sauce into a blender or food processor and process until smooth and well blended.

6 Return the sauce to the pan and stir in the sun-dried tomatoes and chicken. Bring back to the boil and then simmer for 10 minutes until the chicken is cooked. Adjust the seasoning.

7 Drain the pasta thoroughly and toss in the sauce. Serve at once, garnished with sprigs of fresh mint.

> **Cook's Tip**
> Try serving the sauce with a mix of white, green and pink fusilli.

Piquant Chicken with Spaghetti

The addition of cucumber and tomatoes adds a deliciously fresh flavour to this unusual dish.

Serves 4

1 onion, finely chopped
1 carrot, diced
1 garlic clove, crushed
300ml/½ pint/1¼ cups vegetable stock
4 chicken breast fillets, skinned
bouquet garni
115g/4oz button mushrooms, thinly sliced
5ml/1 tsp wine vinegar or lemon juice
350g/12oz fresh or dried spaghetti
½ cucumber, peeled and cut into fingers
2 tomatoes, peeled, seeded and chopped
30ml/2 tbsp crème fraîche
15ml/1 tbsp chopped fresh parsley
15ml/1 tbsp snipped chives
salt and ground black pepper

1 Put the onion, carrot, garlic, vegetable stock, chicken and bouquet garni into a pan. Bring to the boil, cover and simmer for 15–20 minutes or until the chicken is tender. Transfer the chicken to a plate with a slotted spoon and cover with foil.

2 Strain the remaining cooking liquid in the pan. Discard the vegetables and return the liquid to the pan. Add the sliced mushrooms, wine vinegar or lemon juice, then stir and simmer for 2–3 minutes.

3 Bring a pan of lightly salted water to the boil, add the pasta and cook until *al dente*. Drain thoroughly.

4 Blanch the cucumber in boiling water for 10 seconds. Drain and rinse under cold water.

5 Cut the chicken breasts into bite-size pieces. Boil the stock to reduce by half, then add the chicken, tomatoes, crème fraîche, cucumber and herbs. Season with salt and pepper to taste.

6 Transfer the spaghetti to a warmed serving dish and cover with the piquant chicken and tomato sauce. Serve immediately.

Chicken with Eliche & Olives

A delicious way to use up leftover cooked chicken, this colourful salad is fresh tasting yet satisfying.

Serves 4

225g/8oz cooked green beans
225g/8oz/2 cups mixed white, red and green dried eliche
1 beefsteak tomato
30ml/2 tbsp pesto sauce
15ml/1 tbsp olive oil
12 pitted black olives
350g/12oz cooked chicken, cubed
salt and ground black pepper
fresh basil, to garnish

1 Top and tail the green beans, then cut into 4cm/1½in lengths. Cook in a pan of lightly salted water until tender, then drain and refresh under cold running water. Drain again and set aside.

2 Bring a pan of lightly salted water to the boil, add the pasta and cook until *al dente*.

3 Meanwhile, plunge the tomato into a bowl of boiling water for 45 seconds, then plunge into a bowl of cold water for 30 seconds to loosen the skin. Slip off the skin. Halve the tomato and remove the seeds and core.

4 Drain the pasta and rinse in plenty of cold running water. Place the cooked pasta in a large bowl and pour in the pesto sauce and olive oil. Mix well to combine.

5 Cut the tomato into small cubes and add to the pasta mixture in the bowl with the olives and green beans. Season with salt and pepper and add the cubed chicken. Toss gently together and transfer to a serving platter or individual bowls. Garnish with fresh basil.

> **Cook's Tip**
> *Eliche shapes are similar to fusilli but have a slightly looser spiral: hence their name, which translates as "propeller". To ring the changes, use the twisted fusilli casareccia instead.*

Energy 315Kcal/1331kJ; Fat 5.6g; Saturated Fat 2.7g; Carbohydrate 26.6g; Fibre 2.6g

Energy 426Kcal/1794kJ; Fat 12.2g; Saturated Fat 2.2g; Carbohydrate 44.4g; Fibre 3.4g

Pasta with Chicken Livers

Rich-tasting chicken livers are coated in a piquant sauce and tossed with "little ears" in this appetizing dish.

Serves 4
225g/8oz chicken livers, defrosted if frozen
30ml/2 tbsp olive oil
2 garlic cloves, crushed
175g/6oz rindless smoked back bacon, roughly chopped
400g/14oz can chopped Italian plum tomatoes
150ml/¼ pint/⅔ cup chicken stock
15ml/1 tbsp tomato purée (paste)
15ml/1 tbsp dry sherry
30ml/2 tbsp chopped mixed fresh herbs, such as parsley, rosemary and basil
350g/12oz/3 cups dried orecchiette
salt and ground black pepper
freshly grated Parmesan cheese, to serve

1 Wash and trim the chicken livers. Cut into bite-size pieces. Heat the oil in a frying pan and fry the chicken livers for 3–4 minutes, until tender.

2 Add the garlic and bacon to the pan and fry until golden brown. Add the tomatoes, chicken stock, tomato purée, sherry, herbs and salt and pepper to taste.

3 Bring the sauce to the boil and simmer gently, uncovered, for about 5 minutes, until the sauce has thickened. Stir from time to time.

4 Meanwhile, bring a pan of lightly salted water to the boil, add the pasta and cook until *al dente*. Drain, then toss into the sauce. Serve hot, sprinkled with Parmesan cheese.

> **Cook's Tip**
> Chicken livers are popular for topping crostini as well as for pasta sauces. They also make a delicious salad when lightly sautéed, then tossed with salad leaves and dressed with hot olive oil from the pan, sizzled with vin santo (sweet Tuscan wine).

Two-way Chicken & Vegetables

This tender slow-cooked chicken makes a tasty lunch or supper, with the stock and remaining vegetables providing a nourishing soup as a second meal.

Serves 6
1.5 kg/3½ lb chicken
2 onions, quartered
3 carrots, thickly sliced
2 celery sticks, chopped
1 parsnip or turnip, thickly sliced
50 g/2 oz/½ cup button mushrooms, roughly chopped
1–2 fresh thyme sprigs or 5 ml/ 1 tsp dried thyme
4 bay leaves
1 large bunch of fresh parsley
sea salt and ground black pepper
cooked pasta and mangetouts or green beans, to serve

For the soup
115 g/4oz/1 cup dried wholewheat pasta shapes
chunks of crusty bread, to serve

1 Trim the chicken of any extra fat. Put it in a flameproof casserole and add the vegetables and herbs. Pour in water to cover. Bring to the boil over medium heat, skimming off any scum, then lower the heat and simmer for 2–3 hours.

2 Carve the meat neatly, discarding the skin and bones, but returning any small pieces of chicken to the pan. Serve the sliced chicken with some of the vegetables from the pan, plus the pasta of your choice and mangetouts or green beans.

3 Remove any large pieces of parsley and thyme from the pan, allow the remaining mixture to cool, then cover and chill in the refrigerator overnight.

4 To make the soup the next day, carefully lift off the fat that has solidified on the surface of the pan. Return the pan to medium heat and reheat the soup gently.

5 When the soup comes to the boil, add the pasta shapes, with salt to taste, and cook until the pasta is *al dente*. Season the soup with salt and plenty of ground black pepper and garnish with sprigs of fresh parsley. Serve with chunks of bread.

Penne with Chicken, Broccoli & Cheese

Broccoli, garlic and Gorgonzola meld together beautifully; a combination that complements the chicken brilliantly in this sauce. Serve with tubular pasta for a flavourful meal.

Serves 4

115g/4oz/scant 1 cup broccoli
  florets, divided into tiny sprigs
50g/2oz/¼ cup butter
2 chicken breast fillets, skinned
  and cut into thin strips
2 garlic cloves, crushed
400g/14oz/3½ cups dried penne
120ml/4fl oz/½ cup dry white
  wine
200ml/7fl oz/scant 1 cup panna
  da cucina or double (heavy)
  cream
90g/3½oz Gorgonzola cheese,
  rind removed and diced small
salt and ground black pepper
freshly grated Parmesan cheese,
  to serve

1 Plunge the broccoli into a pan of boiling salted water. Bring back to the boil and boil for 2 minutes, then drain in a colander and refresh under cold running water. Shake well to remove the surplus water and set aside to drain completely.

2 Melt the butter in a large pan, add the chicken and garlic, with salt and pepper to taste, and stir well. Fry over medium heat for 3 minutes, or until the chicken becomes white.

3 Meanwhile, bring a pan of lightly salted water to the boil and start to cook the pasta.

4 Pour the wine and cream over the chicken mixture in the pan, stir to mix, then simmer, stirring occasionally, for about 5 minutes, until the sauce has reduced and thickened. Add the broccoli, increase the heat and toss to heat the broccoli through and mix it with the chicken. Taste for seasoning.

5 Drain the pasta and turn into the sauce. Add the Gorgonzola and toss well. Serve immediately, with freshly grated Parmesan cheese handed separately.

Farfalle with Chicken & Cherry Tomatoes

Chicken flavoured with vermouth and herbs is cooked to succulent perfection in a tomato sauce with a hint of spiciness – unbeatable teamed up with bow-shaped pasta.

Serves 4

350g/12oz chicken breast fillets,
  skinned and cut into bite-size
  pieces
60ml/4 tbsp Italian dry vermouth
10ml/2 tsp chopped fresh
  rosemary, plus sprigs to garnish
15ml/1 tbsp olive oil
1 onion, finely chopped
90g/3½oz piece Italian salami,
  diced
275g/10oz/2½ cups dried
  farfalle
15ml/1 tbsp balsamic vinegar
400g/14oz can Italian cherry
  tomatoes
good pinch of crushed dried
  red chillies
salt and ground black pepper

1 Put the pieces of chicken in a large bowl, pour in the dry vermouth and sprinkle with half the chopped rosemary and salt and pepper to taste. Stir well and set aside.

2 Heat the oil in a large frying pan or pan, add the onion and salami and fry over medium heat for about 5 minutes, stirring frequently.

3 Bring a pan of lightly salted water to the boil, add the pasta and cook until al dente.

4 Add the chicken and vermouth to the onion and salami, increase the heat to high and fry for 3 minutes, or until the chicken is white on all sides. Sprinkle with the vinegar.

5 Add the cherry tomatoes and dried chillies. Stir well and simmer for a few minutes more. Taste the sauce for seasoning.

6 Drain the pasta and turn it into the pan. Add the remaining chopped rosemary and toss to mix the pasta and sauce together. Serve immediately, garnished with the rosemary sprigs.

Energy 490Kcal/2067kJ; Fat 14.1g; Saturated Fat 4.2g; Carbohydrate 55.8g; Fibre 3.2g

Energy 869Kcal/3637kJ; Fat 46.5g; Saturated Fat 28g; Carbohydrate 75.7g; Fibre 3.7g

Pappardelle with Chicken & Mushrooms

Rich and creamy, this is a good supper party dish.

Serves 4

15g/½oz dried porcini mushrooms
175ml/6fl oz/¾ cup warm water
25g/1oz/2 tbsp butter
1 small leek or 4 spring onions
  (scallions), chopped
1 garlic clove, crushed
1 small handful fresh flat leaf
  parsley, roughly chopped

120ml/4fl oz/½ cup dry white
  wine
250ml/8fl oz/1 cup chicken stock
400g/14oz fresh or dried
  pappardelle
2 chicken breast fillets, skinned
  and cut into thin strips
105ml/7 tbsp mascarpone
salt and ground black pepper
fresh basil leaves, shredded, to
  garnish

1 Put the dried mushrooms in a bowl. Pour in the warm water and leave to soak for 15–20 minutes. Turn into a fine sieve (strainer) set over a bowl and squeeze the mushrooms to release as much liquid as possible. Chop the mushrooms finely and set aside the strained soaking liquid until required.

2 Melt the butter in a medium frying pan, add the chopped mushrooms, leek or spring onions, garlic and parsley, with salt and pepper to taste. Cook over low heat, stirring frequently, for about 5 minutes, then pour in the wine and stock and bring to the boil. Lower the heat and simmer for about 5 minutes, or until the liquid has reduced and is thickened.

3 Meanwhile, cook the pasta in lightly salted boiling water, adding the reserved liquid from the mushrooms to the water.

4 Add the chicken to the sauce and simmer for 5 minutes, or until just tender. Add the mascarpone a spoonful at a time, stirring well after each addition, then add one or two spoonfuls of the pasta cooking water. Taste for seasoning.

5 Drain the pasta and turn into a warmed large bowl. Add the chicken and sauce and toss well. Serve, topped with the basil.

Conchiglie with Chicken Livers & Herbs

Fresh herbs and chicken livers are a good combination, often used together on crostini in Tuscany. Here they are tossed with pasta shells to make a tasty supper dish.

Serves 4

50g/2oz/¼ cup butter
115g/4oz pancetta or rindless
  streaky (fatty) bacon, diced
250g/9oz frozen chicken livers,
  thawed, drained and diced

2 garlic cloves, crushed
10ml/2 tsp chopped fresh sage
300g/11oz/2¾ cups dried
  conchiglie
150ml/¼ pint/⅔ cup dry
  white wine
4 ripe Italian plum tomatoes,
  peeled and diced
15ml/1 tbsp chopped fresh flat
  leaf parsley
salt and ground black pepper
fresh parsley sprigs, to garnish
  (optional)

1 Melt half the butter in a medium frying pan or pan, add the pancetta or bacon and fry over medium heat for a few minutes, until it is lightly coloured but not crisp.

2 Add the diced chicken livers, garlic, half the fresh sage and plenty of pepper. Increase the heat and toss the livers for about 5 minutes, until they change colour all over.

3 Meanwhile, bring a pan of lightly salted water to the boil, add the pasta and cook until al dente.

4 Pour the wine over the chicken livers in the pan and let it sizzle, then lower the heat and simmer gently for 5 minutes.

5 Add the remaining butter to the pan. When it has melted, add the diced tomatoes, toss to mix, then add the remaining sage and the parsley. Stir well. Taste and add salt if needed.

6 Drain the pasta well and turn into a warmed serving bowl. Pour the sauce over the pasta and toss well. Serve immediately, garnished with parsley sprigs, if liked.

Energy 567Kcal/2397kJ; Fat 12g; Saturated Fat 6.2g; Carbohydrate 75.9g; Fibre 3.5g

Energy 528Kcal/2220kJ; Fat 20.2g; Saturated Fat 9.6g; Carbohydrate 59g; Fibre 3.2g

Spaghetti with Turkey & Cheese

An Italian-American recipe, this dish makes an excellent family meal. It is quite filling and rich, so serve it with a tossed green salad.

Serves 4–6
75g/3oz/6 tbsp butter
350g/12oz turkey breast fillet, cut into thin strips
2 pieces bottled roasted (bell) pepper, drained, rinsed, dried and cut into thin strips

175g/6oz dried spaghetti
50g/2oz/½ cup plain (all-purpose) flour
900ml/1½ pints/3¾ cups hot milk
115g/4oz/1¼ cups freshly grated Parmesan cheese
1.25–2.5ml/¼–½ tsp mustard powder
salt and ground black pepper

1 Melt about a third of the butter in a pan, add the turkey and sprinkle with a little salt and plenty of pepper. Toss the turkey over medium heat for about 5 minutes, until the meat turns white, then add the roasted pepper strips and toss to mix. Remove with a slotted spoon and set aside.

2 Preheat the oven to 180°C/350°F/Gas 4. Bring a pan of lightly salted water and cook the pasta until it is al dente.

3 Meanwhile, melt the remaining butter over low heat in the pan in which the turkey was cooked. Sprinkle in the flour and cook, stirring, for 1–2 minutes. Increase the heat to medium.

4 Add the hot milk a little at a time, whisking after each addition. Bring to the boil and cook, stirring, until the sauce is smooth and thick. Add two-thirds of the Parmesan, then whisk in the mustard, salt and pepper to taste. Remove from the heat.

5 Drain the pasta and return it to the clean pan. Mix in half the cheese sauce, then spoon the mixture around the edge of a baking dish. Stir the turkey mixture into the remaining cheese sauce and spoon into the centre of the dish. Sprinkle the remaining Parmesan evenly over the dish and bake for 15–20 minutes, until the cheese topping is just crisp.

Pappardelle with Rabbit Sauce

This rich-tasting dish comes from the north of Italy, where rabbit sauces for pasta are very popular.

Serves 4
15g/½oz dried porcini mushrooms
175ml/6fl oz/¾ cup warm water
1 small onion
½ carrot
½ celery stick
25g/1oz/2 tbsp butter
15ml/1 tbsp olive oil

40g/1½oz pancetta or rindless streaky (fatty) bacon, chopped
15ml/1 tbsp roughly chopped fresh flat leaf parsley, plus extra to garnish
250g/9oz boneless rabbit meat
90ml/6 tbsp dry white wine
200g/7oz canned chopped Italian plum tomatoes or 200ml/7fl oz/scant 1 cup passata
2 bay leaves, each torn once
300g/11oz dried pappardelle
salt and ground black pepper

1 Put the dried mushrooms in a bowl, pour over the warm water and leave to soak for 15–20 minutes. Finely chop the vegetables, either in a food processor or by hand.

2 Heat the butter and oil in a frying pan until just sizzling. Add the chopped vegetables, pancetta or bacon and the parsley and cook for about 5 minutes.

3 Add the pieces of rabbit and fry on both sides for 3–4 minutes. Pour the wine over and let it reduce for a few minutes, then add the tomatoes or passata. Drain the mushrooms and pour the soaking liquid into the pan. Chop the mushrooms and add them to the mixture, with the bay leaves and salt and pepper to taste. Stir well, cover and simmer for 35–40 minutes, until the rabbit is tender, stirring occasionally.

4 Remove the pan from the heat and lift out the pieces of rabbit with a slotted spoon. Cut them into bite-size chunks and stir them into the sauce. Remove and discard the bay leaves. Taste the sauce and add more salt and pepper, if needed.

5 Bring a pan of lightly salted water to the boil and cook the pasta until al dente. Meanwhile, reheat the sauce. Drain the pasta and toss with the sauce. Serve garnished with parsley.

Energy 473Kcal/1987kJ; Fat 20.8g; Saturated Fat 12.5g; Carbohydrate 36.3g; Fibre 1.4g

Energy 465Kcal/1961kJ; Fat 14.3g; Saturated Fat 5.7g; Carbohydrate 59.3g; Fibre 3.2g

Baked Vegetable Lasagne

A classic lasagne with a vegetarian twist.

Serves 8

30ml/2 tbsp olive oil
1 onion, very finely chopped
500g/1¼lb tomatoes, fresh or canned, chopped
75g/3oz/6 tbsp butter
675g/1½lb cultivated or wild mushrooms, or a combination of both, wiped and sliced

2 garlic cloves, finely chopped
juice of ½ lemon
10–15 no pre-cook dried lasagne sheets
1 litre/1¾ pints/4 cups white sauce (see previous recipe)
175g/6oz/2 cups freshly grated Parmesan or Cheddar cheese
salt and ground black pepper

1 Butter a large shallow baking dish. In a small frying pan heat the oil and sauté the onion until soft but not coloured. Add the tomatoes and cook for about 6–8 minutes, stirring frequently. Season with salt and pepper and set aside until required.

2 Heat 40g/1½oz/3 tbsp of the butter in a frying pan, add the mushrooms and cook until they start to exude their juices. Add the garlic and lemon juice and season with salt and pepper. Cook until the liquids have almost all evaporated and the mushrooms are starting to brown. Set aside.

3 Preheat the oven to 200°C/400°F/Gas 6. To assemble the lasagne, spread one large spoonful of the white sauce over the base of the dish. Top with a layer of pasta, cutting to fit. Cover with a thin layer of mushrooms, then one of whitel sauce. Sprinkle with a little cheese.

4 Make another layer of pasta, spread with a thin layer of tomatoes, and then one of béchamel. Sprinkle with cheese. Repeat layering in the same order, ending with a layer of pasta coated with white sauce. Do not make more than about six layers of pasta. Sprinkle with more cheese and dot with butter.

5 Bake for 20–30 minutes, until the pasta is tender. Remove from the oven and allow to stand for 5 minutes before serving.

Mushroom & Courgette Lasagne

This is a great meat-free main course; the porcini give it a pronounced mushroomy flavour.

Serves 6

15g/½oz dried porcini mushrooms
175ml/6fl oz/¾ cup warm water
30ml/2 tbsp olive oil
75g/3oz/6 tbsp butter
450g/1lb courgettes (zucchini), thinly sliced
1 onion, finely chopped
450g/1lb/6 cups chestnut mushrooms, thinly sliced
2 garlic cloves, crushed
1 quantity Basic Tomato Sauce (see page 9)

10ml/2 tsp chopped fresh marjoram or 5ml/1 tsp dried marjoram
8–10 no pre-cook dried lasagne sheets
50g/2oz/⅔ cup freshly grated Parmesan cheese
salt and ground black pepper

For the white sauce
40g/1½oz/3 tbsp butter
40g/1½oz/⅓ cup plain (all-purpose) flour
900ml/1½ pints/3¾ cups hot milk
freshly grated nutmeg

1 Put the dried porcini in a bowl. Pour over the warm water and leave to soak for 15–20 minutes. Turn into a fine sieve (strainer) set over a bowl and squeeze the mushrooms to release as much liquid as possible. Chop finely and set aside. Strain the liquid and reserve half for the sauce.

2 Preheat the oven to 190°C/375°F/Gas 5. Heat the olive oil with 25g/1oz/2 tbsp of the butter in a large frying pan. Cook the courgettes, in two batches, in the pan, turning frequently, for 5–8 minutes, until lightly coloured. Remove from the pan with a slotted spoon and drain on kitchen paper.

3 Melt half the remaining butter in the pan, then cook the onion, stirring, for 1–2 minutes. Add half the fresh mushrooms and the garlic and season to taste. Toss over a high heat for 5 minutes, until tender. Transfer to a bowl with a slotted spoon, then repeat with the remaining butter and mushrooms.

4 To make the white sauce, melt the butter in a large pan, add the flour and cook, stirring, over medium heat for 1–2 minutes. Whisk in the hot milk gradually. Bring to the boil and cook, stirring, until the sauce is smooth and thick. Add nutmeg, salt and pepper to taste. Whisk well, then remove from the heat.

5 Place the Basic Tomato Sauce in a blender or food processor with the reserved porcini soaking liquid and blend. Add the courgettes to the bowl of fried mushrooms, then stir in the porcini and marjoram.

6 Adjust the seasoning to taste, then spread a third of the tomato sauce in a baking dish. Add half the vegetable mixture, spreading evenly. Top with a third of the white sauce, then about half the lasagne sheets. Repeat these layers, then top with the remaining tomato sauce and white sauce and sprinkle with the grated Parmesan.

7 Bake the lasagne for 35–40 minutes, or until the pasta is tender. Stand for 10 minutes, before serving.

Energy 466Kcal/1943kJ; Fat 28.7g; Saturated Fat 13g; Carbohydrate 34.8g; Fibre 2.6g

Energy 427Kcal/1784kJ; Fat 28.4g; Saturated Fat 14g; Carbohydrate 31.3g; Fibre 2g

Pansotti with Herbs & Cheese

This is a traditional dish from Liguria.

Serves 6–8
1 quantity handmade Egg Pasta
 (see page 8)
flour, for dusting
50g/2oz/¼ cup butter, melted
grated Parmesan cheese, to serve

For the filling
250g/9oz/1 cup ricotta cheese
150g/5oz/1½ cups grated
 Parmesan cheese

1 handful basil leaves, chopped
1 large handful fresh flat leaf
 parsley, chopped
a few marjoram sprigs, chopped
1 garlic clove, crushed
1 small egg
salt and ground black pepper

For the sauce
90g/3½oz shelled walnuts
1 garlic clove
60ml/4 tbsp extra virgin olive oil
125ml/4fl oz/½ cup panna da
 cucina or double (heavy) cream

1 To make the filling, put the ricotta, Parmesan, herbs, garlic and egg in a bowl with salt and pepper to taste. Beat well to mix.

2 To make the sauce, put the walnuts, garlic clove and oil in a food processor and process to a paste, adding up to 125ml/ 4fl oz/½ cup warm water through the feeder tube to slacken the consistency. Spoon the mixture into a large bowl and add the cream. Beat well to mix, then add salt and pepper to taste.

3 Using a pasta machine, roll out one-quarter of the pasta into a 90cm–1m/36in–3ft strip. Cut into two 45–50cm/18–20in lengths. Using a 5cm/2in square ravioli cutter, cut 8–10 squares from one pasta strip. Put a mound of filling in the centre of each.

4 Brush water around the edge of each square, then fold the square diagonally in half over the filling to make a triangle. Press to seal. Spread out the pansotti on floured dish towels and dust with flour. Repeat to make 64–80 pansotti.

5 Cook the pansotti in a pan of boiling water for 4–5 minutes. Put the walnut sauce in a warmed bowl with a little of the pasta water to thin it. Drain the pansotti and transfer to the bowl of walnut sauce. Drizzle butter over, toss and serve with Parmesan.

Energy 593Kcal/2475kJ; Fat 39.g; Saturated Fat 16.9g; Carbohydrate 43.3g; Fibre 2g

Ravioli with Pumpkin

A tasty, less sweet version of the Christmas Eve speciality from Lombardy.

Serves 8
1 quantity handmade Egg Pasta
 (see page 8)
115g/4oz/½ cup butter
flour, for dusting
grated Parmesan cheese, to serve

For the filling
450g/1lb piece of pumpkin
 with skin, seeded and cut
 into chunks
15ml/1 tbsp olive oil
40g/1½oz/½ cup freshly grated
 Parmesan cheese
freshly grated nutmeg
salt and ground black pepper

1 To make the filling, preheat the oven to 220°C/425°F/Gas 7. Put the pumpkin, skin-side down, in a roasting pan and drizzle with oil. Roast in the oven for 30 minutes, turning twice. When cool enough to handle, scrape the flesh into a mixing bowl. Mash the pumpkin with a fork, then add the Parmesan with nutmeg, salt and pepper to taste. Stir well; set aside until cold.

2 Using a pasta machine, roll out one-quarter of the pasta into a 90cm–1m/36in–3 ft strip. Cut the strip into two 45–50cm/ 18–20in lengths. Using a teaspoon, put 10–12 little mounds of filling evenly along one side of one of the pasta strips.

3 Brush a little water around each mound, then fold the plain side of the pasta strip over the filling. Starting from the folded edge, press down gently around each mound, pushing the air out at the unfolded edge. Sprinkle lightly with flour.

4 With a fluted pasta wheel, cut along each long side, then in between each mound to make small square shapes. Put the ravioli on floured dish towels, sprinkle lightly with flour and leave to dry, while repeating the process to make 80–96 ravioli.

5 Drop the ravioli into a large pan of salted boiling water, bring back to the boil and boil for 4–5 minutes. Meanwhile, melt the butter in a small pan until it is sizzling. Drain the ravioli and divide between eight warmed plates. Drizzle the butter over the ravioli and serve with Parmesan.

Energy 342Kcal/1435kJ; Fat 16g; Saturated Fat 8.9g; Carbohydrate 43g; Fibre 2.2g

Spinach & Ricotta Ravioli

The Italian name for this dish is ravioli di magro which means "lean ravioli". It describes the meat-free ravioli which are served on Christmas Eve.

Serves 8
1 quantity handmade Egg Pasta (see page 8)
flour, for dusting
freshly grated Parmesan cheese, to serve

For the filling
40g/1½oz/3 tbsp butter

175g/6oz fresh spinach leaves, trimmed, washed and shredded
200g/7oz/scant 1 cup ricotta cheese
25g/1oz/⅓ cup freshly grated Parmesan cheese
freshly grated nutmeg
1 small egg
salt and ground black pepper

For the sauce
50g/2oz/¼ cup butter
250ml/8fl oz/1 cup panna da cucina or double (heavy) cream
50g/2oz/⅔ cup freshly grated Parmesan cheese

1 To make the ravioli filling, melt the butter in a medium pan, add the spinach and salt and pepper to taste and cook over medium heat for 5–8 minutes, stirring frequently, until the spinach is wilted and tender. Increase the heat to high and stir to dry out.

2 Turn the spinach into a bowl and leave until cold, then add the ricotta, grated Parmesan and freshly grated nutmeg to taste. Beat well to mix, taste for seasoning, add the egg and beat well.

3 Using a pasta machine, roll out one-quarter of the pasta into a 90cm–1m/36in–3 ft strip. Cut the strip with a sharp knife into two 45–50cm/18–20in lengths (you can do this during rolling if the strip gets too long to manage).

4 Using a teaspoon, put 10–12 little mounds of the filling along one side of one of the pasta strips, spacing them evenly. Brush a little water around each mound, then fold the plain side of the pasta strip over the filling.

5 Starting from the folded edge, press down gently with your fingertips around each mound of filling, pushing the air out at the unfolded edge. Sprinkle lightly with flour.

6 With a fluted pasta wheel, cut along each long side, then in between each mound to make small square shapes. Put the ravioli on floured dish towels, sprinkle lightly with flour and leave to dry while repeating the process with the remaining pasta to get 80–96 ravioli altogether.

7 Drop the ravioli into a large pan of salted boiling water, bring back to the boil and boil for 4–5 minutes.

8 Meanwhile, make the sauce. Gently heat the butter, cream and Parmesan in a medium pan until they have melted.

9 Increase the heat and simmer for 1–2 minutes, until the sauce is slightly reduced, then season. Drain the ravioli and divide between large bowls. Drizzle the sauce over them and serve immediately, sprinkled with grated Parmesan.

Agnolotti with Taleggio

The filling for these little half-moons is very simple – only two ingredients – but the combination is stunning.

Serves 6–8
1 quantity handmade Egg Pasta (see page 8)
flour, for dusting

350–400g/12–14oz taleggio cheese
about 30ml/2 tbsp finely chopped fresh marjoram, plus extra to garnish
115g/4oz/½ cup butter
salt and ground black pepper
freshly grated Parmesan cheese, to serve

1 Using a pasta machine, roll out a quarter of the pasta into a 90cm–1m/36–3ft strip. Cut the strip with a sharp knife into two 45–50cm/18–20cm lengths.

2 Cut 8–10 little cubes of taleggioi and place along one side of one of the pasta strips, spacing them evenly. Sprinkle each cube with a little chopped marjoram and pepper to taste.

3 Brush a little water around each cube of cheese, then fold the plain side of the pasta strip over them. Starting from the folded edge, press down gently with your fingertips around each cube, pushing the air out at the unfolded edge. Sprinkle lightly with flour.

4 Using only half of a 5cm/2in fluted round cutter, cut around each cube of cheese to make a half-moon shape. The folded edge should be the straight edge. Press the cut edges with the tines of a fork to give a decorative effect, if you like.

5 Put the agnolotti on floured dish towels, sprinkle with flour and leave to dry. Repeat the process to make 64–80 agnolotti.

6 Drop the agnolotti into a large pan of salted boiling water and cook for 4–5 minutes, until al dente. Meanwhile, melt the butter in a small pan until sizzling. Drain the pasta and divide between 6–8 warmed plates. Drizzle with the sizzling butter, garnish with chopped marjoram and serve with the freshly grated Parmesan.

Energy 483Kcal/2021kJ; Fat 27.2g; Saturated Fat 17.1g; Carbohydrate 42g; Fibre 1.9g

Energy 547Kcal/2283kJ; Fat 35.6g; Saturated Fat 21.5g; Carbohydrate 43.4g; Fibre 2.1g

Cannelloni Sorrentina-style

A delicious tomato-filled version of the classic dish.

Serves 4–6
60ml/4 tbsp olive oil
1 small onion, finely chopped
900g/2lb ripe Italian tomatoes, peeled and finely chopped
2 garlic cloves, crushed
1 large handful fresh basil leaves, shredded
250ml/8fl oz/1 cup vegetable stock
250ml/8fl oz/1 cup dry white wine
30ml/2 tbsp sun-dried tomato purée (paste)
2.5ml/¹⁄₂ tsp sugar
16–18 fresh or dried lasagne
250g/9oz/generous 1 cup ricotta cheese
130g/4¹⁄₂oz mozzarella cheese, drained and diced small
8 bottled anchovy fillets in olive oil, drained and halved lengthways
50g/2oz/²⁄₃ cup freshly grated Parmesan cheese
salt and ground black pepper

1 Cook the onion in the oil for about 5 minutes, until softened. Stir in the tomatoes, garlic and half the basil. Season with salt and pepper to taste and cook for 5 minutes. Transfer half the tomato mixture to a bowl and allow to cool.

3 Stir the stock, wine, tomato purée and sugar into the mixture in the pan and simmer for 20 minutes, stirring, then purée.

4 Meanwhile, cook the lasagne sheets in batches in a pan of salted boiling water until *al dente*. Drain on clean dish towels.

5 Preheat the oven to 190°C/375°F/Gas 5. Add the cheeses to the tomatoes in the bowl. Stir in most of the remaining basil and season. Spread a little cheese mixture over each lasagne sheet. Place an anchovy fillet across the width of each sheet, close to one of the short ends, then roll up like a Swiss (jelly) roll.

6 Spread a little of the tomato sauce over the bottom of a large baking dish. Arrange the cannelloni seam-side down in a layer in the dish and spoon the remaining sauce over them.

7 Sprinkle the Parmesan over the top and bake for 20 minutes or until golden. Serve, garnished with the remaining basil leaves.

Pasta Pie

A marvellous family dish, packed with Italian flavours.

Serves 4
30ml/2 tbsp olive oil
1 small onion, finely chopped
400g/14oz can chopped Italian plum tomatoes
15ml/1 tbsp sun-dried tomato paste
5ml/1 tsp dried mixed herbs
5ml/1 tsp dried oregano or basil
5ml/1 tsp sugar
175g/6oz/1¹⁄₂ cups dried conchiglie or rigatoni
30ml/2 tbsp freshly grated Parmesan cheese
30ml/2 tbsp dried breadcrumbs
salt and ground black pepper

For the white sauce
25g/1oz/2 tbsp butter
25g/1oz/¹⁄₄ cup plain (all-purpose) flour
600ml/1 pint/2¹⁄₂ cups milk
1 egg

1 Heat the olive oil in a large frying pan and cook the onion gently for about 5 minutes, stirring, until softened. Stir in the tomatoes. Fill the empty can with water and add to the pan, with the tomato paste, herbs and sugar.

2 Add salt and pepper to taste and bring to the boil, stirring. Cover, lower the heat and simmer for 10–15 minutes.

3 Meanwhile, preheat the oven to 190°C/375°F/Gas 5. Cook the pasta in lightly salted boiling water until *al dente*.

4 Meanwhile, make the white sauce. Melt the butter in a pan, add the flour and cook, stirring, for 1 minute. Whisk in the milk gradually. Bring to the boil and cook, stirring, until the sauce is smooth and thick. Season, then remove the pan from the heat.

5 Drain the pasta and turn into a baking dish. Taste the tomato sauce for seasoning. Pour into the dish and stir well to mix.

6 Beat the egg into the white sauce, then pour the sauce over the pasta mixture. With a fork, separate the pasta in several places so that the white sauce fills the gaps. Sprinkle with the Parmesan and breadcrumbs and bake for 15–20 minutes, or until golden brown. Stand for about 10 minutes before serving.

Energy 476Kcal/1995kJ; Fat 22.4g; Saturated Fat 9.9g; Carbohydrate 45g; Fibre 3.7g

Energy 444Kcal/1870kJ; Fat 18.4g; Saturated Fat 7.8g; Carbohydrate 56g; Fibre 3g

Spinach & Hazelnut Lasagne

Hazelnuts add a delicious crunchy texture to the spinach layer of this wholesome lasagne.

Serves 4

900g/2lb fresh spinach
300ml/½ pint/1¼ cups vegetable
  or chicken stock
1 onion, finely chopped
1 garlic clove, crushed

75g/3oz/¾ cup hazelnuts
30ml/2 tbsp chopped fresh basil
6–8 no pre-cook dried lasagne
  sheets
400g/14oz can chopped Italian
  plum tomatoes
200g/7oz/scant 1 cup
  mascarpone
flaked hazelnuts and chopped
  parsley, to garnish

1 Preheat the oven to 200°C/400°F/Gas 6. Wash the fresh spinach and place in a pan with just the water that clings to the leaves. Cook the spinach over fairly high heat for 2 minutes, until wilted. Drain well.

2 Heat 30ml/2 tbsp of the stock in a large pan and simmer the onion and garlic until soft. Stir in the spinach, hazelnuts and chopped fresh basil.

3 Arrange a layer of the spinach mixture in a large rectangular ovenproof dish, top with a layer of lasagne sheets, then spoon over a layer of chopped tomatoes, seasoning well with salt and pepper between the layers.

4 Continuing layering until the ingredients are used up. Pour over the remaining stock. Spread the mascarpone over the top.

5 Bake the lasagne for about 45 minutes or until golden brown. Serve hot, sprinkled with attractive lines of flaked hazelnuts and chopped fresh parsley.

Cook's Tip
If you're short of time, use frozen spinach instead of fresh – you will need 450g/1lb frozen.

Energy 474Kcal/1983kJ; Fat 22.3g; Saturated Fat 5.9g; Carbohydrate 50.4g; Fibre 9.1g

Leek & Goat's Cheese Lasagne

An unusual and lighter than average lasagne using a soft goat's cheese. The pasta sheets are not so chewy if boiled briefly first, or use no pre-cook lasagne instead, if you prefer.

Serves 6

8–10 lasagne sheets
1 large aubergine (eggplant),
  sliced
3 leeks, thinly sliced
30ml/2 tbsp olive oil
2 red (bell) peppers

200g/7oz goat's cheese, broken
  into pieces
50g/2oz/⅔ cup freshly grated
  Pecorino or Parmesan cheese

For the sauce
65g/2½oz/5 tbsp butter
65g/2½oz/9 tbsp plain (all-
  purpose) flour
900ml/1½ pints/3¾ cups milk
2.5ml/½ tsp ground bay leaves
freshly grated nutmeg
salt and ground black pepper

1 If necessary, blanch the pasta sheets in plenty of boiling water for just 2 minutes. Drain and place on a clean dish towel.

2 Lightly salt the aubergine slices and place in a colander to drain for 30 minutes, then rinse and pat dry with kitchen paper.

3 Preheat the oven to 190°C/375°F/Gas 5. Lightly fry the leeks in the oil until softened. Grill (broil) the peppers under a pre-heated grill (broiler) until charred. Cool in a covered bowl, then remove the skins, seeds and cores and cut into strips.

4 To make the sauce, melt the butter in a pan and add the flour. Cook, stirring, for 2–3 minutes. Add the milk and bring to the boil, stirring constantly until thickened. Add the bay leaves, nutmeg and salt and pepper to taste. Simmer for 2 minutes.

5 In a greased shallow casserole, layer the leeks, lasagne sheets, aubergine, goat's cheese and Pecorino or Parmesan. Trickle the sauce over the layers, distributing it over the entire dish.

6 Finish with a layer of sauce and grated cheese. Bake in the oven for 30 minutes, or until bubbling and browned on top.

Energy 524Kcal/2194kJ; Fat 28.1g; Saturated Fat 15.7g; Carbohydrate 47.9g; Fibre 5.1g

Baked Macaroni with Cheese

This delicious dish is perhaps less common in Italy than other pasta dishes, but has become a family favourite around the world.

Serves 6
475ml/16fl oz/2 cups milk
1 bay leaf
3 mace blades
50g/2oz/1¼ cups butter
40g/1½oz/⅓ cup plain (all-purpose) flour
175g/6oz/2 cups grated Parmesan or Cheddar cheese, or a combination of both
40g/1½oz/⅓ cup dry breadcrumbs
450g/1lb/4 cups short-cut macaroni
salt and ground black pepper

1 To make the white sauce, gently heat the milk with the bay leaf and mace in a small pan. Do not let it boil.

2 In a separate medium, heavy pan, melt the butter. Add the flour and mix in well with a wire whisk. Cook for 2–3 minutes, but do not let the butter burn.

3 Strain the hot milk into the flour and butter mixture all at once and mix smoothly with the whisk. Bring the sauce to the boil, stirring constantly, and simmer for a further 4–5 minutes.

4 Season with salt and pepper. Add all but 30ml/2 tbsp of the cheese and stir over low heat, until melted. Place a layer of clear film (plastic wrap) directly on the surface of the sauce to prevent a skin forming and set aside.

5 Preheat the oven to 200°C/400°F/Gas 6. Grease an ovenproof dish and sprinkle with some of the breadcrumbs.

6 Bring a pan of lightly salted water to the boil, add the pasta and cook until *al dente*.

7 Drain the pasta, and combine it with the sauce. Pour it into the prepared dish. Sprinkle the top with the remaining breadcrumbs and grated cheese and bake in the centre of the oven for 20 minutes, until golden and bubbling.

Energy 523Kcal/2202kJ; Fat 19.3g; Saturated Fat 11.7g; Carbohydrate 69.7g; Fibre 2.5g

Aubergine Lasagne

A tasty variation of the classic meat dish, this lasagne is guaranteed to satisfy hearty appetites.

Serves 4
3 aubergines (eggplants), sliced
75ml/5 tbsp olive oil
2 large onions, finely chopped
2 x 400g/14oz cans chopped Italian plum tomatoes
5ml/1 tsp dried mixed herbs
2–3 garlic cloves, crushed
6 no pre-cook dried lasagne sheets
salt and ground black pepper

For the cheese sauce
25g/1oz/2 tbsp butter
25g/1oz/¼ cup plain (all-purpose) flour
300ml/½ pint/1¼ cups milk
2.5ml/½ tsp hot mustard
115g/4oz/1 cup grated mature Cheddar
15g/½oz/1 tbsp grated Parmesan cheese

1 Layer the sliced aubergine in a colander, sprinkling lightly with salt between each layer. Leave to stand for 1 hour, then rinse and pat dry with kitchen paper.

2 Heat 60ml/4 tbsp of the oil in a large pan, fry the aubergine and drain on kitchen paper. Add the remaining oil to the pan, cook the onions for 5 minutes, then stir in the tomatoes, herbs, garlic and salt and pepper. Bring to the boil and simmer, covered, for 30 minutes.

3 To make the cheese sauce, melt the butter in a pan, stir in the flour and cook gently for 1 minute, stirring. Gradually stir in the milk. Bring to the boil, stirring, and cook for 2 minutes. Remove from the heat and stir in the mustard, cheeses and seasoning.

4 Preheat the oven to 200°C/400°F/Gas 6. Arrange half the aubergines in the base of an ovenproof dish, and spoon half the tomato sauce over. Arrange three sheets of lasagne on top. Repeat this layering.

5 Spoon the cheese sauce over, cover and bake for 30 minutes, until lightly browned. Serve immediately.

Energy 541Kcal/2259kJ; Fat 32.7g; Saturated Fat 13.5g; Carbohydrate 44.4g; Fibre 7.3g

Cannelloni with Mixed Vegetables

This version of the classic beef-filled cannelloni introduces a variety of vegetables topped with cheese sauce.

Serves 4

8 dried cannelloni tubes
115g/4oz spinach
tomatoes and green salad, to
 serve (optional)

For the filling
15ml/1 tbsp oil
175g/6oz/3/4 cup minced
 (ground) beef

2 garlic cloves, crushed
25g/1oz/1/4 cup plain (all-
 purpose) flour
120ml/4fl oz/1/2 cup beef stock
1 small carrot, finely chopped
1 small yellow courgette
 (zucchini), chopped
salt and ground black pepper

For the sauce
25g/1oz/2 tbsp butter
25g/1oz/1/4 cup plain (all-
 purpose) flour
250ml/8fl oz/1 cup milk
50g/2oz/2/3 cup freshly grated
 Parmesan cheese

1 Preheat the oven to 180°C/350°F/Gas 4. To make the filling, heat the oil in a large pan. Add the minced beef and garlic, and cook for 5 minutes, stirring frequently.

2 Add the flour and cook for a further 1 minute. Slowly stir in the stock and bring to the boil, stirring. Add the carrot and courgette and season with salt and pepper to taste. Cook over medium heat for 10 minutes.

3 Carefully spoon the beef mixture into the cannelloni tubes and arrange in an ovenproof dish.

4 Blanch the spinach in boiling water for 3 minutes. Drain well and place on top of the cannelloni tubes in the dish.

5 To make the sauce, melt the butter in a pan. Add the flour and cook for 1 minute. Stir in the milk and cook, stirring, until smooth and thick. Add the grated cheese and season well.

6 Pour the sauce over the cannelloni and spinach and bake for 30 minutes. Serve with tomatoes and a green salad, if liked.

Energy 491Kcal/2062kJ; Fat 21.7g; Saturated Fat 10.2g; Carbohydrate 52.6g; Fibre 3.4g

Broccoli & Ricotta Cannelloni

Delicious vegetable-filled cannelloni baked in tomato.

Serves 4

60ml/4 tbsp olive oil, plus extra
 for brushing
12 dried cannelloni tubes
450g/1lb/4 cups broccoli florets
75g/3oz/1½ cups fresh
 breadcrumbs
150ml/¼ pint/²/₃ cup milk
225g/8oz/1 cup ricotta cheese
pinch of freshly grated nutmeg

90ml/6 tbsp grated Parmesan
30ml/2 tbsp pine nuts
salt and ground black pepper

For the tomato sauce
30ml/2 tbsp olive oil
1 onion, finely chopped
1 garlic clove, crushed
2 x 400g/14oz cans chopped
 Italian plum tomatoes
15ml/1 tbsp tomato purée (paste)
4 black olives, pitted and chopped
5ml/1 tsp dried thyme

1 Preheat the oven to 190°C/375°F/Gas 5 and lightly grease an ovenproof dish with olive oil. Bring a large pan of water to the boil, add a little olive oil and simmer the cannelloni tubes, uncovered, for about 6–7 minutes, or until nearly cooked.

2 Meanwhile, steam or boil the broccoli for 10 minutes, until tender. Drain the pasta, rinse under cold water and reserve. Drain the broccoli and leave to cool, then place in a blender or food processor and process until smooth. Set aside.

3 Place the breadcrumbs in a bowl, add the milk and oil and stir until softened. Add the ricotta, broccoli purée, nutmeg, 60ml/4 tbsp of the Parmesan cheese and seasoning; set aside.

4 To make the sauce, heat the oil in a frying pan, add the onion and garlic and fry for 5–6 minutes, until softened but not brown. Stir in the tomatoes, tomato purée, black olives, thyme and seasoning. Boil rapidly for 2–3 minutes, then pour into the dish.

5 Spoon the cheese mixture into a piping bag fitted with a 1cm/½in nozzle. Standing each cannelloni tube upright on a board, pipe the filling into each tube. Lay in rows in the tomato sauce. Brush the tops with oil and sprinkle with the remaining Parmesan and pine nuts. Bake for 25–30 minutes until golden.

Energy 733Kcal/3074kJ; Fat 36.3g; Saturated Fat 13.1g; Carbohydrate 74.3g; Fibre 7.6g

Tuna Lasagne

Two popular Italian ingredients, tuna and pasta, combine to make a tasty lasagne that is sure to be a big hit with all the family.

Serves 6
12–16 fresh or dried lasagne
   sheets
15g/1/2oz butter
1 small onion, finely chopped
1 garlic clove, finely chopped
115g/4oz mushrooms, thinly
   sliced
60ml/4 tbsp dry white wine
   (optional)
600ml/1 pint/2^{1}/2 cups white
   sauce (see page 120)
150ml/1/4 pint/2/3 cup whipping
   cream
45ml/3 tbsp chopped fresh
   parsley
2 x 200g/7oz cans tuna, drained
2 canned pimientos, cut into strips
65g/21/2oz/generous 1/2 cup
   frozen peas, thawed
115g/4oz mozzarella cheese,
   grated
30ml/2 tbsp freshly grated
   Parmesan cheese
salt and ground black pepper

1 For fresh lasagne, cook in a pan of salted boiling water until *al dente*. For dried, soak in a bowl of hot water for 3–5 minutes. Place the lasagne in a colander and rinse with cold water. Lay on a dish towel to drain.

2 Preheat the oven to 180°C/350°F/Gas 4. Melt the butter in a pan and cook the onion until soft.

3 Add the garlic and mushrooms to the pan and cook until soft, stirring occasionally. Pour in the wine, if using. Boil for 1 minute, then stir in the white sauce, cream and parsley. Season.

4 Spoon a thin layer of sauce over the base of a 30 x 23cm/ 12 x 9in baking dish. Cover with a layer of lasagne sheets.

5 Flake the tuna. Scatter half the tuna, pimiento strips, peas and mozzarella over the lasagne. Spoon one-third of the remaining sauce over the top and cover with another layer of lasagne.

6 Repeat the layers, ending with pasta and sauce. Sprinkle with the Parmesan. Bake for 30–40 minutes, or until lightly browned.

Smoked Trout Cannelloni

The smoked trout filling gives this cannelloni dish a deliciously different taste.

Serves 4–6
1 large onion, finely chopped
1 garlic clove, crushed
60ml/4 tbsp vegetable stock
2 x 400g/14oz cans chopped
   Italian plum tomatoes
2.5ml/1/2 tsp dried mixed herbs
1 smoked trout, about
   400g/14oz, or 225g/8oz fillets
75g/3oz/3/4 cup frozen peas,
   thawed
75g/3oz/11/2 cups fresh
   breadcrumbs
16 cannelloni tubes
salt and ground black pepper
25ml/11/2 tbsp freshly grated
   Parmesan cheese

For the cheese sauce
25g/1oz/2 tbsp butter
25g/1oz/1/4 cup plain (all-
   purpose) flour
350ml/12fl oz/11/2 cups skimmed
   milk
freshly grated nutmeg

1 Simmer the onion, garlic and stock in a large covered pan for 3 minutes. Uncover and continue to cook, stirring the mixture occasionally, until the stock has reduced entirely.

2 Stir the tomatoes and herbs into the onion mixture. Simmer, uncovered, for a further 10 minutes, until very thick.

3 Meanwhile, skin the smoked trout. Carefully flake the flesh and discard the bones. Mix the fish together with the tomato mixture, peas, breadcrumbs, salt and ground black pepper.

4 Preheat the oven to 190°C/375°F/Gas 5. Spoon the filling into the cannelloni tubes and arrange them side by side in a lightly greased ovenproof dish.

5 To make the sauce, melt the butter in a pan, add the flour and cook for 2–3 minutes, whisking constantly. Pour in the milk and bring to the boil, whisking, until the sauce thickens. Simmer for 2–3 minutes, stirring. Season with salt, pepper and nutmeg.

6 Pour the sauce over the cannelloni and sprinkle with the Parmesan. Bake in the oven for 35–40 minutes, until golden.

Energy 410Kcal/1735kJ; Fat 9.3g; Saturated Fat 2.1g; Carbohydrate 62.3g; Fibre 4.5g

Energy 653Kcal/2744kJ; Fat 27.7g; Saturated Fat 14g; Carbohydrate 69.1g; Fibre 3.2g

Baked Tortellini with Three Cheeses

In this gloriously rich dish, stuffed pasta shapes are smothered in cheese and baked until meltingly tender. Bay leaves and basil add a delicate herbal touch to the finished dish. For the best balance of flavours, choose tortellini with a meat or vegetable filling.

Serves 4–6

450g/1lb fresh tortellini
2 eggs
350g/12oz/1½ cups ricotta or curd (farmer's) cheese
25g/1oz/2 tbsp butter
25g/1oz fresh basil leaves
115g/4oz smoked mozzarella cheese
60ml/4 tbsp freshly grated Parmesan cheese
salt and ground black pepper

1 Preheat the oven to 190°C/375°F/Gas 5. Bring a pan of lightly salted water to the boil, add the tortellini and cook until *al dente*. Drain well.

2 Beat the eggs with the ricotta or curd cheese and season well with salt and pepper.

3 Use the butter to grease an ovenproof dish. Spoon in half the tortellini, pour half the cheese mixture over and cover with half the basil leaves.

4 Cover with the mozzarella and remaining basil. Top with the rest of the tortellini and spread the remaining ricotta or curd cheese mixture over.

5 Sprinkle evenly with the Parmesan cheese. Bake in the oven for 35–45 minutes, or until golden brown and bubbling.

Cook's Tip

If smoked mozzarella cheese is not available, try using a smoked German cheese or even grated smoked Cheddar as an alternative. Grated mature Cheddar cheese can also be used instead of some of the grated Parmesan.

Lasagne with Three Cheeses

This rich lasagne was invented in the United States by Italian immigrants who made use of the abundant ingredients available to them.

Serves 6–8

25g/1oz/2 tbsp butter
15ml/1 tbsp olive oil
225–250g/8–9oz/2–2¼ cups button mushrooms, quartered
30ml/2 tbsp chopped fresh flat leaf parsley
1 quantity Classic Bolognese Sauce (see page 10)
250–350ml/8–12fl oz/1–1½ cups hot beef stock
9–12 fresh lasagne sheets, pre-cooked if necessary
450g/1lb/2 cups ricotta cheese
1 large (US extra large) egg
3 x 130g/4½oz packets mozzarella cheese, drained and thinly sliced
115g/4oz/1¼ cups freshly grated Parmesan cheese
salt and ground black pepper

1 Preheat the oven to 190°C/375°F/Gas 5. Melt the butter in the oil in a frying pan. Add the mushrooms, with salt and pepper to taste, and toss over medium to high heat for 5–8 minutes, until the mushrooms are tender and quite dry. Remove the pan from the heat and stir in the parsley.

2 Heat the Bolognese Sauce and stir in enough hot beef stock to make the sauce quite runny. Stir in the mushroom and parsley mixture, then spread about a quarter of this sauce over the bottom of a baking dish. Cover with 3–4 sheets of lasagne.

3 Beat together the ricotta and egg in a bowl, with salt and pepper to taste, then spread about a third of the mixture over the lasagne sheets. Cover with a third of the mozzarella slices, then sprinkle with about a quarter of the grated Parmesan.

4 Repeat these layers twice, using half the remaining meat sauce each time, and finishing with the remaining Parmesan.

5 Bake the lasagne for 30–40 minutes, or until the cheese topping is golden brown and bubbling. Allow to stand for about 10 minutes before serving.

Energy 484Kcal/2034kJ; Fat 18.5g; Saturated Fat 10.6g; Carbohydrate 57.6g; Fibre 2.2g

Energy 533Kcal/2226kJ; Fat 32.4g; Saturated Fat 18.7g; Carbohydrate 29.7g; Fibre 1.4g

Cannelloni with Tuna

Children love this pasta dish. Fontina cheese has a sweet, nutty flavour and very good melting qualities. Look for it in large supermarkets and Italian delicatessens.

Serves 4–6

50g/2oz/¼ cup butter
50g/2oz/½ cup plain (all-purpose) flour
about 900ml/1½ pints/3¾ cups hot milk
2 x 200g/7oz cans tuna, drained
115g/4oz/1 cup grated Fontina cheese
1.5ml/¼ tsp grated nutmeg
12 no pre-cook cannelloni tubes
50g/2oz/⅔ cup freshly grated Parmesan cheese
salt and ground black pepper
fresh herbs, to garnish

1 Melt the butter in a heavy pan, add the flour and stir over low heat for 1–2 minutes. Remove the pan from the heat and gradually add 350 ml/12 fl oz/1½ cups of the milk, beating vigorously after each addition. Return the pan to the heat and whisk for 1–2 minutes, until the sauce is very thick and smooth. Remove from the heat.

2 Mix the drained tuna with about 120 ml/4 fl oz/½ cup of the warm white sauce in a bowl. Add salt and black pepper to taste. Preheat the oven to 180°C/350°F/Gas 4.

3 Gradually whisk the remaining milk into the rest of the sauce, return to the heat and simmer, whisking, until thickened. Add the grated Fontina and nutmeg, and season with salt and pepper to taste. Simmer for a few minutes, stirring frequently. Pour one-third of the sauce into a baking dish.

4 Fill the cannelloni tubes with the tuna mixture, pushing it in with the handle of a teaspoon. Place the cannelloni in a single layer in the dish. Thin the remaining sauce with a little more milk if necessary, then pour it over the cannelloni.

5 Sprinkle the sauce with freshly grated Parmesan cheese and bake for 30 minutes, or until the top is golden. Serve immediately, garnished with herbs.

Energy 502Kcal/2110kJ; Fat 22.7g; Saturated Fat 11.4g; Carbohydrate 44.3g; Fibre 1.7g

Shellfish Lasagne

This is a luxury lasagne with a superb flavour.

Serves 4–6

4–6 fresh scallops, shelled
450g/1lb raw large peeled prawns (shrimp)
1 garlic clove, crushed
75g/3oz/6 tbsp butter
50g/2oz/½ cup plain (all-purpose) flour
600ml/1 pint/2½ cups hot milk
100ml/3½fl oz/scant ½ cup double (heavy) cream
100ml/3½fl oz/scant ½ cup dry white wine
2 sachets saffron powder
good pinch of cayenne pepper
130g/4½oz Fontina cheese, thinly sliced
75g/3oz/1 cup freshly grated Parmesan cheese
6–8 fresh lasagne sheets, pre-cooked if necessary
salt and ground black pepper

1 Preheat the oven to 190°C/375°F/Gas 5. Cut the scallops, their corals and the prawns into bite-size pieces and spread in a dish. Sprinkle with the garlic and salt and pepper to taste. Melt a third of the butter in a medium pan, add the scallops, corals and prawns and toss over medium heat for 1–2 minutes, or just until the prawns turn pink. Remove with a slotted spoon.

2 Add the remaining butter to the pan and melt over low heat. Sprinkle in the flour and cook, stirring, for 1–2 minutes, then increase the heat to medium and add the hot milk a little at a time, whisking vigorously after each addition. Bring to the boil and cook, stirring, until the sauce is smooth and very thick. Whisk in the cream, wine, saffron powder, cayenne and salt and pepper to taste, then remove the sauce from the heat.

3 Spread about a third of the sauce in a baking dish. Arrange half the Fontina slices over the sauce and sprinkle with about a third of the grated Parmesan. Scatter about half the shellfish evenly on top, then cover with half the lasagne sheets. Repeat the layers, then cover with the remaining sauce and Parmesan.

4 Bake the lasagne for 30–40 minutes, or until golden brown and bubbling. Allow to stand for 10 minutes before serving.

Energy 638Kcal/2670kJ; Fat 34g; Saturated Fat 20.8g; Carbohydrate 38.1g; Fibre 1.2g

Cannelloni al Forno

This traditional recipe takes time to prepare, but is well worth the effort.

Serves 6
15ml/1 tbsp olive oil
1 small onion, finely chopped
450g/1lb/2 cups minced (ground)
 beef
1 garlic clove, finely chopped
5ml/1 tsp dried mixed herbs
120ml/4fl oz/¹/₂ cup beef stock
1 egg
75g/3oz cooked ham or
 mortadella sausage, chopped
45ml/3 tbsp fresh breadcrumbs
150g/5oz/1¹/₂ cups freshly grated
 Parmesan cheese
18 no pre-cook cannelloni tubes

salt and ground black pepper

For the tomato sauce
30ml/2 tbsp olive oil
1 small onion, finely chopped
¹/₂ carrot, finely chopped
1 celery stick, finely chopped
1 garlic clove, crushed
400g/14oz can chopped Italian
 plum tomatoes
a few sprigs of fresh basil
2.5ml/¹/₂ tsp dried oregano

For the white sauce
50g/2oz/¹/₄ cup butter
50g/2oz/¹/₂ cup plain (all-
 purpose) flour
900ml/1¹/₂ pints/3³/₄ cups milk
freshly grated nutmeg

1 Heat the olive oil in a medium pan and cook the onion over gentle heat, stirring occasionally, for 5 minutes, until softened.

2 Add the beef and garlic and cook gently for 10 minutes, stirring to break up any lumps. Add the mixed herbs and salt and pepper to taste, then moisten with half the stock. Cover the pan and simmer for 25 minutes, stirring occasionally and adding more stock as it reduces. Spoon into a bowl and cool.

3 Meanwhile, make the tomato sauce. Heat the olive oil in a pan, add the vegetables and garlic and cook, stirring frequently, for about 10 minutes. Add the tomatoes. Fill the empty can with water, pour it into the pan, then stir in the herbs, with salt and pepper to taste. Bring to the boil, lower the heat, cover and simmer for 25–30 minutes, stirring occasionally. Purée the sauce in a blender or food processor and set aside.

4 Add the egg, ham, breadcrumbs and 90ml/6 tbsp grated Parmesan to the meat and stir well to mix. Taste for seasoning.

5 Spread a little of the tomato sauce over the bottom of a baking dish. Using a teaspoon, fill the cannelloni tubes with the meat mixture and place them in a layer in the dish on top of the tomato sauce. Pour over the remaining tomato sauce.

6 Preheat the oven to 190°C/375°F/Gas 5. To make the white sauce, melt the butter in a pan, add the flour and cook, stirring, for 1–2 minutes. Gradually whisk in the milk. Bring to the boil and cook, stirring, until the sauce is smooth and thick. Add nutmeg, salt and pepper to taste. Whisk well to mix and remove from the heat.

7 Pour the white sauce over the stuffed cannelloni, then sprinkle with the remaining Parmesan. Place in the oven and bake for 40–45 minutes, or until the cannelloni tubes feel tender when pierced with a skewer. Allow the cannelloni to stand for about 10 minutes before serving.

Lasagne with Lamb

Layered with lamb rather than beef, this is a different take on the classic lasagne.

Serves 4–6
15ml/1 tbsp olive oil
1 small onion, finely chopped
450g/1lb/2 cups minced (ground)
 lamb
1 garlic clove, crushed
45ml/3 tbsp dry white wine
5ml/1 tsp dried mixed herbs
450ml/³/₄ pint/scant 2 cups
 passata

12–16 fresh lasagne sheets,
 pre-cooked if necessary
30ml/2 tbsp freshly grated
 Parmesan cheese
salt and ground black pepper

For the white sauce
50g/2oz/¹/₄ cup butter
50g/2oz/¹/₂ cup flour
900ml/1¹/₂ pints/3³/₄ cups hot
 milk
30ml/2 tbsp freshly grated
 Parmesan cheese
freshly grated nutmeg

1 Heat the oil in a pan and gently cook the onion for about 5 minutes, until softened. Add the minced lamb and garlic and cook gently for 10 minutes, stirring frequently. Stir in salt and pepper to taste, then add the wine and cook rapidly for about 2 minutes, stirring constantly. Stir in the herbs and passata. Simmer gently for 45 minutes to 1 hour, stirring occasionally.

2 Preheat the oven to 190°C/375°F/Gas 5. To make the white sauce, melt the butter in a pan, add the flour and cook, stirring, for 1–2 minutes. Add the milk a little at a time, whisking vigorously after each addition. Bring to the boil and cook, stirring, until the sauce is smooth and thick. Add the Parmesan, grate in fresh nutmeg to taste, season with a little salt and pepper and whisk well. Remove the pan from the heat.

3 Spread a few spoonfuls of meat sauce over the bottom of a baking dish and cover with three or four sheets of lasagne. Spread a quarter of the remaining meat sauce over the lasagne, then a quarter of the white sauce. Repeat the layers three times, finishing with white sauce.

4 Sprinkle the Parmesan over the surface and bake for 30–40 minutes, or until the topping is golden brown and bubbling.

Energy 587Kcal/2468kJ; Fat 25.7g; Saturated Fat 13g; Carbohydrate 59.9g; Fibre 2.5g

Energy 764Kcal/3204kJ; Fat 38.1g; Saturated Fat 17.7g; Carbohydrate 67.1g; Fibre 3.3g

Mixed Meat Cannelloni

Combining beef, pork and chicken for the filling makes this a rich and succulent cannelloni dish.

Serves 4
60ml/4 tbsp olive oil
1 onion, finely chopped
1 carrot, finely chopped
2 garlic cloves, crushed
2 ripe Italian plum tomatoes, peeled and finely chopped
130g/4¹/₂oz/¹/₂ cup minced (ground) beef
130g/4¹/₂oz/¹/₂ cup minced (ground) pork

250g/9oz minced (ground) chicken
30ml/2 tbsp brandy
25g/1oz/2 tbsp butter
90ml/6 tbsp panna da cucina or double (heavy) cream
16 dried cannelloni tubes
75g/3oz/1 cup freshly grated Parmesan cheese
salt and ground black pepper

For the white sauce
50g/2oz/¹/₄ cup butter
50g/2oz/¹/₂ cup plain (all-purpose) flour
900ml/1¹/₂ pints/3³/₄ cups milk
freshly grated nutmeg

1 Heat the oil in a medium frying pan, add the onion, carrot, garlic and tomatoes and cook over low heat, stirring, for about 10 minutes, or until very soft.

2 Add all the minced meats to the pan and cook gently for about 10 minutes, stirring frequently to break up any lumps. Add the brandy, increase the heat and stir until it has reduced, then add the butter and cream and cook gently, stirring occasionally, for about 10 minutes. Allow to cool.

3 Preheat the oven to 190°C/375°F/Gas 5. To make the white sauce, melt the butter in a medium pan, add the flour and cook, stirring, for 1–2 minutes. Gradually whisk in the milk, bring to the boil and cook, stirring, until the sauce is smooth and thick. Add nutmeg, salt and pepper to taste. Remove from the heat.

4 Spoon a little of the white sauce into a baking dish. Carefully fill the cannelloni tubes with the meat mixture and place in a single layer in the dish. Pour the remaining white sauce over the tubes, then sprinkle with the Parmesan. Bake for 35–40 minutes, or until golden. Allow to stand for 10 minutes before serving.

Lasagne 'Bolognese'

This is the classic lasagne *al forno*. Use your favourite Bolognese sauce recipe for the filling.

Serves 6
1 quantity Classic Bolognese Sauce (see page 10)
150–250ml/5–8fl oz/²/₃–1 cup hot beef stock

12 no pre-cook dried lasagne sheets
50g/2oz/²/₃ cup freshly grated Parmesan cheese

For the white sauce
50g/2oz/¹/₄ cup butter
50g/2oz/¹/₂ cup plain (all-purpose) flour
900ml/1¹/₂ pints/3³/₄ cups milk
salt and ground black pepper

1 Preheat the oven to 190°C/375°F/Gas 5. Reheat the meat sauce, if cold, then stir in enough stock to make it quite runny.

2 To make the white sauce, melt the butter in a medium pan, add the flour and cook, stirring, for 1–2 minutes. Heat the milk and add a little at a time, whisking vigorously after each addition. Bring to the boil and cook, stirring, until the sauce is smooth and thick. Season to taste, then remove from the heat.

3 Spread about a third of the meat sauce over the bottom of a baking dish. Cover the meat sauce with about a quarter of the white sauce, followed by four sheets of lasagne. Repeat the layers twice more, then cover the top layer of lasagne with the remaining white sauce and sprinkle evenly with Parmesan.

4 Bake for 40–45 minutes, or until the pasta is tender. Allow to stand for about 10 minutes before serving.

> **Cook's Tips**
> • The lasagne is best baked straight after layering or the pasta will begin to absorb the sauces and dry out.
> • To reheat leftover lasagne, prick it all over with a skewer, then pour a little milk over to moisten. Cover with foil and reheat in a 190°C/375°F/Gas 5 oven for 20 minutes, or until bubbling.

Energy 1025Kcal/4284kJ; Fat 59g; Saturated Fat 28.9g; Carbohydrate 71.3g; Fibre 3.4g

Energy 472Kcal/1994kJ; Fat 16g; Saturated Fat 8.8g; Carbohydrate 66g; Fibre 2g

Lasagne with Béchamel Sauce

Nothing beats a lasagne for keeping family and friends happy. The béchamel sauce is flavoured with bay and mace to give it a lift.

Serves 8–10
1 quantity Classic Bolognese
Sauce (see page 10)
10–12 dried lasagne sheets

115g/4oz/1 cup grated Parmesan
40g/1½oz/3 tbsp butter

For the béchamel sauce
700ml/1¼ pints/3 cups milk
1 bay leaf
3 blades mace
115g/4oz/½ cup butter
75g/3oz/¾ cup flour
salt and ground black pepper

1 To make the béchamel sauce, heat the milk with the bay leaf and mace in a pan. Set aside. Melt the butter in a pan, add the flour, and mix well with a wire whisk. Cook for 2–3 minutes.

2 Strain the hot milk into the flour and butter mixture, and combine smoothly with the whisk. Bring the sauce to a boil, stirring constantly, and cook for 4–5 minutes more. Season with salt and pepper, and set aside.

3 Preheat the oven to 200°C/F400°F/Gas 6. Cook the lasagne, sheets in a pan of lightly salted boiling water until al dente. Place in a colander and rinse with cold water. Lay out flat on a dish towel to drain.

4 To assemble the lasagne, spread one large spoonful of the meat sauce over the bottom of the dish. Arrange a layer of pasta in the dish, cutting it to fit.

5 Cover with a thin layer of meat sauce, then one of béchamel. Sprinkle with cheese. Repeat the layers in the same order, ending with a layer of pasta coated with béchamel. Do not make more than about 6 layers of pasta. Use the pasta trimmings to patch any gaps. Sprinkle the top with Parmesan and dot with butter.

6 Bake in the oven for 20 minutes, or until golden brown on top. Let stand for 5 minutes before serving.

Lasagne with Meatballs

In southern Italy, where this type of lasagne is popular, salami and cheese are often added to the layers.

Serves 6–8
300g/11oz/1½ cups minced
(ground) beef
300g/11oz/1½ cups minced
(ground) pork
1 large (US extra large) egg
50g/2oz/1 cup fresh breadcrumbs
75ml/5 tbsp freshly grated
Parmesan cheese
30ml/2 tbsp chopped fresh parsley

2 garlic cloves, crushed
60ml/4 tbsp olive oil
1 onion, finely chopped
1 carrot, finely chopped
1 celery stick, finely chopped
2 x 400g/14oz cans chopped
Italian plum tomatoes
10ml/2 tsp dried oregano or basil
8–10 fresh lasagne sheets, pre-
cooked if necessary
750ml/1¼ pints/3 cups
béchamel sauce (see previous
recipe)
salt and ground black pepper

1 First make the meatballs. Put 175g/6oz/¾ cup each of the minced beef and pork in a large bowl. Add the egg, bread-crumbs, 30ml/2 tbsp of the grated Parmesan, half the parsley and garlic and salt and pepper. Mix together, then squeeze and knead the mixture to bind. With cold hands roll into 60 very small balls. Place on a tray and chill for about 30 minutes.

2 To make the meat sauce, heat half the oil in a frying pan, add the onion, carrot, celery and remaining garlic and stir over low heat for 5 minutes, until softened. Add the remaining minced beef and pork and cook gently for 10 minutes. Season, then add the tomatoes, remaining parsley and the oregano. Cover and simmer gently for 45 minutes to 1 hour. Meanwhile, heat the remaining oil in a large, non-stick frying pan and cook the meatballs for 5–8 minutes, until brown. As they cook, transfer the meatballs to kitchen paper to drain.

3 Preheat the oven to 190°C/375°F/Gas 5. Spread one-third of the meat sauce in a large baking dish. Add half the meatballs, spread with a third of the béchamel and cover with half the lasagne. Repeat these layers, then top with the remaining béchamel. Sprinkle Parmesan on top. Bake for 30–40 minutes.

Energy 367Kcal/1548kJ; Fat 14.5g; Saturated Fat 8.2g; Carbohydrate 47.7g; Fibre 1.5g

Energy 553Kcal/2320kJ; Fat 27g; Saturated Fat 11.3g; Carbohydrate 51g; Fibre 3g

Ravioli with Pork & Turkey

These Roman-style meat ravioli are delightfully scented with fresh herbs.

Serves 8

1 quantity handmade Egg Pasta (see page 8)
50g/2oz/¼ cup butter flour, for dusting
1 bunch sage, leaves chopped
60ml/4 tbsp freshly grated Parmesan cheese

For the filling
25g/1oz/2 tbsp butter
150g/5oz/generous ½ cup minced (ground) pork
115g/4oz/½ cup minced (ground) turkey
4 fresh sage leaves, chopped
1 fresh sprig rosemary, leaves removed and finely chopped
30ml/2 tbsp dry white wine
65g/2½oz/¼ cup ricotta cheese
45ml/3 tbsp freshly grated Parmesan cheese
1 egg, lightly beaten
freshly grated nutmeg
salt and ground black pepper

1 To make the filling, melt the butter in a pan, add the pork and turkey and the herbs and cook for 5–6 minutes. Season and stir. Add the wine and simmer for 1–2 minutes, until reduced slightly. Cover and simmer gently for about 20 minutes. With a slotted spoon, transfer the meat to a bowl; cool.

2 Add the cheeses to the bowl with the egg and freshly grated nutmeg to taste. Stir well to mix the ingredients thoroughly.

3 Using a pasta machine, roll out one-quarter of the pasta into a 90cm–1m/35in–3ft strip. Cut into two 45–50cm/18–20in lengths. Using a teaspoon, put 10–12 little mounds of the filling evenly along one side of one of the pasta strips. Brush water around each mound, then fold the plain side of the pasta strip over the filling. Starting from the folded edge, press down around each mound, pushing the air out. Dust with flour.

4 With a pasta wheel, cut into square shapes. Dust with flour. Put the ravioli on floured dish towels. Repeat with the rest of the pasta to make 80–96 ravioli. Cook in boiling water for 4–5 minutes. Meanwhile, heat the sage in the butter until sizzling. Drain the ravioli and serve with the sage butter and Parmesan.

Cheese & Prosciutto Ravioli

Typical of southern Italian cuisine, these tasty ravioli are layered with tomato sauce.

Serves 4–6

1 quantity handmade Egg Pasta (see page 8)
flour, for dusting
60ml/4 tbsp freshly grated Pecorino cheese

For the filling
175g/6oz/¾ cup ricotta cheese
30ml/2 tbsp freshly grated Parmesan cheese
115g/4oz prosciutto, finely chopped
150g/5oz mozzarella cheese, drained and finely chopped
1 small egg
15ml/1 tbsp chopped fresh parsley

For the tomato sauce
30ml/2 tbsp olive oil
1 onion, finely chopped
400g/14oz can chopped Italian plum tomatoes
15ml/1 tbsp sun-dried tomato purée (paste)
5–10ml/1–2 tsp dried oregano
salt and ground black pepper

1 To make the sauce, heat the oil in a medium pan, add the onion and cook gently, stirring, for about 5 minutes, until soft. Add the tomatoes. Fill the empty can with water, pour into the pan, then stir in the tomato paste, oregano and salt and pepper to taste. Bring to the boil, cover the pan and simmer gently for 30 minutes, stirring occasionally. Add more water if necessary. Meanwhile, put all the filling ingredients in a bowl with salt and pepper to taste. Mix well with a fork.

2 Using a pasta machine, roll out one-quarter of the pasta into a 90cm–1m/36in–3ft strip. Cut into two 45–50cm/18–20in lengths. Using 2 teaspoons, put 10–12 little mounds of the filling evenly along one side of one of the pasta strips. Brush water around each mound, then fold the plain side of the pasta strip over the filling. Starting from the folded edge, press down gently around each mound, pushing the air out.

3 Sprinkle with flour. With a fluted pasta wheel, cut into small square shapes. Put the ravioli on floured dish towels. Repeat with the remaining pasta to make 80–96 ravioli. Cook in a large pan of boiling water for 4–5 minutes, until tender. Drain the ravioli and layer in a bowl with Pecorino and tomato sauce.

Energy 521Kcal/2194kJ; Fat 21g; Saturated Fat 10.4g; Carbohydrate 59.5g; Fibre 3g

Energy 393Kcal/1653kJ; Fat 17.1g; Saturated Fat 9.4g; Carbohydrate 42g; Fibre 1.6g

Turkey Pasta Bake

Layers of turkey and macaroni topped with a light cheese sauce make up this healthy pasta bake.

Serves 4–6

450g/1lb/2 cups lean minced (ground) turkey
1 large onion, finely chopped
60ml/4 tbsp tomato purée (paste)
250ml/8fl oz/1 cup red wine or stock
5ml/1 tsp ground cinnamon
300g/11oz/2¾ cups dried macaroni
25g/1oz/2 tbsp sunflower margarine
25g/1oz/3 tbsp plain (all-purpose) flour
300ml/½ pint/1¼ cups skimmed milk
5ml/1 tsp grated nutmeg
2 tomatoes, sliced
60ml/4 tbsp wholemeal breadcrumbs
salt and ground black pepper
green salad, to serve

1 Preheat the oven to 220°C/425°F/Gas 7. Fry the turkey and onion in a non-stick pan without any fat, stirring until lightly browned and the turkey fat has reduced.

2 Stir in the tomato purée, red wine or stock and cinnamon. Season with salt and pepper to taste, then cover and simmer for about 5 minutes.

3 Bring a pan of lightly salted water to the boil, add the pasta and cook until al dente. Drain the pasta.

4 Layer the macaroni with the turkey mixture in a wide ovenproof dish.

5 Melt the margarine in a pan and add the flour, stirring. Cook for 2–3 minutes, stirring constantly, then gradually add the milk and whisk over medium heat, until thickened and smooth.

6 Whisk the nutmeg and salt and pepper to taste into the sauce, then pour evenly over the pasta. Arrange the tomato slices on top and sprinkle with lines of breadcrumbs.

7 Bake in the oven for 30–35 minutes, or until golden brown.

Energy 397Kcal/1683kJ; Fat 7.2g; Saturated Fat 1.2g; Carbohydrate 53.3g; Fibre 2.5g

Chicken Lasagne

A variation of the traditional beef lasagne, this is an excellent dish for all-round entertaining. Serve simply with a green salad.

Serves 8

30ml/2 tbsp olive oil
900g/2lb/4 cups minced (ground) raw chicken
225g/8oz rindless streaky (fatty) bacon rashers (strips), chopped
2 garlic cloves, crushed
450g/1lb leeks, sliced
225g/8oz carrots, diced
30ml/2 tbsp tomato purée (paste)
450ml/¾ pint/1¾ cups chicken stock
12 no pre-cook dried lasagne sheets

For the cheese sauce
50g/2oz/¼ cup butter
50g/2oz/½ cup plain (all-purpose) flour
600ml/1 pint/2½ cups milk
115g/4oz/1 cup grated mature Cheddar cheese
1.5ml/¼ tsp English mustard powder
salt and ground black pepper

1 Heat the oil in a large flameproof casserole and brown the minced chicken and bacon briskly, separating the pieces with a wooden spoon. Add the crushed garlic cloves, chopped leeks and diced carrots and cook for about 5 minutes, until softened. Add the tomato purée, stock and seasoning. Bring to the boil, cover and simmer for 30 minutes.

2 To make the sauce, melt the butter in a pan, add the flour and gradually blend in the milk, stirring until smooth. Bring to the boil, stirring all the time until thickened, and simmer for several minutes. Add half the grated Cheddar cheese and the mustard and season to taste.

3 Preheat the oven to 190°C/375°F/Gas 5. Layer the chicken mixture, lasagne and half the cheese sauce in a 2.5 litre/4 pints/10½ cups ovenproof dish, starting and finishing with the chicken mixture.

4 Pour the remaining cheese sauce over, sprinkle with the remaining cheese and bake for 1 hour, or until lightly browned.

Energy 558Kcal/2347kJ; Fat 23g; Saturated Fat 10.4g; Carbohydrate 45.2g; Fibre 3.5g

Rotolo di Pasta

A giant Swiss (jelly) roll of pasta with a spinach filling, which is poached, sliced and baked with béchamel sauce. This recipe is made the traditional way with sheets of fresh egg pasta.

Serves 6

700g/1½lb frozen chopped spinach, thawed
50g/2oz/¼ cup butter
1 onion, chopped
100g/4oz ham or bacon, diced
225g/8oz/1 cup ricotta or curd (farmer's) cheese
1 egg
freshly grated nutmeg
6 fresh spinach lasagne sheets
1.2 litres/2 pints/5 cups béchamel sauce, warmed (see page 132)
50g/2oz/⅔ cup freshly grated Parmesan cheese
salt and ground black pepper

1 Squeeze the excess moisture from the spinach and set aside. Melt the butter in a saucepan and fry the onion until golden. Add the ham and fry until beginning to brown. Take off the heat and stir in the spinach. Cool slightly, then beat in the ricotta or curd cheese and the egg. Season with salt, pepper and nutmeg.

2 Roll the pasta out to a rectangle about 30 × 40cm/12 × 16in. Spread the filling all over, leaving a 1cm/½in border all round the edge of the rectangle.

3 Roll up the pasta and filling from the shorter end and wrap in muslin to form a sausage shape, tying the ends with string.

4 Poach the pasta roll in a very large pan (or fish kettle) of simmering water for about 20 minutes, or until firm. Carefully remove, drain and then unwrap. Leave to cool.

5 When you are ready to finish the dish, preheat the oven to 200°C/400°F/Gas 6. Cut the pasta roll into 2.5cm/1in slices. Spoon a little béchamel sauce over the base of a shallow baking dish and arrange the slices on top, slightly overlapping.

6 Spoon the remaining sauce over the roll slices, sprinkle with cheese and bake for 15–20 minutes, or until browned. Allow to stand for a few minutes before serving.

Chicken Cannelloni al Forno

A lighter alternative to the usual beef-filled, béchamel-coated version. Try filling with ricotta cheese, onion and mushroom for a vegetarian dish.

Serves 4–6

450g/1lb chicken breast fillets, cooked
225g/8oz mushrooms
2 garlic cloves, crushed
30ml/2 tbsp chopped fresh parsley
15ml/1 tbsp chopped fresh tarragon
1 egg, beaten
freshly squeezed lemon juice
12–18 fresh or dried cannelloni tubes
1 quantity Basic Tomato Sauce (see page 9)
50g/2oz/⅔ cup grated Parmesan cheese
salt and freshly ground black pepper
fresh parsley sprig, to garnish

1 Preheat the oven to 200°C/400°F/Gas 6. Place the chicken in a blender or food processor and process until finely minced (ground). Transfer to a bowl.

2 Place the mushrooms, garlic, parsley and tarragon in the blender or food processor and process until finely minced.

3 Beat the mushroom mixture into the chicken with the egg, salt and ground black pepper and lemon juice to taste.

4 Bring a large pan of lightly salted water to the boil, add the cannelloni tubes and cook until al dente. Drain well and pat dry on a clean dish towel.

5 Place the filling in a piping bag fitted with a large plain nozzle. Use to fill each tube of cannelloni.

6 Lay the filled cannelloni tightly together in a single layer in a buttered shallow ovenproof dish. Spoon the Tomato Sauce over and sprinkle with Parmesan cheese. Bake in the oven for 30 minutes or until brown and bubbling. Serve the cannelloni garnished with a sprig of parsley.

Energy 703Kcal/2932kJ; Fat 38.9g; Saturated Fat 18g; Carbohydrate 62.3g; Fibre 4.4g

Energy 458Kcal/1938kJ; Fat 10.1g; Saturated Fat 3.7g; Carbohydrate 62.2g; Fibre 3.6g

Fiorentina Pizza

An egg adds the finishing
touch to this spinach pizza;
it's best when the yolk is
still slightly soft.

1 small red onion, thinly sliced
175g/6oz fresh spinach, stalks
   removed
350ml/12fl oz/1½ cups Basic
   Tomato Sauce (see page 13)
freshly grated nutmeg
150g/5oz mozzarella cheese
1 egg
25g/1oz/¼ cup grated Gruyère
   cheese

Serves 3–4
1 quantity Basic Pizza Dough (see
   page 12)
flour, for dusting
45ml/3 tbsp olive oil

1 Roll out the dough on a lightly floured surface to a
25–30cm/10–12cm round and place on a baking sheet.

2 Heat 15ml/1 tbsp of the olive oil. Add the onion and fry over
a low heat, stirring occasionally, for 5 minutes, until soft. Add the
spinach and fry until wilted. Drain any excess liquid.

3 Preheat the oven to 220°C/425°F/Gas 7. Brush the pizza
base with half the remaining olive oil. Spread the Tomato Sauce
evenly over the base, using the back of a spoon, to within
1cm/½in of the edge. Then cover the top of the pizza with the
spinach mixture. Sprinkle over a little freshly grated nutmeg.

4 Slice the mozzarella thinly and arrange it over the spinach.
Drizzle over the remaining oil. Bake for 10 minutes, then
remove from the oven.

5 Make a small well in the centre of the pizza topping and
carefully break the egg into the hole. Sprinkle over the Gruyère.
Return the pizza to the oven for 5–10 minutes, until crisp and
golden. Serve immediately.

Variation
*For an instant meal, buy a ready-prepared pizza base and use
a bottled tomato pasta sauce, flavoured with basil.*

Energy 689Kcal/2886kJ; Fat 37g; Saturated Fat 12.8g; Carbohydrate 67.9g; Fibre 4.9g

Butternut Squash & Sage Pizza

The combination of the
sweet butternut squash,
pungent sage and sharp
goat's cheese works
wonderfully on this pizza.

30ml/2 tbsp olive oil
1 shallot, finely chopped
1 small butternut squash, peeled,
   seeded and cubed
8 fresh sage leaves
350ml/12fl oz/1½ cups Basic
   Tomato Sauce (see page 13)
75g/3oz mozzarella cheese, sliced
75g/3oz firm goat's cheese
salt and ground black pepper

Serves 2–3
1 quantity Basic Pizza Dough (see
   page 12)
15g/½ oz/1 tbsp butter

1 Preheat the oven to 200°C/400°F/Gas 6. Roll out the dough
on a lightly floured surface to a 25–30cm/10–12cm round and
place on a baking sheet.

2 Melt the butter in the oil in a roasting pan. Add the shallot,
squash and half the sage leaves. Toss well to coat all over in oil.
Roast the vegetables for 15–20 minutes, until tender.

3 Increase the oven temperature to 220°C/425°F/Gas 7.
Spread the Tomato Sauce evenly over the surface of the pizza,
to within 1cm/½in of the edge.

4 Spoon the squash mixture evenly over the pizza, arrange the
mozzarella on top and crumble over the goat's cheese.

5 Scatter the remaining sage leaves over the pizza and season
with plenty of salt and pepper. Bake for 15–20 minutes, until the
cheese has melted and the crust is golden. Serve immediately.

Cook's Tip
*For a quick scone base, mix 225g/8oz/2 cups self-raising (self-
rising) flour with a pinch of salt, then rub in 50g/2oz/¼ cup
diced butter. Pour in about 150ml/¼ pint/⅔ cup milk and mix
to a soft dough. Pat out to a 25cm/10in round, top as
suggested above and bake for about 20 minutes.*

Energy 674Kcal/2828kJ; Fat 34.6g; Saturated Fat 13.9g; Carbohydrate 73.8g; Fibre 6g

Quattro Formaggi Pizzettes

As the Italian title suggests, these tasty little pizzas are topped with four different types of cheese and have a very rich flavour.

Serves 4
1 quantity Basic Pizza Dough (see page 12
flour, for dusting

15ml/1 tbsp olive oil
1 small red onion, very thinly sliced
50g/2oz dolcelatte cheese
50g/2oz mozzarella cheese
50g/2oz Gruyère cheese
30ml/2 tbsp freshly grated Parmesan cheese
15ml/1 tbsp chopped fresh thyme
ground black pepper

1 Preheat the oven to 220°C/425°F/Gas 7. Divide the dough into four pieces and roll out each one on a lightly floured surface into a 13cm/5in circle.

2 Place well apart on two greased baking sheets, then push up the dough edges to make a thin rim.

3 Heat the olive oil in a small frying pan. Add the red onion slices and fry over low heat, stirring occasionally, for 4–5 minutes, until softened. Divide them among the pizza bases, then brush over any oil remaining in the pan.

4 Cut the dolcelatte and mozzarella into cubes and scatter over the pizza bases. Grate the Gruyère cheese into a bowl. Add the Parmesan and thyme and mix thoroughly. Sprinkle the mixture over the bases.

5 Grind over plenty of black pepper. Bake for 15–20 minutes, until the crust on each pizza is crisp and golden and the cheese is bubbling. Serve immediately.

> **Variation**
> There's no need to stick slavishly to the suggested cheeses. Any variety that melts readily can be used, but a mixture of soft and hard cheeses gives the best result.

New Potato, Rosemary & Garlic Pizza

New potatoes, smoked mozzarella, rosemary and garlic make the flavour of this pizza unique.

Serves 2–3
1 quantity Basic Pizza Dough (see page 12)
flour, for dusting

350g/12oz new potatoes
45ml/3 tbsp olive oil
2 garlic cloves, crushed
1 red onion, very thinly sliced
150g/5oz/1¼ cups grated smoked mozzarella cheese
10ml/2 tsp chopped rosemary
salt and ground black pepper
30ml/2 tbsp freshly grated Parmesan cheese, to serve

1 Preheat the oven to 220°C/425°F/Gas 7. Roll out the dough on a lightly floured surface to a 25–30cm/10–12cm round and place on a baking sheet.

2 Bring a large pan of lightly salted water to the boil and cook the potatoes for 5 minutes. Drain well. When cool, peel the potatoes and slice them thinly.

3 Heat 30ml/2 tbsp of the oil in a frying pan. Add the sliced potatoes and garlic and fry over medium heat, stirring occasionally, for 5–8 minutes, until tender.

4 Brush the pizza base with the remaining oil. Scatter over the onion, then arrange the potatoes on top. Sprinkle over the mozzarella and rosemary. Grind over plenty of black pepper. Bake for 15–20 minutes, until the crust is crisp and golden. Sprinkle over the grated Parmesan and serve.

> **Cook's Tips**
> • Next time you find yourself with leftover new potatoes, use them to make this tasty pizza.
> • Smoked mozzarella, also known as mozzarella affumicata, is available from supermarkets and delicatessens.

Spring Vegetable & Pine Nut Pizza

With its colourful topping of tender young vegetables, the pizza makes a lovely, fresh tasting meal.

Serves 2–3

1 quantity Basic Pizza Dough (see page 12)
flour, for dusting
45ml/3 tbsp olive oil
1 garlic clove, crushed
4 spring onions (scallions), sliced
2 courgettes (zucchini), sliced
1 leek, thinly sliced
115g/4oz asparagus tips, sliced
15ml/1 tbsp chopped fresh oregano

30ml/2 tbsp pine nuts
50g/2oz/½ cup grated mozzarella cheese
30ml/2 tbsp freshly grated Parmesan cheese
salt and ground black pepper

For the tomato sauce

15ml/1 tbsp olive oil
1 onion, finely chopped
1 garlic clove, crushed
400ml/14oz can chopped Italian plum tomatoes
15ml/1 tbsp tomato purée (paste)
15ml/1 tbsp chopped fresh herbs
pinch of sugar

1 To make the tomato sauce, heat the oil in a pan and fry the onion and garlic over low heat, stirring occasionally, for about 5 minutes, until softened but not browned. Add the remaining ingredients, stir well and simmer for 15–20 minutes, until the mixture is thick and flavoursome.

2 Preheat the oven to 220°C/425°F/Gas 7. Roll out the dough on a lightly floured surface to a 25–30cm/10–12cm round and place on a baking sheet. Brush the pizza base with 15ml/1 tbsp of the olive oil, then spread the tomato sauce evenly over the top to within 1cm/½in of the edge.

3 Heat half the remaining olive oil in a frying pan and fry the garlic, spring onions, courgettes, leek and asparagus, stirring over medium heat for 3–5 minutes.

4 Arrange the vegetables over the tomato sauce, then sprinkle the oregano and pine nuts over the top. Mix the cheeses and sprinkle over. Drizzle with the remaining olive oil and season well. Bake for 15–20 minutes, until crisp and golden.

Roasted Vegetable & Goat's Cheese Pizza

This pizza incorporates the smoky flavours of roasted vegetables and the tangy taste of goat's cheese.

Serves 3

1 aubergine (eggplant), cut into thick chunks
2 courgettes (zucchini), sliced lengthways
1 red (bell) pepper, quartered and seeded

1 yellow (bell) pepper, quartered and seeded
1 small red onion, cut into wedges
90ml/6 tbsp olive oil
1 quantity Basic Pizza Dough (see page 12)
400g/14oz can chopped Italian plum tomatoes, well drained
115g/4oz goat's cheese, cubed
15ml/1 tbsp chopped fresh thyme
ground black pepper
green olive paste, to serve

1 Preheat the oven to 220°C/425°F/Gas 7. Place the vegetables in a roasting pan. Brush with 60ml/4 tbsp of the oil. Roast for 30 minutes, until charred, turning the peppers once. Remove the vegetables but leave the oven on. Put the peppers in a bowl and cover with crumpled kitchen paper. When cool enough to handle, peel off the skins and cut the flesh into thick strips.

2 Roll out the dough on a lightly floured surface to a 25–30cm/ 10–12cm round. Brush the base with half the remaining oil and spread over the drained tomatoes. Arrange the vegetables on top and dot with the goat's cheese. Scatter over the thyme.

3 Drizzle over the remaining oil and season. Bake for 15–20 minutes, until crisp. Spoon the olive paste over to serve.

> **Cook's Tip**
> To make a tasty green olive paste, put 40 pitted green olives and 5ml/1 tsp capers in a food processor. Add four pieces of drained sun-dried tomatoes in oil, 5ml/1 tsp ground almonds, one chopped garlic clove and a pinch of ground cumin. Process briefly, add 60ml/4 tbsp olive oil and process to a paste.

Wild Mushroom Pizzettes

With their delicate earthy flavour, wild mushrooms make a delicious topping for these little pizzas. Serve as an unusual starter or for a stylish light meal.

Serves 4

45ml/3 tbsp olive oil
350g/12oz/4½ cups fresh wild
   mushrooms, sliced
2 shallots, chopped

2 garlic cloves, finely chopped
30ml/2 tbsp chopped fresh mixed
   thyme and flat leaf parsley
1 quantity Basic Pizza Dough (see
   page 12)
flour, for dusting
40g/1½ oz/s ½ cup grated
   Gruyère cheese
30ml/2 tbsp freshly grated
   Parmesan cheese
salt and ground black pepper

1 Preheat the oven to 220°C/425°F/Gas 7. Heat 30ml/2 tbsp of the oil in a frying pan. Add the mushrooms, shallots and garlic and fry over medium heat, stirring occasionally, until all the juices have evaporated.

2 Stir in half the mixed herbs and season to taste with salt and pepper, then set aside to cool.

3 Divide the dough into four pieces and roll out each one on a lightly floured surface to a 13cm/5in circle. Place well apart on two greased baking sheets, then push up the dough edges on each to form a thin rim. Brush the bases with oil and top with the mushroom mixture, leaving a small rim all the way around.

4 Mix the Gruyère and Parmesan cheeses, then sprinkle one-quarter of the mixture over each of the pizzettes. Bake for 15–20 minutes, until crisp and golden. Remove from the oven and scatter over the remaining herbs to serve.

Cook's Tip
Fresh wild mushrooms add a distinctive flavour to the topping, but a mixture of cultivated mushrooms, such as shiitake, oyster and chestnut mushrooms, would do just as well.

Cheese & Pimiento Pizzettes

Great party food with lots of Italian style, these tempting mini pizzas take only minutes to make and will be eaten even quicker.

Makes 24

2 quantities Basic Pizza Dough
   (see page 12)

60ml/4 tbsp olive oil
30ml/2 tbsp olive paste
175g/6oz goat's cheese
1 large canned or bottled
   pimiento, drained
30ml/2 tbsp chopped fresh thyme
30ml/2 tbsp pine nuts
ground black pepper
fresh thyme sprigs, to garnish

1 Preheat the oven to 220°C/425°F/Gas 7. Divide the pizza dough into 24 pieces and roll out each one on a lightly floured surface to a small oval, about 3mm/⅛in thick.

2 Place well apart on greased baking sheets and prick all over with a fork. Brush with 30ml/2 tbsp of the oil.

3 Spread a thin layer of the olive paste on each oval and crumble over the feta. Cut the pimiento into thin strips and pile on top of the cheese.

4 Sprinkle each pizzette with thyme and pine nuts. Drizzle over the remaining oil and grind over plenty of black pepper. Bake for 10–15 minutes, until crisp and golden. Garnish with thyme sprigs and serve immediately.

Cook's Tip
Use a goat's cheese with a firm texture, suitable for crumbling.

Variations
• *Feta makes an interesting change to goat's cheese.*
• *Either black or green olive paste can be used for this recipe. Tapenade is also widely available from supermarkets and delicatessens and makes a good substitute.*

Calzone

A calzone is like a folded pizza, with the dough wrapped around a cheese and vegetable filling. Here the traditional tomato and garlic filling is enlivened with chunks of sweet melting cheese, olives and sliced peppery sausage.

Makes 4

30ml/2 tbsp extra virgin olive oil
1 small red onion, thinly sliced
2 garlic cloves, crushed

400g/14oz can chopped Italian plum tomatoes
50g/2oz sliced pepperoni or chorizo sausage
50g/2oz/1/2 cup pitted black olives
1 quantity Basic Pizza Dough (see page 12)
flour, for dusting
200g/7oz mozzarella or other semi-soft cheese, diced
5ml/1 tsp dried oregano
salt and ground black pepper
oregano sprigs, to garnish

1 Heat the oil in a frying pan and fry the sliced onion and crushed garlic for 5 minutes. Add the chopped tomatoes and cook for a further 5 minutes, or until slightly reduced. Add the sliced pepperoni and pitted black olives. Season with plenty of salt and pepper.

2 Divide the dough into four portions. Roll out each portion on a lightly flour surface into a round measuring about 20cm/8in. Preheat the oven to 200°C/400°F/Gas 6. Lightly grease two baking sheets.

3 Spread the tomato filling on half of each dough circle, leaving a margin around the edge. Scatter the mozzarella cheese on top. Sprinkle the filling with the dried oregano.

4 Dampen the edges of the dough circle with cold water. Fold the dough in half and press the edges together with your fingers to seal securely.

5 Place two calzones on each baking sheet. Bake for 12–15 minutes, until the dough is risen and golden. Cool for 2 minutes, then loosen from the sheet with a palette knife and transfer to individual serving plates. Serve at once, garnished with oregano.

Energy 625Kcal/2626kJ; Fat 28.2g; Saturated Fat 9.8g; Carbohydrate 75g; Fibre 4g

Sun-dried Tomato Calzone

Hot things up with a few more red chilli flakes.

Serves 2

3 shallots, chopped
30ml/2 tbsp olive oil
4 baby aubergines (eggplant), cubed
1 garlic clove, chopped

50g/2oz/1/3 cup sun-dried tomatoes in oil, drained
1.5ml/1/4 tsp dried red chilli flakes
10ml/2 tsp chopped fresh thyme
75g/3oz mozzarella cheese
1/2 quantity Basic Pizza Dough (see page 12)
salt and ground black pepper
flour, for dusting

1 Preheat the oven to 220°C/425°F/Gas 7. Fry the shallots in oil until soft. Add the aubergines, garlic, tomatoes, chilli, thyme and seasoning. Cook for 5 minutes. Divide the dough in half and roll out each piece on a lightly floured surface to an 18cm/7in round.

2 Spread the aubergine mixture over half of each round, leaving a 2.5cm/1in border, then scatter the diced mozzarella on top. Dampen the edges with water, then fold over the dough to enclose the filling. Press the edges together. Place on greased baking sheets. Brush with oil and make a small hole in the top of each calzone. Bake for 15–20 minutes, until golden.

Margherita Pizza

This is a quick version of an ever-popular classic.

Serves 2

half a 300g/11oz packet pizza base mix

15ml/1 tbsp herb-infused olive oil
45ml/3 tbsp ready-made tomato and basil sauce
150g/5oz mozzarella, sliced
salt and ground black pepper

1 Make the pizza base mix following the packet instructions. Preheat the oven as instructed. Brush the base with a little of the oil and spread the tomato and basil sauce over the top.

2 Top with the mozzarella and bake for 25–30 minutes, or until golden. Drizzle with the remaining oil, season and serve.

Top Energy 732Kcal/3071kJ; Fat 32g; Saturated Fat 8.7g; Carbohydrate 97.4g; Fibre 7.8g
Above Energy 349Kcal/1466kJ; Fat 14.6g; Saturated Fat 6g; Carbohydrate 44g; Fibre 1.7g

Mushroom & Pesto Pizza

Capture all the wonderful flavours of home-baked Italian pizza with this recipe.

Serves 4
350g/12oz/3 cups strong white
  bread flour
1.5ml/¼ tsp salt
15g/½oz easy-blend (rapid-rise)
  dried yeast
15ml/1 tbsp olive oil
150ml/¼ pint warm water

For the topping
50g/2oz dried porcini mushrooms
25g/1oz/¾ cup fresh basil
25g/1oz/⅓ cup pine nuts
40g/1½oz Parmesan cheese,
  thinly sliced
105ml/7 tbsp olive oil
2 onions, thinly sliced
225g/8oz chestnut mushrooms,
  sliced
salt and ground black pepper

1 To make the pizza base, put the flour in a bowl with the salt, dried yeast and olive oil. Add 250ml/8fl oz/1 cup hand-hot water and mix to a dough using a round-bladed knife.

2 Turn on to a work surface and knead for 5 minutes until smooth. Place in a clean bowl, cover with clear film (plastic wrap) and leave in a warm place until doubled in bulk.

3 Meanwhile, make the topping. Soak the dried mushrooms in hot water for 20 minutes. Place the basil, pine nuts, Parmesan and 75ml/5 tbsp of the olive oil in a blender or food processor and process to make a smooth paste. Set the paste aside.

4 Fry the onions in the remaining olive oil for 3–4 minutes, until beginning to colour. Add the chestnut mushrooms and fry for 2 minutes. Stir in the drained porcini mushrooms and season lightly with salt and pepper.

5 Preheat the oven to 220°C/425°F/Gas 7. Lightly grease a large baking sheet. Turn the pizza dough on to a floured surface and roll out to a 30cm/12in round. Place on the baking sheet.

6 Spread the basil and pine nut mixture to within 1cm/½in of the edges. Spread the mushroom mixture on top. Bake the pizza for 35–40 minutes, until risen and golden.

Ricotta & Fontina Pizzas

The combination of delicate mushrooms and a delicious creamy cheese makes a winning topping for pizza.

Serves 4
400g/14oz can chopped Italian
  plum tomatoes
150ml/¼ pint/⅔ cup passata
5ml/1 tsp dried oregano
1 bay leaf
10ml/2 tsp malt vinegar
2 large garlic cloves, chopped
30ml/2 tbsp olive oil, plus extra
  for brushing

350g/12oz/4 cups mixed
  mushrooms (chestnut, flat or
  button), sliced
1 quantity Basic Pizza Dough (see
  page 12)
flour, for dusting
30ml/2 tbsp chopped fresh
  oregano, plus whole leaves, to
  garnish
250g/9oz/generous 1 cup
  ricotta cheese
225g/8oz Fontina cheese, sliced
salt and ground black pepper

1 To make the topping, place the tomatoes, passata, herbs, vinegar and half of the garlic in a pan, cover and bring to the boil. Lower the heat, remove the lid and simmer for 20 minutes, stirring occasionally, until reduced.

3 Heat the oil in a frying pan. Add the mushrooms and remaining garlic. Season with salt and pepper to taste. Cook, stirring, for about 5 minutes, or until the mushrooms are tender. Set aside.

4 Preheat the oven to 220°C/425°F/Gas 7. Divide the pizza dough into four equal pieces. Roll out each piece on a lightly floured surface to a 25cm/10in round and place on four lightly oiled baking sheets.

5 Spoon the tomato sauce over each dough round and spread evenly over the surface to within 1cm/½in of the edge. Brush the edge with a little olive oil. Top the sauce with the mushrooms, fresh oregano and ricotta and Fontina cheeses.

6 Bake for about 15 minutes, until golden brown and crisp. Scatter the oregano leaves over the top.

Energy 862Kcal/3617kJ; Fat 40.7g; Saturated Fat 19.9g; Carbohydrate 94g; Fibre 5.7g

Energy 631Kcal/2642kJ; Fat 31.3g; Saturated Fat 5.7g; Carbohydrate 76.6g; Fibre 5.3g

Peppery Tomato Pizza

Peppery rocket and aromatic fresh basil add colour and flavour to this crisp pizza, a perfect addition to any picnic.

Serves 2

225g/8oz/2 cups strong white bread flour
5ml/1 tsp salt
2.5ml/½ tsp easy-blend (rapid-rise) dried yeast
30ml/2 tbsp olive oil
150ml/¼ pint/⅔ cup warm water

For the topping
10ml/2 tsp olive oil
1 garlic clove, crushed
150g/5oz canned chopped Italian plum tomatoes
2.5ml/½ tsp caster (superfine) sugar
30ml/2 tbsp torn fresh basil
2 tomatoes, seeded and chopped
150g/5oz mozzarella cheese, sliced
20g/¾oz rocket (arugula) leaves
salt and ground black pepper

1 To make the pizza base, place the dry ingredients in a bowl. Add the oil and the warm water. Mix to form a soft dough. Turn out the dough and knead until it is smooth and elastic. Place in an oiled bowl and cover. Leave in a warm place for 45 minutes, or until doubled in bulk.

2 Preheat the oven to 220°C/425°F/Gas 7. To make the topping, heat the oil in a frying pan and fry the garlic for 1 minute. Add the canned tomatoes and sugar and cook for 10 minutes, stirring occasionally.

3 Knead the risen dough lightly, then roll out to form a rough 30cm/12in round. Place on a lightly oiled baking sheet and push up the edges of the dough to form a shallow, even rim.

4 Season the tomato mixture and stir in the basil. Spoon on to the pizza base, then top with the fresh tomatoes. Arrange the mozzarella slices on top of the tomato mixture. Season with salt and pepper and drizzle with a little olive oil.

5 Bake for 10–12 minutes, until crisp and golden. Scatter the rocket leaves over the pizza just before serving.

Grilled Vegetable Pizza

Grilled vegetables are good at any time, but are particularly tasty when teamed with melted cheese.

Serves 4

1 courgette (zucchini), sliced
2 baby aubergines (eggplants) or 1 small aubergine, sliced
30ml/2 tbsp olive oil
1 yellow (bell) pepper, seeded and thickly sliced
115g/4oz/1 cup cornmeal
50g/2oz/½ cup potato flour

50g/2oz/½ cup soya flour
5ml/1 tsp baking powder
2.5ml/½ tsp salt
50g/2oz/¼ cup butter or soft margarine
about 105ml/7 tbsp milk
4 plum tomatoes, peeled and chopped
30ml/2 tbsp chopped fresh basil
115g/4oz mozzarella cheese, sliced
salt and ground black pepper
fresh basil leaves, to garnish

1 Preheat the grill (broiler). Brush the sliced courgette and aubergine slices with a little oil and place on a grill rack with the pepper slices. Cook under the grill, until lightly browned, turning once.

2 Meanwhile, preheat the oven to 200°C/400°F/Gas 6. Place the cornmeal, potato flour, soya flour, baking powder and salt in a mixing bowl and stir to mix. Lightly rub in the butter or margarine until the mixture resembles coarse breadcrumbs. Stir in enough of the milk to make a soft but not sticky dough.

3 Place the dough on a sheet of non-stick baking parchment on a baking sheet and roll or press it out to form a 25cm/10in round, pushing up the edges to form a shallow, even rim.

4 Brush the pizza dough with any remaining oil, then spread the chopped tomatoes over the dough. Sprinkle with the chopped basil and season with salt and pepper. Arrange the grilled (broiled) vegetables over the tomatoes and top with the sliced mozzarella cheese.

5 Bake for 25–30 minutes, until crisp and golden brown. Garnish the pizza with fresh basil and serve immediately.

Energy 735Kcal/3087kJ; Fat 31.3g; Saturated Fat 12.7g; Carbohydrate 93g; Fibre 5.5g

Energy 400Kcal/1666kJ; Fat 23.9g; Saturated Fat 5.3g; Carbohydrate 34.6g; Fibre 4.4g

Radicchio Pizza

With its quick-to-make scone dough base, this tasty vegetable pizza is very easy to prepare.

Serves 2

225g/8oz/2 cups self-raising (self-rising) flour
2.5ml/½ tsp salt
50g/2oz/¼ cup butter
about 120ml/4fl oz/½ cup milk

For the topping
400ml/14fl oz/1⅔ cups passata
pinch of dried basil

2 garlic cloves, crushed
25ml/1½ tbsp olive oil, plus extra for dipping
2 leeks, sliced
100g/3½oz radicchio, roughly chopped
20g/¾oz Parmesan cheese, grated
115g/4oz mozzarella cheese, sliced
10–12 pitted black olives
salt and ground black pepper
fresh basil leaves, to garnish

1 Preheat the oven to 220°C/425°F/Gas 7 and grease a baking sheet. Mix the flour and salt in a bowl, rub in the butter and stir in enough milk to make a soft dough. Roll it out on a lightly floured surface to a 25–28cm/10–11in round. Place on the baking sheet.

2 Mix the passata, basil and half of the garlic in a small pan. Season with salt and pepper, then simmer over medium heat until the mixture is thick and has reduced by about half.

3 Heat the olive oil in a large frying pan and fry the leeks and remaining garlic for 4–5 minutes, until slightly softened. Add the radicchio and cook, stirring continuously for a few minutes, then cover and simmer gently for about 5–10 minutes. Stir in the Parmesan cheese and season to taste.

4 Cover the dough base with the passata mixture and then spoon the leek and radicchio mixture on top. Arrange the mozzarella slices on top and scatter with the black olives.

5 Dip a few basil leaves in olive oil, arrange on top and bake the pizza for 15–20 minutes, until the top is golden brown.

Onion Focaccia

This pizza-like flat bread is characterized by its soft dimpled surface, sometimes dredged simply with coarse salt, or with onions, herbs or olives. It tastes delicious served warm with soup.

Makes 2

675g/1½lb/6 cups strong plain bread flour
2.5ml/½ tsp salt

2.5ml/½ tsp caster (superfine) sugar
15ml/1 tbsp easy-blend (rapid-rise) dried yeast
60ml/4 tbsp extra virgin olive oil
450ml/¾ pint/scant 2 cups warm water

To finish
2 red onions, thinly sliced
45ml/3 tbsp extra virgin olive oil
15ml/1 tbsp coarse salt

1 Sift the flour, salt and sugar into a large bowl. Stir in the yeast, oil and water and mix to a dough using a round-bladed knife. (Add a little extra water if the dough is dry.)

2 Turn out on to a lightly floured surface and knead for about 10 minutes, until smooth and elastic. Put the dough in a clean, lightly oiled bowl and cover with clear film (plastic wrap). Leave to rise in a warm place, until doubled in bulk.

3 Place two 25cm/10in plain metal flan rings on baking sheets. Oil the insides of the rings and the baking sheets.

4 Preheat the oven to 200°C/400°F/Gas 6. Halve the dough and roll each piece to a 25cm/10in round. Press into the flan rings, cover with a dampened dish cloth and leave for 30 minutes to rise.

5 Make deep holes, about 2.5cm/1in apart, in the dough. Cover and leave for a further 20 minutes.

6 To finish, scatter with the onions and drizzle over the oil. Sprinkle with the salt, then a little cold water, to stop a crust from forming. Bake the focaccia for about 25 minutes, lightly sprinkling with water again during cooking. Cool on a wire rack before serving.

Energy 970Kcal/4066kJ; Fat 52.4g; Saturated Fat 26g; Carbohydrate 99.4g; Fibre 8.5g

Energy 1508Kcal/6362kJ; Fat 42.9g; Saturated Fat 6.2g; Carbohydrate 264.6g; Fibre 10.9g

Mediterranean Pizza

The combination of
favourite Mediterranean
ingredients makes a delicious
modern pizza topping. Serve
with a mixed green salad for
an easy lunch dish.

Serves 4
12 sun-dried tomatoes, dry or in
    oil, drained
1 quantity Basic Pizza Dough (see
    page 12)

flour, for dusting
350g/12oz/1¾ cups goat's
    cheese, sliced as thinly as
    possible
30ml/2 tbsp capers in brine or
    salt, rinsed
10 fresh basil leaves
60ml/4 tbsp olive oil
salt and ground black pepper

1 Preheat the oven to 240°C/475°F/Gas 9. To prepare the
topping, if using dry sun-dried tomatoes, place in a small bowl,
cover with hot water and leave to soak for 15 minutes. Drain
and cut into thin slices. If using sun-dried tomatoes in oil, drain
and slice thinly.

2 Roll out the pizza dough to a 30cm/12in round on a floured
surface. Place on a large baking sheet.

3 Arrange the cheese on the pizza base, to within 1cm/½in of
the edge. Dot the pizza with the tomato pieces.

4 Sprinkle with the capers and basil leaves. Allow to rise for
10 minutes before baking.

5 Sprinkle the pizza with salt, pepper and olive oil. Place the
pizza in the oven. Bake for about 20–30 minutes, or until the
crust is golden.

> **Cook's Tips**
> • *The soaking water from the sun-dried tomatoes can be saved
> for adding to a pasta sauce or soup.*
> • *For a more moist pizza, spread a thin layer of home-made
> tomato sauce on the base before add the topping ingredients.*

Energy 489Kcal/2046kJ; Fat 26.9g; Saturated Fat 11.6g; Carbohydrate 46g; Fibre 2.3g

Vegetable Wholemeal Pizza

For a satisfying meal, serve
this pizza with a mixed bean
salad and crusty bread.

Serves 2
10ml/2 tsp olive oil
30ml/2 tbsp tomato purée
    (paste)
10ml/2 tsp dried basil
1 onion, sliced
1 garlic clove, finely chopped
2 small courgettes (zucchini),
    sliced
115g/4oz mushrooms, sliced
115g/4oz/⅔ cup canned or
    frozen sweetcorn

4 plum tomatoes, sliced
50g/2oz/1½ cup grated Red
    Leicester cheese
50g/2oz mozzarella cheese,
    grated
salt and ground black pepper
basil sprigs, to garnish

For the pizza base
225g/8oz/2 cups plain (all-
    purpose) wholemeal (whole-
    wheat) flour
pinch of salt
10ml/2 tsp baking powder
50g/2oz/¼ cup margarine
about 150ml/¼ pint/⅔ cup milk

1 Preheat the oven to 220°C/425°F/Gas 7. Grease a baking
sheet with a little oil. To make the pizza base, put the flour, salt
and baking powder in a bowl and rub the margarine lightly into
the flour until it resembles breadcrumbs. Add enough milk to
form a soft dough and knead. Roll out to a 25cm/10in round.

2 Place the dough on the prepared baking sheet, then push up
the edges to make a thin rim. Spread the tomato purée over
the base and sprinkle the basil on top.

3 Heat the oil in a frying pan, add the onion, garlic, courgettes
and mushrooms, and cook gently for 10 minutes, stirring
occasionally. Spread the mixture over the pizza base, sprinkle
the corn on top and season with salt and pepper. Arrange the
tomato slices on top. Mix together the cheeses and sprinkle
over the pizza. Bake for 25–30 minutes, until cooked.

Pizza with Onions & Olives

The sweetness of slow-
cooked onions contrasts
nicely with the tangy olives.

Serves 4
90ml/6 tbsp olive oil
4 onions, finely sliced
salt and ground black pepper

1 quantity Basic Pizza Dough (see
    page 12), rolled out to a
    30cm/12in round
350g/12oz/1¾ cups diced
    mozzarella cheese
32 black olives, pitted and halved
45ml/3 tbsp chopped fresh parsley

1 Preheat the oven to 240°C/475°F/Gas 9. Heat half the olive
oil in a large frying pan. Add the sliced onions and cook over
low heat for 12–15 minutes, until soft and just beginning to turn
brown. Season with salt and pepper and remove from the heat.

2 Spread the onions over the prepared pizza dough to within
1cm/½in of the edge. Sprinkle with the mozzarella. Dot with
the olives. Sprinkle with parsley and the remaining olive oil and
bake for 15–20 minutes, or until the crust is golden brown and
the cheese is bubbling.

Top Energy 913Kcal/3833kJ; Fat 42.6g; Saturated Fat 11g; Carbohydrate 102g; Fibre 15.4g
Above Energy 551Kcal/2300kJ; Fat 30.8g; Saturated Fat 8g; Carbohydrate 57g; Fibre 4.8g

Classic Marinara Pizza

The combination of simple ingredients gives this pizza its truly Italian flavour.

Serves 2
60ml/4 tbsp extra virgin olive oil or sunflower oil
675g/1½lb plum tomatoes, peeled, seeded and chopped
4 garlic cloves, cut into slivers
15ml/1 tbsp chopped oregano
salt and ground black pepper

For the pizza base
225g/8oz/2 cups plain (all-purpose) white flour
pinch of salt
10ml/2 tsp baking powder
50g/2oz/¼ cup margarine
about 150ml/¼ pint/⅔ cup milk

1 Preheat the oven to 220°C/425°F/Gas 7. Use non-stick baking parchment to line a baking sheet. To make the base, sieve the flour, salt and baking powder in a bowl and rub the margarine lightly into the flour until it resembles breadcrumbs.

2 Pour in enough milk to form a soft dough and knead. Roll the dough out to a circle about 25cm/10in in diameter. Place the dough on the prepared baking sheet, then push up the dough edges to make a thin rim.

3 Heat 30ml/2 tbsp of the oil in a pan. Add the tomatoes and cook, stirring for about 5 minutes, until soft. Place the tomatoes in a sieve (strainer) over a bowl and leave to drain for 5 minutes. Discard the juice in the bowl, then purée the flesh in the sieve.

4 Brush the pizza base with half the remaining oil. Spoon over the tomatoes and sprinkle with garlic and oregano. Drizzle over the remaining oil and season. Bake for 15–20 minutes in the oven, until the pizza is crisp and golden. Serve immediately.

Pizza with Four Cheeses

Any combination of cheeses can be used, but they must be different in character.

Serves 4
1 quantity Basic Pizza Dough (see page 12), rolled out
75g/3oz/½ cup Gorgonzola or other blue cheese, thinly sliced
75g/3oz/½ cup diced mozzarella cheese
75g/3oz/½ cup goat's cheese, thinly sliced
7g/3oz/½ cup grated mature (sharp) Cheddar cheese
4 fresh sage leaves, torn into pieces, or 45ml/3tbsp chopped fresh parsley
salt and ground black pepper
45ml/3 tbsp olive oil

1 Preheat the oven to 240°C/475°F/Gas 9. Arrange the Gorgonzola on one quarter of the pizza and the mozzarella on another, leaving the edge free.

2 Arrange the goat's and Cheddar cheeses on the remaining two quarters.

3 Sprinkle with the herbs, salt and pepper, and olive oil. Bake for about 15–20 minutes, or until the crust is golden brown and the cheeses are bubbling.

Pizza with Sausage

In unfussy Italian style, sausage meat, tomatoes and mozzarella are simply flavoured with oregano to make a mouth-watering pizza topping.

Serves 4
450g/1lb drained, peeled plum tomatoes, fresh or canned
225g/8oz/1½ cups Italian pure sausage meat
1 quantity Basic Pizza Dough (see page 12)
flour, for dusting
350g/12oz/1¾ cups diced mozzarella cheese
5ml/1 tsp oregano leaves, fresh or dried
45ml/3 tbsp olive oil
salt and ground black pepper

1 Preheat the oven to 240°C/475°F/Gas 9. Strain the tomatoes through the medium holes of a food mill or sieve (strainer) placed over a bowl, scraping in all the pulp.

2 Snip the end off the sausage skin and squeeze out the sausage meat.

2 Roll out the dough on a lightly floured surface to a 30cm/12in round. Place on a baking sheet.

3 Spread some of the puréed tomatoes on the prepared pizza dough, leaving the rim uncovered. Sprinkle evenly with the mozzarella. Add the sausage meat in small lumps.

4 Sprinkle with oregano, salt and pepper, and olive oil. Bake for about 15–20 minutes, or until the crust is golden brown and the cheese is bubbling.

> **Cook's Tip**
> For the best flavour, try to find salsiccia (fresh Italian-style sausage) from Italian delicatessens. Salsiccia puro suino is the best. If you have difficulty finding salsiccia, you can substitute good-quality sausages with a high meat content; ones flavoured with herbs or spices will add zing to the topping.

Top Energy 429Kcal/1798kJ; Fat 23g; Saturated Fat 2.3g; Carbohydrate 50.8g; Fibre 3.4g
Above Energy 546Kcal/2283kJ; Fat 32g; Saturated Fat 15g; Carbohydrate 43.7g; Fibre 1.6g

Energy 632Kcal/2641kJ; Fat 37.9g; Saturated Fat 14g; Carbohydrate 55.4g; Fibre 3.1g

Pumpkin & Pistachio Risotto

An elegant combination of creamy, golden rice and orange pumpkin, this stunning risotto is Italian cooking at its best.

Serves 4

1.2 litres/2 pints/5 cups vegetable stock or water
generous pinch of saffron threads
30ml/2 tbsp olive oil
1 onion, chopped
2 garlic cloves, crushed
900g/2lb pumpkin, peeled, seeded and cut into 2cm/³⁄₄in cubes

400g/14oz/2 cups risotto rice
200ml/7fl oz/scant 1 cup dry white wine
30ml/2 tbsp freshly grated Parmesan cheese
50g/2oz/¹⁄₂ cup pistachios, coarsely chopped
45ml/3 tbsp chopped fresh marjoram or oregano, plus leaves to garnish
salt, freshly grated nutmeg and ground black pepper

1 Bring the stock or water to the boil and reduce to a low simmer. Ladle a little of it into a small bowl. Add the saffron threads and leave to infuse.

2 Heat the oil in a large, heavy pan or deep frying pan. Add the onion and garlic and cook gently for about 5 minutes, until softened. Add the pumpkin cubes and rice and stir to coat everything in oil. Cook for a few more minutes, until the rice looks transparent.

3 Pour in the wine and allow it to bubble hard. When it has been absorbed, add a quarter of the hot stock or water and the saffron liquid. Stir until all the liquid has been absorbed. Gradually add the remaining stock or water, a little at a time, allowing the rice to absorb the liquid before adding more, and stirring constantly. After 20–30 minutes the rice should be golden yellow, creamy and *al dente*.

4 Stir in the Parmesan cheese, cover the pan and leave to stand for 5 minutes. To finish, stir in the pistachios and marjoram or oregano. Season to taste with a little salt, nutmeg and pepper, and scatter over a few marjoram or oregano leaves.

Energy 589Kcal/2458kJ; Fat 16g; Saturated Fat 3.5g; Carbohydrate 87.6g; Fibre 3.9g

Risotto with Parmesan

This traditional risotto is simply flavoured with grated Parmesan cheese and golden, fried chopped onion.

Serves 3–4

1 litre/1³⁄₄ pints/4 cups beef, chicken or vegetable stock
65g/2¹⁄₂oz/5 tbsp butter

1 small onion, finely chopped
275g/10oz/1¹⁄₂ cups risotto rice
120ml/4fl oz/¹⁄₂ cup dry white wine
75g/3oz/1 cup freshly grated Parmesan cheese, plus extra to garnish
salt and ground black pepper
basil leaves, to garnish

1 Heat the stock in a pan and leave to simmer until needed.

2 Melt two-thirds of the butter in a large heavy pan or deep frying pan. Stir in the chopped onion and cook gently until softened and golden.

3 Add the risotto rice and stir to coat the grains with butter. After 1–2 minutes, pour in the white wine. Increase the heat slightly and cook until the wine evaporates. Add one small ladleful of the hot stock. Cook until the stock has been absorbed, stirring constantly.

4 Gradually add the remaining stock, a little at a time, allowing the rice to absorb the liquid before adding more, and stirring constantly. After 20–30 minutes the rice should be creamy and *al dente*. Season to taste.

5 Remove the pan from the heat. Stir in the remaining butter and the Parmesan cheese. Taste again for seasoning. Allow the risotto to stand for 3–4 minutes before serving, garnished with basil leaves and shavings of Parmesan, if you like.

> **Cook's Tip**
> If you run out of stock when cooking the risotto, just continue using hot water. Do not worry if the rice is done before all the stock is used up: only add as much as you need.

Energy 479Kcal/1991kJ; Fat 19.9g; Saturated Fat 12.3g; Carbohydrate 56.3g; Fibre 0.2g

Rosemary Risotto with Borlotti Beans

This is a classic risotto with a subtle and complex taste, from the heady flavours of rosemary to the savoury beans and the fruity-sweet flavours of mascarpone and Parmesan.

Serves 3–4

400g/14oz can borlotti beans
30ml/2 tbsp olive oil
1 onion, chopped
2 garlic cloves, crushed

275g/10oz/1½ cups risotto rice
175ml/6fl oz/¾ cup dry
    white wine
900ml–1 litre/1½–1¾ pints/
    3¾–4 cups simmering
    vegetable or chicken stock
60ml/4 tbsp mascarpone cheese
65g/2½oz/scant 1 cup freshly
    grated Parmesan cheese, plus
    extra, to serve (optional)
5ml/1 tsp chopped fresh
    rosemary
salt and ground black pepper

1 Drain the beans, rinse under cold water and drain again. Purée about two-thirds of the beans fairly coarsely in a food processor or blender. Set the remaining beans aside.

2 Heat the olive oil in a large pan and gently fry the onion and garlic for 6–8 minutes, until very soft. Add the rice and cook over a medium heat for a few minutes, stirring constantly, until the grains are thoroughly coated in oil and are slightly translucent.

3 Pour in the wine. Cook over medium heat for 2–3 minutes, stirring all the time, until the wine has been absorbed. Add the stock gradually, a ladleful at a time, allowing the rice to absorb the liquid before adding more, and continuing to stir.

4 When the rice is three-quarters cooked, stir in the bean purée. Continue to cook the risotto, adding the remaining stock, until it is creamy and the rice is *al dente*. Add the reserved beans, with the mascarpone, Parmesan and rosemary, then season to taste. Stir, then cover and leave to stand for about 5 minutes so that the rice completes cooking and absorbs all the flavours. Serve with extra Parmesan, if you like.

Risotto with Ricotta & Basil

This is a well-flavoured risotto, which benefits from the distinct pungency of basil, mellowed with smooth, mild ricotta.

Serves 3–4

1 litre/1¾ pints/4 cups chicken
    or vegetable stock
45ml/3 tbsp olive oil

1 onion, finely chopped
275g/10oz/1½ cups risotto rice
175g/6oz/¾ cup ricotta cheese
50g/2oz/generous 1 cup fresh
    basil leaves, finely chopped, plus
    extra to garnish
75g/3oz/1 cup freshly grated
    Parmesan cheese
salt and ground black pepper

1 Heat the stock in a pan and leave to simmer. Heat the oil in a large heavy pan and fry the onion over gentle heat until soft.

2 Stir in the rice. Cook for a few minutes, stirring, until the rice is coated with oil and is slightly translucent.

3 Pour in about a quarter of the stock. Cook, stirring, until all the stock has been absorbed. Gradually add the remaining stock, a ladleful at a time, allowing the rice to absorb the liquid before adding more, and stirring constantly. After 20–30 minutes the rice should be creamy and *al dente*. Season to taste with salt and pepper.

4 Spoon the ricotta into a bowl and break it up a little with a fork. Stir into the risotto along with the basil and Parmesan. Taste and adjust the seasoning, then cover and allow to stand for 2–3 minutes before serving, garnished with basil leaves.

> **Cook's Tip**
> *The short grain rice that grows in the Po Valley in Piedmont is ideal for the slow cooking method used in risottos. The grains are able to absorb all the cooking liquid, acquiring a creamy smoothness while at the same time retaining their shape. The three types of risotto rice to look out for in Italian delicatessens are Carnaroli, Arborio and Vialone Nano.*

Porcini & Parmesan Risotto

This variation on the classic Risotto alla Milanese includes saffron, porcini mushrooms and Parmesan.

Serves 4

15g/¹⁄₂oz/2 tbsp dried porcini mushrooms
150ml/¹⁄₄ pint/²⁄₃ cup warm water
1 litre/1³⁄₄ pints/4 cups vegetable stock
generous pinch of saffron threads

30ml/2 tbsp olive oil
1 onion, finely chopped
1 garlic clove, crushed
350g/12oz/1³⁄₄ cups risotto rice
150ml/¹⁄₄ pint/²⁄₃ cup dry white wine
25g/1oz/2 tbsp butter
50g/2oz/²⁄₃ cup freshly grated Parmesan cheese
salt and ground black pepper
pink and yellow oyster mushrooms, to serve (optional)

1 Put the dried porcini in a bowl and pour over the warm water. Leave the mushrooms to soak for 20 minutes, then lift out with a slotted spoon. Filter the soaking water through a layer of kitchen paper in a sieve (strainer), then place it in a pan with the stock. Bring the liquid to a gentle simmer.

2 Spoon about 45ml/3 tbsp of the hot stock into a cup and stir in the saffron strands. Set aside. Finely chop the porcini. Heat the oil in a separate pan and lightly sauté the onion, garlic and mushrooms for 5 minutes. Gradually add the rice, stirring to coat the grains in oil. Cook for 2 minutes, stirring constantly. Season with salt and pepper.

3 Pour in the white wine. Cook, stirring, until it has been absorbed, then ladle in a quarter of the stock. Cook, stirring, until the stock has been absorbed. Gradually add the remaining stock, a little at a time, allowing the rice to absorb the liquid before adding more, and stirring constantly.

4 After about 20 minutes, when all the stock has been absorbed and the rice is cooked but still *al dente*, stir in the butter, saffron water (with the strands) and half the Parmesan. Serve, sprinkled with the remaining Parmesan. Garnish with pink and yellow oyster mushrooms, if you like.

Risotto with Four Vegetables

This is one of the prettiest risottos; fresh green vegetables highlight the sweet yellow squash.

Serves 3–4

115g/4oz/1 cup shelled fresh peas
115g/4oz/1 cup green beans, cut into short lengths
1 litre/1³⁄₄ pints/4 cups chicken stock

30ml/2 tbsp olive oil
75g/3oz/6 tbsp butter
1 acorn squash, skin and seeds removed, cut into matchsticks
1 onion, finely chopped
275g/10oz/1¹⁄₂ cups risotto rice
120ml/4fl oz/¹⁄₂ cup Italian dry white vermouth
75g/3oz/1 cup freshly grated Parmesan cheese
salt and ground black pepper

1 Bring a pan of lightly salted water to the boil, add the peas and beans and cook for 2–3 minutes, until the vegetables are just tender. Drain, refresh under cold running water, drain again and set aside. Bring the stock to a simmer in a pan.

2 Heat the oil with 25g/1oz/2 tbsp of the butter in a medium pan until foaming. Add the squash and cook gently for 2–3 minutes or until just softened. Remove with a slotted spoon and set aside. Add the onion to the pan and cook gently for about 3 minutes, stirring frequently, until softened.

3 Stir in the rice until the grains start to swell and burst, then add the vermouth. Stir until the vermouth stops sizzling and most of it has been absorbed by the rice, then add a few ladlefuls of the stock, with salt and pepper to taste. Stir over low heat, until the stock has been absorbed.

4 Gradually add the remaining stock, a few ladlefuls at a time, allowing the rice to absorb the liquid before adding more, and stirring all the time. After about 20 minutes, when all the stock has been absorbed and the rice is cooked and creamy but still *al dente*, gently stir in the vegetables, the remaining butter and about half the grated Parmesan. Heat through, then taste for seasoning and serve with the remaining grated Parmesan served separately.

Energy 497Kcal/2069kJ; Fat 15.2g; Saturated Fat 6.6g; Carbohydrate 71.3g; Fibre 0.2g

Energy 624Kcal/2611kJ; Fat 31.2g; Saturated Fat 14.6g; Carbohydrate 63.9g; Fibre 3.5g

Green Risotto

You could use spinach-flavoured risotto rice to give this stunning dish even greater dramatic impact. However, white risotto rice makes a pretty contrast to the spinach.

Serves 3–4

1 litre/1¾ pints/4 cups chicken stock
30ml/2 tbsp olive oil

1 onion, finely chopped
275g/10oz/1½ cups risotto rice
75ml/5 tbsp white wine
about 400g/14oz tender baby spinach leaves
15ml/1 tbsp chopped fresh basil
5ml/1 tsp chopped fresh mint
60ml/4 tbsp freshly grated Parmesan cheese
salt and ground black pepper
knob of butter or more grated Parmesan cheese, to serve

1 Heat the stock in a pan and leave to simmer until needed.

2 Heat the oil in a heavy pan and fry the onion for 3–4 minutes until soft. Add the rice and stir to coat each grain. Pour in the white wine. Cook, stirring, until it has been absorbed.

3 Add a few ladlefuls of the stock and cook, stirring, until the stock has been absorbed. Gradually add the remaining stock, a little at a time, allowing the rice to absorb the liquid before adding more, and stirring constantly.

4 Stir in the spinach leaves and herbs with the last of the liquid, and add a little salt and pepper. Continue cooking until the rice is cooked but still al dente and the spinach leaves have wilted. Stir in the Parmesan cheese, with a knob of butter, if you like, or serve with extra Parmesan.

> **Cook's Tip**
> The secret to risotto is to add the hot liquid gradually, about a ladleful at a time, and to stir constantly until the liquid has been absorbed before adding more. It is easy to overcook Arborio rice and it is often recommended to turn off the heat when the risotto is almost cooked and "resting" for a few minutes.

Oven-baked Porcini Risotto

This risotto is easy to make because you don't have to stand over it, stirring constantly as it cooks, as you do with a traditional risotto.

Serves 4

25g/1oz/½ cup dried porcini mushrooms
30ml/2 tbsp garlic-infused olive oil
1 onion, finely chopped
225g/8oz/generous 1 cup risotto rice
salt and ground black pepper

1 Put the porcini mushrooms in a heatproof bowl and pour over 750ml/1½ pints/3 cups boiling water. Leave them to soak for 30 minutes. Drain the mushrooms through a sieve lined with kitchen paper, reserving the soaking liquor. Rinse the mushrooms thoroughly under cold running water to remove any grit, and dry on kitchen paper.

2 Preheat the oven to 180°C/350°F/Gas 4. Heat the olive oil in a large roasting pan on the hob on medium heat and add the chopped onion. Cook for 2–3 minutes, or until softened but not coloured.

3 Add the risotto rice and stir for 1–2 minutes, then add the reserved mushrooms and stir well. Pour in the mushroom liquor and mix thoroughly. Season with salt and pepper to taste, and cover with foil.

4 Bake in the oven for 30 minutes, stirring occasionally, until all the stock has been absorbed and the rice is tender. Divide between warm serving bowls and serve immediately.

> **Cook's Tip**
> In Italy, dried porcini mushrooms are used all year round, not as a substitute for fresh porcini, but as a valued ingredient in its own right. Don't buy cheap porcini, but look for packets containing large pale-coloured pieces. Although they will seem expensive, a little goes a long way.

Two Cheese Risotto

This undeniably rich and creamy risotto is just the thing to serve on cold winter evenings when everyone needs warming up.

Serves 3–4
1 litre/1³/4 pints/4 cups vegetable or chicken stock
7.5ml/1¹/2 tsp olive oil
50g/2oz/¹/4 cup butter
1 onion, finely chopped
1 garlic clove, crushed
275g/10oz/1¹/2 cups risotto rice, preferably Vialone Nano
175ml/6fl oz/³/4 cup dry white wine
75g/3oz/³/4 cup Fontina cheese, cubed
50g/2oz/²/3 cup freshly grated Parmesan cheese, plus extra, to serve
salt and ground black pepper

1 Heat the stock in a pan and leave to simmer until needed.

2 Heat the olive oil with half the butter in a pan and gently fry the onion and garlic for 5–6 minutes, until soft. Add the rice and cook, stirring all the time, until the grains are coated in fat and have become slightly translucent around the edges.

3 Pour in the white wine. Cook, stirring, until it has been absorbed, then add a ladleful of hot stock. Cook, stirring, until the stock has been absorbed. Gradually add the remaining stock, a little at a time, allowing the rice to absorb the liquid before adding more, and stirring constantly.

4 When the rice is half cooked, stir in the Fontina cheese, and continue cooking and adding stock gradually. Keep stirring.

5 When the risotto is creamy and the grains are tender but still *al dente*, stir in the remaining butter and the Parmesan. Season with salt and pepper, then remove the pan from the heat. Cover and leave to stand for 3–4 minutes before serving.

> **Variation**
> Stir in a handful of chopped fresh herbs with the Parmesan.

Brown Rice Risotto with Mushrooms

A classic risotto of mixed mushrooms, herbs and fresh Parmesan cheese, but made using brown long-grain rice. Serve with a mixed leaf salad tossed in a balsamic dressing for a stylish lunch.

Serves 4
15g/¹/2oz/2 tbsp dried porcini mushrooms
150ml/¹/4 pint/²/3 cup warm water
15ml/1 tbsp olive oil
4 shallots, finely chopped
2 garlic cloves, crushed
250g/9oz/1¹/3 cups brown long-grain rice
900ml/1¹/2 pints/3³/4 cups well-flavoured vegetable stock
450g/1lb/6 cups mixed mushrooms, such as closed cup, chestnut and field mushrooms, sliced if large
30–45ml/2–3 tbsp chopped fresh flat leaf parsley
50g/2oz/²/3 cup freshly grated Parmesan cheese
salt and ground black pepper

1 Put the dried porcini in a bowl and pour over the warm water. Leave the mushrooms to soak for 20 minutes, then lift out with a slotted spoon. Filter the soaking water through a layer of kitchen paper in a sieve (strainer) and reserve. Roughly chop the porcini.

2 Heat the oil in a large pan, add the shallots and garlic and cook gently for 5 minutes, stirring. Add the brown rice to the shallot mixture and stir to coat the grains in oil.

3 Stir the vegetable stock and the porcini soaking liquid into the rice mixture in the pan. Bring to the boil, lower the heat and simmer, uncovered, for about 20 minutes, or until most of the liquid has been absorbed, stirring frequently.

4 Add all the mushrooms, stir well and cook the risotto for a further 10–15 minutes, until the liquid has been absorbed.

5 Season with salt and pepper to taste, stir in the chopped parsley and grated Parmesan and serve immediately.

Energy 547Kcal/2273kJ; Fat 25.1g; Saturated Fat 13.8g; Carbohydrate 56.4g; Fibre 0.2g

Energy 338Kcal/1412kJ; Fat 7.8g; Saturated Fat 3.1g; Carbohydrate 54.3g; Fibre 2g

Fried Rice Balls Stuffed with Mozzarella

These deep-fried balls of risotto are stuffed with mozzarella cheese. They are very popular snacks in Italy, which is hardly surprising as they are quite delicious.

Serves 4

I quantity Risotto with Parmesan (see page 146)
3 eggs
115g/4oz/²⁄₃ cup diced mozzarella cheese
oil, for deep-frying
breadcrumbs and flour, to coat
dressed frisée lettuce and cherry tomatoes, to serve

1 Put the risotto in a bowl and allow it to cool completely. Beat two of the eggs together, then stir them into the cold risotto until well mixed.

2 Use your hands to form the rice mixture into balls the size of a large egg. If the mixture is too moist to hold its shape well, stir in a few tablespoons of breadcrumbs. Poke a hole into the centre of each ball with your finger, then fill it with a few small cubes of mozzarella, and close the hole over again with the rice mixture.

3 Heat the oil for deep-frying until a small piece of bread sizzles as soon as it is dropped in.

4 Spread some flour on a plate. Beat the remaining egg in a shallow bowl. Sprinkle another plate with breadcrumbs. Roll the balls in the flour, then in the egg, and finally in the breadcrumbs.

5 Fry them a few at a time in the hot oil, until golden and crisp. Drain on kitchen paper while the remaining balls are being fried. Serve hot, with a salad of frisée lettuce and tomatoes.

Cook's Tip
This is the perfect way to use leftover risotto.

Champagne Risotto

This may seem rather extravagant, but it makes a really beautifully flavoured risotto, perfect for that special anniversary dinner.

Serves 3–4

750ml/1¼ pints/3 cups light vegetable or chicken stock
25g/1oz/2 tbsp butter
2 shallots, finely chopped
275g/10oz/1½ cups risotto rice, preferably Carnaroli
½ bottle or 300ml/½ pint/1¼ cups champagne
150ml/¼ pint/²⁄₃ cup double (heavy) cream
40g/1½oz/½ cup freshly grated Parmesan cheese
10ml/2 tsp very finely chopped fresh chervil
salt and ground black pepper
black truffle shavings, to garnish (optional)

1 Heat the stock in a pan and leave to simmer until needed.

2 Melt the butter in a pan and fry the shallots for 2–3 minutes until softened. Add the rice and cook, stirring all the time, until the grains are evenly coated in butter and are beginning to look translucent around the edges.

3 Pour in about two-thirds of the champagne and cook over a high heat so that the liquid bubbles fiercely. Cook, stirring constantly, until all the liquid has been absorbed, then begin to add the hot stock.

4 Add the stock, a ladleful at a time, making sure that each addition has been completely absorbed before adding the next. The risotto should gradually become creamy and velvety and all the stock should be absorbed.

5 When the rice is tender but still al dente, stir in the remaining champagne and the double cream and grated Parmesan. Taste for seasoning.

6 Remove from the heat, cover and leave to stand for a few minutes. Stir in the chervil and serve topped with a few truffle shavings, if you like.

Energy 468Kcal/1941kJ; Fat 23.1g; Saturated Fat 14.3g; Carbohydrate 48.3g; Fibre 0.1g

Energy 505Kcal/2111kJ; Fat 30.9g; Saturated Fat 8.5g; Carbohydrate 44.8g; Fibre 0.7g

Pesto Risotto

If you buy the pesto – and there are some excellent varieties available nowadays from Italian delicatessens – this is just about as easy as a risotto gets.

Serves 3–4
1 litre/1³/₄ pints/4 cups vegetable
    stock
30ml/2 tbsp olive oil
2 shallots, finely chopped
1 garlic clove, crushed
275g/10oz/1¹/₂ cups risotto rice
175ml/6fl oz/³/₄ cup dry white
    wine
45ml/3 tbsp pesto sauce
25g/1oz/¹/₃ cup freshly grated
    Parmesan cheese, plus extra,
    to serve (optional)
salt and ground black pepper

1 Heat the stock in a pan and leave to simmer until needed.

2 Heat the olive oil in a pan and fry the shallots and garlic for 4–5 minutes, until the shallots are soft but not browned.

3 Add the rice and cook over medium heat, stirring all the time, until the grains of rice are coated in oil and the outer part of the grain is translucent and the inner part opaque.

4 Pour in the wine. Cook, stirring, until all of it has been absorbed, then add a ladleful of the hot stock. Cook, stirring, until the stock has been absorbed. Gradually add the remaining stock, a little at a time, allowing the rice to absorb the liquid before adding more, and stirring constantly.

5 After about 20 minutes, when all the stock has been absorbed and the rice is creamy and tender but *al dente*, stir in the pesto and Parmesan. Taste and add salt and pepper to taste, then cover and leave to stand for 3–4 minutes. Spoon into a bowl and serve, with extra Parmesan, if you like.

> **Variation**
> Green basil pesto sauce is used for this recipe, but red pesto, made with red peppers, can also be used.

Pumpkin & Apple Risotto

Pumpkin and other winter squash appear in many classic Italian recipes. If pumpkins are out of season, butternut or onion squash work well as a substitute.

Serves 3–4
225g/8oz butternut squash
    or pumpkin flesh, peeled
    and seeded
1 cooking apple
25g/1oz/2 tbsp butter
900ml–1 litre/1¹/₂–1³/₄
    pints/3³/₄–4 cups vegetable
    stock
25ml/1¹/₂ tbsp olive oil
1 onion, finely chopped
1 garlic clove, crushed
275g/10oz/1¹/₂ cups risotto rice,
    such as Vialone Nano
175ml/6fl oz/³/₄ cup fruity
    white wine
75g/3oz/1 cup freshly grated
    Parmesan cheese
salt and ground black pepper

1 Cut the squash into small pieces. Peel, core and roughly chop the apple. Place in a pan and pour in 120ml/4fl oz/¹/₂ cup water. Bring to the boil, then simmer for 15–20 minutes, until the squash is very tender. Drain, return the squash mixture to the pan and add half the butter. Mash the mixture roughly with a fork to break up any large pieces, but leave the mixture chunky.

2 Heat the stock in a pan and leave to simmer until needed.

3 Heat the oil and remaining butter in a pan and fry the onion and garlic until the onion is soft. Add the rice and cook, stirring constantly, over medium heat for 2 minutes, until the rice is coated in oil and the grains are slightly translucent.

4 Add the wine and stir into the rice. When all the liquid has been absorbed, begin to add the stock a ladleful at a time, making sure each addition has been absorbed before adding the next. This should take about 20 minutes.

5 When roughly two ladlefuls of stock are left, add the squash and apple mixture together with another addition of stock. Continue to cook, stirring well and adding the rest of the stock, until the risotto is very creamy. Stir in the Parmesan, season to taste and serve immediately.

Energy 421Kcal/1751kJ; Fat 14.1g; Saturated Fat 3.2g; Carbohydrate 56.5g; Fibre 0.3g

Energy 439Kcal/1831kJ; Fat 13.3g; Saturated Fat 7.4g; Carbohydrate 59.1g; Fibre 1.1g

Roasted Pepper Risotto

The smoky flavour of the red (bell) peppers gives this risotto a divinely earthy taste.

Serves 3–4
1 red (bell) pepper
1 yellow (bell) pepper
1 litre/1¾ pints/4 cups vegetable stock

15ml/1 tbsp olive oil
25g/1oz/2 tbsp butter
1 onion, chopped
2 garlic cloves, crushed
275g/10oz/1½ cups risotto rice
50g/2oz/²/₃ cup freshly grated Parmesan cheese
salt and ground black pepper
freshly grated Parmesan cheese, to serve (optional)

1 Preheat the grill (broiler) to high. Cut the peppers in half, remove the seeds and cores and arrange, cut-side down, on a baking sheet. Place under the grill for 5–6 minutes, until the skin is charred. Put the peppers in a plastic bag, tie the ends and leave for 4–5 minutes.

2 Peel the peppers when they are cool enough to handle and the steam has loosened the skin. Cut into thin strips. Bring the stock to the boil in a pan and leave to simmer until required.

3 Heat the oil and butter in a pan and fry the onion and garlic for 4–5 minutes over low heat, until the onion begins to soften. Add the peppers and cook the mixture for a further 3–4 minutes, stirring occasionally.

4 Stir in the rice. Cook over medium heat for 3–4 minutes, stirring all the time, until the rice is evenly coated in oil and the outer part of each grain has become translucent.

5 Add a ladleful of stock. Cook, stirring, until all the liquid has been absorbed. Continue to add the stock, a ladleful at a time, making sure that each quantity has been absorbed before adding the next.

6 When the rice is tender but is still al dente, stir in the Parmesan and season to taste. Cover and leave to stand for 3–4 minutes, then serve, with extra Parmesan, if using.

Jerusalem Artichoke Risotto

This is a simple and warming risotto, which benefits from the delicious and distinctive flavour of Jerusalem artichokes.

Serves 3–4
400g/14oz Jerusalem artichokes
40g/1½oz/3 tbsp butter
1 litre/1¾ pints/4 cups vegetable stock
15ml/1 tbsp olive oil

1 onion, finely chopped
1 garlic clove, crushed
275g/10oz/1½ cups risotto rice
120ml/4fl oz/½ cup fruity white wine
10ml/2 tsp fresh thyme, finely chopped
40g/1½oz/½ cup freshly grated Parmesan cheese, plus extra, to serve
salt and ground black pepper
fresh thyme sprigs, to garnish

1 Peel the artichokes, cut them into pieces and immediately add them to a pan of lightly salted water. Simmer them until tender, then drain and mash with 15g/½oz/1 tbsp of the butter. Add a little more salt, if needed.

2 Boil the stock in a pan and leave to simmer until required.

3 Heat the oil and the remaining butter in a pan and fry the onion and garlic for 5–6 minutes, until soft. Add the rice and cook over a medium heat for about 2 minutes, until the grains are translucent around the edges.

4 Pour in the wine, stir until it has been absorbed, then start adding the simmering stock, a ladleful at a time, making sure each quantity has been absorbed before adding the next.

5 When you have just one ladleful of stock to add, stir in the mashed artichokes and the chopped thyme. Season with salt and pepper. Continue cooking until the risotto is creamy and the artichokes are hot.

6 Stir in the Parmesan cheese. Remove from the heat, cover the pan and leave the risotto to stand for a few minutes. Spoon into a warmed serving dish, garnish with fresh thyme and serve with Parmesan.

Energy 362Kcal/1509kJ; Fat 7.6g; Saturated Fat 3.1g; Carbohydrate 61.7g; Fibre 1.6g

Energy 418Kcal/1741kJ; Fat 14.8g; Saturated Fat 7.7g; Carbohydrate 56g; Fibre 1.1g

Risotto with Four Cheeses

This is a very rich, heady dish, made with four flavourful Italian cheeses. Serve it for a special dinner-party first course, with a light, dry sparkling white wine.

Serves 4
40g/1½oz/3 tbsp butter
1 small onion, finely chopped
1.2 litres/2 pints/5 cups chicken
  stock
350g/12oz/1¾ cups risotto rice

200ml/7fl oz/scant 1 cup dry
  white wine
50g/2oz/½ cup grated
  Gruyère cheese
50g/2oz/½ cup diced
  taleggio cheese
50g/2oz/½ cup diced
  Gorgonzola cheese
50g/2oz/⅔ cup freshly grated
  Parmesan cheese
salt and ground black pepper
chopped fresh flat leaf parsley,
  to garnish

1 Melt the butter in a large, heavy pan or deep frying pan and fry the onion over gentle heat for about 4–5 minutes, stirring frequently, until softened and lightly browned.

2 Pour the stock into another pan and heat it to simmering point. Keep simmering until required.

3 Add the rice to the onion mixture, and stir until the grains of rice are coated in oil and the outer part of the grain is translucent and the inner part opaque. Add the wine. Stir until it stops sizzling and most of it has been absorbed by the rice, then pour in a little of the hot stock. Add salt and pepper to taste. Stir over low heat, until the stock has been absorbed.

4 Gradually add the remaining stock, a ladleful at a time, allowing the rice to absorb the liquid before adding more, and stirring constantly. After 20–25 minutes the rice should be al dente and the risotto creamy.

5 Turn off the heat under the pan, then add the Gruyère, taleggio, Gorgonzola and 30ml/2 tbsp of the Parmesan. Stir gently until the cheeses have melted, then taste for seasoning. Garnish with parsley and serve with the remaining Parmesan.

Risotto with Asparagus

Fresh farm asparagus only has a short season, so make the most of it with this elegant risotto.

Serves 3–4
225g/8oz fresh asparagus
750ml/1¼ pints/3 cups vegetable
  or chicken stock

65g/2½oz/5 tbsp butter
1 small onion, finely chopped
275g/10oz/1½ cups risotto rice,
  such as Arborio or Carnaroli
75g/3oz/1 cup freshly grated
  Parmesan cheese
salt and ground black pepper

1 Bring a pan of water to the boil. Cut off any woody pieces on the ends of the asparagus stalks, peel the lower portions, then cook in the water for 5 minutes. Drain the asparagus, reserving the cooking water, refresh under cold water and drain again. Cut the asparagus diagonally into 4cm/1¼in pieces. Keep the tip and next-highest sections separate from the stalks.

2 Place the stock in a pan and add 450ml/¾ pint/scant 2 cups of the asparagus cooking water. Heat to simmering point and keep it hot.

3 Melt two-thirds of the butter in a large, heavy pan or deep frying pan. Add the onion and fry until it is soft and golden. Stir in all the asparagus except the top two sections. Cook for 2–3 minutes. Add the rice and cook for 1–2 minutes, mixing well to coat it with butter.

4 Stir in a ladleful of the hot liquid. Using a wooden spoon, stir until the stock has been absorbed. Gradually add the remaining stock, a little at a time, allowing the rice to absorb the liquid before adding more, and stirring all the time.

5 After 10 minutes, add the remaining asparagus sections. Continue to cook as before, for about 15 minutes, until the rice is al dente and the risotto is creamy.

6 Off the heat, stir in the remaining butter and the Parmesan. Grind in a little black pepper, and taste again for salt. Serve.

Energy 467Kcal/1940kJ; Fat 20.2g; Saturated Fat 12.4g; Carbohydrate 56.1g; Fibre 1g

Energy 630Kcal/2624kJ; Fat 24.6g; Saturated Fat 15.6g; Carbohydrate 71.4g; Fibre 0.2g

Risotto-stuffed Aubergines with Spicy Tomato Sauce

Glossy, purple aubergines from the south of Italy are wonderful filled with a rice stuffing, then baked with a cheese and pine nut topping.

Serves 4
4 small aubergines (eggplants)
105ml/7 tbsp olive oil
1 small onion, chopped
175g/6oz/scant 1 cup risotto rice
750ml/1¼ pints/3 cups vegetable
   stock
15ml/1 tbsp white wine vinegar
25g/1oz/⅓ cup freshly grated
   Parmesan cheese
15g/½oz/2 tbsp pine nuts

For the tomato sauce
300ml/½ pint/1¼ cups thick
   passata or puréed tomatoes
5ml/1 tsp mild curry paste
pinch of salt

1 Preheat the oven to 200°C/400°F/Gas 6. Cut the aubergines in half lengthways and remove the flesh with a small knife. Brush the shells with 30ml/2 tbsp of the oil and bake on a baking sheet, supported by crumpled foil, for 6–8 minutes.

2 Chop the aubergine flesh. Heat the remaining oil in a medium pan. Add the aubergine flesh and the onion, and cook over gentle heat for 3–4 minutes, until soft. Add the rice and stock, and leave to simmer, uncovered, for about 15 minutes. Stir in the the vinegar.

3 Increase the oven temperature to 230°C/450°F/Gas 8. Carefully spoon the rice mixture into the aubergine skins, top with the cheese and pine nuts, return to the oven and brown for 5 minutes.

4 To make the tomato sauce, mix the passata or puréed tomatoes with the curry paste in a small pan. Heat through and add salt to taste.

5 Spoon the tomato sauce on to four individual plates and arrange two aubergine halves on each one.

Energy 478Kcal/1985kJ; Fat 28.9g; Saturated Fat 7g; Carbohydrate 41.3g; Fibre 3.5g

Leek, Mushroom & Lemon Risotto

Leeks and lemon go together beautifully in this light risotto, while brown cap mushrooms add texture and extra flavour.

Serves 4
225g/8oz trimmed leeks
1.2 litres/2 pints/5 cups vegetable
   stock
30ml/2 tbsp olive oil
3 garlic cloves, crushed
225g/8oz/2–3 cups brown cap
   mushrooms, chopped roughly
75g/3oz/6 tbsp butter
1 large onion, roughly chopped
350g/12oz/1¾ cups risotto rice
grated rind of 1 lemon
45ml/3 tbsp lemon juice
50g/2oz/⅔ cup freshly grated
   Parmesan cheese
60ml/4 tbsp mixed chopped fresh
   chives and flat leaf parsley
salt and ground black pepper

1 Slice the leeks in half lengthways, wash them well and then slice evenly. Heat the stock to simmering point.

2 Heat the oil in a large pan and cook the garlic for 1 minute. Add the leeks, mushrooms and plenty of seasoning and cook over medium heat for about 10 minutes, or until the leeks have softened and browned. Spoon into a bowl and set aside.

3 Add 25g/1oz/2 tbsp of the butter to the pan. As soon as it has melted, add the onion and cook over medium heat for 5 minutes, until it has softened and is golden.

4 Stir in the rice and cook for about 1 minute until the grains begin to look translucent and are coated in the fat. Add a ladleful of stock and cook gently, stirring occasionally, until the liquid has been absorbed.

5 Continue to add stock, a ladleful at a time, stirring constantly, until all of it has been absorbed. This should take about 25–30 minutes. The risotto should be creamy and the rice should be tender but still al dente.

6 Just before serving, add the leeks and mushrooms, with the remaining butter. Stir in the grated lemon rind and juice. Add the Parmesan and herbs. Taste for seasoning before serving.

Energy 606Kcal/2522kJ; Fat 26.2g; Saturated Fat 13.2g; Carbohydrate 77.7g; Fibre 2.9g

Seafood Risotto

You can use any shellfish or seafood for this risotto, as long as the total weight is similar to that used here.

Serves 4–6

450g/1lb fresh mussels, in
   their shells
about 250ml/8fl oz/1 cup dry
   white wine
225g/8oz sea bass fillet, skinned
   and cut into pieces
seasoned flour, for dusting
60ml/4 tbsp olive oil
8 scallops with corals separated,
   white parts halved or sliced
225g/8oz squid, cleaned and cut
   into rings
12 large raw prawns (shrimp) or
   langoustines, heads removed
2 shallots, finely chopped
1 garlic clove, crushed
400g/14oz/2 cups risotto rice
3 tomatoes, peeled, seeded and
   chopped
1.5 litres/2½ pints/6¼ cups
   simmering fish stock
30ml/2 tbsp chopped fresh
   parsley
30ml/2 tbsp double (heavy)
   cream
salt and ground black pepper

1 Scrub the mussels, discarding any that do not close when sharply tapped. Place in a large pan and add 90ml/6 tbsp of the wine. Bring to the boil, cover the pan and cook for 3–4 minutes, until all the mussels have opened, shaking the pan occasionally. Drain, reserving the liquid; discard any mussels that have not opened. Reserve a few mussels in their shells for garnishing; remove the rest from their shells. Strain the cooking liquid.

2 Dust the pieces of sea bass in seasoned flour. Heat 30ml/ 2 tbsp of the olive oil in a frying pan and fry the fish for 3–4 minutes, until cooked. Transfer to a plate. Add a little more oil to the pan and fry the white parts of the scallops for 1–2 minutes on both sides, until tender. Transfer to a plate.

3 Fry the squid for 3–4 minutes in the same pan, adding a little more oil if necessary, then set aside. Lastly, add the prawns and fry for a further 3–4 minutes, turning frequently until pink. Towards the end of cooking, add about 30ml/2 tbsp wine and continue cooking until the prawns are tender, but do not burn. Remove the prawns from the pan. When cool enough to handle, remove the shells and legs, leaving the tails intact.

4 In a large pan, heat the remaining olive oil and fry the shallots and garlic for 3–4 minutes over gentle heat until the shallots are soft. Add the rice and cook for a few minutes, stirring, until the rice is coated with oil and the grains are slightly translucent. Stir in the tomatoes, with the reserved liquid from the mussels.

5 When all the free liquid has been absorbed, add the remaining wine, stirring constantly. When it has also been absorbed, gradually add the hot stock, one ladleful at a time, continuing to stir the rice constantly and waiting until each quantity of stock has been absorbed before adding the next.

6 When the risotto is three-quarters cooked, carefully stir in all the seafood, except the mussels reserved for the garnish. Continue to cook until all the stock has been absorbed and the rice is tender but is still al dente. Stir in the parsley and cream and taste for seasoning. Cover the pan and leave the risotto to stand for 2–3 minutes. Serve, garnished with reserved mussels.

Mussel Risotto

Fresh root ginger and coriander add a distinctive flavour to this dish, while chillies give it a little heat.

Serves 3–4

900g/2lb fresh mussels, in
   their shells
about 250ml/8fl oz/1 cup dry
   white wine
30ml/2 tbsp olive oil
1 onion, chopped
2 garlic cloves, crushed
1–2 fresh green chillies, seeded
   and finely sliced
2.5cm/1in piece of fresh root
   ginger, grated
275g/10oz/1½ cups risotto rice
900ml/1½ pints/3¾ cups
   simmering fish stock
30ml/2 tbsp chopped fresh
   coriander (cilantro)
30ml/2 tbsp double (heavy) cream
salt and ground black pepper

1 Scrub the mussels; discard any that do not close when tapped. Place in a large pan. Add 120ml/4fl oz/½ cup of the wine and bring to the boil. Cover and cook for 4–5 minutes, until they have opened, shaking the pan occasionally. Drain, reserving the liquid; discard any unopened mussels. Remove the mussels from their shells, reserving a few in their shells. Strain the mussel liquid.

2 Heat the oil and fry the onion and garlic for 3–4 minutes, until beginning to soften. Add the chillies. Continue to cook over low heat for 1–2 minutes, stirring frequently, then stir in the ginger and fry gently for 1 minute more.

3 Add the rice and cook over a medium heat for 2 minutes, stirring, until the rice is coated in oil and becomes translucent. Stir in the reserved mussel liquid. When absorbed, add the remaining wine and cook, stirring, until this has been absorbed. Add the hot fish stock, a little at a time, making sure each addition has been absorbed before adding the next.

4 When the rice is three-quarters cooked, stir in the mussels. Add the coriander and season. Continue adding stock to the risotto until it is creamy and the rice is al dente. Remove from the heat, stir in the cream, cover and leave to rest for a few minutes. Spoon into a warmed serving dish, decorate with the reserved mussels in their shells and serve immediately.

Energy 439Kcal/1833kJ; Fat 11.3g; Saturated Fat 3.5g; Carbohydrate 56.6g; Fibre 0.2g

Energy 541Kcal/2265kJ; Fat 13.9g; Saturated Fat 3.5g; Carbohydrate 58.8g; Fibre 0.6g

Squid Risotto with Chilli

Tenderized squid is lightly
cooked in an exotic risotto.

Serves 3–4
about 450g/1lb squid, cleaned
    and cut into rings
about 45ml/3 tbsp olive oil
15g/½oz/1 tbsp butter
1 onion, finely chopped
2 garlic cloves, crushed
1 fresh red chilli, seeded and sliced
275g/10oz/1½ cups risotto rice

175ml/6fl oz/¾ cup dry
    white wine
1 litre/1¾ pints/4 cups
    simmering fish stock
30ml/2 tbsp chopped fresh
    coriander (cilantro)
salt and ground black pepper

For the marinade
2 ripe kiwi fruit, mashed
1 fresh red chilli, seeded and sliced
30ml/2 tbsp fresh lime juice

1 Mash the kiwi fruit for the marinade in a bowl, then stir in the
chilli and lime juice. Add the squid, stirring to coat all the strips
in the mixture. Season with salt and pepper, cover with clear
film (plastic wrap) and chill for 4 hours or overnight.

2 Drain the squid. Heat 15ml/1 tbsp of the olive oil in a frying
pan and cook the strips, in batches if necessary, for 30–60
seconds over high heat; cook them very quickly. Transfer to a
plate and set aside. If too much juice accumulates in the pan,
reserve it in a jug and add more olive oil to the pan.

3 Heat the remaining oil with the butter in a large pan and
gently fry the onion and garlic for 5–6 minutes, until soft. Add
the sliced chilli to the pan and fry for 1 minute more.

4 Add the rice. Cook for a few minutes, stirring, until the rice is
coated with oil and is slightly translucent, then stir in the wine
until it has been absorbed. Gradually add the hot stock and the
squid cooking liquid, a ladleful at a time, stirring and waiting until
each quantity has been absorbed before adding the next.

5 When the rice is three-quarters cooked, stir in the squid and
continue cooking the risotto until all the stock has been
absorbed and the rice is tender. Season. Stir in the coriander,
cover and leave to stand for a few minutes before serving.

Scallop Risotto

Try to buy fresh scallops for
this dish, as they taste much
better than frozen ones.
Fresh scallops come with
the coral attached, which
adds flavour and colour.

Serves 3–4
about 12 shelled scallops, with
    their corals
1 litre/1¾ pints/4 cups fish stock
50g/2oz/¼ cup butter

15ml/1 tbsp olive oil
30ml/2 tbsp Pernod
2 shallots, finely chopped
275g/10oz/1½ cups risotto rice
generous pinch of saffron threads,
    dissolved in 15ml/1 tbsp
    warm milk
30ml/2 tbsp chopped fresh
    parsley
60ml/4 tbsp double (heavy)
    cream
salt and ground black pepper

1 Separate the scallops from their corals. Cut the white flesh in
half or into 2cm/¾in slices. Heat the stock until simmering.

2 Melt half the butter with 5ml/1 tsp oil. Fry the white parts of
the scallops for 2–3 minutes. Pour over the Pernod, heat for a
few seconds, then ignite and allow to flame for a few seconds.
When the flames have died down, remove pan from the heat.

3 Heat the remaining butter and olive oil in another pan and
fry the shallots for about 3–4 minutes, until soft but not
browned. Add the rice and cook for a few minutes, stirring, until
the rice is coated with oil and is beginning to turn translucent.

4 Gradually add the hot stock, a ladleful at a time, stirring
constantly and waiting for each ladleful of stock to be absorbed
before adding the next.

5 When the rice is very nearly cooked, add the scallops and all
the juices from the pan, together with the corals, saffron milk,
parsley and seasoning. Stir well to mix. Continue cooking,
adding the remaining stock and stirring occasionally, until the
risotto is thick and creamy.

6 Remove from the heat, stir in the cream and cover. Leave the
risotto to stand for about 3 minutes before serving.

Energy 460Kcal/1924kJ; Fat 10.9g; Saturated Fat 1.6g; Carbohydrate 59.9g; Fibre 0.5g

Energy 550Kcal/2290kJ; Fat 22.5g; Saturated Fat 12.2g; Carbohydrate 58.9g; Fibre 0.2g

Shellfish Risotto with Mixed Mushrooms

A quick and easy risotto, where all the liquid is added in one go. The method is well-suited to this shellfish dish, as it means everything cooks together undisturbed.

Serves 6

225g/8oz fresh mussels, in
   their shells
225g/8oz fresh Venus or carpet
   shell clams, in their shells
1.75 litres/3 pints/7½ cups
   chicken or vegetable stock
45ml/3 tbsp olive oil

1 onion, chopped
450g/1lb/2⅓ cups risotto rice
150ml/¼ pint/⅔ cup dry white
   wine
225g/8oz/2–3 cups assorted wild
   and cultivated mushrooms,
   trimmed and sliced
115g/4oz raw peeled prawns
   (shrimp), deveined
1 medium or 2 small squid,
   cleaned and sliced
3 drops truffle oil (optional)
75ml/5 tbsp chopped mixed fresh
   parsley and chervil
celery salt and cayenne pepper

1 Scrub the mussels and clams clean, discarding any that are open and do not close when tapped with a knife. Set aside.

2 Heat the stock and leave simmering until needed. Heat the oil in a large frying pan and fry the onion for 6–8 minutes, until soft but not browned.

3 Add the rice, stirring to coat the grains in oil, then pour in the stock and wine and cook for 5 minutes. Add the mushrooms and cook for 5 minutes more, stirring occasionally.

4 Add the prawns, squid, mussels and clams and stir into the rice. Cover the pan and simmer over low heat for 15 minutes, until the prawns have turned pink and the mussels and clams have opened. Discard any of the shellfish that remain closed.

5 Switch off the heat. Add the truffle oil, if using, and stir in the herbs. Cover tightly and leave to stand for 5–10 minutes to allow all the flavours to blend. Season to taste with celery salt and a pinch of cayenne and serve immediately.

Energy 423Kcal/1768kJ; Fat 7.5g; Saturated Fat 1.2g; Carbohydrate 62.5g; Fibre 0.6g

Risotto with Prawns

A dash of tomato purée gives this delicate prawn risotto a soft pink colour.

Serves 3–4

350g/12oz large raw prawns
   (shrimp), in their shells
1 bay leaf
1–2 fresh parsley sprigs
5ml/1 tsp whole peppercorns

2 garlic cloves, peeled and
   left whole
65g/2½oz/5 tbsp butter
2 shallots, finely chopped
275g/10oz/1½ cups risotto rice
15ml/1 tbsp tomato purée
   (paste), softened in 120ml/
   4fl oz/½ cup dry white wine
salt and ground black pepper

1 Put the prawns in a large pan with 1 litre/1¾ pints/4 cups water and the herbs, peppercorns and garlic. Bring to the boil over medium heat. As soon as the prawns turn pink, lift them out, peel them and return the shells to the pan. Boil the stock with the shells for a further 10 minutes, then strain. Return the stock to the clean pan and simmer gently until needed.

2 Slice the prawns in half lengthways, removing the dark vein along the back. Set four halves aside for the garnish, then roughly chop the rest.

3 Heat two-thirds of the butter in a flameproof casserole and fry the shallots until golden. Add the rice, mixing well to coat it with butter. Pour in the tomato purée and wine and cook until it has been absorbed. Add a ladleful of the simmering stock and stir until the stock has been absorbed.

4 Gradually add the remaining stock, a ladleful at a time, allowing the rice to absorb the liquid before adding more, and stirring constantly.

5 After 20–25 minutes, when all the stock has been absorbed, the risotto is creamy and the rice is al dente, stir in the chopped prawns and the remaining butter. Season to taste with salt and pepper. Cover and allow the risotto rest for 3–4 minutes. Spoon into a serving bowl, garnish with the reserved prawns and serve.

Energy 457Kcal/1905kJ; Fat 14.3g; Saturated Fat 8.6g; Carbohydrate 55.7g; Fibre 0.1g

Truffle & Lobster Risotto

To capture the precious qualities of truffle, partner it with lobster and serve in a silky smooth risotto. Both truffle shavings and truffle oil are added towards the end of cooking to preserve their flavour.

Serves 4
1.2 litres/2 pints/5 cups chicken
   stock
50g/2oz/4 tbsp unsalted butter
1 onion, chopped
350g/12oz/1¾ cups risotto rice
1 fresh thyme sprig
150ml/¼ pint/⅔ cup dry
   white wine
1 freshly cooked lobster
45ml/3 tbsp chopped mixed fresh
   parsley and chervil
3–4 drops truffle oil
2 hard-boiled eggs, cut into
   wedges
1 fresh black or white truffle
salt and ground black pepper

1 Heat the stock and keep at a gentle simmer until needed. Melt the butter in a pan, add the onion and fry until the onion is soft. Add the rice and stir well to coat with fat.

2 Add the thyme, then pour in the wine and cook until it has been absorbed. Add the chicken stock a little at a time, stirring. Allow each ladleful to be absorbed before adding the next.

3 Twist off the lobster tail, cut the underside with scissors and remove the white tail meat. Carefully break open the claws with a small kitchen hammer and remove the flesh. Cut half the meat into big chunks, then roughly chop the remainder.

4 Stir in the chopped lobster meat, half the chopped herbs and the truffle oil. Remove the rice from the heat, cover and leave to stand for 5 minutes. Divide among plates and top with the lobster chunks and hard-boiled eggs. To serve, shave fresh truffle over each portion and sprinkle with the remaining herbs.

> **Cook's Tip**
> To make the most of the aromatic truffle scent, keep the tuber in the rice jar for a few days before use.

Crab Risotto

A luxurious way to serve fresh crab, this dish is laced with Marsala and cream.

Serves 3–4
2 large cooked crabs
15ml/1 tbsp olive oil
25g/1oz/2 tbsp butter
2 shallots, finely chopped
275g/10oz/1½ cups risotto rice
75ml/5 tbsp Marsala or brandy
1 litre/1¾ pints/4 cups
   simmering fish stock
5ml/1 tsp chopped fresh tarragon
5ml/1 tsp chopped fresh parsley
60ml/4 tbsp double (heavy)
   cream
salt and ground black pepper

1 To remove the crabmeat, hold a crab firmly in one hand and hit the underside firmly with the heel of your hand to loosen the shell. Using your thumbs, push against the body and pull away from the shell. From the inside of the shell, remove and discard the intestines. Discard the grey gills – "dead man's fingers". Break off the claws and legs from the body, then use a small hammer or crackers to break them open. Using a pick, remove the meat from the claws and legs. Set the meat aside.

2 Using a pick or a skewer, pick out the white meat from the body cavities and add to the rest of the meat. Reserve some white meat to garnish. Scoop out the brown meat from inside the shell and set aside with the white meat.

3 Heat the oil and butter in a pan and gently fry the shallots until soft but not brown. Add the rice. Cook for a few minutes, stirring, until the rice is slightly translucent. Add the Marsala, bring to the boil and cook, stirring, until the liquid evaporates.

4 Add a ladleful of hot stock and cook, stirring, until all the stock has been absorbed. Continue cooking in this way until about two-thirds of the stock has been added, then carefully stir in all the crabmeat and the herbs.

5 Continue to cook the risotto, adding the remaining stock. When the rice is al dente, remove it from the heat, stir in the cream and taste for seasoning. Cover and leave to stand for 3 minutes. Serve garnished with the reserved white crabmeat.

Monkfish Risotto

Monkfish is a versatile, firm-textured fish, ideal for cooking in a risotto.

Serves 3–4

about 450g/1lb monkfish, cut into cubes
seasoned flour, for coating
1 litre/1³⁄₄ pints/4 cups fish stock
30ml/2 tbsp olive oil
40g/1¹⁄₂oz/3 tbsp butter
2 shallots, finely chopped
1 lemon grass stalk, finely chopped
275g/10oz/1¹⁄₂ cups risotto rice, preferably Carnaroli
175ml/6fl oz/³⁄₄ cup dry white wine
30ml/2 tbsp chopped fresh parsley
salt and white pepper
dressed salad leaves, to serve

1 Place the monkfish cubes in a bowl and toss in seasoned flour until coated. Heat the stock in a pan and leave to simmer gently until needed.

2 Heat 15ml/1 tbsp of the oil with half the butter in a frying pan. Fry the monkfish cubes over medium to high heat for 3–4 minutes, until cooked, turning occasionally. Transfer to a plate and set aside.

3 Heat the remaining oil and butter in a pan and fry the shallots over low heat for about 4 minutes, until soft but not brown. Add the lemon grass and cook for 1–2 minutes more.

4 Add the rice. Cook for 2–3 minutes, stirring, until the rice is coated with oil and is slightly translucent. Gradually add the wine and the hot stock, stirring and waiting until each ladleful has been absorbed before adding the next.

5 When the rice is about three-quarters cooked, stir in the monkfish. Continue to cook the risotto, adding the remaining stock and stirring constantly until the grains of rice are tender, but still al dente. Season with salt and white pepper.

6 Remove the pan from the heat, stir in the parsley and cover with the lid. Leave the risotto to stand for a few minutes before serving with a garnish of dressed salad leaves.

Salmon Risotto with Cucumber & Tarragon

This simple risotto is cooked all in one go, and is easier to make than the traditional version.

Serves 4

1.2 litres/2 pints/5 cups chicken or fish stock
25g/1oz/2 tbsp butter
small bunch of spring onions (scallions), white parts only, chopped
¹⁄₂ cucumber, peeled, seeded and chopped
350g/12oz/1³⁄₄ cups risotto rice
150ml/¹⁄₄ pint/²⁄₃ cup dry white wine
450g/1lb salmon fillet, skinned and diced
45ml/3 tbsp chopped fresh tarragon
salt and ground black pepper

1 Heat the stock in a pan and keep at a gentle simmer. Melt the butter in a large pan and add the spring onions and cucumber. Cook for 2–3 minutes, stirring frequently, without allowing the spring onions to colour.

2 Stir in the rice, then pour in the stock and wine. Bring to the boil, then lower the heat and simmer, uncovered, for 10 minutes, stirring occasionally.

3 Stir in the diced salmon and season to taste with salt and black pepper. Continue cooking for a further 5 minutes, stirring occasionally, then switch off the heat. Cover and leave to stand for 5 minutes.

4 Remove the lid, add the chopped tarragon and mix lightly. Spoon into a warmed serving bowl and serve.

> **Cook's Tip**
> If you prefer to cook the traditional way, add the liquid gradually, adding the salmon about two-thirds of the way through cooking. Carnaroli risotto rice would be best for this recipe.

Energy 431Kcal/1802kJ; Fat 9.1g; Saturated Fat 5.3g; Carbohydrate 56.5g; Fibre 0.3g

Energy 594Kcal/2477kJ; Fat 18.1g; Saturated Fat 5.4g; Carbohydrate 70.9g; Fibre 0.4g

Risotto with Bacon, Baby Courgettes & Peppers

A medley of colours, this creamy vegetable risotto would make a perfect light lunch or supper, served with chunks of rustic bread and a glass of dry white wine.

Serves 4

30ml/2 tbsp olive oil
115g/4oz rindless streaky (fatty) bacon rashers (strips), cut into thick strips
1.2 litres/2 pints/5 cups vegetable or chicken stock
350g/12oz/1¾ cups risotto rice
30ml/2 tbsp single (light) cream
45ml/3 tbsp dry sherry

50g/2oz/²⁄₃ cup freshly grated Parmesan cheese
50g/2oz/²⁄₃ cup chopped fresh parsley
salt and ground black pepper

For the vegetables

1 small red (bell) pepper, seeded
1 small green (bell) pepper, seeded
25g/1oz/2 tbsp butter
75g/3oz horse mushrooms, sliced
225g/8oz baby courgettes (zucchini), halved
1 onion, halved and sliced
1 garlic clove, crushed

1 Heat half the oil in a frying pan. Add the bacon and heat gently until the fat runs. Increase the heat and fry until crisp, then drain on kitchen paper and set aside. Heat the stock in a pan and leave to simmer gently until required.

2 Heat the remaining oil in a heavy pan over medium heat. Add the rice, stir to coat the grains, then ladle in a little of the hot stock. Stir until it has been absorbed. Gradually add the rest of the stock in the same way, stirring constantly.

3 To prepare the vegetables, cut the peppers into chunks. Melt the butter in a separate pan and fry the peppers, mushrooms, courgettes, onion and garlic until the onion is just tender. Season well with salt and pepper, then stir in the bacon.

4 When all the stock has been absorbed by the rice, stir in the cream, sherry, Parmesan, parsley and seasoning. Spoon on to individual plates and top with the vegetables and bacon.

Risotto with Smoked Bacon & Tomato

A classic risotto, with plenty of onions, smoked bacon and sun-dried tomatoes. You'll want to keep going back for more!

Serves 4–6

8 sun-dried tomatoes in olive oil
1 litre/1¾ pints/4 cups vegetable stock
275g/10oz rindless smoked back bacon, cut into 2.5cm/1in pieces

75g/3oz/6 tbsp butter
450g/1lb onions, roughly chopped
2 garlic cloves, crushed
350g/12oz/1¾ cups risotto rice
300ml/½ pint/1¼ cups dry white wine
50g/2oz/²⁄₃ cup freshly grated Parmesan cheese
45ml/3 tbsp mixed chopped fresh chives and flat leaf parsley
salt and ground black pepper

1 Drain the sun-dried tomatoes and reserve 15ml/1 tbsp of the oil. Roughly chop the tomatoes and set aside. Heat the stock in a pan and leave to simmer gently until required.

2 Heat the oil from the sun-dried tomatoes in a large pan and fry the bacon until well cooked and golden. Remove with a slotted spoon and drain on kitchen paper.

3 Melt 25g/1oz/2 tbsp of the butter in a pan and fry the onions and garlic over medium heat for 10 minutes, until soft and golden brown. Stir in the rice. Cook for 1 minute, until the grains turn translucent. Stir the wine into the stock. Add a ladleful of the mixture to the rice and cook gently, stirring, until the liquid has been absorbed.

4 Stir in another ladleful of the stock and wine mixture and allow it to be absorbed. Repeat this process until all the liquid has been used up. This should take 25–30 minutes. The risotto will turn thick and creamy, and the rice should be al dente.

5 Just before serving, stir in the bacon, sun-dried tomatoes, Parmesan, half the herbs and the remaining butter. Add salt and pepper to taste and serve sprinkled with the remaining herbs.

Energy 624Kcal/2595kJ; Fat 24.2g; Saturated Fat 10g; Carbohydrate 78.4g; Fibre 3g

Energy 507Kcal/2110kJ; Fat 21.2g; Saturated Fat 11.1g; Carbohydrate 54.4g; Fibre 1.6g

Leek & Prosciutto Risotto

Flavoured with tasty Italian cured ham, this simple risotto makes an easy supper that is full of flavour.

Serves 3–4
1 litre/1¾ pints/4 cups chicken stock
7.5ml/1½ tsp olive oil
40g/1½oz/3 tbsp butter
2 leeks, cut in slices
175g/6oz prosciutto, torn into pieces
75g/3oz/generous 1 cup button mushrooms, sliced
275g/10oz/1½ cups risotto rice
45ml/3 tbsp chopped fresh flat leaf parsley
40g/1½oz/1½ cup freshly grated Parmesan cheese
salt and ground black pepper

1 Heat the stock in a pan and simmer gently until needed.

2 Heat the oil and butter in another pan and fry the leeks until soft. Set aside a few strips of prosciutto for the garnish and add the rest to the pan. Fry for 1 minute, then add the mushrooms and fry, stirring, for 2–3 minutes, until lightly browned.

3 Add the rice. Cook, stirring, for 1–2 minutes, until the grains are evenly coated in oil and have become translucent around the edges. Add a ladleful of hot stock. Stir until this has been absorbed completely, then add the next ladleful. Continue in this way until all the stock has been absorbed.

4 When the risotto is creamy and the rice is tender but still *al dente*, stir in the parsley and Parmesan. Taste for seasoning, remove from the heat and cover. Rest for a few minutes, then spoon into a bowl and garnish with the reserved prosciutto.

> **Cook's Tip**
> *Italy is well known for its prosciutto crudo, salted and air-dried ham. The most famous of these, prosciutto di Parma, comes from the area around Parma, where Parmesan cheese is also made. The pigs from this region are fed on the whey from the cheese-making process, which makes their flesh mild and sweet.*

Risi e Bisi

A classic pea and ham risotto from the Veneto region, northern Italy. Traditionally this is served as an appetizer in Italy, but it also makes a fine light supper dish.

Serves 4
75g/3oz/6 tbsp butter
1 small onion, finely chopped
about 1 litre/1¾ pints/4 cups chicken stock
275g/10oz/1½ cups risotto rice
150ml/¼ pint/⅔ cup dry white wine
225g/8oz/2 cups frozen petits pois, thawed
115g/4oz cooked ham, diced
salt and ground black pepper
50g/2oz/⅔ cup freshly grated Parmesan cheese, to serve

1 Heat the stock in a pan and keep at a gentle simmer until needed. Melt 50g/2oz/¼ cup of the butter in a pan until foaming. Add the onion and cook gently for about 3 minutes, stirring frequently, until softened.

2 Add the rice to the onion mixture. Stir until the grains start to swell, then pour in the wine. Stir until it stops sizzling and most of it has been absorbed, then pour in a little hot stock, with salt and pepper to taste. Stir continuously, over low heat, until all the stock has been absorbed.

3 Add the remaining stock, a ladleful at a time, allowing the rice to absorb the liquid before adding more, and stirring constantly. Add the peas after about 20 minutes. After 25–30 minutes, the rice should be *al dente* and the risotto moist and creamy.

4 Gently stir in the cooked ham and the remaining butter. Heat through until the butter has melted, then taste for seasoning. Transfer to a warmed serving bowl. Grate or shave a little Parmesan over the top and serve the rest separately.

> **Cook's Tip**
> *Always use fresh Parmesan cheese, grated off a block. It has a far superior flavour to ready-grated Parmesan.*

Quick Risotto

This is a cheat's risotto as the rice is cooked quickly in a conventional way, and the other ingredients are simply added at the last minute.

Serves 3–4
275g/10oz/1½ cups risotto rice
1 litre/1¾ pints/4 cups chicken stock
115g/4oz/1 cup diced mozzarella cheese
2 egg yolks
30ml/2 tbsp freshly grated Parmesan cheese
75g/3oz cooked ham, cut into small cubes
30ml/2 tbsp chopped fresh parsley
salt and ground black pepper

1 Put the rice in a pan and pour in the stock. Bring to the boil and then cover and simmer for about 18–20 minutes, until the rice is tender.

2 Remove the pan from the heat and quickly stir in the mozzarella, egg yolks, Parmesan, ham and parsley. Season well with salt and pepper. Cover the pan and stand for 2–3 minutes to allow the cheese to melt, then stir again. Serve immediately.

Risotto alla Milanese

This classic risotto is always served with the hearty beef stew, Osso Buco, but also makes a delicious first course or light supper dish in its own right.

Serves 3–4
about 1.2 litres/2 pints/5 cups beef or chicken stock
good pinch of saffron threads
75g/3oz/6 tbsp butter
1 onion, finely chopped
275g/10oz/1½ cups risotto rice
75g/3oz/1 cup freshly grated Parmesan cheese
salt and ground black pepper

1 Bring the stock to the boil, then reduce to a low simmer. Ladle a little stock into a small bowl. Add the saffron strands and leave to infuse.

2 Melt 50g/2oz/¼ cup of the butter in a large pan until foaming. Add the onion and cook gently for about 3 minutes, stirring frequently, until softened but not browned.

3 Add the rice. Stir until the grains start to swell and burst, then add a few ladlefuls of the stock, with the saffron liquid and salt and pepper to taste. Stir over low heat, until the stock has been absorbed.

4 Add the remaining stock, a few ladlefuls at a time, allowing the rice to absorb all the liquid before adding more, and stirring constantly. After 20–25 minutes, the rice should be tender but still al dente and the risotto golden yellow, moist and creamy.

5 Gently stir in about two-thirds of the grated Parmesan and the remaining butter. Heat through until the butter has melted, then taste for seasoning. Transfer the risotto to a warmed bowl and serve with the remaining Parmesan handed separately.

Pancetta & Broad Bean Risotto

This delicious risotto makes a healthy and filling meal when served with cooked fresh seasonal vegetables or a mixed green salad.

Serves 4
1.5 litres/2½ pints/6¼ cups chicken stock
15ml/1 tbsp olive oil
1 onion, chopped
2 garlic cloves, finely chopped
175g/6oz smoked pancetta, diced
350g/12oz/1¾ cups risotto rice
225g/8oz/2 cups frozen baby broad beans
30ml/2 tbsp chopped fresh mixed herbs, such as parsley, thyme and oregano
salt and ground black pepper
shavings of Parmesan cheese, to serve

1 Pour the stock into a pan and simmer gently until required.

2 Heat the oil in a large pan. Add the onion, garlic and pancetta and cook gently for about 5 minutes, stirring occasionally. Do not allow the onion and garlic to brown.

3 Add the rice to the pan and cook for 1 minute, stirring, until the rice turns translucent. Add a ladleful of stock and cook, stirring constantly, until the liquid has been absorbed.

4 Continue adding the remaining stock, a ladleful at a time, allowing the rice to absorb the liquid before adding more, and stirring all the time. Cook until all the stock has been absorbed and the rice is cooked and creamy but still al dente. This should take 25-30 minutes.

5 Meanwhile, cook the broad beans in a pan of lightly salted boiling water for about 3 minutes, until tender. Drain well and stir into the risotto, with the mixed herbs. Add salt and pepper to taste. Serve sprinkled with shavings of fresh Parmesan.

> **Cook's Tip**
> If the broad beans are large, or if you prefer skinned beans, remove the outer skin after cooking in boiling water.

Top Energy 405Kcal/1692kJ; Fat 12g; Saturated Fat 6.5g; Carbohydrate 55.1g; Fibre 0g
Above Energy 477Kcal/1981kJ; Fat 22g; Saturated Fat 13.6g; Carbohydrate 56g; Fibre 0.2g

Energy 511Kcal/2132kJ; Fat 13.9g; Saturated Fat 4g; Carbohydrate 77.6g; Fibre 3.9g

Duck Risotto

Brandy-flavoured duck is enhanced with orange in this spectacular risotto.

Serves 3–4
2 duck breasts
30ml/2 tbsp brandy
30ml/2 tbsp orange juice
15ml/1 tbsp olive oil (optional)
1 onion, finely chopped
1 garlic clove, crushed

275g/10oz/1½ cups risotto rice
1–1.2 litres/1¾–2 pints/4–5 cups
   hot duck or chicken stock
5ml/1 tsp chopped fresh thyme
5ml/1 tsp chopped fresh mint
10ml/2 tsp grated orange rind
40g/1½oz/½ cup freshly grated
   Parmesan cheese
salt and ground black pepper
strips of thinly pared orange rind,
   to garnish

1 Score the skin of the duck breasts and rub with salt. Fry, skin-side down, in a heavy frying pan and dry-fry over medium heat for 6–8 minutes to render the fat. Transfer to a plate and discard the skin. Cut into strips about 2cm/¾in wide.

2 Pour all but 15ml/1 tbsp of the rendered duck fat from the pan into a cup, then reheat the fat in the pan. Fry the duck slices for 2–3 minutes over medium high heat, until evenly brown but not overcooked. Add the brandy, heat to simmering point and then ignite. When the flames have died down, add the orange juice and season. Remove from the heat; set aside.

3 In a pan, heat either 15ml/1 tbsp of the remaining duck fat or use olive oil. Fry the onion and garlic over gentle heat, until the onion is soft but not browned. Add the rice and cook, stirring all the time, until the grains are coated in oil and have become slightly translucent around the edges.

4 Add the stock, a ladleful at a time, waiting for each quantity to be absorbed completely before adding the next. Just before adding the final ladleful of stock, stir in the duck, with the thyme and mint. Cook until the risotto is creamy and the rice *al dente*.

5 Add the orange rind and Parmesan. Taste for seasoning, then remove from the heat, cover the pan and leave to stand for a few minutes. Serve garnished with orange rind.

Chicken Liver Risotto

The combination of chicken livers, bacon, parsley and thyme gives this risotto a wonderfully rich flavour.

Serves 2–4
175g/6oz chicken livers
900ml–1 litre/1½–1¾ pints/
   3¾–4 cups chicken stock
about 15ml/1 tbsp olive oil
about 25g/1oz/2 tbsp butter
about 40g/1½oz speck or 3
   rindless streaky (fatty) bacon
   rashers (strips), finely chopped

2 shallots, finely chopped
1 garlic clove, crushed
1 celery stick, finely sliced
275g/10oz/1½ cups risotto rice
175ml/6fl oz/¾ cup dry white
   wine
5ml/1 tsp chopped fresh thyme
15ml/1 tbsp chopped fresh
   parsley
salt and ground black pepper
parsley and thyme sprigs,
   to garnish

1 Clean the chicken livers carefully, removing any fat or membrane. Rinse well, pat dry with kitchen paper and cut into small, even pieces. Heat the stock and simmer until needed.

2 Heat the oil and butter in a frying pan and fry the speck or bacon for 2–3 minutes. Add the shallots, garlic and celery and continue frying for 3–4 minutes over low heat, until the vegetables are slightly softened. Increase the heat and add the chicken livers, stir-frying for a few minutes, until they are brown.

3 Add the rice. Cook, stirring, for a few minutes, then pour over the wine. Allow to boil, stirring frequently, taking care not to break up the chicken livers. When all the wine has been absorbed, add the hot stock, a ladleful at a time, stirring.

4 About halfway through cooking, add the thyme and season with salt and pepper. Continue to add the stock as before, making sure that it is absorbed before adding more.

5 When the risotto is creamy and the rice is tender but *al dente*, stir in the parsley. Taste for seasoning. Remove the pan from the heat, cover and leave to stand for a few minutes before serving, garnished with parsley and thyme.

Energy 408Kcal/1708kJ; Fat 8.5g; Saturated Fat 3g; Carbohydrate 56.7g; Fibre 0.2g

Energy 418Kcal/1742kJ; Fat 11.6g; Saturated Fat 4.8g; Carbohydrate 55.8g; Fibre 0.2g

Risotto with Chicken

This is a classic combination of chicken and rice, cooked with prosciutto, white wine and Parmesan cheese.

Serves 6

1.75 litres/3 pints/7½ cups chicken stock
30ml/2 tbsp olive oil
225g/8oz skinless chicken breast fillets, cut into 2.5cm/1in cubes
1 onion, finely chopped
1 garlic clove, finely chopped
450g/1lb/2⅓ cups risotto rice
120ml/4fl oz/½ cup dry white wine
1.5ml/¼ tsp saffron threads
50g/2oz prosciutto, cut into thin strips
25g/1oz/2 tbsp butter, cubed
25g/1oz/⅓ cup freshly grated Parmesan cheese, plus extra to serve
salt and ground black pepper
flat leaf parsley, to garnish

1 Heat the stock in a pan and simmer gently until needed. Heat the oil in a frying pan over medium-high heat. Add the chicken cubes and cook, stirring, until they start to turn white.

2 Reduce the heat to low and add the onion and garlic. Cook, stirring, until the onion is soft. Stir in the rice. Sauté for 1–2 minutes, stirring constantly, until all the rice grains are coated.

3 Add the wine and bubble, stirring, until the wine has been absorbed. Stir the saffron into the simmering stock, then add ladlefuls of stock to the rice, allowing each ladleful to be absorbed before adding the next.

4 When the rice is three-quarters cooked, add the prosciutto and continue cooking until the rice is just tender and the risotto creamy. Add the butter and the Parmesan and stir in well. Season with salt and pepper to taste. Serve the risotto hot, sprinkled with more Parmesan, and garnish with parsley.

> **Cook's Tip**
> Try turkey for a modern version of this classic recipe.

Rabbit & Lemon Grass Risotto

The addition of exotic lemon grass adds a pleasant tang to this country risotto.

Serves 3–4

225g/8oz rabbit meat
seasoned flour, for coating
50g/2oz/¼ cup butter
15ml/1 tbsp olive oil
45ml/3 tbsp dry sherry
1 litre/1¾ pints/4 cups chicken stock
1 onion, finely chopped
1 garlic clove, crushed
1 lemon grass stalk, peeled and very finely sliced
275g/10oz/1½ cups risotto rice, preferably Carnaroli
10ml/2 tsp finely chopped fresh thyme
45ml/3 tbsp double (heavy) cream
25g/1oz/⅓ cup freshly grated Parmesan cheese
salt and ground black pepper

1 Cut the rabbit into strips and coat in the seasoned flour. Heat half the butter and oil in a frying pan and fry the rabbit quickly until evenly brown. Add the sherry and allow to boil briefly to burn off the alcohol. Season with salt and pepper and set aside.

2 Pour the stock into a pan and simmer gently until required.

3 Heat the remaining olive oil and butter in a large pan. Fry the onion and garlic over low heat for 4–5 minutes, until the onion is soft. Add the lemon grass and cook for a few minutes.

4 Add the rice and stir to coat in the oil. Add a ladleful of stock and cook, stirring, until the liquid has been absorbed. Continue adding the stock in this way, stirring constantly. When the rice is almost cooked, stir in three-quarters of the rabbit strips, with the pan juices. Add the thyme and seasoning.

5 Continue cooking until the rice is tender but is still *al dente*. Stir in the cream and Parmesan, remove from the heat and cover. Leave to stand before serving, garnished with rabbit strips.

> **Cook's Tip**
> If rabbit is not available, use chicken or turkey instead.

Energy 418kcal/1744kJ; Fat 9.5g; Saturated Fat 3.8g; Carbohydrate 60.9g; Fibre 0.1g

Energy 477Kcal/1981kJ; Fat 21.9g; Saturated Fat 13.6g; Carbohydrate 56.2g; Fibre 0.2g

Lemon & Herb Risotto Cake

This unusual rice dish can be served as a main course with salad, or as a satisfying side dish. It is also good served cold, and packs well for picnics.

Serves 4
oil, for greasing
1 small leek, finely sliced
600ml/1 pint/2½ cups chicken
stock
225g/8oz/generous 1 cup risotto
rice
finely grated rind of 1 lemon
30ml/2 tbsp snipped fresh chives
30ml/2 tbsp chopped fresh
parsley
75g/3oz/¾ cup grated
mozzarella cheese
salt and ground black pepper

1 Preheat the oven to 200°C/400°F/Gas 6. Lightly oil a 21cm/8½ in round loose-based cake tin (pan).

2 Put the leek in a large pan with 45ml/3 tbsp of the stock. Cook over a medium heat, stirring occasionally, until softened. Stir in the rice, then add the remaining stock.

3 Bring to the boil. Lower the heat, cover the pan and simmer gently, stirring occasionally, for about 20 minutes, or until all the liquid has been absorbed.

4 Stir in the lemon rind, herbs, cheese and seasoning. Spoon the mixture into the tin, cover with foil and bake for 30–35 minutes, or until lightly browned. Leave to stand for 5 minutes, then turn out. Serve hot or cold, in slices.

> **Cook's Tip**
> *The risotto rice is cooked with less liquid than normal and therefore has a drier consistency.*

> **Variation**
> *Add 50g/2oz finely diced cooked ham with the mozzarella.*

Timballo of Rice with Peas

This dish is made like a risotto, but is given a final baking in the oven.

Serves 4–6
75g/3oz/6 tbsp butter
30ml/2 tbsp olive oil
1 small onion, finely chopped
50g/2oz ham, cut into small dice
45ml/3 tbsp finely chopped fresh
parsley, plus sprigs to garnish
2 garlic cloves, very finely chopped
225g/8oz/2 cups shelled peas,
thawed if frozen
60ml/4 tbsp water
1.3 litres/2¼ pints/5½ cups
chicken or vegetable stock
350g/12oz/1¾ cups risotto rice
75g/3oz/1 cup freshly grated
Parmesan cheese
175g/6oz Fontina cheese, very
thinly sliced
salt and ground black pepper

1 Preheat the oven to 180°C/350°F/Gas 4. Heat half the butter and all the oil in a large, heavy pan. Cook the onion until soft, then add the ham and stir over medium heat for 3–4 minutes. Stir in the parsley and garlic. Cook for 2 minutes. Add the peas, then season and add 60ml/4 tbsp water.

2 Cover the pan, and cook for 8 minutes for fresh peas, or 4 minutes for frozen peas. Remove the lid and cook until the liquid has evaporated. Spoon half the mixture into a dish. Heat the stock and keep it simmering. Grease a flat-based baking dish and line with non-stick parchment paper.

3 Stir the rice into the pea mixture in the pan. Heat through, then add a ladleful of stock. Cook until absorbed, stirring. Add the remaining stock in the same way. After about 20 minutes, when the rice is just tender, remove from the heat. Season. Mix in most of the remaining butter and half the Parmesan.

4 To assemble, sprinkle the bottom of the dish with Parmesan, and spoon in half the rice. Add a layer of Fontina and spoon over the pea and ham mixture. Sprinkle with Parmesan. Cover with the remaining Fontina and end with the remaining rice. Sprinkle with the last of Parmesan and dot with butter. Bake for 10–15 minutes. Remove from the oven and stand for 10 minutes. Unmould on to a plate. Remove the paper and serve.

Energy 811Kcal/3369kJ; Fat 40.3g; Saturated Fat 23.8g; Carbohydrate 77.7g; Fibre 2.9g

Energy 264Kcal/1103kJ; Fat 4.5g; Saturated Fat 2.6g; Carbohydrate 46.5g; Fibre 1.6g

Vermicelli Frittata

An Italian version of an omelette, eggs are baked with fine pasta strands, cheese and vegetables to create a delicious supper dish. Serve hot or cold with a fresh-tasting rocket salad.

Serves 4–6
50g/2oz dried vermicelli
6 eggs
60ml/4 tbsp panna da cucina or double (heavy) cream
1 handful fresh basil leaves, shredded
1 handful fresh flat leaf parsley, chopped
75g/3oz/1 cup freshly grated Parmesan cheese
25g/1oz/2 tbsp butter
15ml/1 tbsp olive oil
1 onion, finely sliced
3 large pieces bottled roasted red (bell) pepper, drained, rinsed, dried and cut into strips
1 garlic clove, crushed
salt and ground black pepper

1 Preheat the oven to 190°C/375°F/Gas 5. Bring a pan of lightly salted water to the boil, carefully coil in the pasta and cook until *al dente*.

2 Meanwhile, break the eggs into a bowl and add the cream and herbs. Whisk in about two-thirds of the grated Parmesan and add salt and pepper to taste.

3 Drain the pasta well and allow to cool, then snip it into short lengths with scissors. Add to the egg mixture and whisk again. Set the mixture aside.

4 Melt the butter in the oil in a large, ovenproof non-stick frying pan. Add the onion and cook gently, stirring frequently, for 5 minutes, until softened. Add the peppers and garlic.

5 Pour the egg and pasta mixture into the pan and stir well. Cook over low to medium heat, without stirring, for 3–5 minutes or until the frittata is just set underneath. Sprinkle the remaining Parmesan over and bake in the oven for 5 minutes, or until set. Before serving, leave the frittata to stand for at least 5 minutes. Serve cut into wedges.

Risotto Frittata

Half omelette, half risotto, this makes a delightful light meal. Try to cook in a cast-iron pan, so that the eggs cook quickly underneath but stay moist on top.

Serves 4
400–475ml/14–16fl oz/
 1²/₃–2 cups chicken stock
30–45ml/2–3 tbsp olive oil
1 small onion, finely chopped
1 garlic clove, crushed
1 large red (bell) pepper, seeded and cut into thin strips
150g/5oz/³/₄ cup risotto rice
25–40g/1–1¹/₂oz/2–3 tbsp butter
175g/6oz/2¹/₂ cups button mushrooms, finely sliced
60ml/4 tbsp freshly grated Parmesan cheese
6–8 eggs
salt and ground black pepper

1 Pour the stock into a pan and simmer gently until required. Heat 15ml/1 tbsp oil in a large frying pan and fry the onion and garlic over gentle heat for 2–3 minutes, until the onion begins to soften but does not brown. Add the pepper and cook, stirring, for 4–5 minutes, until soft.

2 Stir in the rice and cook gently for 2–3 minutes, stirring all the time, until the grains are evenly coated with oil.

3 Add a quarter of the hot chicken stock and season. Stir over low heat until the stock has been absorbed. Continue to add more stock, a little at a time, allowing the rice to absorb the liquid before adding more. Continue cooking in this way until the rice is *al dente*.

4 Meanwhile, heat a little of the remaining oil and some butter and quickly fry the mushrooms until golden. Remove the rice from the heat and stir in the mushrooms and Parmesan cheese.

5 Beat together the eggs with 40ml/8 tsp cold water and season well. Heat the remaining oil and butter in an omelette pan and add the risotto mixture. Spread the mixture out in the pan, then immediately add the beaten egg, tilting the pan so that the omelette cooks evenly. Fry over moderately high heat for 1–2 minutes and serve immediately.

Energy 434Kcal/1804kJ; Fat 24.5g; Saturated Fat 9.5g; Carbohydrate 34.1g; Fibre 1.4g

Energy 270Kcal/1118kJ; Fat 20.4g; Saturated Fat 9.9g; Carbohydrate 9.4g; Fibre 0.6g

Semolina & Pesto Gnocchi

These Roman gnocchi are made from rounds of semolina paste, which are brushed with melted butter and topped with cheese, then baked until golden. They taste wonderful, especially when served with a home-made tomato sauce.

Serves 4

750ml/1¼ pints/3 cups milk
200g/7oz/generous 1 cup
  semolina
45ml/3 tbsp pesto sauce
60ml/4 tbsp finely chopped sun-
  dried tomatoes, patted dry
  if oily
50g/2oz/¼ cup butter
75g/3oz/1 cup freshly grated
  Pecorino cheese
2 eggs, beaten
freshly grated nutmeg, to taste
salt and ground black pepper
home-made tomato sauce,
  to serve
fresh basil sprigs, to garnish

1 Heat the milk in a large non-stick pan. When it is on the point of boiling, sprinkle in the semolina, stirring constantly until the mixture is smooth and very thick. Lower the heat and simmer for 2 minutes until the paste starts to come away from the sides.

2 Remove from the heat and stir in the pesto and sun-dried tomatoes, with half of the butter and half of the Pecorino. Add the eggs, with nutmeg, salt and pepper to taste. Spoon into a clean shallow baking dish or pan to a depth of 1cm/½in, and level the surface. Allow to cool, then chill.

3 Preheat the oven to 190°C/375°F/Gas 5. Lightly grease a shallow baking dish, then, using a 4cm/1½in scone cutter or a glass, stamp out as many rounds as possible from the chilled semolina paste. Place the leftover semolina paste on the bottom of the greased dish and arrange the cut-out rounds on top, in overlapping circles.

4 Melt the remaining butter and brush it over the gnocchi. Sprinkle over the remaining Pecorino. Bake for 30–40 minutes, until golden. Garnish with basil and serve with tomato sauce.

Pumpkin Gnocchi

The addition of pumpkin makes these potato gnocchi extra delicious. A mushroom sauce gives added richness.

Serves 4

450g/1lb floury potatoes
450g/1lb pumpkin, peeled and
  chopped
2 egg yolks
200g/7oz/1¾ cups flour
pinch of ground allspice
1.5ml/¼ tsp ground cinnamon
pinch of grated nutmeg
finely grated rind of ½ orange
flour, for dusting
salt and ground black pepper
50g/2oz Parmesan cheese,
  shaved, to garnish

For the sauce

30ml/2 tbsp olive oil
1 shallot, chopped
175g/6oz/2¼ cups fresh
  chanterelles, sliced
10ml/2 tsp almond butter
150ml/¼ pint/⅔ cup crème
  fraîche
a little milk or water
75ml/5 tbsp chopped parsley

1 Cover the potatoes with salted water, bring to the boil and cook for 20 minutes. Preheat the oven to 180°C/350°F/Gas 4. Wrap the pumpkin in foil and bake for 30 minutes. Drain, add to the potato and pass through a vegetable mill into a bowl.

2 Add the egg yolks, flour, spices, orange rind and seasoning to the pumpkin and mix to a soft dough, adding more flour if needed. Spoon into a piping bag fitted with a 1cm/½in nozzle. Pipe on to a floured surface to make a 15cm/6in sausage. Roll in the flour and cut into 2.5cm/1in pieces. Repeat with the rest.

3 Mark the gnocchi lightly with a fork and cook in boiling salted water for 3–4 minutes.

4 Meanwhile, make the sauce. Heat the oil in a non-stick frying pan and fry the shallot until soft, without colouring. Add the chanterelles and cook briefly, then stir in the almond butter. Stir in the crème fraîche. Simmer briefly and adjust the consistency with milk or water. Add the parsley and season to taste.

5 Lift the gnocchi out of the water, turn into bowls and spoon the sauce over the top. Scatter with the Parmesan.

Energy 560Kcal/2347kJ; Fat 31.1g; Saturated Fat 15.3g; Carbohydrate 47.8g; Fibre 1.1g

Energy 576Kcal/2411kJ; Fat 31g; Saturated Fat 16g; Carbohydrate 62.1g; Fibre 5.1g

Spinach & Ricotta Gnocchi

The success of this Italian dish lies in not overworking the dough mixture, to achieve delicious, light mouthfuls.

Serves 4
900g/2lb fresh spinach
350g/12oz/1½ cups ricotta cheese
60ml/4 tbsp freshly grated Parmesan cheese
3 large eggs, beaten
1.5ml/¼ tsp grated nutmeg
45–60ml/3–4 tbsp plain (all-purpose) flour
115g/4oz/½ cup butter, melted
salt and ground black pepper
freshly grated Parmesan cheese, to serve

1 Place the spinach in a large pan and cook for 5 minutes, until wilted. Leave to cool, then squeeze the spinach as dry as possible. Process in a blender or food processor, then transfer to a bowl.

2 Add the ricotta cheese, Parmesan, eggs and grated nutmeg. Season with salt and pepper and mix together. Add enough flour to make the mixture into a soft dough. Using your hands, shape the mixture into 7.5cm/3in sausages, then dust lightly with flour.

3 Bring a large pan of salted water to the boil. Gently slide the gnocchi into the water and cook for 1–2 minutes, until they float to the surface.

4 Remove the gnocchi with a slotted spoon and transfer to a warmed dish. Pour over the melted butter and sprinkle with Parmesan cheese. Serve at once.

> **Variation**
> *For baked spinach gnocchi, place the gnocchi in a buttered baking dish as they are poached, then pour over 50g/2oz/¼ cup melted butter. Scatter the top with 50g/2oz/⅔ cup freshly grated Parmesan and cook in an oven preheated to 180°C/350°F/Gas 4 for 5 minutes until the cheese has melted.*

Polenta with Mushroom Sauce

In Italy, polenta is often used as a starchy base for a meal. Its subtle taste works well with this mushroom sauce.

Serves 4
1.2 litres/2 pints/5 cups vegetable stock
350g/12oz/2½ cups polenta
50g/2oz/⅔ cup freshly grated Parmesan cheese
salt and ground black pepper

For the sauce
15g/½oz/1 cup dried porcini mushrooms
150ml/¼ pint/⅔ cup hot water
15ml/1 tbsp olive oil
50g/2oz/¼ cup butter
1 onion, finely chopped
1 carrot, finely chopped
1 celery stick, finely chopped
2 garlic cloves, crushed
450g/1lb/6 cups mixed chestnut and large flat mushrooms, roughly chopped
120ml/4fl oz/½ cup red wine
400g/14oz can chopped Italian plum tomatoes
5ml/1 tsp tomato purée (paste)
15ml/1 tbsp chopped fresh thyme leaves

1 To make the sauce, put the dried mushrooms in a bowl with the hot water and soak for 20 minutes. Drain the mushrooms, reserving the liquid, and chop them roughly.

2 Heat the oil and butter in a pan. Fry the onion, carrot, celery and garlic over low heat until beginning to soften. Increase the heat and add the fresh and soaked, dried mushrooms. Cook for 8–10 minutes, until the mushrooms are soft and golden.

3 Pour in the wine and cook rapidly for 2–3 minutes, until reduced, then add the tomatoes and the reserved mushroom liquid. Stir in the tomato purée, thyme and plenty of salt and pepper. Lower the heat and simmer for 20 minutes.

4 Meanwhile, heat the stock in a large, heavy pan. Add a generous pinch of salt. When simmering, pour in the polenta in a fine stream, whisking until smooth. Cook for 30 minutes, stirring constantly, until the polenta comes away from the pan. Remove from heat and stir in half of the Parmesan and pepper. Divide among four heated bowls and top each with the mushroom sauce. Sprinkle with the remaining grated Parmesan.

Energy 566Kcal/2342kJ; Fat 45.7g; Saturated Fat 26.4g; Carbohydrate 15.2g; Fibre 5.1g

Energy 572Kcal/2384kJ; Fat 21g; Saturated Fat 9.7g; Carbohydrate 72.2g; Fibre 5.4g

Polenta Elisa

This dish comes from the valley around Lake Como. Serve it solo as a starter, or with a mixed salad and salami or prosciutto for a midweek supper.

Serves 4
250ml/8fl oz/1 cup milk
225g/8oz/2 cups quick-cook
  polenta
115g/4oz/1 cup Gruyère cheese
115g/4oz/1 cup torta di
  Dolcelatte cheese, crumbled
50g/2oz/¼ cup butter
2 garlic cloves, roughly chopped
a few fresh sage leaves, chopped
salt and ground black pepper

1 Bring the milk and 750ml/1¼ pints/3 cups water to the boil in a large pan. Add 5ml/1 tsp salt, then pour in the polenta in a steady stream, whisking to incorporate. Change to a wooden spoon and continue to cook, stirring constantly, for 5 minutes, until the polenta comes away from the sides of the pan.

2 Preheat the oven to 200°C/400°F/Gas 6. Lightly grease a 20–25cm/8–10in baking dish.

3 Spoon half of the polenta into the greased baking dish and level the surface. Cover with half of the grated Gruyère and crumbled Dolcelatte. Spoon the remaining polenta over the top and sprinkle with the remaining cheeses.

4 Melt the butter in a small pan until foaming, then fry the garlic and sage, stirring, until the butter turns golden brown.

5 Drizzle the butter mixture over the polenta and cheese and grind black pepper liberally over the top. Bake for 5 minutes. Serve immediately.

> **Cook's Tip**
> When cooking the polenta in step 1, do not stop stirring until your remove the polenta from the heat.

Grilled Polenta with Gorgonzola

Golden squares of grilled polenta look and taste delicious. Serve spread with any flavourful soft cheese or as an accompaniment to soups and salads.

Serves 6–8
15ml/1 tbsp salt
350g/12oz/2½ cups quick-cook
  polenta
225g/8oz/1¼ cups Gorgonzola
  cheese, at room temperature

1 Bring 1.5 litres/2½ pints/6¼ cups water to the boil in a large heavy pan. Add the salt. Reduce the heat to a simmer and gradually add the polenta in a fine, steady stream, whisking to incorporate. Change to a wooden spoon and cook, stirring, until the polenta comes away from the sides of the pan. This may take 25–50 minutes depending on the type of polenta used.

2 When the polenta is cooked, sprinkle a work surface or large board with a little water. Spread the polenta out onto the surface in a layer 2cm/¾in thick. Allow to cool completely. Preheat the grill (broiler).

3 Cut the polenta into triangles. Grill (broil) on both sides, until hot and speckled with brown. Serve spread with the cheese.

Baked Cheese Polenta with Tomato

In this Italian classic, cooked polenta is cut into shapes and baked, layered with tomato sauce and cheese.

Serves 4
5ml/1 tsp salt
250g/9oz/2¼ cups quick-cook
  polenta
5ml/1tsp paprika
2.5ml/½ tsp ground nutmeg
30ml/2 tbsp olive oil
1 large onion, finely chopped
2 garlic cloves, crushed
2 x 400g/14oz cans chopped
  Italian plum tomatoes
15ml/1tbsp tomato purée (paste)
5ml/1 tsp sugar
75g/3 oz Gruyère cheese, grated
salt and ground black pepper

1 Preheat the oven to 200°C/400°F/Gas 6. Line a 28 × 18cm/11 × 7in baking tin (pan) with clear film (plastic wrap). Bring 1 litre/1¾ pints/4 cups water to the boil in a large heavy pan, with 5ml/1 tsp salt.

2 Pour in the polenta in a steady stream, whisking to incorporate. Change to a wooden spoon and cook, stirring constantly, for 5 minutes, until the polenta comes away from the sides of the pan. Beat in the paprika and nutmeg, then pour into the prepared tin and smooth the surface. Leave until cold.

3 Heat the oil in a pan and cook the onion and garlic until soft. Add the tomatoes, purée and sugar. Season with salt and pepper, then simmer gently for 20 minutes.

4 Turn out the polenta on to a chopping board and cut into 5cm/2in squares. Place half the squares in a greased ovenproof dish. Spoon over half the tomato sauce and sprinkle with half the cheese. Repeat the layers. Bake for about 25 minutes, until golden. Serve immediately.

Energy 454Kcal/1892kJ; Fat 21.8g; Saturated Fat 12.8g; Carbohydrate 44.1g; Fibre 1.3g

Top Energy 252Kcal/1052kJ; Fat 5.7g; Saturated Fat 2.5g; Carbohydrate 41g; Fibre 1.2g
Above Energy 404Kcal/1687kJ; Fat 14.3g; Saturated Fat 5g; Carbohydrate 54.7g; Fibre 3.7g

Grilled Chilli & Herb Polenta

Chillies and fresh herbs transform mild tasting polenta into a palate-tingling snack. Perfect served with a tangy tomato sauce.

Serves 6–12
10ml/2 tsp crushed dried chilli flakes
250g/9oz/2¼ cups quick-cook polenta
50g/2oz/¼ cup butter
75g/3oz Parmesan cheese, finely grated
30ml/2 tbsp chopped fresh dill
30ml/2 tbsp chopped fresh coriander (cilantro)
30ml/2 tbsp olive oil
salt
home-made tomato sauce, to serve

1 Finely, chop the dried chilli flakes. Put them in a pan with 1.3 litres/2¼ pints/5⅔ cups water. Bring to the boil and add salt to taste.

2 Pour the polenta into the water in a steady stream, whisking constantly. Reduce the heat and continue to stir with a wooden spoon for 5 minutes, until the polenta comes away from the sides of the pan. Whisk in the butter, Parmesan and herbs. Season with salt. Pour into a greased 33 × 23cm/13 × 9in baking tin (pan) and leave to cool. Leave uncovered so that the surface firms up and chill overnight.

3 Remove the polenta from the refrigerator and leave for about 30 minutes. Cut into 12 even triangles and brush the tops with oil. Heat a griddle until a few drops of water sprinkled on the surface evaporate instantly. Lower the heat to medium and cook the polenta triangles, oiled-side down, for about 2 minutes, then turn 180 degrees and cook for 1 minute more for a chequered effect. Serve with tomato sauce.

> **Cook's Tip**
> The polenta triangles can be cooked directly on an oiled grill rack on the barbecue, if you prefer. Make sure they are well seared on one side before turning over to cook the other side.

Mushroom Polenta

This simple dish of squares of set polenta baked with mushrooms and cheese is quite sublime. Any combination of mushrooms will work – try a mixture of button and wild mushrooms. Serve with a leafy salad and crisp, white wine.

Serves 4
250g/9oz/2½ cups quick-cook polenta
50g/2oz/¼ cup butter
400g/14oz chestnut mushrooms, sliced
175g/6oz/1½ cups grated Gruyère cheese
salt and ground black pepper

1 Line a 28 × 18cm/11 × 7in shallow baking tin (pan) with baking parchment. Bring 1 litre/1¾ pints/4 cups water with 5ml/1 tsp salt to the boil in a large pan.

2 Add the polenta in a steady stream, whisking constantly. Bring back to the boil, stirring with a wooden spoon, and cook for 5 minutes, until thick and smooth. Turn the polenta into the prepared tin and smooth the surface. Leave to cool.

3 Preheat the oven to 200°C/400°F/Gas 6. Melt the butter in a frying pan and cook the mushrooms for 3–5 minutes, until golden. Season with salt and lots of black pepper.

4 Turn out the polenta on to a chopping board. Peel away the parchment and cut the polenta into large squares. Pile the squares into a shallow, ovenproof dish.

5 Sprinkle with half the cheese, then pile the mushrooms on top and pour over their buttery juices. Sprinkle with the remaining cheese and bake for about 20 minutes, until the cheese is melting and pale golden.

> **Cook's Tip**
> The cheesy mushroom topping is also delicious on toasted herb or sun-dried tomato bread as a light lunch or supper. For extra flavour, add crushed garlic to the pan of mushrooms.

Tuna, Courgette & Pepper Frittata

This nutritious Italian-style
omelette is quick and easy
to make. Serve it simply,
with a mixed leaf salad for
a tasty lunch or supper.

Serves 4

15ml/1 tbsp sunflower oil
1 onion, chopped
1 courgette (zucchini), thinly sliced
1 red (bell) pepper, seeded
   and sliced

4 eggs
30ml/2 tbsp semi-skimmed
   (low-fat) milk
200g/7oz can tuna in brine or
   water, drained and flaked
10ml/2 tsp dried herbes de
   Provence
50g/2oz/¹⁄₂ cup grated half-fat
   Cheddar cheese
salt and ground black pepper
mixed leaf salad, to serve

1 Heat half the oil in a shallow, non-stick pan. Add the onion,
courgette and red pepper and cook, stirring frequently, for
5 minutes.

2 Beat the eggs with the milk in a small bowl. Heat the
remaining oil in a heavy, non-stick omelette pan. Add the
cooked onion, courgette and red pepper, flaked tuna and dried
herbs, and season well with salt and pepper.

3 Pour the egg mixture evenly into the frying pan over the
vegetable mixture and cook over medium heat until the eggs
are beginning to set. Pull the sides into the middle to allow the
uncooked egg to run on to the pan, then continue cooking
undisturbed, until the frittata is golden underneath. Meanwhile,
preheat the grill (broiler) to medium.

4 Sprinkle the cheese over the top of the frittata and grill
(broil) until the cheese has melted and the top is golden.

Variations
• Use 25g/1oz/¹⁄₃ cup freshly grated Parmesan cheese in place
of Red Leicester or Cheddar cheese.
• Use canned pink or red salmon in place of tuna.

Frittata with Onions

Gently cooked onions give
this simple frittata a
beautifully sweet flavour.
Serve with a leafy salad and
ciabatta for an easy light
lunch or supper.

Serves 3–4

60ml/4 tbsp olive oil
2 onions, thinly sliced
30ml/2 tbsp chopped fresh
   parsley or basil
6 eggs
salt and ground black pepper

1 Heat the oil in a large non-stick or heavy frying pan. Stir in
the onions and cook over low heat, until they are soft and
golden. This may take 10–15 minutes. Season with salt and
pepper. Stir in the herbs.

2 Break the eggs into a bowl and beat them lightly with a fork.
Increase the heat under the onions to medium and, when they
are sizzling, pour in the eggs. Quickly stir into the onions to
distribute well. Stop stirring.

3 Cook for about 5 minutes, or until the frittata is puffed and
golden brown underneath. If the frittata seems to be sticking to
the pan, shake the pan backwards and and forwards to help
release it.

4 Place a large plate upside down over the pan, then, holding
them firmly together with oven gloves, invert the frittata on to
the plate. Slide the frittata back into the pan and continue to
cook for a further 3–4 minutes, until golden brown on the
second side. Remove from the heat, transfer to a plate and
cut into wedges to serve.

Cook's Tip
A frittata is basically a flat baked omelette and is incredibly
versatile, as you can add anything to it. For instance, in this
recipe you could replace some of the onions with chopped
salami or cooked chicken. Lightly fried mushrooms, courgettes
(zucchini) and aubergines (eggplants) would also be good.

Pasta Frittata

This is a great way to use up cold leftover pasta.

Serves 4
225g/8oz/1½ cups cold cooked pasta, with any sauce
59g/2oz/½ cup freshly grated Parmesan cheese
5 eggs, lightly beaten
65g/2½oz/5 tbsp butter
salt and ground black pepper

1 Stir the pasta and Parmesan into the eggs. Season to taste. Heat half the butter in a large pan. Pour in the egg mixture. and cook for 4–5 minutes, gently shaking the pan.

2 Invert the frittata on to a plate. Melt the remaining butter in the pan, slide the frittata back in and cook for 3–4 minutes.

Sliced Frittata Salad

A refreshing idea for a summer's lunch – cold frittata with tomato sauce.

Serves 3–4
6 eggs
30ml/2 tbsp mixed fresh herbs, such as basil, parsley, thyme or tarragon, finely chopped
35g/1½oz/¼ cup freshly grated Parmesan or Romano cheese
45ml/3 tbsp olive oil
salt and ground black pepper

For the tomato sauce
30ml/2 tbsp olive oil
1 small onion, finely chopped
350g/12oz fresh tomatoes, or 400g/14oz can tomatoes, chopped
1 garlic clove, chopped

1 To make the frittata, break the eggs into a large bowl and beat them lightly with a fork. Beat in the herbs and cheese. Season to taste with salt and ground black pepper. Heat the oil in a large non-stick or heavy frying pan until hot but not smoking.

2 Pour in the egg mixture. Cook, without stirring, until the frittata is puffed and golden brown underneath.

3 Place a large plate upside down over the pan and, holding together firmly with oven gloves, invert the frittata on to the plate. Carefully slide the frittata back into the pan and continue cooking for a further 3–4 minutes, until golden brown on the second side. Remove from the heat and allow to cool completely.

4 To make the tomato sauce, heat the oil in a heavy pan. Add the onion and cook slowly until it is soft. Add the tomatoes, garlic and 60ml/4 tbsp water, then season with salt and pepper. Cover the pan and cook over medium heat for about 15 minutes (or 5 minutes for canned), until the tomatoes are soft.

5 Remove from the heat, cool slightly, then pass the sauce through a food mill or sieve (strainer). Leave to cool completely.

6 Cut the frittata into thin slices, place in a serving bowl and toss lightly with the sauce. Serve at room temperature or chilled.

Frittata with Spinach & Ham

In Italy, frittate are often used as fillings for sandwiches. This hearty version would make an excellent filling.

Serves 6
200g/7oz/1 cup cooked leaf spinach, fresh or frozen
45ml/3 tbsp olive oil
4 spring onions (scallions), finely sliced
1 garlic clove, finely chopped
50g/2oz/⅓ cup diced ham or prosciutto
8 eggs
salt and ground black pepper

1 Squeeze any excess moisture out of the spinach with your hands. Chop it roughly and set aside.

2 Heat the oil in a large non-stick or heavy frying pan. Stir in the spring onions and cook for 3–4 minutes. Add the garlic and ham and stir over medium heat, until just golden. Stir in the spinach and cook for 3–4 minutes, or until just heated through. Season with salt and pepper.

3 Break the eggs into a bowl and beat lightly with a fork. Increase the heat under the vegetables. After about 1 minute pour in the eggs. Mix them quickly into the other ingredients, and stop stirring. Cook over medium heat for about 5–6 minutes, or until the frittata is puffed and golden brown underneath. Shake the pan if the frittata seems to be sticking.

4 Place a large plate upside down over the pan and, holding it firmly with oven gloves, invert the frittata on to the plate. Slide the frittata back into the pan and continue cooking for a further 3–4 minutes, until golden brown on the second side. Remove from the heat. Serve hot or cold. Cut into wedges to serve.

> **Cook's Tip**
> If preferred, do not turn the frittata over, but put the pan under the grill (broiler) to finish the uncooked top side.

Energy 184Kcal/763kJ; Fat 14g; Saturated Fat 3.1g; Carbohydrate 1.6g; Fibre 1.7g

Top Energy 410Kcal/1710kJ; Fat 28.5g; Saturated Fat 15g; Carbohydrate 22g; Fibre 1.2g
Above Energy 285Kcal/1180kJ; Fat 24.4g; Saturated Fat 6g; Carbohydrate 4.3g; Fibre 1.2g

Pan-fried Prawns in their Shells

Large prawns (shrimp) sizzled with garlic, vermouth and tomato make a stylish supper for friends. Serve with hot crusty Italian bread, such as ciabatta, to mop up the juices.

Serves 4

60ml/4 tbsp extra virgin olive oil

32 large raw prawns (shrimp), in their shells
4 garlic cloves, finely chopped
120ml/4fl oz/½ cup Italian dry white vermouth
45ml/3 tbsp passata
salt and ground black pepper
chopped fresh flat leaf parsley, to garnish
crusty bread and lemon wedges (optional), to serve

I Heat the olive oil in a large heavy frying pan until just sizzling. Add the prawns and toss over medium to high heat until their shells just begin to turn pink.

2 Sprinkle the chopped garlic over the prawns in the pan and toss again, then add the vermouth and let it bubble, tossing the prawns constantly so that they cook evenly and absorb the flavours of the garlic and vermouth.

3 Keeping the pan on the heat, add the passata and season to taste. Stir until the prawns are thoroughly coated in the sauce. Serve at once, sprinkled with the parsley and accompanied by plenty of hot crusty bread, and lemon wedges, if desired.

Cook's Tips
• *Prawns in their shells are sweet and juicy, and fun to eat with your fingers. They can be quite messy though, so provide guests with finger bowls and napkins.*
• *When buying fresh prawns check that they have bright shells that feel firm; if they are limp or seem to smell of ammonia, do not buy them.*
• *If you do not have dry vermouth to hand, you could use dry white wine instead. Passata can be replaced by puréed canned or fresh tomatoes.*

Chargrilled Squid

Squid is very popular in the coastal regions of Italy where it is usually cooked simply with few ingredients to preserve its delicate texture.

Serves 2

2 whole prepared squid, with tentacles

75ml/5 tbsp olive oil
30ml/2 tbsp balsamic vinegar
2 fresh red chillies, finely chopped
60ml/4 tbsp dry white wine
salt and ground black pepper
sprigs of fresh parsley, to garnish
hot cooked risotto rice, to serve

I Make a lengthways cut down the body of each squid, then open out the body flat. Score the flesh on both sides of the bodies in a criss-cross pattern with the tip of a sharp knife. Chop the tentacles. Place all the squid in a china or glass dish. Whisk the oil and vinegar in a small bowl. Add salt and pepper to taste and pour over the squid. Cover and leave to marinate for about 1 hour.

2 Heat a ridged cast-iron pan until hot. Add the body of one of the squid. Cook over medium heat for 2–3 minutes, pressing the squid with a fish slice or metal spatula to keep it flat. Repeat on the other side. Cook the other squid body in the same way.

3 Cut the squid bodies into diagonal strips. Pile the hot risotto rice in the centre of heated soup plates and top with the strips of squid, arranging them criss-cross fashion. Keep hot.

4 Add the chopped tentacles and chillies to the pan and toss over medium heat for 2 minutes. Stir in the wine, then pour the mixture over the squid and rice. Garnish with the parsley and serve at once.

Cook's Tip
If you like your food spicy, chop some, or all, of the chilli seeds with the flesh. If not, cut the chillies in half lengthways, scrape out the seeds and discard them before chopping the flesh.

Spicy Seafood & Mussel Stew

This spicy seafood dish, packed with Mediterranean flavours, is irresistible with herby brown rice.

Serves 4
10ml/2 tsp olive oil
1 onion, chopped
1 garlic clove, crushed
2 celery sticks, chopped
1 red (bell) pepper, seeded and diced
5ml/1 tsp each ground coriander, ground cumin and ground ginger
2.5ml/½ tsp hot chilli powder
2.5ml/½ tsp garam masala
30ml/2 tbsp plain (all-purpose) wholemeal (whole-wheat) flour
300ml/½ pint/1¼ cups each fish stock and dry white wine
225g/8oz can chopped tomatoes
225g/8oz mushrooms, sliced
450g/1lb frozen cooked, shelled mixed seafood, thawed
175g/6oz/1 cup frozen corn kernels
225g/8oz fresh mussels
225g/8oz/generous 1 cup long grain brown rice
30–45ml/2–3 tbsp chopped mixed fresh herbs
salt and ground black pepper
fresh parsley sprigs, to garnish

1 Heat the oil in a large, non-stick pan. Add the onion, garlic, celery and red pepper and cook, stirring occasionally, for 5 minutes. Add the ground spices and cook, stirring, for 1 minute, then add the flour and cook, continuing to stir, for 1 minute.

2 Gradually stir in the stock and wine, then add the tomatoes and mushrooms. Bring to the boil, stirring continuously, then cover and simmer, stirring occasionally, for 20 minutes.

3 Stir in the rest of the seafood, corn kernels and mussels and cook, stirring occasionally, for a further 10–15 minutes, until hot. Discard any unopened mussels.

4 Meanwhile, cook the brown rice in a large pan of lightly salted boiling water for about 35 minutes, or until just tender.

5 Rinse the cooked rice in fresh boiling water and drain thoroughly, then toss the rice together with the mixed herbs. Season the stew to taste and serve on a bed of the herbed rice. Garnish with fresh parsley sprigs and serve immediately.

Italian Prawn Skewers

These simple and delicious mouthfuls are typical of the cooking found along the Amalfi Coast.

Serves 4
900g/2lb large raw prawns (shrimp), peeled
60ml/4 tbsp olive oil
45ml/3 tbsp vegetable oil
75g/3oz/1½ cups breadcrumbs
1 garlic clove, crushed
15ml/1 tbsp chopped fresh parsley
salt and ground black pepper
lemon wedges, to serve

1 Slit the prawns down their backs and remove the dark vein. Rinse in cold water and pat dry.

2 Put the olive oil and vegetable oil in a large bowl and add the prawns, mixing them to coat evenly. Add the breadcrumbs, garlic and parsley and season with salt and pepper. Toss the prawns thoroughly, to give them an even coating of breadcrumbs. Cover and leave to marinate for 1 hour.

3 Thread the prawns on to four metal or wooden skewers, curling them up as you do so, so that the tails are firmly skewered in the middle.

4 Preheat the grill (broiler). Place the skewers in the grill pan and cook for about 2 minutes on each side, until the breadcrumbs are golden. Serve with lemon wedges.

Cook's Tip
Soak wooden skewers in cold water for a few hours before threading so that they do not burn.

Variation
To give a citrus zing to the prawns, add the finely grated rind of half a lemon or 1 lime to the breadcrumb mixture.

Energy 298Kcal/1252kJ; Fat 8.1g; Saturated Fat 1.1g; Carbohydrate 14.8g; Fibre 1g

Energy 513Kcal/2172kJ; Fat 7.3g; Saturated Fat 1.6g; Carbohydrate 72.5g; Fibre 4.2g

Stewed Mussels & Clams

Casseroles of mixed shellfish are very popular along the Ligurian coast.

Serves 4

675g/1½lb fresh mussels, in their shells
675g/1½lb fresh clams, in their shells
75ml/5 tbsp olive oil

3 garlic cloves, peeled and crushed
300ml/½ pint/1¼ cups dry white wine
75ml/5 tbsp chopped fresh parsley
ground black pepper
rounds of crusty bread, toasted, to serve

1 Cut off the beards from the mussels with a small sharp knife. Scrub and rinse the mussels and clams in several changes of water. Discard any mussels or clams with broken shells.

2 Heat the oil in a large pan, add the garlic and as soon as the garlic is golden, add the mussels, clams and the wine. Cover and cook over medium to high heat for about 5–8 minutes, shaking the pan occasionally, until all the shells have opened. (Discard any shellfish that do not open.)

3 Lift the clams and mussels out of the pan, pouring any liquid in the shells back into the pan. Place the shellfish in a warmed serving bowl. Remove and discard the garlic.

4 Strain the liquid in the pan through a sieve (strainer) lined with a layer of kitchen paper, pouring it over the shellfish in the bowl. Sprinkle with parsley and season with black pepper. To serve, place rounds of toasted bread in the bottom of individual soup bowls and ladle in the mussels and clams with the liquid.

> **Cook's Tip**
> Mussels and clams should be firmly closed when fresh. If one is slightly open, give it a sharp tap to check that it is alive; it should close immediately. Discard any mussels or clams that do not close, as they are probably dead.

Grilled Prawns with Herbs

Large prawns are delicious marinated with fresh herbs, lemon and garlic, then grilled to succulent perfection. This is a simple dish, ideal for al fresco entertaining.

Serves 4

24 large raw prawns (shrimp), in their shells
3 garlic cloves, finely chopped
45ml/3 tbsp finely chopped fresh basil leaves

15ml/1 tbsp fresh thyme leaves
30ml/2 tbsp finely chopped fresh parsley
15ml/1 tbsp coarsely crushed black pepper
juice of 1 lemon
60ml/4 tbsp olive oil
8 bay leaves
50g/2oz salt pork or pancetta, cut into 8 small squares
fresh flat leaf parsley sprigs, to garnish

1 Pull off the heads of the prawns, peel the tails, then slit them down the back to reveal the long dark vein. Remove and discard this vein.

2 Place the prawns in a bowl with the garlic, chopped herbs, pepper, lemon juice and olive oil. Mix well to coat, then cover and leave to marinate in the refrigerator for at least 6 hours, or preferably overnight.

3 Preheat the grill (broiler). Arrange 6 prawns on each of 4 skewers so that they lie flat, threading a bay leaf and a square of salt pork between every 2 prawns. Brush with the remaining marinade in the bowl.

4 Place the skewers in a single layer under the grill and cook for about 3 minutes. Turn and cook for a further 3 minutes. Serve, garnished with parsley sprigs.

> **Cook's Tip**
> This dish is also suitable for barbecuing; brush the prawns with the remaining marinade every now and again during cooking.

Energy 278Kcal/1162kJ; Fat 15.5g; Saturated Fat 2.4g; Carbohydrate 2.2g; Fibre 0g

Energy 243Kcal/1012kJ; Fat 15.9g; Saturated Fat 3.7g; Carbohydrate 0.4g; Fibre 0.6g

Baked Mussels & Potatoes

This dish originates from Puglia in the south of Italy, an area noted for its imaginative casseroles.

Serves 2–3

675g/1½lb large fresh mussels, in their shells
225g/8oz potatoes, unpeeled

75ml/5 tbsp olive oil
2 garlic cloves, finely chopped
8 fresh basil leaves, torn
225g/8oz tomatoes, peeled and thinly sliced
45ml/3 tbsp fresh white breadcrumbs
ground black pepper

1 Cut off the beards from the mussels with a small sharp knife, then scrub and soak in several changes of cold water. Discard any mussels with broken shells.

2 Place the mussels with a cupful of water in a large pan over medium heat. As soon as the mussels open, lift them out, pouring any liquid in the shells back into the pan.

3 Remove and discard the empty half shells, leaving the mussels attached to the other half. (Discard any mussels that do not open.) Strain the liquid in the pan through a layer of kitchen paper and reserve.

4 Place the potatoes in a pan, with water to cover. Bring to the boil and cook until they are still quite firm. Drain and peel, then slice them evenly.

5 Preheat the oven to 180°C/350°F/Gas 4. Spread 30ml/2 tbsp of the olive oil in the bottom of a shallow ovenproof dish. Cover with the potato slices in one layer. Cover with the mussels in their half shells. Sprinkle evenly with finely chopped garlic and torn fresh basil leaves.

6 Cover with a layer of the tomato slices. Sprinkle with breadcrumbs and black pepper, the strained mussel liquid and the remaining olive oil. Bake for about 20 minutes, or until the tomatoes are soft and the breadcrumbs golden. Serve directly from the baking dish.

Energy 348Kcal/1457kJ; Fat 20.5g; Saturated Fat 3g; Carbohydrate 25.8g; Fibre 1.7g

Prawns in Spicy Tomato Sauce

The tomato sauce base can be spiced up by adding a few hot chillies.

Serves 6

90ml/6 tbsp olive oil
1 onion, finely chopped
1 celery stick, finely chopped
1 small red (bell) pepper, seeded and chopped
120ml/4fl oz/½ cup red wine
15ml/1 tbsp wine vinegar

400g/14oz can plum tomatoes, chopped, with their juice
1 kg/2lb large raw prawns (shrimp), in their shells
2–3 garlic cloves, finely chopped
45ml/3 tbsp finely chopped fresh parsley
1 piece dried chilli, crumbled or chopped (optional)
salt and ground black pepper
fresh flat leaf parsley sprigs, to serve

1 Heat half the olive oil in a heavy pan. Add the chopped onion and cook over low heat, until soft. Stir in the chopped celery and pepper and cook gently for a further 5 minutes.

2 Increase the heat to medium high and add the wine, vinegar and tomatoes. Season with salt and pepper. Bring to a boil and cook for about 5 minutes.

3 Lower the heat, cover the pan, and simmer the mixture for about 30 minutes, until the vegetables are soft. Purée the sauce through a food mill.

4 Pull off the heads of the prawns, peel the tails, then slit them down the back to reveal the long dark intestinal vein. Remove and discard this vein.

5 Heat the remaining oil in a clean heavy pan. Stir in the garlic, parsley and chilli, if using. Cook over medium heat, stirring constantly, until the garlic is golden. Do not let the garlic brown. Add the tomato sauce and bring to the boil. Taste to check the seasoning.

6 Stir in the prawns and bring the sauce back to the boil. Reduce the heat slightly and simmer for 6–8 minutes, until the prawns are pink and stiff. Remove from the heat and serve.

Energy 191Kcal/793kJ; Fat 12.5g; Saturated Fat 1.8g; Carbohydrate 4.3g; Fibre 1.2g

Stuffed Squid

A truly Italian dish in which the squid are filled with a tasty anchovy, tomato and breadcrumb stuffing.

Serves 4

1kg/2lb fresh squid (about 16 medium)
juice of ½ lemon
2 anchovy fillets, chopped
2 garlic cloves, finely chopped
3 tomatoes, peeled, seeded and finely chopped
30ml/2 tbsp chopped fresh parsley
50g/2oz/1 cup fresh breadcrumbs
1 egg
30ml/2 tbsp olive oil
120ml/4fl oz/½ cup dry white wine
salt and ground black pepper

1 Working near the sink, clean the squid by first peeling off the thin skin from the body section. Rinse well. Pull the head and tentacles away from the body sac. Some of the intestines will come away with the head. Remove and discard the translucent quill and any remaining insides from the sac. Sever the tentacles from the head. Discard the head and intestines.

2 Remove and discard the small hard beak from the base of the tentacles. Place the tentacles in a bowl of water with the lemon juice. Rinse the sacs well under cold running water. Pat the insides dry with kitchen paper.

3 Preheat the oven to 180°C/350°F/Gas 4. Drain the tentacles. Chop them coarsely and place in a mixing bowl. Stir in the next 6 ingredients and season. Use this mixture to loosely stuff the squid sacs. Close the sacs with wooden toothpicks.

4 Oil a shallow baking dish large enough to fit the squid in one layer. Arrange the squid sacs in the dish. Pour over the oil and wine. Bake uncovered for 35–45 minutes, or until tender.

Cook's Tip
Do not be tempted to overstuff the squid sacs otherwise they may burst during cooking.

Energy 335Kcal/1414kJ; Fat 11.5g; Saturated Fat 2.2g; Carbohydrate 15.9g; Fibre 1.8g

Deep-fried Prawns & Squid

The Italian name of this dish is Fritto Misto, which means "mixed fry". The seafood is coated in a light batter and deep fried until deliciously crisp. No one will be able to resist these lovely morsels.

Serves 6

vegetable oil, for deep-frying
500g/1¼lb medium-sized fresh prawns (shrimp), shelled and deveined
500g/1¼lb squid (about 12 medium), cleaned, cut into bite-size pieces
115g/4oz/1 cup flour
lemon wedges, to serve

For the batter
2 egg whites
30ml/2 tbsp olive oil
15ml/1 tbsp white wine vinegar
100g/3½oz/scant 1 cup flour
10ml/2 tsp baking soda
40g/1½oz/⅓ cup cornflour (cornstarch)
salt and ground black pepper

1 To make the batter, place the egg whites in a large bowl with the olive oil and vinegar and beat together lightly with a wire whisk. Gradually beat in the dry ingredients, season and whisk until well blended. Beat in 250ml/8fl oz/1 cup water, a little at a time. Cover the bowl and leave to stand for 15 minutes.

2 Heat the oil for deep-frying until a small piece of bread sizzles as soon as it is dropped in – about 180°C/350°F.

3 Place the flour on a plate and coat the prawn and squid pieces in the flour, shaking off any excess. Dip the seafood quickly into the batter. Fry in small batches for about 1 minute, stirring with a slotted spoon to prevent the pieces from sticking to each other. Remove and drain on kitchen paper. Allow the oil to come back up to the correct temperature between batches. Sprinkle lightly with salt and serve with lemon wedges.

Cook's Tip
Any mixture of seafood can be used; it must be completely fresh.

Energy 318Kcal/1340kJ; Fat 13.3g; Saturated Fat 1.9g; Carbohydrate 24.1g; Fibre 0.7g

Baked Aromatic Sea Bass

The silvery sea bass from Mediterranean waters has a delicate white flesh which benefits from simple cooking. Baked with fresh herbs, the fish tastes exquisite.

Serves 4
1 large sea bass, about 1.3kg/3lb
4 bay leaves
a few fresh thyme sprigs
8–10 fresh parsley sprigs
a few fresh fennel, tarragon or basil leaves
15ml/1 tbsp peppercorns
135ml/9 tbsp extra virgin olive oil
flour, for coating
salt and ground black pepper
herb sprigs or lemon wedges, to garnish

1 Gut the fish, leaving the head on. Wash carefully in cold water. Pat dry with kitchen paper. Place half the herbs and peppercorns in the bottom of a shallow platter and lay the fish on top. Arrange the remaining herbs on top of the fish and in its cavity. Sprinkle with 15ml/1 tbsp of the oil. Cover lightly with foil, and refrigerate for 2 hours.

2 Preheat the oven to 200°C/400°F/Gas 6. Remove and discard all the herbs from around the fish, then pat it dry with kitchen paper. Spread a little flour in a platter and season it with salt and pepper. Roll the fish in the flour, then shake off the excess.

3 Heat the remaining olive oil in a flameproof dish just large enough to hold the fish comfortably. When the oil is hot, add the fish and brown it quickly on both sides.

4 Transfer the dish to the oven and bake for 25–40 minutes, depending on the size of the fish. The fish is cooked when the dorsal fin (in the middle of the backbone) comes out easily when pulled. Garnish with herb sprigs or lemon wedges and serve immediately.

> **Cook's Tip**
> You could always use two smaller 500g/1¼lb sea bass instead of one large fish; just double the quantities of fresh herbs.

Grilled Fresh Sardines

The oily flesh of sardines is ideal for barbecuing.

Serves 4–6
1kg/2lb very fresh sardines, gutted and with heads removed
olive oil, for brushing
salt and ground black pepper
45ml/3 tbsp chopped fresh parsley, to garnish
lemon wedges, to serve

1 Preheat the grill (broiler). Rinse the sardines in water. Pat dry with kitchen paper.

2 Brush the sardines with olive oil, season and grill (broil) for 3–4 minutes on each side. Serve with parsley and lemon wedges.

Sardine Gratin

Flavourful sardines demand a robust filling.

Serves 4
15ml/1 tbsp light olive oil
½ small onion, finely chopped
2 garlic cloves, crushed
40g/1½oz/⅓ cup blanched almonds, chopped
25g/1oz/3 tbsp sultanas (golden raisins), roughly chopped
10 pitted black olives
30ml/2 tbsp capers, roughly chopped
30ml/2 tbsp roughly chopped fresh parsley
50g/2oz/1 cup dry breadcrumbs
16 large sardines, scaled and gutted
25g/1oz/⅓ cup freshly grated Parmesan cheese
salt and ground black pepper

1 Preheat the oven to 200°C/400°F/Gas 6. Lightly oil a shallow ovenproof dish. Heat the oil in a frying pan and fry the onion and garlic gently for 3 minutes. Stir in the almonds, sultanas, olives, capers, parsley and half the breadcrumbs. Season lightly.

2 Make 2–3 diagonal cuts on each side of the sardines. Pack the stuffing into the cavities and arrange the sardines in the dish. Mix the remaining breadcrumbs with the cheese and scatter over the fish. Bake for about 20 minutes, until cooked through.

Top Energy 214Kcal/893kJ; Fat 13.2g; Saturated Fat 3.2g; Carbohydrate 0.2g; Fibre 0.4g
Above Energy 346Kcal/1445kJ; Fat 20g; Saturated Fat 4.6g; Carbohydrate 16.2g; Fibre 2.2g

Energy 219Kcal/914kJ; Fat 11.2g; Saturated Fat 1.7g; Carbohydrate 0.2g; Fibre 0.4g

Pan-fried Sole with Lemon

The delicate flavour and texture of sole is brought out in this simple cooking method, and creates a wonderfully healthy dish.

Serves 2

30–45 ml/2–3 tbsp plain (all-purpose) flour

4 lemon sole fillets
45ml/3 tbsp olive oil
50g/2 oz/¼ cup butter
60ml/4 tbsp lemon juice
30ml/2 tbsp rinsed bottled capers
salt and ground black pepper
fresh flat leaf parsley, to garnish
lemon wedges, to serve

1 Season the flour with salt and black pepper. Coat the sole fillets evenly on both sides.

2 Heat the oil with half the butter in a large shallow pan until foaming. Add two sole fillets and fry over a medium heat for 2–3 minutes on each side.

3 Lift out the sole fillets with a fish slice or metal spatula and place on a warmed serving platter. Keep hot. Fry the remaining sole fillets.

4 Remove the pan from the heat and add the lemon juice and remaining butter. Return the pan to high heat and stir vigorously until the pan juices are sizzling and beginning to turn golden brown. Remove from the heat and stir in the capers.

5 Pour the pan juices over the sole, sprinkle with salt and pepper to taste and garnish with the parsley. Add the lemon wedges and serve at once.

> **Cook's Tip**
> It is important to cook the pan juices to the right colour after removing the fish. Too pale, and they will taste insipid, too dark, and they may taste bitter. Take great care not to be distracted at this point so that you can watch the colour of the juices change to a golden brown.

Three-colour Fish Kebabs

Made with three different types of fish, these colourful kebabs are straight from the Italian Riviera.

Serves 4

120ml/4 fl oz/½ cup olive oil
finely grated rind and juice of 1 large lemon
5ml/1 tsp crushed chilli flakes
350g/12 oz monkfish fillet, cubed
350g/12 oz swordfish fillet, cubed
350g/12 oz thick salmon fillet or steak, cubed
2 red, yellow or orange (bell) peppers, cored, seeded and cut into squares

30ml/2 tbsp finely chopped fresh flat leaf parsley
salt and ground black pepper

For the tomato chilli sauce

225g/8 oz ripe tomatoes, finely chopped
1 garlic clove, crushed
1 fresh red chilli, seeded and chopped
45ml/3 tbsp extra virgin olive oil
15ml/1 tbsp lemon juice
15ml/1 tbsp finely chopped fresh flat leaf parsley
pinch of sugar

1 Put the oil in a shallow glass or china bowl and add the lemon rind and juice, the chilli flakes and pepper to taste. Whisk to combine, then add the fish chunks. Turn to coat evenly. Add the pepper squares, stir, then cover and marinate in a cool place for 1 hour, turning occasionally.

2 Thread the fish and peppers on to eight oiled metal skewers, reserving the marinade. Barbecue or grill (broil) the skewered fish for 5–8 minutes, turning once.

3 Meanwhile, mix all the ingredients for the sauce together and season to taste. Heat the reserved marinade in a small pan, then stir in the parsley, with salt and pepper to taste and spoon over the kebabs. Serve the kebabs accompanied by the sauce.

> **Cook's Tip**
> Don't marinate the fish for more than an hour or the lemon will break down the fibres, making it easy to overcook by mistake.

Energy 526Kcal/2186kJ; Fat 40.2g; Saturated Fat 15.8g; Carbohydrate 6g; Fibre 0.3g

Energy 458Kcal/1913kJ; Fat 25.9g; Saturated Fat 4.5g; Carbohydrate 7.8g; Fibre 2.6g

Roast Sea Bass

The subtle flavour of cooked fennel harmonizes perfectly with the delicate taste of sea bass in this simple roasted dish.

Serves 4
1 fennel bulb with fronds, about 275g/10oz
2 lemons
120ml/4fl oz/½ cup olive oil
1 small red onion, diced
2 sea bass, about 500g/1¼lb each, cleaned, with heads left on
120ml/4fl oz/½ cup dry white wine
salt and ground black pepper
lemon slices, to garnish

1 Preheat the oven to 190°C/375°F/Gas 5. Cut the fronds off the top of the fennel and reserve for the garnish. Cut the fennel bulb lengthways into thin wedges, then into dice.

2 Cut one lemon half into four slices. Squeeze the juice from the remaining lemon half and the other lemon.

3 Heat 30 ml/2 tbsp of the oil in a frying pan, add the diced fennel and onion and cook gently, stirring frequently, for about 5 minutes, until softened. Remove from the heat.

4 Make three diagonal slashes on both sides of each sea bass with a sharp knife. Brush a roasting pan generously with oil, add the fish and tuck two lemon slices into each cavity. Scatter the softened fennel and onion over the fish.

5 Whisk the remaining oil with the lemon juice and salt and pepper to taste and pour over the fish. Cover with foil and roast for 30 minutes, or until the flesh flakes, removing the foil for the last 10 minutes. Discard the lemon slices, transfer the fish to a heated serving platter and keep hot.

6 Put the roasting pan on top of the stove. Add the wine and stir over medium heat to incorporate all the pan juices. Bring to the boil, then spoon the juices over the fish on the platter. Garnish the fish with the reserved fennel fronds and lemon slices and serve immediately.

Stuffed Swordfish Rolls

An unusual way of serving swordfish, this elaborate dish is packed with robust Italian flavours.

Serves 4
30ml/2 tbsp olive oil
1 small onion, finely chopped
1 celery stick, finely chopped
450g/1lb ripe Italian plum tomatoes, chopped
115g/4oz pitted green olives, half roughly chopped, half left whole
45ml/3 tbsp drained bottled capers
4 large swordfish steaks, each about 1cm/½in thick and 115g/4oz in weight
1 egg
50g/2oz/⅔ cup grated Pecorino cheese
25g/1oz/½ cup fresh breadcrumbs
salt and ground black pepper
fresh parsley sprigs, to garnish

1 Heat the oil in a large heavy frying pan. Add the onion and celery and cook gently for about 3 minutes, stirring frequently. Stir in the tomatoes, olives and capers, with salt and pepper to taste. Bring to the boil, then lower the heat, cover and simmer for about 15 minutes. Stir occasionally and add a little water if the sauce becomes too thick.

2 Remove the fish skin and place each steak between two sheets of clear film (plastic wrap). Pound lightly with a rolling pin until each steak is reduced to about 5mm/¼in thick.

3 Beat the egg in a bowl. Add the cheese, breadcrumbs and a few spoonfuls of the sauce, then mix to a moist stuffing. Spread one-quarter of the stuffing over each swordfish steak, then roll up into a sausage shape. Secure with wooden cocktail sticks.

4 Add the rolls to the sauce in the pan and bring to the boil. Lower the heat, cover and simmer for about 30 minutes, turning once. Add a little water as the sauce reduces.

5 Remove the rolls from the sauce and discard the sticks. Place the fish on warmed dinner plates and spoon the sauce over and around. Garnish with the parsley and serve immediately.

Energy 282Kcal/1174kJ; Fat 17g; Saturated Fat 2.5g; Carbohydrate 2.6g; Fibre 1.9g

Energy 327Kcal/1364kJ; Fat 19.4g; Saturated Fat 5.4g; Carbohydrate 9.6g; Fibre 2.4g

Grilled Red Mullet with Garlic & Rosemary

This recipe is very simple – the succulent flesh of red mullet – *triglia* – in Italian, with its prawn-like taste, is so good in itself that the fish only needs a simple method of cooking to bring out its robust and distinctive flavour.

Serves 4

4 red mullet, cleaned, weighing
   about 275g/10oz each

4 garlic cloves, cut lengthways
   into thin slivers
75ml/5 tbsp olive oil
30ml/2 tbsp balsamic vinegar
10ml/2 tsp very finely chopped
   fresh rosemary or 5ml/1 tsp
   dried rosemary
coarse sea salt and ground black
   pepper, to serve
fresh rosemary sprigs and lemon
   wedges, to garnish

1 Cut three diagonal slits in both sides of each fish. Push the garlic slivers into the slits.

2 Place the fish in a single layer in a shallow dish. Whisk the oil, vinegar and rosemary together, then whisk in ground black pepper to taste.

3 Pour the mixture over the fish, cover with clear film (plastic wrap) and leave to marinate in a cool place for about 1 hour.

4 Put the fish on the rack of a grill (broiler) pan and grill (broil) for 5–6 minutes on each side, turning once and brushing with the marinade, until lightly browned. Sprinkle the cooked fish with coarse sea salt, then garnish with fresh rosemary sprigs and serve immediately with lemon wedges.

Variation
Red mullet are extra delicious cooked on the barbecue. If possible, enclose them in a hinged basket grill so that they are easy to turn over.

Pan-fried Red Mullet with Basil & Citrus

Red mullet is popular all over the Mediterranean. This Italian recipe combines it with oranges and lemons, which grow in abundance in the south of the country.

Serves 4

4 red mullet, weighing about
   225g/8oz each, filleted
90ml/6 tbsp olive oil

10 peppercorns, crushed
2 oranges, one peeled and sliced,
   and one squeezed
1 lemon
flour, for dusting
15g/½oz/1 tbsp butter
2 canned anchovies, drained
   chopped
60ml/4 tbsp shredded fresh basil
salt and ground black pepper

1 Place the fish fillets in a shallow dish in a single layer. Pour over the olive oil and sprinkle with the crushed peppercorns. Arrange the orange slices on top of the fish. Cover the dish, and leave to marinate in the refrigerator for at least 4 hours.

2 Halve the lemon. Remove the skin and pith from one half using a small sharp knife, and slice thinly. Squeeze the juice from the other half.

3 Lift the fish out of the marinade and pat dry on kitchen paper. Reserve the marinade and orange slices. Season the fish with salt and pepper and dust lightly with flour.

4 Heat 45ml/3 tbsp of the marinade in a frying pan. Add the fish and fry for 2 minutes on each side. Remove from the pan and keep warm. Discard the residue that is left in the pan.

5 Melt the butter in the pan with any of the remaining original marinade. Add the anchovies and cook, stirring, until completely softened and mashed.

6 Stir in the orange and lemon juice, then check the seasoning and simmer until slightly reduced. Stir in the basil. Pour the sauce over the fish. Serve with the orange and lemon slices.

Energy 350Kcal/1462kJ; Fat 22.4g; Saturated Fat 4g; Carbohydrate 12.2g; Fibre 1.5g

Energy 270Kcal/1122kJ; Fat 19.1g; Saturated Fat 2g; Carbohydrate 0.3g; Fibre 0.5g

Monkfish with Tomato & Olive Sauce

This dish comes from the coast of Calabria in southern Italy. Serve with garlic-flavoured mashed potato to soak up the sauce.

Serves 4
450g/1lb fresh mussels, scrubbed
a few fresh basil sprigs, plus extra
    leaves, to garnish
2 garlic cloves, roughly chopped
300ml/¹/₂pint/1¹/₄ cups dry
    white wine
30ml/2 tbsp olive oil
15g/¹/₂oz/1 tbsp butter
900g/2lb monkfish fillets, skinned
    and cut into large chunks
1 onion, finely chopped
500g/1¹/₄lb jar sugocasa or
    passata
15ml/1 tbsp sun-dried tomato
    paste
115g/4oz/1 cup pitted black olives
salt and ground black pepper

1 Put the mussels in a flameproof casserole with some basil leaves, the garlic and the wine. Cover and bring to the boil. Lower the heat and simmer for 5 minutes, shaking the pan frequently. Remove the mussels, discarding any that are not open. Strain the cooking liquid and reserve.

2 Heat the oil and butter in the casserole until foaming, add the monkfish pieces and sauté over medium heat, until they just change colour. Remove with a slotted spoon.

3 Add the onion to the juices in the casserole and cook gently for 5 minutes, stirring frequently. Add the sugocasa or passata, the reserved cooking liquid from the mussels and the tomato paste. Season to taste. Bring to the boil, stirring, then lower the heat, cover and simmer for 20 minutes, stirring occasionally.

4 Pull off and discard the top shells from the mussels. Add the monkfish pieces to the tomato sauce and cook gently for 5 minutes. Gently stir in the olives and remaining basil, then taste for seasoning. Place the mussels in their half shells on top of the sauce, cover the pan and heat the mussels through for 1–2 minutes. Garnish with basil and serve immediately.

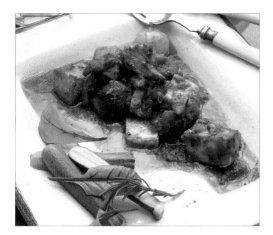

Fresh Tuna & Tomato Stew

A deliciously simple dish that relies on good basic ingredients. For real Italian flavour, serve with polenta or pasta.

Serves 4
12 baby onions, peeled
900g/2lb ripe tomatoes
675g/1¹/₂lb fresh tuna
45ml/3 tbsp olive oil
2 garlic cloves, crushed
45ml/3 tbsp chopped fresh herbs,
2 bay leaves
2.5ml/¹/₂ tsp sugar
30ml/2 tbsp sun-dried tomato
    paste
150ml/¹/₄ pint/²/₃ cup dry white
    wine
salt and ground black pepper
baby courgettes (zucchini), to
    serve
fresh herbs, to garnish

1 Leave the onions whole and cook in a pan of boiling water for 4–5 minutes until softened. Drain.

2 Plunge the tomatoes into boiling water for 30 seconds, then refresh in cold water. Peel away the skins and chop roughly.

3 Cut the tuna into 2.5cm/1in chunks. Heat the oil in a large frying or sauté pan and quickly fry the tuna on both sides, until browned. Remove from the pan with a slotted spoon.

4 Add the onions, garlic, tomatoes, chopped herbs, bay leaves, sugar, tomato paste and wine and bring to the boil, breaking up the tomatoes with a wooden spoon.

5 Reduce the heat and simmer gently for 5 minutes. Return the fish to the pan and cook for a further 5 minutes. Season. Serve with baby courgettes and garnished with fresh herbs.

> **Variation**
> Two large mackerel make a readily available alternative to tuna. Fillet and cut into chunks or simply lay the whole fish over the sauce and cook, covered with a lid, until the mackerel is cooked through.

Energy 393Kcal/1647kJ; Fat 16.8g; Saturated Fat 3.4g; Carbohydrate 13.8g; Fibre 3.3g

Energy 357Kcal/1505kJ; Fat 13.4g; Saturated Fat 3.6g; Carbohydrate 5.4g; Fibre 1.8g

Trout Baked in Paper with Olives

Wrapped in a parcel, the fish remains moist and succulent.

Serves 4
4 medium trout, about
   275g/10oz each, gutted
75ml/5 tbsp olive oil
4 bay leaves
4 slices pancetta or bacon
60ml/4 tbsp chopped shallots
60ml/4 tbsp chopped fresh
   parsley
120ml/4fl oz/½ cup dry
   white wine
24 green olives, pitted
salt and ground black pepper

1 Preheat the oven to 200°C/400°F/Gas 6. Wash the trout well under cold running water. Drain. Pat dry with kitchen paper.

2 Lightly brush oil onto 4 pieces of parchment paper, each large enough to enclose one fish. Arrange one fish on each. Place a bay leaf in each cavity; sprinkle with salt and pepper.

3 Wrap a slice of pancetta around each fish. Divide the shallots, parsley, oil, wine and olives between the 4 packets. Close loosely around the fish, rolling the edges together. Bake for 25 minutes.

Grilled Salmon Steaks with Fennel

The mild aniseed flavour of fennel goes well with fish.

Serves 4
juice of 1 lemon
45ml/3 tbsp chopped fresh fennel
   herb, or fennel bulb tops
5ml/1 tsp fennel seeds
45ml/3 tbsp olive oil
4 even-sized salmon steaks, about
   675g/1½lb in total
salt and ground black pepper

1 Combine the lemon juice, fennel and fennel seeds with the olive oil in a bowl. Add the salmon steaks, turning to coat. Sprinkle with salt and pepper. Marinate for 2 hours.

2 Preheat the grill (broiler) and cook the fish for 3 minutes. Turn. Cook for 3–4 minutes until the edges begin to brown. Serve.

Seafood Stew

Stews of mixed fish and shellfish are specialities of the Mediterranean.

Serves 6–8
45ml/3 tbsp olive oil
1 medium onion, sliced
1 carrot, sliced
½ stalk celery, sliced
2 garlic cloves, chopped
400g/14oz can chopped
   tomatoes
225g/8oz fresh shrimp, peeled
   and deveined (reserve the shells)
450g/1lb white fish bones and
   heads, gills removed
1 bay leaf
1 sprig fresh thyme, or 1.5ml/¼
   tsp dried thyme leaves
a few peppercorns
salt and ground black pepper
675g/1½lb fresh mussels, in their
   shells, scrubbed and rinsed
450g/1lb fresh small clams, in
   their shells, scrubbed and rinsed
250ml/8fl oz/1 cup white wine
900g/2lb mixed fish fillets, such as
   cod, monkfish, or hake, bones
   removed and cut into chunks
45ml/3 tbsp finely chopped fresh
   parsley

1 Heat the oil in a medium pan. Add the sliced onion, and cook slowly until soft. Stir in the carrot and celery, and cook for 5 minutes more. Add the garlic, tomatoes and their juice, and 250ml/8fl oz/1 cup of water. Cook until the vegetables are soft, about 15 minutes. Purée in a food processor and set aside.

2 Place the shrimp shells in a large pan with the fish bones and heads. Add the herbs and peppercorns, and pour in 750ml/1¼ pints/3 cups of water. Bring to the boil, reduce the heat, and simmer for 25 minutes, skimming off any scum that rises to the surface. Strain and pour into a pan with the tomato sauce.

3 Place the mussels and clams in a pan with the wine. Cover, and steam until all the shells have opened. Lift the clams and mussels out and set aside. Strain the cooking liquid and add it to the stock and tomato sauce. Check the seasoning.

4 Bring the sauce to a boil. Add the fish, and boil for 5 minutes. Add the shrimp and boil for 3–4 minutes. Stir in the mussels and clams and cook for 2–3 minutes more. Transfer the stew to a warmed casserole. Sprinkle with parsley and serve.

Top Energy 479Kcal/1996kJ; Fat 29.2g; Saturated Fat 6.4g; Carbohydrate 1.4g; Fibre 1.1g
Above Energy 369Kcal/1534kJ; Fat 26g; Saturated Fat 4.3g; Carbohydrate 0.2g; Fibre 0.4g

Energy 391Kcal/1651kJ; Fat 14.7g; Saturated Fat 1.8g; Carbohydrate 4.9g; Fibre 1.4g

Sea Bass with an Almond Crust

In this delicious dish the almond crust is almost a biscuit, and its sweetness complements the flavour of the sea bass, as well as keeping the fish succulent.

Serves 4

1 large or 2 small sea bass, about 1.5kg/3–3¹/₂ lb total weight, cleaned and scaled, with head and tail left on
15ml/1 tbsp sunflower oil
175g/6oz/1¹/₂ cups blanched almonds
65g/2¹/₂ oz/¹/₃ cup butter, softened
2.5–5ml/¹/₂–1 tsp ground cinnamon
25g/1oz/¹/₄ cup icing (confectioner's) sugar
1 onion, finely sliced
a good pinch of saffron strands
salt and ground black pepper
lime wedges and fresh flat leaf parsley sprigs, to garnish

1 Rinse the fish in cold running water and pat dry.

2 Heat the oil in a small frying pan and fry the almonds for 2–3 minutes, until golden, stirring frequently. Drain on kitchen paper until cool and then grind in a spice or coffee mill. Pour the ground almonds into the bowl of a food processor and blend with 25g/1oz/2 tbsp of the butter, the cinnamon, icing sugar and 60ml/4 tbsp water to make a smooth paste.

3 Preheat the oven to 190°C/375°F/Gas 5. Grease a large ovenproof dish, using about 15g/½oz/1 tbsp of the butter. Scatter the sliced onion in the dish. Dissolve the saffron threads in 15ml/1 tbsp boiling water and add to the dish.

4 Stuff the fish with half of the almond mixture and place it on top of the onion. Using a spatula, spread the remaining almond paste evenly over the top of the fish.

5 Melt the remaining butter and pour over the fish. Season to taste and then bake in the oven, uncovered, for about 45–50 minutes until the fish flakes easily and the almond topping is crusty. Transfer the fish to a serving plate. Garnish with lime wedges and parsley.

Octopus with Lemon & Garlic

Fresh octopus is widely appreciated in Italy. Dressed with olive oil and lemon juice, it makes a delectable light dish.

Serves 3–4

900g/2lb octopus (young and small if possible)
30ml/2 tbsp chopped fresh parsley
2 garlic cloves, very finely chopped
60ml/4 tbsp extra virgin olive oil
45ml/3 tbsp fresh lemon juice
ground black pepper

1 If your fishmonger has not prepared the octopus, beat the octopus repeatedly against a strong table or marble surface. To prepare, pull the head and tentacles from the body to remove the soft body contents. Cut off the tentacles just below the eyes. Wash carefully under cold running water.

2 Place the octopus in a large pan with cold water to cover. Bring to a boil, cover the pan tightly, and simmer gently until tender – 45 minutes for small octopus and up to 2 hours for larger ones. Skim off any scum which rises to the surface.

3 Remove from the pan and allow to cool slightly. Rub the octopus lightly with a clean cloth to remove any loose dark skin. Slice the warm octopus into rounds 2cm/¾in wide.

4 Place the octopus pieces in a serving bowl. Toss with the parsley, garlic, olive oil and lemon juice. Sprinkle with pepper. Mix well. Allow to stand for at least 20 minutes before serving at room temperature.

> **Cook's Tips**
> • *In Italy, a wine cork is placed in the pan with the octopus to reduce the amount of scum.*
> • *The octopus must be pounded (99 times, some say) to tenderize them before they are cooked. The ink has a strong pungent taste and is not usually used.*

Energy 290Kcal/1216kJ; Fat 14.1g; Saturated Fat 2.3g; Carbohydrate 0.4g; Fibre 0.6g

Energy 619Kcal/2572kJ; Fat 44.9g; Saturated Fat 11.4g; Carbohydrate 10.8g; Fibre 3.5g

Baked Cod with Garlic Mayonnaise

Although cod is not native to Italian waters, a similar native species is used for this dish. Baked with a crisp anchovy-flavoured topping, the fish combines perfectly with tasty garlic mayonnaise.

Serves 4

4 canned anchovy fillets, drained
45ml/3 tbsp finely chopped
  fresh parsley
coarsely ground black pepper

90ml/6 tbsp olive oil
4 cod or hake fillets, about
  675g/1½lb total, skinned
40g/1½oz/⅔ cup fresh
  breadcrumbs

For the mayonnaise
2 garlic cloves, finely chopped
1 egg yolk
1 tsp Dijon mustard
175ml/6fl oz/¾ cup vegetable oil
salt and ground black pepper

1 To make the mayonnaise, mash the garlic to a paste using a pestle and mortar, then beat into the egg yolk and mustard in a medium bowl. Add the oil in a thin stream, whisking vigorously with a small wire whisk. When the mixture is thick and smooth, season with salt and pepper. Cover the bowl and keep cool.

2 Preheat the oven to 200°C/400°F/Gas 6. Chop the anchovy fillets very finely. Place in a small bowl with the parsley, then add pepper and 45ml/3 tbsp of the oil. Stir until the anchovies have disintegrated to a paste.

3 Place the cod fillets in a single layer in an oiled baking dish. Spread the anchovy paste on the top of the cod fillets. Sprinkle with the breadcrumbs and the remaining oil.

4 Bake for 20–25 minutes or until the breadcrumbs are golden. Serve hot with the garlic mayonnaise.

> **Variation**
> Hake, haddock or salmon steaks could be substituted for the cod equally successfully. Try sprinkling the topping with freshly grated Parmesan cheese before cooking.

Energy 637Kcal/2642kJ; Fat 49.8g; Saturated Fat 6.5g; Carbohydrate 10g; Fibre 0.9g

Monkfish Medallions with Thyme & Olives

The firm, sweet flesh of monkfish marries well with Italian flavours.

Serves 4

500g/1¼lb monkfish fillet,
  preferably in one piece
45ml/3 tbsp extra virgin olive oil
75g/3oz/½ cup small black
  olives, pitted

1 large or 2 small tomatoes,
  seeded and diced
1 fresh thyme sprig, or 5ml/1 tsp
  dried thyme leaves
salt and ground black pepper
15ml/1 tbsp very finely chopped
  fresh parsley, to serve

1 Preheat the oven to 200°C/400°F/Gas 6. Remove the grey membrane from the monkfish, if necessary. Cut the fish into slices 1cm/½in thick.

2 Heat a non-stick frying pan until quite hot, without oil. Add the fish and sear quickly on both sides. Transfer to a side dish.

3 Spread 15ml/1 tbsp of the olive oil in the bottom of a shallow baking dish. Arrange the fish in a single layer. Scatter the olives and diced tomato evenly over the top of the fish.

4 Sprinkle with thyme, salt and pepper, together with the remaining oil. Bake for 10–12 minutes, until the fish is cooked when tested with a fork.

5 To serve, divide the medallions between 4 warmed plates. Spoon on the vegetables and any cooking juices. Sprinkle with the chopped parsley and serve immediately.

> **Cook's Tip**
> Monkfish has a huge, ugly head and only the flesh on the tail is eaten. This is usually sold as fillets. The delicious flesh is not dissimilar to lobster.

Energy 211Kcal/882kJ; Fat 12.2g; Saturated Fat 1.9g; Carbohydrate 1.3g; Fibre 1.4g

Salt Cod with Parsley & Garlic

Salt cod is very popular in Italy. For centuries the fish has been imported from Scandinavia. When planning a salt cod recipe, bear in mind that the fish must be soaked in water for 24 hours to reduce its salt content.

Serves 4–5
675g/1½lb boneless and skinless
   salt cod, preferably in one piece

seasoned flour with ground black
   pepper, for coating
30ml/2 tbsp extra virgin olive oil
45ml/3 tbsp finely chopped
   fresh parsley
2 garlic cloves, finely chopped
25g/1oz/2 tbsp butter, cut into
   small pieces
flat leaf parsley sprigs, to serve

1 Cut the salt cod into 5cm/2in squares. Place the fish in a large bowl and cover with cold water. Allow to stand for at least 24 hours, changing the water several times.

2 Preheat the oven to 190°C/375°F/Gas 5. Drain the fish, shaking out the excess moisture. Remove any remaining bones or skin. Dredge lightly in the seasoned flour.

3 Spread 15ml/1 tbsp of the oil over the bottom of a baking dish large enough to hold the fish in a single layer.

4 Place the fish in the dish. Combine the chopped parsley and garlic, then sprinkle evenly over the fish. Sprinkle with the remaining oil and dot with butter.

5 Bake in the oven for 15 minutes, then turn the fish and bake for a further 15–20 minutes, or until tender. Garnish with flat leaf parsley and serve immediately.

> **Cook's Tip**
> Salt cod is called baccalà in Italian and it is often combined with strong flavourings. When buying salt cod, choose meaty, white pieces; sometimes it is sold skinned which is convenient.

Red Mullet with Tomatoes

Both the pretty colour and distinctive taste of red mullet are enhanced by the garlicky tomato sauce.

Serves 4
4 red mullet or red snapper,
   about 175–200g/6–7oz each
450g/1lb tomatoes, peeled, or
   400g/14oz can plum tomatoes

60ml/4 tbsp olive oil
60ml/4 tbsp finely chopped
   fresh parsley
2 garlic cloves, finely chopped
120ml/4fl oz/½ cup white wine
4 thin lemon slices, cut in half
salt and ground black pepper

1 Scale and clean the fish without removing the liver. Wash and pat dry with kitchen paper. Chop the tomatoes.

2 Heat the oil in a pan large enough to hold the fish in a single layer. Add the parsley and garlic and sauté for 1 minute. Stir in the tomatoes and cook over medium heat for 15–20 minutes, stirring occasionally. Season with salt and pepper.

3 Add the fish to the tomato sauce and cook over medium to high heat for 5 minutes. Add the wine and the lemon slices. Bring back to the boil and cook for about 5 minutes. Turn the fish and cook for a further 4–5 minutes, until tender. Transfer the fish and lemon to a warmed serving platter; keep warm.

4 Boil the sauce for 3–4 minutes to reduce it slightly. Spoon the sauce over the fish and serve immediately.

> **Cook's Tip**
> The liver of red mullet is regarded as a great delicacy and is therefore not removed during cooking.

> **Variation**
> Two smallish sea bass can be substituted for the red mullet.

Energy 234Kcal/974kJ; Fat 14.9g; Saturated Fat 1.7g; Carbohydrate 3.4g; Fibre 1.2g

Energy 278Kcal/1171kJ; Fat 10.6g; Saturated Fat 4g; Carbohydrate 0.1g; Fibre 0.2g

Beef Stew with Tomatoes, Wine & Peas

It seems there are as many recipes for this rich beef stew as there are Italian cooks. This one is very traditional, perfect for a winter lunch or dinner. Serve it with boiled or mashed potatoes to soak up the delicious sauce.

Serves 4

flour, for coating
10ml/2 tsp chopped fresh thyme
　or 5 ml/1 tsp dried thyme
1kg/2¼lb braising or stewing
　steak, cut into large cubes
45ml/3 tbsp olive oil
1 onion, roughly chopped
450g/1lb jar sugocasa
　or passata
250ml/8 fl oz/1 cup beef stock
250ml/8 fl oz/1 cup red wine
2 garlic cloves, crushed
30ml/2 tbsp tomato purée
　(paste)
275g/10oz/2 cups shelled
　fresh peas
5ml/1 tsp sugar
salt and ground black pepper
fresh thyme, to garnish

1 Preheat the oven to 160°C/325°F/Gas 3. Put the flour in a shallow dish and season with the thyme and salt and pepper. Add the beef cubes and coat evenly.

2 Heat the oil in a large flameproof casserole, add the beef and brown on all sides over medium to high heat. Remove with a slotted spoon and drain on kitchen paper.

3 Add the onion to the pan, scraping the base of the pan to mix in any sediment. Cook gently for about 3 minutes, stirring frequently, until softened.

4 Stir in the sugocasa or passata, stock, wine, garlic and tomato purée. Bring to the boil, stirring. Return the beef to the pan and stir well to coat. Cover and cook in the oven for 1½ hours.

5 Stir in the peas and sugar. Return the casserole to the oven and cook for 30 minutes more, or until the beef is tender. Taste for seasoning. Garnish with fresh thyme before serving.

Energy 572Kcal/2391kJ; Fat 23.7g; Saturated Fat 7.4g; Carbohydrate 19.3g; Fibre 4.4g

Meatballs with Peperonata

The famous Italian sweet pepper sauce is the ideal partner to meatballs.

Serves 4

400g/14oz/1¾ cups minced
　(ground) beef
115g/4oz/2 cups fresh
　breadcrumbs
50g/2oz/⅔ cup freshly grated
　Parmesan cheese
2 eggs, beaten
pinch of paprika
pinch of freshly grated nutmeg
5ml/1 tsp dried mixed herbs
2 thin slices of mortadella or
　prosciutto, chopped
vegetable oil, for shallow frying
salt and ground black pepper

For the peperonata
30ml/2 tbsp olive oil
1 small onion, thinly sliced
2 yellow (bell) peppers, cored,
　seeded and cut lengthways into
　thin strips
2 red (bell) peppers, cored,
　seeded and cut lengthways into
　thin strips
275g/10oz/1¼ cups finely
　chopped tomatoes or passata
15ml/1 tbsp chopped fresh
　parsley

1 Put the beef in a bowl. Add half the breadcrumbs and the next six ingredients. Season with salt and pepper. Mix well with clean wet hands. Divide into 12 equal portions and roll each into a ball. Flatten slightly to about 1cm/½in thick. Roll the meatballs in the remaining breadcrumbs to evenly coat. Place on a plate, cover with clear film (plastic wrap) and chill for about 30 minutes to firm up.

2 Meanwhile, make the peperonata. Heat the oil and cook the onion gently for 3 minutes, stirring frequently, until softened. Add the pepper strips and cook for 3 minutes, stirring. Stir in the tomatoes and parsley, with salt and pepper to taste. Bring to the boil, stirring. Cover and cook for 15 minutes, remove the lid and continue to cook, stirring frequently, for 10 minutes, or until reduced and thick. Taste for seasoning. Keep hot.

3 Pour oil into a frying pan to a depth of about 2.5cm/1in. When hot but not smoking, shallow fry the meatballs for 10–12 minutes, turning 3–4 times and pressing them flat with a metal spatula. Drain on kitchen paper. Serve hot, with the peperonata.

Energy 563Kcal/2348kJ; Fat 35.5g; Saturated Fat 11.5g; Carbohydrate 30.9g; Fibre 2.8g

Polpettes with Mozzarella & Tomato

Beef patties are baked with cheese and anchovies to make an attractive-looking dish in typical Italian style. Serve with a green salad and sautéed potatoes for a satisfying meal that will go down well with all the family.

Serves 6
½ slice white bread, crusts removed
45ml/3 tbsp milk

675g/1½lb minced (ground) beef
1 egg, beaten
50g/2½oz/1 cup breadcrumbs
vegetable oil for frying
2 beefsteak or other large tomatoes, sliced
15ml/1 tbsp chopped fresh oregano
1 mozzarella cheese, cut into 6 slices
6 drained canned anchovies, cut in half lengthways
salt and ground black pepper

1 Preheat the oven to 200°C/400°F/Gas 6. Put the bread and milk into a small pan and heat very gently, until the bread absorbs all the milk. Mash it to a pulp and leave to cool.

2 Put the beef into a bowl with the bread mixture and the egg and season with salt and pepper. Mix together well with clean wet hands, then shape the mixture into six patties. Spread the breadcrumbs out on to a plate and press the patties in them to coat thoroughly.

3 Heat about 5mm/¼ in oil in a large frying pan. Add the patties in batches and fry for 2 minutes on each side, until browned all over. Transfer the patties to a greased ovenproof dish, arranging in a single layer.

4 Lay a slice of tomato on top of each patty, sprinkle with oregano and season with salt and pepper. Place the mozzarella slices on top. Arrange two strips of anchovy, placed in a cross, on top of each slice of mozzarella.

5 Bake for 10–15 minutes, until the mozzarella has melted. Serve hot, straight from the dish.

Polpettini with Fontina

These Italian meatballs are filled with Fontina cubes, then rolled in crumbs and fried. They are delicious served with pasta and a rich tomato sauce.

Serves 6–8
500g/1¼lb lean minced (ground) beef
500g/1¼lb lean minced (ground) pork
3 garlic cloves, crushed
grated rind and juice of 1 lemon
2 slices of day-old bread, crumbled

40g/1½oz/½ cup freshly grated Parmesan cheese
2.5ml/½ tsp ground cinnamon
5ml/1 tsp dried oregano
2 eggs, beaten
5ml/1 tsp salt
150g/5oz Fontina cheese, cut into 16 cubes
50–75g/3–4oz/1–2 cups dried breadcrumbs
olive oil, for shallow frying
ground black pepper
fresh herbs and freshly grated Parmesan cheese, to garnish
tomato sauce, to serve
tagliatelle, to serve

1 Preheat the oven to 180°C/350°F/Gas 4. Put the lean minced beef and pork into a bowl. Add the garlic, lemon rind and juice, crumbled bread, Parmesan, cinnamon and oregano and stir. Beat in the eggs, salt and plenty of pepper.

2 Knead to mix the ingredients. Shape into 16 balls. Cup each ball in turn in your hand and press a piece of Fontina into the centre. Reshape each ball, making sure the cheese is covered.

3 Roll the meatballs in the dried breadcrumbs. Heat about 5mm/¼ in oil in a large frying pan. Add the meatballs in batches and cook them quickly all over, until lightly browned and sealed. Transfer the meatballs to a roasting pan and bake for 20 minutes, until cooked through. Garnish with fresh herbs and Parmesan and serve immediately with pasta and tomato sauce.

Variation
Try using minced veal instead of the beef and serve in a pool of basil-flavoured tomato sauce.

Meatballs with Porcini

These meatballs, flavoured with Italian mushrooms, are delicious served hot with pasta or rice. They are also good cold as picnic food.

Serves 3–4

7.5g/¼oz/2 tbsp dried porcini
   mushrooms
150ml/¼ pint/⅔ cup warm
   water
450g/1lb/2 cups lean minced
   (ground) beef
2 garlic cloves, finely chopped

60ml/4 tbsp chopped fresh
   parsley
45ml/3 tbsp chopped fresh basil
1 egg
90ml/6 tbsp fresh breadcrumbs
30ml/2 tbsp freshly grated
   Parmesan cheese
60ml/4 tbsp olive oil
1 onion, very finely chopped
50ml/2fl oz/¼ cup dry white
   wine
chopped fresh parsley, to garnish
salt and ground black pepper

1 Soak the dried mushrooms in the warm water for 20 minutes. Drain, reserving the liquid, and chop the mushrooms finely. Strain the soaking liquid through a sieve (strainer) lined with kitchen paper and set aside.

2 Combine the meat with the chopped mushrooms, garlic, parsley and basil in a mixing bowl. Stir in the egg. Add the breadcrumbs and Parmesan, then season with salt and pepper. Mix well with clean wet hands, then form into small balls about 4cm/1½in in diameter.

3 Heat the oil in a large heavy frying pan. Add the onion and cook over low heat, until soft. Increase the heat and add the meatballs, rolling them often to brown them evenly all over. After about 5 minutes, add the strained mushroom soaking water. Cook for a further 5–8 minutes, or until the meatballs are cooked through.

4 Transfer the meatballs to a heated serving plate with a slotted spoon. Add the wine to the pan and cook for 1–2 minutes, stirring to scrape up any residues on the bottom of the pan. Pour the sauce over the meatballs. Garnish with parsley and serve immediately.

Energy 389Kcal/1623kJ; Fat 20.3g; Saturated Fat 7g; Carbohydrate 16.1g; Fibre 1.1g

Beef Stew with Red Wine

For an authentic Italian touch, serve this rich, hearty dish with soft polenta.

Serves 6

75ml/5 tbsp olive oil
1.2kg/2½lb boneless beef chuck,
   cut into 3cm/1¼in cubes
1 onion, very finely sliced
2 carrots, chopped
45ml/3 tbsp finely chopped fresh
   parsley
1 garlic clove, chopped

1 bay leaf
a few fresh thyme sprigs, or pinch
   of dried thyme leaves
pinch of freshly grated nutmeg
250ml/8fl oz/1 cup red wine
400g/14oz can plum tomatoes,
   chopped, with their juice
120ml/4fl oz/½ cup beef or
   chicken stock
about 15 black olives, pitted and
   halved
1 large red (bell) pepper, cored,
   seeded and cut into strips
salt and ground black pepper

1 Preheat the oven to 180°C/350°F/Gas 4. Heat 45ml/3 tbsp of the oil in a large, flameproof casserole. Brown a batch of the meat, turning to sear on all sides. Transfer to a plate and brown the remaining meat.

2 When all the meat has been browned and removed from the pan, add the remaining oil, with the onion and carrots. Cook over low heat, until the onion has softened. Add the parsley and garlic and cook for a further 3–4 minutes.

3 Return the meat to the pan, increase the heat and stir well to mix the vegetables with the meat. Stir in the bay leaf, thyme and nutmeg. Add the wine, bring to the boil and cook, stirring, for 4–5 minutes.

4 Stir in the tomatoes, stock and olives, and mix well. Season with salt and pepper and bring back to the boil. Cover the casserole and cook in the oven for 1½ hours.

5 Remove the casserole from the oven. Stir in the strips of pepper, then return the casserole to the oven and cook, uncovered, for a further 30 minutes, or until the beef is tender. Serve immediately.

Energy 474Kcal/1973kJ; Fat 28.8g; Saturated Fat 8.7g; Carbohydrate 6.1g; Fibre 2.6g

Pizzaiola Steak

This tasty steak dish is a speciality of Naples. It is accompanied by a characteristic tomato sauce.

Serves 4

450g/1lb beef steaks, preferably rump, thinly sliced
45ml/3 tbsp flour, for coating
45ml/3 tbsp olive oil
3 garlic cloves, peeled and crushed
400g/14oz can plum tomatoes, with their juice, passed through a food mill
30ml/2 tbsp chopped fresh basil or parsley
salt and ground black pepper
fresh parsley sprigs, to garnish

1 Trim any excess fat from the steaks, and notch the edges slightly with a sharp knife to prevent them from curling during cooking. Pat the steaks dry with kitchen paper, then coat lightly in the flour.

2 Heat 30ml/2 tbsp of the oil in a large heavy frying pan with the garlic cloves. As soon as they are golden, increase the heat, push them to the side of the pan and add the steaks. Brown quickly on both sides. Transfer the meat to a dish.

3 Add the tomatoes, the remaining oil and the herbs to the pan. Season with salt and pepper. Cook over medium heat for about 15 minutes. Discard the garlic cloves.

4 Return the steaks to the pan, stir to cover them with the sauce and cook for a further 4–5 minutes. Do not overcook: for the most tender results, the meat should still be slightly pink. Transfer to a warmed serving platter, garnish with parsley sprigs and serve immediately.

> **Variation**
> For an extra-rich flavour, add some red wine to the pan in step 3, before adding the tomatoes. Sizzle the wine for a minute, stirring, then continue as described. You may prefer to remove the garlic before adding the wine.

Herbed Burgers

Beef burgers are given the Italian treatment and transformed into a tasty family meal with the addition of fresh herbs and a tomato sauce.

Serves 4

675g/1½lb/3 cups lean minced (ground) beef
1 garlic clove, finely chopped
1 spring onion (scallion), very finely chopped
45ml/3 tbsp chopped fresh basil
30ml/2 tbsp chopped fresh parsley
40g/1½oz/3 tbsp butter
salt and ground black pepper

For the tomato sauce
45ml/3 tbsp olive oil
1 onion, finely chopped
300g/11oz tomatoes, chopped
a few fresh basil leaves
5ml/1 tsp sugar
15ml/1 tbsp white wine vinegar

1 To make the tomato sauce, heat the oil in a large pan and sauté the onion gently, until translucent. Add the tomatoes and cook for 2–3 minutes. Add the basil, cover the pan and cook for 7–8 minutes over medium heat.

2 Add 45–60ml/3–4 tbsp water, the sugar and vinegar and cook for a further 2–3 minutes. Season the sauce with salt and pepper to taste. Remove from the heat, allow to cool slightly, then pass the sauce through a food mill or sieve (strainer). Check the seasoning.

3 Combine the meat with the garlic, spring onion and herbs in a mixing bowl. Season with salt and pepper. With clean hands, form into 4 burgers, patting the meat as lightly as possible.

4 Heat the butter in a frying pan. When the foam subsides, add the burgers, and cook over medium heat, until brown on the underside. Turn the burgers over and continue cooking until done. Transfer to a warmed plate.

5 Tilt the frying pan and spoon off any surface fat. Pour in the sauce, increase the heat and bring to the boil, scraping up the meat residue from the bottom of the pan. Divide the burgers between individual plates and serve with the tomato sauce.

Energy 290Kcal/1212kJ; Fat 15.3g; Saturated Fat 4g; Carbohydrate 12.2g; Fibre 1.1g

Energy 555Kcal/2301kJ; Fat 44.3g; Saturated Fat 18.4g; Carbohydrate 6.2g; Fibre 1.8g

Beef Rolls with Garlic & Tomato Sauce

Italy has many regional variations on the technique of wrapping thin slices of beef around a richly flavoured stuffing. This recipe incorporates some of the classic ingredients.

Serves 4

4 thin slices of rump steak, about 115g/4oz each
4 slices smoked ham
150g/5oz Pecorino cheese, grated
2 garlic cloves, crushed
75ml/5 tbsp chopped fresh parsley
2 eggs, soft-boiled, shelled and chopped
45ml/3 tbsp olive oil
1 large onion, finely chopped
150ml/¼ pint/⅔ cup passata
75ml/2½fl oz/⅓ cup red wine
2 bay leaves
150ml/¼ pint/⅔ cup beef stock
salt and ground black pepper
flat leaf parsley, to garnish

1 Preheat the oven to 160°C/325°F/Gas 3. Lay the beef slices on a sheet of greaseproof paper. Cover the beef with another sheet of greaseproof paper or clear film (plastic wrap) and beat with a mallet or rolling pin until very thin.

2 Lay a ham slice over each. Mix the cheese with the garlic, parsley, eggs and a little salt and pepper. Stir well until all the ingredients are evenly mixed. Spoon the stuffing on to the ham and beef slices. Fold two opposite sides of the meat over the stuffing, then roll up the meat to form parcels. Secure with string.

3 Heat the oil in a frying pan. Add the parcels and fry quickly on all sides to brown. Transfer to an ovenproof dish.

4 Add the onion to the frying pan and fry for 3 minutes. Stir in the passata, wine, bay leaves and stock and season with salt and pepper. Bring to the boil, then pour the sauce over the meat.

5 Cover the dish and bake in the oven for 1 hour. Drain the meat and remove the string. Spoon on to warmed serving plates. Taste the sauce, adding extra salt and pepper if necessary, and spoon it over the meat. Serve garnished with parsley.

Corsican Beef Stew with Macaroni

The Italian-influenced cuisine in Corsica often features pasta served with gravy as a sauce or, as in this recipe, in a rich beef stew.

Serves 4

25g/1oz dried mushrooms (ceps or porcini)
6 garlic cloves
900g/2lb stewing beef, cut into 5cm/2in cubes
115g/4oz lardons, or thick streaky
(fatty) bacon cut into strips
45ml/3 tbsp olive oil
2 onions, sliced
300ml/½ pint/1¼ cups dry white wine
30ml/2 tbsp passata
pinch of ground cinnamon
sprig of rosemary
1 bay leaf
225g/8oz/2 cups large macaroni
50g/2oz/⅔ cup freshly grated Parmesan cheese
salt and ground black pepper

1 Soak the dried mushrooms in warm water for 20 minutes. Drain, reserving the liquid, and set the mushrooms aside. Cut three of the garlic cloves into thin strips and insert into the pieces of beef by making little slits with a sharp knife. Push the lardons or pieces of bacon into the beef with the garlic. Season the meat with salt and pepper.

2 Heat the oil in a heavy pan, add half the beef and brown well on all sides. Transfer to a plate. Repeat with the remaining beef. Add the sliced onions to the pan and cook until lightly browned. Crush the remaining garlic and add to the onions with the meat.

3 Stir in the white wine, passata, mushrooms, cinnamon, rosemary and bay leaf and season with salt and pepper. Cook gently for 30 minutes, stirring frequently. Strain the mushroom liquid and add to the stew with enough water to cover. Bring to the boil, cover and simmer very gently for 3 hours, until the meat is very tender.

4 Cook the macaroni in a large pan of boiling, salted water until al dente. Lift the pieces of meat out of the gravy and transfer to a warmed serving platter. Drain the pasta and layer in a serving bowl with the gravy and cheese. Serve with the meat.

Escalope of Veal with Cream Sauce

Pan-fried escalopes make a
quick, easy dinner-party dish
and are delicious served
with hot buttered tagliatelle
and lightly steamed green
vegetables.

Serves 4

15ml/1 tbsp plain (all-purpose)
   flour
4 veal escalopes (scallops), each
   weighing about 75–115g/3–4oz

30ml/2 tbsp sunflower oil
1 shallot, chopped
150g/5oz/2 cups oyster
   mushrooms, sliced
30ml/2 tbsp Marsala or
   medium-dry sherry
200ml/7fl oz/scant 1 cup
   crème fraîche
30ml/2 tbsp chopped fresh
   tarragon
salt and ground black pepper

1 Season the flour with salt and pepper and use to dust the veal escalopes, then set aside.

2 Heat the oil in a large non-stick frying pan and cook the shallot and sliced mushrooms for 5 minutes. Add the veal escalopes and cook over a high heat for about 1½ minutes on each side. Pour in the Marsala or sherry and cook until reduced by half.

3 Remove the veal escalopes from the pan. Stir the crème fraîche, tarragon and seasoning into the juices remaining in the pan and simmer gently for 3–5 minutes.

4 Return the escalopes to the pan and heat through for 1 minute before serving.

Cook's Tips
• If the sauce seems to be too thick, add 30ml/2 tbsp water.
• To tenderize veal escalopes before pan-frying, place the escalope between two sheets of clear film or greaseproof paper, or on a chopping board, and cover with clear film. Use the flat wooden side of a meat mallet or a rolling pin to firmly, but gently, beat the veal out thinly and evenly.

Calf's Liver with Balsamic Vinegar

This sweet and sour liver
dish is a speciality of Venice.
Serve it very simply, with a
side vegetable such as lightly
cooked green beans.

Serves 2

15ml/1 tbsp plain (all-purpose)
   flour
2.5ml/½ tsp finely chopped
   fresh sage
4 thin slices of calf's liver, cut into
   serving pieces

45ml/3 tbsp olive oil
25g/1oz/2 tbsp butter
2 small red onions, sliced and
   separated into rings
150ml/¼ pint/⅔ cup dry
   white wine
45ml/3 tbsp balsamic vinegar
a pinch of sugar
salt and ground black pepper
fresh sage sprigs, to garnish

1 Spread out the flour in a shallow bowl. Season it with the sage and plenty of salt and pepper. Turn the liver in the flour until well coated.

2 Heat 30ml/2 tbsp of the oil with half of the butter in a wide heavy pan or frying pan until foaming. Add the onion rings and cook gently, stirring frequently, for about 5 minutes until softened but not coloured. Remove the onion rings with a slotted spoon and set aside on a plate.

3 Heat the remaining oil and butter in the pan until foaming, add the liver and cook over a medium heat for 2–3 minutes on each side, until tender. Transfer to warmed plates and keep hot.

4 Add the wine and vinegar to the pan, then stir to mix with the pan juices and any sediment. Return the onions to the pan, add the sugar and heat through, stirring. Spoon the sauce over the liver, garnish with sage and serve immediately.

Cook's Tip
Never overcook calf's liver because it can soon become tough; it is most tender when served slightly pink.

Veal Escalopes with Marsala

The mild flavour of veal is enlivened with the sweetness of Marsala in this quick and delicious dish.

Serves 4

450g/1lb veal escalopes (scallops), preferably cut across the grain, about 5mm/¼in thick

50g/2oz/½ cup seasoned flour, for coating
50g/2oz/¼ cup butter
75ml/5 tbsp Marsala
75ml/5 tbsp stock or water

1 Pound the escalopes flat to a thickness of about 4mm/⅛in. If they have not been cut across the grain or from one muscle, cut small notches around the edges to prevent the escalopes from curling during cooking.

2 Spread the flour out on a plate. Heat the butter in a large frying pan. Lightly coat the veal slices in the flour, shaking off any excess. As soon as the foam from the butter subsides, put the veal into the pan in a single layer and brown the slices quickly on both sides, in two batches if necessary. Transfer with a metal spatula to a warmed serving plate.

3 Pour in the Marsala and the stock or water. Cook over medium to high heat for 3–4 minutes, scraping up any meat residues from the bottom of the pan. Pour the sauce over the meat and serve immediately.

> **Cook's Tips**
> • Young milk-fed veal is ideal for scaloppine (escalopes) as it needs very little cooking. When buying veal, bear in mind that young veal should have very pale, slightly rosy, fine-grained flesh with no trace of fat.
> • Marsala is made in the west of Sicily, near the town from which it takes its name. It is a rich brown fortified wine with a sweet, musky flavour and is used in Italian cooking for both sweet and savoury dishes.

Ham & Cheese Veal Escalopes

In this traditional dish from Bologna, veal escalopes are baked with a topping of cheese to make a meltingly succulent dish. Serve with a green salad as a foil to the richness.

Serves 4

8 veal escalopes (scallops), about 450g/1lb total, preferably cut across the grain

50g/2oz/½ cup seasoned flour, for coating
25g/1oz/2 tbsp butter
30ml/2 tbsp olive oil
45ml/3 tbsp dry white wine
8 thin slices ham
40g/1½oz/½ cup freshly grated Parmesan, or 8 thin slices Gruyère
fresh parsley sprigs, to garnish

1 Preheat the oven to 200°C/400°F/Gas 6. Pound the escalopes flat. If they have not been cut across the grain or from one muscle, cut small notches around the edges to prevent them from curling during cooking. Spread the seasoned flour over a plate.

2 Heat the butter with the oil in a large frying pan. Lightly coat the veal slices in the flour, shaking off any excess. As soon as the foam from the butter subsides, put the veal into the pan in a single layer and brown the slices quickly on both sides. Transfer with a metal spatula to a shallow baking dish. Cook the escalopes in two batches.

3 Add the white wine to the pan and cook gently for 1–2 minutes, scraping up the brown residue from the bottom of the pan with a wooden spoon. Pour the sauce over the veal escalopes.

4 Place one slice of ham on top of each escalope. Sprinkle with one tablespoon of Parmesan, or top with one slice of Gruyère. Place in the oven and cook for 5–7 minutes, until the cheese has melted.

5 Divide the escalopes between warmed individual plates, garnish with parsley sprigs and serve immediately.

Energy 263Kcal/1104kJ; Fat 11.3g; Saturated Fat 6.6g; Carbohydrate 11.1g; Fibre 0.4g

Energy 315Kcal/1317kJ; Fat 18.5g; Saturated Fat 8.2g; Carbohydrate 0.4g; Fibre 0g

Milanese Veal Chops

A juicy veal chop encased in a crisp breadcrumb coating is a mouthwatering classic from Milan. The success of the dish depends on taking great care when cooking the veal chops in the butter.

Serves 2
2 veal chops or cutlets, on the bone
1 egg
90–120ml/6–8 tbsp dried breadcrumbs
50g/2oz/¼ cup butter
15ml/1 tbsp vegetable oil
salt and ground black pepper
lemon wedges, to serve

1 Trim any gristle or thick fat from the chops. Cut along the rib bone, if necessary, to free the meat on one side. Pound the meat slightly to flatten.

2 Beat the egg in a shallow bowl and season it with salt and pepper. Spread the breadcrumbs over a plate. Dip the chops into the egg, and then into the breadcrumbs. Gently pat the breadcrumbs to help them to stick.

3 Heat the butter with the oil in a heavy frying pan large enough to hold both chops side by side. Do not allow the butter to brown. Add the chops to the pan, and cook slowly over low to medium heat, until the breadcrumbs are golden and the meat is cooked through. The timing will depend on the thickness of the chops. The important thing is not to overcook the breadcrumb coating while undercooking the meat. Serve hot with lemon wedges.

Cook's Tips
• To make your own breadcrumbs, use bread that is a couple of days old. Remove the crusts and process the bread in a blender or food processor to form crumbs of a suitable size. They can then be dried out in a low oven.
• The trick with this recipe is to keep the butter hot enough to cook the veal, without allowing it to turn brown.

Veal Rolls with Sage & Ham

These rolls are so good that, as their Italian name Saltimbocca implies, they "jump into your mouth". For the best results, make sure you use a well-flavoured stock, preferably home-made.

Serves 4
8 small veal escalopes (scallops)
8 small slices prosciutto
8 leaves fresh sage
40g/1½oz/3 tbsp butter
120ml/4fl oz/½ cup beef or chicken stock, warmed
salt and ground black pepper
fresh sage leaves, to garnish

1 Gently pound the veal slices with a mallet until thin. Lay a piece of prosciutto over each slice. Top with a sage leaf and season with salt and pepper.

2 Roll an escalope around the filling and secure the roll with a wooden toothpick. Repeat this process with the remaining filled escalopes.

3 Heat half the butter in a frying pan just large enough to hold the rolls in a single layer. When the butter is bubbling add the veal, turning the rolls to brown them on all sides. Cook for about 7–10 minutes, or until the veal is cooked. Transfer with a slotted spoon to a warmed serving platter.

4 Add the remaining butter and the hot stock to the frying pan and bring to the boil, scraping up the brown residue on the bottom of the pan with a wooden spoon. Pour the sauce over the veal rolls, garnish with sage leaves and serve immediately.

Cook's Tip
To make an authentic meat stock or broth, place about 1kg/2lb of meat scraps and bones in a large pan. Add an onion, carrot, celery stick, ripe tomato and a handful of parsley. Add about 1.5 litres/2½ pints/6¼ cups water to cover, season and bring to the boil. Reduce the heat and simmer very gently for 2–3 hours, skimming the surface regularly. Strain before using.

Energy 431Kcal/1804kJ; Fat 23.1g; Saturated Fat 9.3g; Carbohydrate 19.5g; Fibre 0.6g

Per roll Energy 115Kcal/481kJ; Fat 6g; Saturated Fat 3.4g; Carbohydrate 0.2g; Fibre 0g

Osso Buco

This dish is traditionally served with Risotto alla Milanese, but plain rice is just as good. "Osso buco" means "hollow bone" and the recipe calls for shin of veal cut across the bone – the marrow centre is considered a great delicacy.

Serves 4

seasoned flour, for coating
4 pieces of shin of veal
2 small onions
30ml/2 tbsp olive oil
1 large celery stick, finely chopped

1 carrot, finely chopped
2 garlic cloves, finely chopped
400g/14oz can chopped tomatoes
300ml/½ pint/1¼ cups dry
    white wine
300ml/½ pint/1¼ cups chicken
    or veal stock
1 strip of thinly pared lemon rind
2 bay leaves, plus extra to garnish
salt and ground black pepper

For the gremolata
30 ml/2 tbsp finely chopped fresh
    flat leaf parsley
finely grated rind of 1 lemon
1 garlic clove, finely chopped

1 Preheat the oven to 160°C/325°F/Gas 3. Season the flour with salt and pepper and use to coat the shin of veal. Slice one of the onions and separate it into rings. Heat the oil in a large flameproof casserole, add the veal and onion rings and cook until the veal is browned. Drain the veal on kitchen paper.

2 Chop the remaining onion and add to the pan with the celery, carrot and garlic. Scrape up the residue on the bottom of the pan and cook gently, stirring frequently, for about 5 minutes, until the vegetables soften slightly.

3 Add the chopped tomatoes, wine, stock, lemon rind and bay leaves, then season to taste with salt and pepper. Bring to the boil, stirring. Return the veal to the pan and coat with the sauce. Cover and cook in the oven for 2 hours or until tender.

4 Meanwhile, make the gremolata. In a small bowl, mix together the parsley, lemon rind and garlic. Remove the casserole from the oven, discard the strip of lemon rind and the bay leaves. Taste the sauce for seasoning. Serve sprinkled with the gremolata and garnished with extra bay leaves.

Energy 317Kcal/1335kJ; Fat 8.7g; Saturated Fat 1.8g; Carbohydrate 12.5g; Fibre 2.6g

Veal Escalopes with Lemon

Popular in Italian restaurants, this dish is very easy to make at home. Lightly cooked green beans and Peperonata – a chunky tomato and sweet red (bell) pepper dip – make the perfect accompaniment.

Serves 4
4 veal escalopes (scallops)

30–45ml/2–3 tbsp flour, for
    coating
50g/2oz/¼ cup butter
60ml/4 tbsp olive oil
60ml/4 tbsp Italian dry white
    vermouth or dry white wine
45ml/3 tbsp lemon juice
salt and ground black pepper
lemon wedges and fresh parsley,
    to garnish

1 Put each escalope between two sheets of clear film (plastic wrap) and pound until very thin.

2 Cut the pounded escalopes in half or into quarters. Season the flour with salt and pepper and use to coat the veal.

3 Melt the butter with half the oil in a large heavy frying pan until sizzling. Add as many escalopes as the pan will hold. Fry over medium to high heat for 1–2 minutes on each side, until lightly coloured. Transfer with a metal spatula to a plate and keep hot. Add the remaining oil to the pan and cook the remaining veal in the same way.

4 Remove the pan from the heat and add the vermouth or wine and the lemon juice. Stir vigorously to mix with the pan juices, then return to the heat and return all the veal to the pan. Spoon the sauce over the veal. Shake the pan over medium heat, until the escalopes are coated and heated through.

5 Serve immediately, garnished with lemon wedges and parsley.

> **Variation**
> Use skinless boneless chicken breasts instead of the veal. If they are thick, cut them in half before pounding.

Energy 453Kcal/1898kJ; Fat 23g; Saturated Fat 8.5g; Carbohydrate 43.9g; Fibre 1.8g

Calf's Liver with Onions

This classic Venetian dish is very good served with grilled polenta. Allow enough time for the onions to cook very slowly, to produce a sweet flavour.

800g/1¾lb calf's liver, sliced thinly
salt and ground black pepper
45ml/3 tbsp finely chopped fresh parsley, to garnish
grilled polenta wedges, to serve (optional)

Serves 6
75g/3oz/⅓ cup butter
45ml/3 tbsp olive oil
675g/1½lb onions, finely sliced

1 Heat two-thirds of the butter with the oil in a large heavy frying pan. Add the onions and cook over low heat for 40–50 minutes, stirring frequently, until soft and tender. Season with salt and pepper. Transfer to a dish.

2 Heat the remaining butter in the pan over medium to high heat. When it has stopped bubbling, add the liver and brown on both sides. Cook for about 5 minutes, until browned on the outside but still rosy in the middle. Transfer with a metal spatula to a warmed side dish.

3 Return the onions to the pan. Increase the heat slightly and stir the onions to mix them into the liver cooking juices.

4 When the onions are hot, turn them out onto a heated serving platter. Arrange the liver on top and sprinkle with parsley. Serve with grilled polenta wedges, if desired.

Cook's Tip
For grilled (broiled) polenta, bring 1.5 litres/2½ pints/6¼ cups water to the boil in a large pan, whisk in 350g/12oz/2½ cups polenta, then cook, beating, for about 30 minutes. Spread out on a damp surface, 2cm/¾ thick, and leave until cold. Cut into squares and grill (broil) until browned.

Veal with Anchovies & Mozzarella

Scaloppine are thin escalopes of veal cut across the grain. For this dish, they are rolled around an anchovy, tomato and mozzarella filling and served with a Marsala sauce.

Serves 4–6
50g/2oz/¼ cup butter
50g/2oz can anchovies
4 fresh tomatoes, peeled and chopped
30ml/2 tbsp chopped fresh flat leaf parsley
6 veal escalopes (scallops), about 100g/3¾oz each
200g/7oz mozzarella cheese, cut in thin slices
30ml/2 tbsp olive oil
175ml/6fl oz/¾ cup Marsala or medium dry sherry
30–45ml/2–3 tbsp single (light) cream
salt and ground black pepper
fresh herbs, to garnish
cooked linguine, to serve

1 Melt half the butter in a small pan. Drain the anchovies and add them to the pan. Cook gently, stirring with a wooden spoon, until they break down to a pulp. Stir in the tomatoes and cook for about 3 minutes, until they have softened and reduced. Transfer to a bowl, cool, then stir in the parsley.

2 Place each veal escalope in turn between two sheets of baking parchment and beat with a mallet or rolling pin until thin. Spread the escalopes out on a board and sprinkle with ground black pepper. Divide the anchovy and tomato mixture among them, leaving the edges free.

3 Top with the slices of cheese. Fold the long edges of each escalope towards the centre, then bring up the sides to form a neat parcel. Secure with kitchen string (twine).

4 Heat the remaining butter with the oil in a large frying pan. Brown the rolled escalopes, then pour in the Marsala or sherry. Cook, uncovered, for 5 minutes or until the Marsala or sherry has reduced and thickened.

5 Transfer the rolls to a serving plate, stir the pan juices, then pour in the cream. Reheat without boiling, then strain over the rolls. Garnish with fresh herbs and serve with linguine.

Calf's Liver with Honey

Calf's liver, with its meltingly soft texture, is a great favourite in Italy. This is a quick and easy, slightly contemporary, treatment of this delicacy.

Serves 4

4 slices calf's liver, each about
175g/ 6oz and 1.5cm/½in thick
flour, for dusting

25g/1oz/2 tbsp butter
30ml/2 tbsp vegetable oil
30ml/2 tbsp sherry vinegar or red
  wine vinegar
30–45ml/2–3 tbsp chicken stock
15ml/1 tbsp clear honey
salt and ground black pepper
watercress sprigs, to garnish

1 Wipe the liver slices with damp kitchen paper, then season both sides with a little salt and pepper. Dust the slices lightly with flour, shaking off any excess. Place the coated liver on a board and set aside.

2 In a large heavy frying pan, melt half of the butter with the oil over high heat and swirl the pan to mix them together.

3 Add the liver slices to the pan and cook for 1–2 minutes, until browned on one side, then turn and cook for a further 1 minute. Transfer to heated plates and keep warm.

4 Stir the vinegar, stock and honey into the pan and boil for about 1 minute, stirring constantly, then add the remaining butter, stirring until melted and smooth. Spoon the honey-flavoured sauce over the liver slices, garnish each portion with watercress and serve immediately.

> **Cook's Tips**
> • Cook the liver until it is browned on the outside but still rosy-pink in the centre. Calf's liver should never be overcooked, otherwise the delicate texture will be lost.
> • Use a mild-flavoured honey, such as acacia, for the sauce so that it does not overpower other flavours.

Energy 302Kcal/1260kJ; Fat 16.6g; Saturated Fat 5.7g; Carbohydrate 5.8g; Fibre 0.1g

Cold Veal with Tuna Sauce

This classic summer dish is best when prepared in advance and refrigerated for a few hours before serving. The dish can be kept for up to 3 days in the refrigerator.

Serves 6–8

800g/1¾lb boneless roasting
  veal, in one piece
1 carrot, peeled
1 stalk celery
1 small onion, peeled and
  quartered
1 bay leaf

1 clove
5ml/1 tsp whole peppercorns

For the tuna sauce
400g/14oz canned tuna,
  preferably in olive oil
4 anchovy fillets
10ml/2 tsp capers, rinsed and
  drained
45ml/3 tbsp fresh lemon juice
300ml/½ pint/1¼ cups
  mayonnaise
salt and ground black pepper
capers and pickled cornichons,
  to garnish

1 Place the veal, vegetables, bay leaf, clove and peppercorns in a medium pan (not aluminium or copper). Cover with water. Bring to the boil and simmer for 50–60 minutes, until tender. Skim off any scum that rises to the surface. Do not overcook, or the veal will fall apart when sliced. Allow it to cool in its cooking liquid for several hours, or overnight.

2 To make the tuna sauce, drain the tuna. Place in a food processor or blender and add the anchovies, capers and lemon juice. Process to a creamy paste. If it seems too thick, add 30–45ml/2–3 tbsp of the cool veal stock and process again.

3 Scrape the tuna paste into a bowl. Fold in the mayonnaise. Check the seasoning and adjust as necessary.

4 Slice the veal as thinly as possible. Spread a little of the tuna sauce over the bottom of a serving platter.

5 Arrange a layer of the veal slices on top of the sauce. Cover with a thin layer of sauce. Make another layer or two of veal slices and sauce, ending with the sauce. Garnish with capers and cornichons. Cover and chill until needed.

Energy 262Kcal/1093kJ; Fat 15.4g; Saturated Fat 2.8g; Carbohydrate 1.6g; Fibre 0.4g

Pork with Marsala and Juniper

Although most frequently used in desserts, Sicilian Marsala gives savoury dishes a rich, fruity and alcoholic tang. Here it combines beautifully with wild mushrooms, herbs and berries to make a tasty sauce for pork.

Serves 4
*25g/1oz dried cep or porcini
mushrooms
4 pork escalopes (scallops)
10ml/2 tsp balsamic vinegar
8 whole garlic cloves
15g/½oz/1 tbsp butter
45ml/3 tbsp Marsala
several rosemary sprigs
10 juniper berries, crushed
salt and ground black pepper*

1 Put the dried mushrooms in a bowl and add enough hot water to just cover. Leave to soak for 20 minutes. Drain, reserving the liquid. Strain the soaking liquid through a sieve (strainer) lined with kitchen paper and reserve.

2 Brush the pork escalopes with 5ml/1 tsp of the balsamic vinegar and season with salt and pepper. Put the garlic cloves in a small pan of boiling water and cook for 10 minutes, until soft. Drain and set aside.

3 Melt the butter in a large frying pan. Add the pork and fry quickly until browned on the underside. Turn the meat over and cook for another minute. Add the Marsala, rosemary, mushrooms, 60ml/4 tbsp of the mushroom juices, the garlic cloves, juniper and remaining balsamic vinegar.

4 Simmer gently for about 3 minutes, until the pork is cooked through. Season lightly with salt and ground black pepper and serve immediately.

Cook's Tip
Use good-quality butcher's pork which won't be drowned by the flavour of the sauce. Free-range, organic pork will provide more taste and a better texture.

Pork in Sweet & Sour Sauce

The combination of sweet and sour flavours is popular in Venetian cooking, especially with meat and liver. This recipe is given extra bite with the addition of crushed mixed peppercorns. Served with shelled broad beans tossed with grilled bacon, the dish is quite delectable.

Serves 2
*1 whole pork fillet (tenderloin), weighing about 350g/12oz
25ml/1½ tbsp flour, for coating
30–45ml/2–3 tbsp olive oil
250ml/8fl oz/1 cup dry white wine
30ml/2 tbsp white wine vinegar
10ml/2 tsp sugar
15ml/1 tbsp mixed peppercorns, coarsely ground
salt and ground black pepper*

1 Cut the pork diagonally into thin slices. Place between two sheets of clear film (plastic wrap) and pound lightly with a rolling pin to flatten them evenly.

2 Spread out the flour in a shallow bowl. Season well with salt and pepper, then lightly coat the meat in the flour.

3 Heat 15ml/1 tbsp of the olive oil in a wide heavy pan or frying pan and add as many slices of pork as the pan will hold. Fry over medium to high heat for 2–3 minutes on each side, until crispy and tender. Remove with a metal spatula and set aside. Repeat with the remaining pork fillets, adding more oil as necessary.

4 Mix the wine, wine vinegar and sugar in a jug. Pour into the pan and stir vigorously over high heat until reduced, scraping the pan to incorporate the sediment. Stir in the peppercorns and return the pork to the pan. Spoon the sauce over the pork until it is evenly coated and heated through.

Cook's Tip
Grind the mixed peppercorns in a pepper grinder, or crush them with a mortar and pestle.

Pork Fillet with Caper Sauce

A piquant sauce flavoured with capers and anchovies gives these medallions of pork plenty of zing. The sauce can be made in advance and reheated while the pork is cooked.

Serves 4–5
450g/1lb pork fillet (tenderloin), cut into thin slices
flour, for coating
25g/1oz/2 tbsp butter
30ml/2 tbsp olive oil
ground black pepper

For the caper sauce
30ml/2 tbsp olive oil
50g/2oz/¼ cup butter
½ small onion, very finely chopped
1 anchovy fillet, rinsed and chopped
15ml/1 tbsp flour
30ml/2 tbsp capers, rinsed
15ml/1 tbsp finely chopped fresh parsley
60ml/4 tbsp wine vinegar
60ml/4 tbsp balsamic vinegar

1 To make the sauce, heat the oil and 25g/1oz/2 tbsp of the butter in a small pan (not aluminum) and slowly cook the onion until softened. Add the anchovy and mash it into the onion with a wooden spoon.

2 Stir in the flour until well amalgamated, then add the capers and parsley. Add the wine vinegar and 60ml/4 tbsp water and stir constantly over low heat to thicken the sauce. Just before serving, stir in the remaining butter and the balsamic vinegar.

3 Meanwhile, place the pork fillets between two sheets of clear film (plastic wrap) and pound with a rolling pin to flatten them evenly and thinly.

4 Spread out the flour in a shallow bowl. Season well with black pepper and coat the pork lightly, shaking off any excess.

5 Heat the butter and the oil in a large frying pan and, when hot, add some of the pork slices in a single layer. Cook for a total of 5–6 minutes to brown the meat on both sides. Transfer to a heated serving dish and repeat with the remaining pork slices. Serve immediately, with the sauce.

Energy 290Kcal/1202kJ; Fat 21.7g; Saturated Fat 8.3g; Carbohydrate 3.6g; Fibre 0.7g

Pork Chops with Mushrooms

The addition of dried porcini helps to enhance the mushroomy flavour of this delicious pork dish. A great Italian-style supper dish.

Serves 4
15g/½oz/3 tbsp dried porcini mushrooms
150ml/8fl oz/1 cup warm water
75g/3oz/6 tbsp butter
2 garlic cloves, peeled and crushed
300g/11oz fresh cultivated mushrooms, thinly sliced
15ml/1 tbsp olive oil
4 pork chops, trimmed of excess fat
2.5ml/½ tsp fresh thyme leaves, or 1.5ml/¼ tsp dried
120ml/4fl oz/½ cup dry white wine
75ml/3fl oz/⅓ cup single (light) cream
salt and ground black pepper

1 Soak the porcini mushrooms in the warm water for 20 minutes. Drain the mushrooms, reserving the soaking water. Strain the soaking liquid through a layer of kitchen paper placed in a sieve (strainer) and reserve.

2 Melt two-thirds of the butter in a large frying pan. Add the garlic. When the foam subsides, stir in all the mushrooms. Season with salt and pepper and cook for 8–10 minutes over medium heat, until the mushrooms give up their liquid. Using a slotted spoon, transfer the mushrooms to a dish.

3 Heat the oil and remaining butter in the frying pan. Add the pork in a single layer and sprinkle with thyme. Cook over medium to high heat for about 3 minutes on each side to seal. Reduce the heat and cook for a further 15–20 minutes. Transfer to a warmed plate.

4 Spoon off any fat in the pan. Pour in the wine and the mushroom water. Cook over high heat, until reduced by about half, stirring to scrape up the residues on the bottom of the pan and mixing in well.

5 Add the mushrooms and the cream and cook for 4–5 minutes more. Serve the chops with the sauce.

Energy 420Kcal/1742kJ; Fat 30.7g; Saturated Fat 16.6g; Carbohydrate 1.4g; Fibre 0.8g

Basil & Pecorino Stuffed Pork Fillet

This is a very easy dish to make and looks extremely impressive.

Serves 6–8
2 pork fillet (tenderloins), each
   about 350g/12oz
45ml/3 tbsp olive oil

40g/1½oz/1½ cups fresh basil
   leaves, chopped
50g/2oz Pecorino cheese, grated
2.5ml/½ tsp chilli flakes
salt and ground black pepper

1 Make a 1cm/½in slit down the length of one of the pork fillets. Continue to slice, cutting along the fold of the meat, until you can open it out flat.

2 Lay between two sheets of baking parchment and pound with a rolling pin to an even thickness of about 1cm/½in. Lift off the top sheet of parchment and brush the meat with a little oil.

3 Press half the basil leaves on to the surface, then scatter over half the Pecorino cheese and chilli flakes. Add a little pepper.

4 Roll up lengthways to form a sausage shape and tie with kitchen string (twine). Repeat with the second fillet. Season both with salt.

5 Heat the remaining oil in a large frying pan and brown the fillets for 5 minutes, turning to sear on all sides. Transfer them to a roasting pan and cook in the oven for about 20 minutes, or until the pork is cooked through. Leave to stand for 10 minutes before slicing into rounds and serving.

> **Variation**
> The pork can be barbecued: first sear on all sides over hot coals, then cook over gentler heat until done, covering with a foil tent or lid, and moving the pork often to avoid burning.

Pork Braised in Milk with Carrots

This method of slowly cooking a joint of pork produces a deliciously creamy gravy and makes the meat meltingly tender. This recipe is a speciality of the Veneto region.

Serves 4–5
675g/1½lb lean loin of pork
45ml/3 tbsp olive oil
25g/1oz/2 tbsp butter

1 small onion, finely chopped
1 celery stick, finely chopped
8 carrots, cut into 5cm/2in strips
2 bay leaves
15ml/1 tbsp peppercorns
salt and ground black pepper
475ml/16fl oz/2 cups milk,
   scalded

1 Trim any excess fat from the pork and tie it into a roll with string. Preheat the oven to 180°C/350°F/Gas 4.

2 Heat the oil and butter in a large flameproof casserole. Add the vegetables and cook over low heat for 8–10 minutes, until softened. Increase the heat, push the vegetables to one side and add the pork, browning it on all sides. Add the bay leaves and peppercorns, then season with salt.

3 Pour in the hot milk. Cover the casserole and place it in the centre of the oven. Bake for about 90 minutes, turning and basting the pork with the sauce about once every 20 minutes. Remove the cover for the last 20 minutes of baking.

4 Remove the meat from the casserole, then cut off the string. Place the meat on a warmed serving platter and cut into slices.

5 Discard the bay leaves from the pan. Press about one-third of the carrots and all the liquids in the pan through a sieve (strainer). Arrange the remaining carrots around the meat.

6 Place the sauce in a small pan, taste for seasoning, and bring to the boil. If the sauce seems too thin, boil it for a few minutes to reduce slightly. Serve the sliced meat with the carrots, and hand the hot sauce separately.

Energy 331Kcal/1378kJ; Fat 19.8g; Saturated Fat 7.7g; Carbohydrate 9.6g; Fibre 2.6g

Energy 174Kcal/725kJ; Fat 9.7g; Saturated Fat 3.1g; Carbohydrate 0.1g; Fibre 0.3g

Roast Lamb with Herbs

Succulent tender lamb, bathed in fresh herbs and wine, this dish from southern Italy is very simple but full of flavour.

Serves 4–6

1.3kg/3lb leg of lamb
45–60ml/3–4 tbsp olive oil
4 garlic cloves, peeled and halved
2 fresh sage sprigs, or pinch of dried sage leaves
2 fresh rosemary sprigs, or 5ml/1 tsp dried
2 bay leaves
2 fresh thyme sprigs, or 2.5ml/ ½ tsp dried
175ml/6fl oz/¾ cup dry white wine
salt and ground black pepper

1 Cut any excess fat from the lamb. Rub with olive oil. Using a sharp knife, make small cuts just under the skin all around the meat. Insert the garlic pieces in some of the cuts, and a few of the fresh herbs in the others. (If using dried herbs, sprinkle them over the surface of the meat.)

2 Rub the remaining fresh herbs all over the lamb and allow it to stand in a cool place for at least 2 hours before cooking. Preheat the oven to 190°C/375°F/Gas 5.

3 Place the lamb in a large roasting pan, surrounded by the herbs. Pour on 30ml/2 tbsp of the olive oil. Season with salt and pepper. Place in the oven and roast for 35 minutes, basting the meat occasionally.

4 Pour the wine over the lamb. Roast for a further 15 minutes or until the meat is cooked. Transfer the lamb to a heated serving dish, tent with foil and leave to stand for 10 minutes.

5 Tilt the pan, spooning off any fat on the surface. Strain the pan juices into a gravy boat and serve with the sauce.

> **Cook's Tip**
> Both rosemary and sage have a pungent aromatic flavour that combines well with lamb, but don't be tempted to overdo it.

Lamb Stewed with Tomatoes & Garlic

This rustic stew comes from the plateau of Puglia, where sheep graze happily alongside vineyards.

Serves 5–6

2 large garlic cloves
1 sprig fresh rosemary (or 45ml/ 3 tbsp chopped fresh parsley if fresh rosemary is not available)
90ml/6 tbsp olive oil
1.2kg/2½lb stewing lamb, trimmed and cut into chunks
flour seasoned with ground black pepper, for coating
175ml/6fl oz/¾ cup dry white wine
10ml/2 tsp salt
450g/1lb fresh tomatoes, chopped, or 400g/14oz can tomatoes
120ml/4fl oz/½ cup beef stock, heated

1 Preheat the oven to 180°C/350°F/Gas 4. Chop the garlic with the parsley, if using.

2 Heat 60ml/4 tbsp of the oil in a wide flameproof casserole. Add the garlic and rosemary or parsley and cook over medium heat until the garlic is golden.

3 Coat the lamb in the flour. Add a batch of lamb chunks to the pan in a single layer and cook, turning, until they are evenly browned. Using a slotted spoon, transfer them to a plate. Add a little more oil to the casserole and brown the remaining lamb.

4 When all the lamb has been browned, return it to the casserole with the wine. Increase the heat and bring to the boil, scraping up any residues from the bottom. Sprinkle with the salt, then stir in the tomatoes and the stock. Stir well. Cover and cook in the oven for 1¾–2 hours or until the meat is tender.

> **Cook's Tip**
> For a delicious garlic toast accompaniment. drizzle thick slices of rustic bread with extra virgin olive oil, then rub with a peeled garlic clove and toast on both sides until golden.

Roast Lamb with Rosemary

In Italy, lamb is traditionally served at Easter. This simple roast with potatoes owes its wonderful flavour to the fresh rosemary and garlic.

Serves 4
½ leg of lamb, about 1.3kg/3lb
2 garlic cloves, cut lengthways into thin slivers
105ml/7 tbsp olive oil
leaves from 4 fresh rosemary sprigs, finely chopped
about 250ml/8fl oz/1 cup lamb or vegetable stock
675g/1½lb potatoes, cut into 2.5cm/1in cubes
a few fresh sage leaves, chopped
salt and ground black pepper
cooked baby carrots, to serve

1 Preheat the oven to 230°C/450°F/Gas 8. Using the point of a sharp knife, make deep incisions in the lamb, especially near the bone, and insert the slivers of garlic.

2 Put the lamb in a roasting pan and rub all over with 45 ml/3 tbsp of the oil. Sprinkle over about half of the chopped rosemary, patting it on firmly, and season with plenty of salt and pepper. Roast for 30 minutes, turning once.

3 Lower the oven temperature to 190°C/375°F/Gas 5. Turn the lamb over again and add 120 ml/4 fl oz/½ cup of the stock.

4 Roast for a further 1½ –1½ hours, until the lamb is tender, turning the joint two or three times more and adding the rest of the stock in two or three batches. Baste the lamb each time it is turned.

5 Meanwhile, put the potatoes in a separate roasting pan and toss with the remaining oil and rosemary and the sage. Roast, on the same oven shelf as the lamb, if possible, for 45 minutes, turning the potatoes several times until they are golden and cooked through.

6 Transfer the lamb to a carving board, tent with foil and leave in a warm place for 10 minutes so that the flesh firms for easier carving. Serve whole or carved into thin slices, surrounded by the potatoes and accompanied by baby carrots.

Mediterranean Lamb with Artichokes

A delicious lamb stew, flavoured with heady spices and preserved lemon.

Serves 4–6
675g/1½lb lean lamb, trimmed and cut into cubes
2 onions, very finely chopped
2 garlic cloves, crushed
60ml/4 tbsp chopped fresh parsley
60ml/4 tbsp chopped fresh coriander (cilantro)
a good pinch of ground ginger
5ml/1 tsp ground cumin
90ml/6 tbsp olive oil
350–400ml/12–14fl oz/1½–1⅔ cups water or stock
1 preserved lemon, salt washed off
400g/14oz can artichoke hearts, drained and halved
15ml/1 tbsp chopped fresh mint
1 egg, beaten (optional)
salt and ground black pepper
chopped fresh mint, to garnish
couscous, to serve

1 Place the meat in a shallow dish. Stir together the onions, garlic, parsley, coriander, ginger, cumin, seasoning and olive oil. Stir into the meat, cover with clear film (plastic wrap) and set aside to marinate for at least 3 hours or preferably overnight.

2 Heat a large heavy pan and stir in the meat with all the marinade. Cook for 5–6 minutes, until the meat is browned, then stir in enough water or stock to just cover the meat. Bring to the boil, cover and simmer for 45–60 minutes, until tender.

3 Discard the lemon flesh and cut the peel into pieces. Stir into the meat and simmer for 15 minutes. Add the artichokes and mint. Simmer for a few minutes to heat through. If you wish to thicken the sauce, remove the pan from the heat and stir in some of the egg. Garnish with mint and serve with couscous.

> **Cook's Tip**
> To preserve lemons, scrub and quarter them almost through to the base, then rub the cut sides with salt. Pack into a large sterilized jar, and half-fill with more salt, adding peppercorns and cinnamon. Cover completely with lemon juice. Store for 2 weeks, shaking daily. Add a little olive oil to seal; use within 1–3 months.

Energy 777Kcal/3265kJ; Fat 34.2g; Saturates 12.4g; Carbohydrate 27.2g; Fibre 1.7g

Energy 330Kcal/1374kJ; Fat 23.9g; Saturated Fat 7.4g; Carbohydrate 5.9g; Fibre 1.9g

Chicken with Chianti

The full-flavoured wine and red pesto give this sauce a rich colour and almost spicy flavour, while the grapes add a delicious sweetness.

Serves 4
45ml/3 tbsp olive oil
4 part-boned chicken breasts, skinned

1 red onion, cut into wedges
30ml/2 tbsp red pesto
300ml/½ pint/1¼ cups Chianti
115g/4oz red grapes, halved lengthways and seeded if necessary
salt and ground black pepper
fresh basil leaves, to garnish
rocket (arugula) salad, to serve

1 Heat 30 ml/2 tbsp of the oil in a large frying pan, add the chicken breasts and sauté over medium heat for about 5 minutes, until they have changed colour on all sides. Remove with a slotted spoon and drain on kitchen paper.

2 Heat the remaining oil in the pan, add the onion wedges and red pesto and cook gently, stirring constantly, for about 3 minutes until the onion is softened, but not browned.

3 Add the Chianti and 300ml/½ pint/1¼ cups water to the pan and bring to the boil, stirring, then return the chicken to the pan and add salt and pepper to taste.

4 Reduce the heat, then cover the pan and simmer gently, stirring occasionally, for 20 minutes, or until the chicken is tender.

5 Add the grapes to the pan and cook over low to medium heat, until heated through, then taste the sauce for seasoning. Garnish with basil and serve accompanied by the rocket salad.

> **Variations**
> Use green pesto instead of red, and substitute a dry white wine such as Pinot Grigio for the Chianti, then finish with seedless green grapes. A few spoonfuls of mascarpone cheese can be added at the end if you like, to enrich the sauce.

Chicken with Tomatoes & Prawns

This Piedmontese dish was created especially for Napoleon after the battle of Marengo. Versions of it appear in both Italian and French recipe books.

Serves 4
120ml/4 1 oz/½ cup olive oil
8 chicken thighs on the bone, skinned
1 onion, finely chopped
1 celery stick, finely chopped
1 garlic clove, crushed

350g/12oz ripe Italian plum tomatoes, peeled and chopped
250ml/8fl oz/1 cup dry white wine
2.5ml/½tsp finely chopped fresh rosemary
15ml/1 tbsp butter
8 small triangles of white bread
175g/6oz large raw prawns (shrimp), peeled
salt and ground black pepper
finely chopped flat leaf parsley and whole cooked prawns (shrimp), to garnish

1 Heat about 30 ml/2 tbsp of the oil in a frying pan, add the chicken thighs and sauté over medium heat for about 5 minutes, until they have changed colour on all sides. Transfer to a flameproof casserole.

2 Add the onion and celery to the frying pan and cook gently, stirring frequently, for about 3 minutes, until softened. Add the garlic, tomatoes, wine, rosemary and salt and pepper to taste. Bring to the boil, stirring.

3 Pour the tomato sauce over the chicken. Cover and cook gently for 40 minutes, or until the chicken is tender.

4 About 10 minutes before serving, add the remaining oil and the butter to the frying pan and heat until hot but not smoking. Add the triangles of bread and shallow fry until crisp and golden on each side. Drain on kitchen paper.

5 Add the peeled prawns to the tomato sauce and heat until the prawns are cooked through. Taste the sauce for seasoning. Dip one of the tips of each fried bread triangle in chopped parsley. Serve the dish hot, garnished with the bread triangles and the whole prawns.

Stuffed Chicken Rolls

These tasty chicken rolls are filled with a delicious rice, ricotta and herb stuffing. They are perfect served on a bed of tagliatelle tossed with fried wild mushrooms.

Serves 4

25g/1oz/2 tbsp butter
1 garlic clove, chopped
150g/5oz/1¼ cups cooked white
   long grain rice
45ml/3 tbsp ricotta cheese
10ml/2 tsp chopped fresh flat
   leaf parsley
5ml/1 tsp chopped fresh tarragon
4 boneless chicken breasts,
   skinned
3–4 slices prosciutto
15ml/1 tbsp olive oil
120ml/4fl oz/½ cup white wine
salt and ground black pepper
fresh flat leaf parsley sprigs, to
   garnish

1 Preheat the oven to 180°C/350°F/Gas 4. Melt about 10g/¼oz/2 tsp of the butter in a small pan and fry the garlic for a few seconds without browning. Spoon into a bowl.

2 Add the rice, ricotta, parsley and tarragon to the garlic in the bowl and season with salt and pepper. Stir to mix.

3 Place each chicken breast in turn between two sheets of clear film (plastic wrap) and flatten by beating lightly, but firmly, with a rolling pin.

4 Divide the slices of prosciutto between the chicken breasts, trimming the ham to fit, if necessary. Place a spoonful of the rice stuffing at the wider end of each ham-topped breast. Roll up carefully and tie in place with cooking string, or secure with a cocktail stick.

5 Heat the oil and the remaining butter in a frying pan and lightly fry the chicken rolls until browned on all sides. Place side by side in a shallow baking dish and pour over the white wine.

6 Cover the dish with greaseproof paper and cook in the oven for 30–35 minutes, until the chicken is tender. Cut the rolls into slices, garnish with sprigs of flat leaf parsley and a generous grinding of black pepper, if you like. Serve immediately.

Energy 329Kcal/1375kJ; Fat 11.5g; Saturated Fat 5.1g; Carbohydrate 21.3g; Fibre 1.3g

Hunter's Chicken

This famous dish, known in Italy as Pollo alla Cacciatora, sometimes has strips of green pepper added to the sauce for extra colour and flavour instead of the fresh mushrooms.

Serves 4

15g/½oz/1 cup dried porcini
   mushrooms
250ml/8fl oz/1 cup warm water
30ml/2 tbsp olive oil
15g/½oz/1 tbsp butter
4 chicken pieces, on the bone,
   skinned
1 large onion, thinly sliced
400g/14oz can chopped Italian
   plum tomatoes
150ml/¼ pint/⅔ cup red wine
1 garlic clove, crushed
1 fresh rosemary sprig, leaves
   removed and finely chopped
115g/4oz/1¾ cups fresh field
   mushrooms, thinly sliced
salt and ground black pepper
fresh rosemary sprigs, to garnish

1 Put the dried porcini in a bowl with the warm water and leave to soak for 20 minutes. Remove the porcini from the liquid and squeeze over the bowl. Strain the liquid and reserve. Finely chop the soaked porcini.

2 Heat the oil and butter in a large flameproof casserole until foaming. Add the chicken and sauté over medium heat for 5 minutes, or until golden. Remove and drain on kitchen paper.

3 Add the onion and soaked mushrooms to the pan. Cook gently, stirring frequently, for about 3 minutes, until the onion has softened but not browned. Stir in the chopped tomatoes, wine and reserved mushroom soaking liquid, then add the crushed garlic and chopped rosemary, with salt and pepper to taste. Bring to the boil, stirring constantly.

4 Return the chicken to the pan and coat with the sauce. Cover and simmer gently for 30 minutes.

5 Add the fresh mushrooms and stir well to mix into the sauce. Continue simmering gently for 10 minutes, or until the chicken is tender. Taste for seasoning. Garnish with fresh rosemary and serve immediately.

Energy 287Kcal/1206kJ; Fat 10.7g; Saturated Fat 3.3g; Carbohydrate 4.7g; Fibre 1.5g

Chicken with Prosciutto & Cheese

This dish appears as Pollo alla Valdostana on Italian menus; the name Valdostana derives from Val d'Aosta, home of the Fontina cheese used on top of the chicken.

Serves 4
2 thin slices of prosciutto
2 thin slices of Fontina cheese

4 part-boned chicken breasts
4 basil sprigs
30ml/2 tbsp olive oil
15g/¹/₂oz/1 tbsp butter
120ml/4fl oz/¹/₂ cup dry
    white wine
salt and ground black pepper
tender young salad leaves, to
    serve

I Preheat the oven to 200°C/400°F/Gas 6. Lightly oil a large baking dish. Cut the prosciutto and Fontina slices in half crossways.

2 Skin the chicken breasts. Open out the slit in the centre of each one. Fill each cavity with half a ham slice and a basil sprig.

3 Heat the oil and butter in a wide heavy frying pan until foaming. Cook the chicken breasts over medium heat for 1–2 minutes on each side, until they change colour, then transfer with a slotted spoon to the prepared baking dish.

4 Add the wine to the pan juices, stir until sizzling, then pour over the chicken and season to taste. Top each chicken breast with a slice of Fontina. Bake for 20 minutes, or until the chicken is tender. Serve hot, with tender young salad leaves.

> **Cook's Tip**
> *There is nothing quite like the buttery texture and nutty flavour of Fontina cheese. It also has superb melting qualities. If unavailable, you can use a mountain cheese, such as Gruyère or Emmental. Ask for the cheese to be sliced thinly on the machine slicer, as you will find it difficult to slice it thinly yourself.*

Devilled Chicken

You can tell that this spicy, barbecued chicken dish comes from southern Italy because it has dried red chillies in the marinade. Serve with rice and a tossed salad for an easy supper.

Serves 4
120ml/4fl oz/¹/₂ cup olive oil
finely grated rind and juice of 1
    large lemon

2 garlic cloves, finely chopped
10ml/2 tsp finely chopped or
    crumbled dried red chillies
12 boneless chicken thighs,
    skinned and each cut into
    3 or 4 pieces
salt and ground black pepper
flat leaf parsley leaves, to garnish
lemon wedges, to serve

I To make a marinade, mix the oil, lemon rind and juice, garlic and chillies in a large, shallow glass or china dish. Add salt and pepper to taste. Whisk well, then add the chicken pieces, turning to coat with the marinade. Cover and marinate in the refrigerator for at least 4 hours, or preferably overnight.

2 When ready to cook, prepare the barbecue or preheat the grill (broiler) and thread the chicken pieces on to eight oiled metal skewers.

3 Cook on the barbecue or under a hot grill for 6–8 minutes, turning frequently, until tender. Garnish with parsley leaves and serve hot, with lemon wedges for squeezing.

> **Cook's Tip**
> *Thread the chicken pieces spiral-fashion on the skewers so they do not fall off during cooking.*

> **Variation**
> *If you prefer a milder taste, this dish is just as good without the chillies. Add chopped fresh herbs instead, for added flavour.*

Energy 299Kcal/1254kJ; Fat 12g; Saturated Fat 2.6g; Carbohydrate 0.4g; Fibre 0.6g

Energy 322Kcal/1346kJ; Fat 14.7g; Saturated Fat 6g; Carbohydrate 0.4g; Fibre 0g

Pan-fried Chicken with Pesto

Make your own delicious pesto sauce and serve it warm with golden chicken pieces for a quick and easy meal with lots of Italian flair.

Serves 4
15ml/1 tbsp olive oil
4 boneless, skinless chicken breast
    fillets, about 175g/6oz each
fresh basil leaves, to garnish
braised baby carrots, to serve

For the pesto
90ml/6 tbsp olive oil
50g/2oz/½ cup pine nuts
50g/2oz/⅔ cup freshly grated
    Parmesan cheese
50g/2oz/1 cup fresh basil leaves
15g/½oz/¼ cup fresh parsley
2 garlic cloves, crushed
salt and ground black pepper

1 Heat the oil in a frying pan. Add the chicken fillets and cook gently for 15–20 minutes, turning several times, until they are tender, lightly browned and thoroughly cooked.

2 Meanwhile, make the pesto. Place the olive oil, pine nuts, Parmesan cheese, basil leaves, parsley and garlic in a blender or food processor with salt and pepper. Process until well mixed and the required texture is achieved.

3 Remove the cooked chicken from the pan, cover and keep hot. Reduce the heat slightly, then add the pesto to the pan and cook gently for a few minutes, stirring constantly, until the pesto has warmed through.

4 Pour the warm pesto over the chicken and garnish with basil leaves. Serve with braised baby carrots and celery.

Variations
To ring the changes, serve the pesto with boneless chicken thighs instead of breast portions. Of course, the pesto also makes a perfect quick sauce for pasta – at the end of step 2, simply stir into hot cooked pasta. The pesto is also good for adding flavour to soups and roasted vegetables.

Chicken with Tomato Salsa

This simple meal is a great way to enjoy the flavour, colour and health benefits of Mediterranean herbs and ingredients. For the best result, marinate the chicken overnight.

Serves 4
4 boneless, skinless chicken breast
    fillets, about 175g/6oz each
30ml/2 tbsp fresh lemon juice
30ml/2 tbsp olive oil
10ml/2 tsp ground cumin
10ml/2 tsp dried oregano
15ml/1 tbsp coarse black pepper

For the salsa
1 green chilli
450g/1lb plum tomatoes, seeded
    and chopped
3 spring onions (scallions),
    chopped
15ml/1 tbsp chopped fresh
    parsley
30ml/2 tbsp chopped fresh
    coriander (cilantro)
30ml/2 tbsp fresh lemon juice
45ml/3 tbsp olive oil

1 With a meat mallet, pound the chicken between two sheets of clear film (plastic wrap) until thin.

2 In a shallow dish, combine the lemon juice, oil, cumin, oregano and pepper. Add the chicken and turn to coat. Cover and leave to marinate for at least 2 hours, or in the refrigerator overnight.

3 To make the salsa, char the chilli skin either over a gas flame or under the grill (broiler). Leave to cool for 5 minutes. Carefully rub off the charred skin, taking care to wash your hands afterwards. For a less hot flavour, discard the seeds.

4 Chop the chilli very finely and place in a bowl. Add the seeded and chopped tomatoes, the chopped spring onions, chopped fresh parsley and coriander, lemon juice and olive oil and mix well. Set aside until ready to serve.

5 Remove the chicken from the marinade. Heat a ridged griddle. Add the chicken fillets and cook on one side until browned, for about 3 minutes. Turn over and cook for a further 4 minutes. Serve with the chilli salsa.

Chicken with Peppers

This colourful dish comes from the sun-baked south of Italy, where sweet peppers grow in abundance.

Serves 4

1.3kg/3lb chicken, cut into serving pieces
3 large (bell) peppers, red, yellow or green
90ml/6 tbsp olive oil
2 red onions, finely sliced
2 garlic cloves, finely chopped
small piece of dried chilli, crumbled (optional)
120ml/4fl oz/½ cup white wine
2 tomatoes, fresh or canned, peeled and chopped
45ml/3 tbsp chopped fresh parsley
salt and ground black pepper

1 Trim any fat off the chicken and remove all excess skin. To prepare the peppers, cut them in half, and discard the seeds, cores and stems. Slice into strips.

2 Heat half the oil in a large heavy pan or flameproof casserole. Add the onions and cook over low heat, until soft. Transfer to a side dish.

3 Add the remaining oil to the pan and increase the heat to medium. Add the chicken and cook for 6–8 minutes to brown on all sides. Return the onions to the pan, then add the garlic and dried chilli, if using.

4 Pour in the wine and cook until it has reduced by half. Add the pepper strips and stir well to coat. Season with salt and pepper to taste, then cook for 3–4 minutes, stirring occasionally. Stir in the chopped tomatoes.

5 Lower the heat, cover the pan and cook for 25–30 minutes, stirring occasionally, until the peppers have softened and the chicken is cooked. Stir in the chopped parsley and serve.

Variation
Use chicken thighs or breast portions to reduce preparation time.

Energy 448Kcal/1872kJ; Fat 19.7g; Saturated Fat 3.1g; Carbohydrate 23g; Fibre 5.7g

Chicken Breasts Cooked in Butter

This simple and delicious way of cooking chicken makes the most of its light, delicate flavour and texture. It is an ideal dish for midweek meals, when time is short.

Serves 4
4 small boneless chicken breast portions, skinned
seasoned flour, for coating
75g/3oz/6 tbsp butter
fresh parsley sprigs, to garnish

1 Separate the two fillets of each breast. They come apart very easily; one is large, the other small. Pound the large fillets lightly to flatten them. Dredge the chicken in the seasoned flour, shaking off any excess.

2 Heat the butter gently in a large heavy frying pan until it bubbles. Place all the chicken fillets in the pan, in a single layer if possible. Cook over medium to high heat for 3–4 minutes, until they are golden brown on the underside.

3 Turn the chicken over. Reduce the heat to low to medium, and continue cooking until the fillets are cooked through but still springy to the touch – about 9–12 minutes in all. If the chicken begins to brown too much, cover the pan for the final minutes of cooking. Serve immediately, garnished with a sprigs of fresh parsley.

Cook's Tips
• Make sure that the heat is not to high during the last part of the cooking process, otherwise the butter will burn and develop an acrid taste. Also, it is important that the chicken has a chance to cook through thoroughly, without the outer parts drying out and turning too brown.
• This chicken dish should be accompanied by delicately flavoured vegetables, such as mange tout or fresh peas, so that its subtle taste is not overpowered.

Energy 311Kcal/1302kJ; Fat 17.1g; Saturated Fat 10.2g; Carbohydrate 3g; Fibre 0.1g

Chicken with Ham & Cheese

This tasty combination comes from Emilia-Romagna, where the dish is also prepared with veal.

Serves 4

4 chicken breast fillets, skinned
seasoned flour, for coating

50g/2oz/¼ cup butter
3–4 fresh sage leaves
4 thin slices prosciutto or cooked ham, cut in half
40g/1½oz/½ cup freshly grated Parmesan cheese

1 Cut each chicken breast in half lengthways to make two flat pieces of about the same thickness. Coat the chicken in the seasoned flour and shake off the excess.

2 Preheat the grill (broiler). Heat the butter in a large heavy frying pan with the sage leaves. Add the chicken in a single layer and cook over low to medium heat, until golden brown on both sides, turning as necessary.

3 Remove the chicken from the heat and arrange on a flameproof serving dish or grill pan. Place one piece of ham on top of each chicken piece and top with the grated Parmesan. Grill (broil) for 3–4 minutes, or until the cheese has melted.

Chicken with Lemon & Garlic

This is a quick supper dish with a hint of paprika, which adds an unusual twist to the Mediterranean flavours of olive oil, lemon and garlic.

Serves 2–4

2 chicken breast fillets, skinned
30ml/2 tbsp olive oil

1 shallot, finely chopped
4 garlic cloves, finely chopped
5ml/1 tsp paprika
juice of 1 lemon
30ml/2 tbsp chopped fresh parsley
salt and ground black pepper
fresh flat leaf parsley, to garnish
lemon wedges, to serve

1 Remove the little fillet from the back of each breast portion. If the breast still looks fatter than a finger, bat it with a rolling pin to make it thinner. Slice all the chicken meat into strips.

2 Heat the oil in a large frying pan. Stir-fry the chicken strips with the shallot, garlic and paprika over high heat for about 3 minutes, until cooked through.

3 Add the lemon juice and parsley and season with salt and pepper to taste. Garnish with flat leaf parsley and serve hot with lemon wedges.

> **Variation**
> Try using strips of turkey breast or pork fillet (tenderloin). They need slightly longer cooking. The whites of spring onions (scallions) can replace the shallots, and the chopped green tops can be used instead of parsley.

Roast Chicken with Fennel

In Italy, this dish is prepared with wild fennel. Cultivated fennel bulb works just as well though.

Serves 4–5

1.6lb/3½lb roasting chicken
1 onion, quartered
120ml/4fl oz/½ cup olive oil

2 medium fennel bulbs
1 garlic clove, peeled
pinch of freshly grated nutmeg
3–4 thin slices pancetta or bacon
120ml/4fl oz/½ cup dry white wine
salt and ground black pepper

1 Preheat the oven to 180°C/350°F/Gas 4. Rinse the chicken in cold water and pat it dry, inside and out, with kitchen paper. Season the cavity with salt and pepper. Place the onion quarters in the cavity. Rub the chicken with about 45ml/3 tbsp of the olive oil, then place in a roasting pan.

2 Cut the green fronds from the tops of the fennel bulbs. Chop the fronds with the garlic, then place in a small bowl and mix with the nutmeg. Season with salt and pepper.

3 Sprinkle the fennel and garlic mixture over the chicken, pressing it onto the oiled skin. Cover the breast with the slices of pancetta or bacon, then sprinkle with 30ml/2 tbsp oil. Place in the oven and roast for 30 minutes.

4 Meanwhile, boil or steam the fennel bulbs until barely tender. Drain the fennel and cut into quarters or sixths lengthways.

5 Remove the roasting pan from the oven and baste the chicken with any oils in the pan. Arrange the fennel pieces around the chicken and sprinkle the fennel with the remaining oil. Pour about half the wine over the chicken and return the pan to the oven for 30 minutes.

6 Baste the chicken again and pour on the remaining wine. Cook for a further 15–20 minutes, until the chicken is cooked. Transfer the chicken to a serving platter, arrange the fennel around it and serve immediately.

Top Energy 335Kcal/1404kJ; Fat 16.8g; Saturated Fat 9.8g; Carbohydrate 0.3g; Fibre 0g
Above Energy 139kcal/580kJ; Fat 6.5g; Saturated Fat 1g; Carbohydrate 1.5g; Fibre 0.8g

Energy 339Kcal/1422kJ; Fat 12.6g; Saturated Fat 2.8g; Carbohydrate 2.8g; Fibre 2.6g

Pan-fried Marinated Poussin

Marinated for several hours before cooking, these little birds are full of tangy flavour and make a supper dish with a difference.

Serves 3–4

2 poussins, weighing about 450g/1lb each

5–6 fresh mint leaves, torn, plus extra whole leaves, to garnish
1 leek, sliced into thin rings
1 garlic clove, finely chopped
60ml/4 tbsp olive oil
30ml/2 tbsp fresh lemon juice
50ml/2fl oz/¼ cup dry white wine
salt and ground black pepper

1 Using sharp kitchen scissors, cut the poussins in half down the backbone, dividing the breast. Flatten the 4 halves with a mallet. Place them in a large bowl with the mint leaves, sliced leek, chopped garlic and a little pepper. Sprinkle with oil and half the lemon juice, cover and leave to marinate in a cool place for 6 hours.

2 Heat a large heavy frying pan. Place the poussins with their marinade in the pan. Cover and cook over medium heat for about 45 minutes, turning occasionally, until the juices run clear when the meat is pierced. Season with salt during the cooking. Transfer to a warm serving dish.

3 Tilt the pan and spoon off any fat on the surface. Pour in the wine and remaining lemon juice, then cook for a few minutes until the sauce reduces.

4 Strain the sauce through a sieve (strainer), pressing the vegetables to extract all the juices. Place the poussins on individual dishes and spoon over the sauce. Sprinkle with mint, and serve immediately.

> **Cook's Tip**
> You could use chicken fillets or boneless chicken thighs instead of the poussins. In this case, reduce the cooking time to 20–30 minutes, or until tender.

Parmesan Chicken Bake

Chicken is layered with tomato sauce and cheese to make a winning supper dish.

Serves 4

4 chicken breast fillets, skinned
60ml/4 tbsp flour, for coating
60ml/4 tbsp olive oil
225g/8oz mozzarella cheese, sliced
60ml/4 tbsp freshly grated Parmesan cheese
30ml/2 tbsp fresh breadcrumbs
salt and ground black pepper

For the tomato sauce

15ml/1 tbsp olive oil
1 onion, finely chopped
1 celery stick, finely chopped
1 red (bell) pepper, seeded, cored and diced
1 garlic clove, crushed
400g/14oz can chopped tomatoes with the juice
150ml/¼ pint/⅔ cup chicken stock
15ml/1 tbsp tomato purée (paste)
10ml/2 tsp sugar
15ml/1 tbsp chopped fresh basil
15ml/1 tbsp chopped fresh parsley

1 To make the tomato sauce, heat the olive oil in a frying pan and gently cook the onion, celery, pepper and crushed garlic in the oil until softened.

2 Add the tomatoes with their juice, the stock, purée, sugar and herbs. Season to taste and bring to the boil. Simmer for 30 minutes to make a thick sauce, stirring occasionally.

3 Place the chicken fillets between sheets of clear film (plastic wrap) and flatten to a thickness of 5mm/¼in with a rolling pin. Season the flour with salt and pepper. Toss the chicken in the flour to coat, shaking to remove the excess.

4 Preheat the oven to 180°C/350°F/Gas 4. Heat the remaining oil in a large frying pan and cook the chicken quickly in batches for 3–4 minutes until coloured.

5 Layer the chicken pieces in a large baking dish with the cheeses and thick tomato sauce, finishing with a layer of cheese and breadcrumbs on top. Bake for 20–30 minutes until golden. Garnish with basil and serve.

Grilled Poussins with Citrus Glaze

This recipe is also suitable for pigeon, snipe and partridge, with the tangy glaze combining perfectly with the flavour of the birds. Serve the dish with baked tomatoes and a leafy salad.

Serves 4

2 poussins (weighing about 675g/1½lb each)
50g/2oz/¼ cup butter, softened
30ml/2 tbsp olive oil
2 garlic cloves, crushed
2.5ml/½ tsp dried thyme
1.5ml/¼ tsp cayenne pepper, or to taste
grated rind and juice of 1 unwaxed lemon
grated rind and juice of 1 unwaxed lime
30ml/2 tbsp clear honey
salt and ground black pepper
fresh dill, to garnish

1 Using kitchen scissors, cut along both sides of the backbone of each bird; remove and discard the spine. Cut the birds in half along the breastbone, then press down firmly with a rolling pin to flatten.

2 Place the butter in a small bowl, then beat in 15ml/1 tbsp of the olive oil, the garlic, thyme, cayenne, half the lemon and lime rind and 15ml/1 tbsp each of the lemon and lime juice. Beat in salt and pepper.

3 Carefully loosen the skin of each poussin breast with your fingertips. Using a round-bladed knife, spread the butter mixture evenly between the skin and the breast meat.

4 Preheat the grill (broiler) and line a grill pan with foil. In a small bowl, mix together the remaining olive oil, lemon and lime juices and the honey. Place the bird halves, skin-side up, on the grill pan and brush with the citrus juice mixture.

5 Grill (broil) on one side for 10–12 minutes, basting once or twice with the juices. Turn over and grill for 7–10 minutes, basting once, or until the meat juices run clear when the thigh is pierced with a knife.

6 Garnish the poussins with the dill and serve immediately.

Duck with Chestnut Sauce

This autumnal dish makes use of the sweet chestnuts that are gathered every year in the Italian woods.

Serves 4–5

1 fresh rosemary sprig
1 garlic clove, thinly sliced
30ml/2 tbsp olive oil
4 duck breasts, boned and fat removed

For the sauce
450g/1lb chestnuts
5ml/1 tsp oil
350ml/12fl oz/1½ cups milk
1 small onion, finely chopped
1 carrot, finely chopped
1 small bay leaf
30ml/2 tbsp cream, warmed
salt and ground black pepper

1 Pull the leaves from the sprig of rosemary and combine them with the garlic and oil in a shallow bowl. Pat the duck breasts dry with kitchen paper. Brush the duck breasts with the rosemary marinade and leave to stand for at least 2 hours.

2 Preheat the oven to 180°C/350°F/Gas 4. Cut a cross in the flat side of each chestnut with a sharp knife.

3 Place the chestnuts in a roasting pan with the oil, then shake the pan until the nuts are coated with the oil. Bake for about 20 minutes, then peel off the skins.

4 Place the chestnuts in a heavy pan with the milk, onion, carrot and bay leaf. Cook slowly for about 10–15 minutes, until the chestnuts are very tender. Season with salt and pepper. Discard the bay leaf, then press the mixture through a sieve (strainer). Return the sauce to the pan.

5 Preheat the grill (broiler), then grill (broil) the duck breasts for about 6–8 minutes, until medium rare: the meat should be pink when sliced.

6 Meanwhile, gently reheat the chestnut sauce. Just before serving, stir the cream into the sauce. If it is too thick, add a little more cream. Slice the duck into rounds and arrange on warm plates. Serve with the chestnut sauce.

Mediterranean Turkey Kebabs

Lean turkey wrapped in strips of courgette and aubergine makes the basis for these delicious lemon- and basil-flavoured kebabs.

Serves 4

90ml/6 tbsp olive oil
45ml/3 tbsp fresh lemon juice
1 garlic clove, finely chopped
30ml/2 tbsp chopped fresh basil

2 courgettes (zucchini)
1 long thin aubergine (eggplant)
300g/11oz boneless turkey, cut into 2in cubes
12–16 pickled onions
1 red or yellow (bell) pepper, seeded, cored and cut into 5cm/2in squares
salt and ground black pepper
fresh basil sprigs, to garnish

1 Mix the oil with the lemon juice, garlic and basil in a small bowl. Season with salt and pepper.

2 Slice the courgettes and aubergine lengthways into strips 4cm/1½in thick. Cut them crossways about two-thirds of the way along their length. Discard the shorter length. Wrap half the turkey pieces with the courgette slices and the other half with the aubergine slices.

3 Thread the turkey, onions and pepper pieces alternately on to metal skewers. Lay the prepared kebabs on a platter and sprinkle with the flavoured oil. Leave to marinate for at least 30 minutes. Preheat the grill (broiler).

4 Grill (broil) the kebabs for about 10 minutes, turning the skewers occasionally, until the vegetables are tender and the turkey is cooked through. Transfer to a serving platter, garnish with fresh basil sprigs and serve immediately.

Cook's Tip
These kebabs are also suitable for cooking on a barbecue, but make sure they do not get too hot, otherwise the vegetables will burn and the turkey will be undercooked. Wedges of onion can be used instead of pickled onions, if you prefer.

Turkey Cutlets with Olives

The mild flavour of turkey is pepped up with garlic and chilli, then served in a tasty tomato and olive sauce. A useful dish for quick and easy entertaining.

Serves 4

90ml/6 tbsp olive oil
1 garlic clove, peeled and lightly crushed

1 dried chilli, lightly crushed
500g/1¼lb boneless turkey breast, cut into 5mm/¼in thick slices
120ml/4fl oz/½ cup dry white wine
4 tomatoes, peeled and seeded, cut into thin strips
about 24 black olives, pitted
6–8 fresh basil leaves, torn
salt and ground black pepper

1 Heat 60ml/4 tbsp of the olive oil in a large frying pan. Add the garlic and dried chilli and cook over low heat, until the garlic is golden: do not allow to burn.

2 Increase the heat to medium. Add the turkey slices to the pan and cook them for about 2 minutes, until lightly browned on both sides. Season with salt and pepper. Using a metal spatula, transfer the turkey to a warmed dish.

3 Remove the garlic and chilli from the pan and discard. Add the wine, tomato strips and olives to the pan. Cook over medium heat for 3–4 minutes, scraping up any meat residue from the bottom of the pan.

4 Return the turkey to the pan and sprinkle with the basil. Heat through for about 30 seconds before serving.

Cook's Tip
All olives start off green and then mature into darker fruit, black olives being the most mature. The varieties kept as table olives and for cooking are preserved by various methods, including dry-curing in salt and preserving in brine. Often they are flavoured with aromatics, such as garlic, herbs and chillies. Any type of black olive can be used in this recipe.

Turkey with Marsala Cream Sauce

Marsala makes a very rich and tasty sauce. The addition of lemon juice gives it a sharp edge, which helps to offset the richness.

Serves 6
6 turkey breast steaks
45ml/3 tbsp flour, for coating
30ml/2 tbsp olive oil

25g/1oz/2 tbsp butter
175ml/6fl oz/³/₄ cup dry Marsala
60ml/4 tbsp lemon juice
175ml/6fl oz/³/₄ cup double
   (heavy) cream
salt and ground black pepper
lemon wedges and chopped fresh
   parsley, to garnish

1 Put each turkey steak between two sheets of clear film (plastic wrap) and pound with a rolling pin to flatten and stretch. Cut each steak in half or into quarters, cutting away and discarding any sinew.

2 Spread out the flour in a shallow bowl. Season well and use to coat the meat.

3 Heat the oil and butter in a wide heavy pan or frying pan until sizzling. Add as many pieces of turkey as the pan will hold and sauté over medium heat for about 3 minutes on each side, until crispy and tender. Transfer to a warmed serving dish and keep hot. Repeat with the remaining turkey.

4 Lower the heat. Mix the Marsala with the lemon juice, add to the pan and increase the heat. Bring to the boil, stirring in the sediment, then add the cream. Simmer, stirring constantly, until the sauce is reduced and glossy. Taste for seasoning. Spoon the sauce over the turkey pieces, garnish with the lemon wedges and chopped parsley and serve immediately.

Variation
Veal or pork escalopes (scallops) or chicken breast fillets can be used instead of the turkey, and 50g/2oz/¹/₂ cup mascarpone cheese instead of the double cream.

Stuffed Turkey Breast with Lemon

This elegant dish of rolled turkey breast makes an impressive main course.

Serves 4–5
675g/1¹/₂lb boneless turkey
   breast, in one piece, skinned
1 carrot, cut into matchsticks
1 courgette (zucchini), cut into
   matchsticks
75g/3oz/¹/₃ cup ham, cut into
   matchsticks
2 thick slices white bread, crusts
   removed and softened in a
   little milk

10 green olives, pitted and finely
   chopped
1 large garlic clove, finely chopped
60ml/4 tbsp chopped parsley
60ml/4 tbsp finely chopped basil
1 egg
1.5ml/¹/₄ tsp grated lemon rind
30ml/2 tbsp freshly grated
   Parmesan cheese
60ml/4 tbsp olive oil
250ml/8fl oz/1 cup chicken stock,
   warmed
¹/₂ lemon, cut into thin wedges
25g/1oz/2 tbsp butter
salt and ground black pepper

1 Cut part of the way through the turkey breast and open the two halves out like a book. Pound to flatten evenly.

2 Preheat the oven to 200°C/400°F/Gas 6. Blanch the carrot and courgette for 2 minutes. Drain and combine with the ham.

3 Squeeze the bread and place in a mixing bowl, breaking it into small pieces. Stir in the olives, garlic and herbs, and the egg. Add the lemon rind and Parmesan. Season with salt and pepper. Spread the bread mixture over the meat, leaving a small border all around. Cover with the ham and vegetable mixture. Roll the turkey up and tie the roll in several places with string.

4 Heat the oil in a flameproof casserole, add the turkey and brown on all sides. Remove from the heat, add the stock and arrange the lemon wedges around the meat. Cover and cook in the oven for 15 minutes. Discard the lemon and baste the meat. Continue cooking, uncovered, for 25–30 minutes, basting occasionally, until the juices run clear when the meat is pierced.

5 Leave the roll to stand for 10 minutes before slicing. Strain the sauce, stir in the butter, taste for seasoning, then serve.

Energy 382Kcal/1595kJ; Fat 21.2g; Saturated Fat 7.5g; Carbohydrate 7.3g; Fibre 1.5g

Energy 385Kcal/1602kJ; Fat 23.7g; Saturated Fat 12.8g; Carbohydrate 9.9g; Fibre 0.2g

Roast Pheasant with Juniper

Sage and juniper are often used in Italian cooking to flavour game birds.

Serves 3–4

1.2–1.6kg/2½–3 lb pheasant
  with liver, chopped (optional)
45ml/3 tbsp olive oil
2 fresh sage sprigs
3 shallots, chopped
1 bay leaf

2 lemon quarters, plus 5ml/
  1 tsp juice
30ml/2 tbsp juniper berries,
  lightly crushed
4 thin slices pancetta or bacon
90ml/6 tbsp dry white wine
250ml/8fl oz/1 cup chicken stock
25g/1oz/2 tbsp butter, softened
30ml/2 tbsp flour
30ml/2 tbsp brandy
salt and ground black pepper

1 Wash the pheasant under cold water. Drain and pat dry with kitchen paper. Rub with 15ml/1 tbsp olive oil. Place the rest of the oil, with the sage, shallots and bay leaf in a shallow bowl. Add the lemon juice and juniper berries. Place the pheasant and lemon quarters in the bowl with the marinade, and spoon it over the bird. Stand for several hours in a cool place, turning the pheasant occasionally. Remove the lemon and reserve.

2 Preheat the oven to 180°C/350°F/Gas 4. Place the pheasant in a roasting pan, reserving the marinade. Season the cavity with salt and pepper; place the lemon quarters and bay leaf inside. Arrange some of the sage leaves on the pheasant breast and lay the pancetta or bacon over the top. Secure with string.

3 Spoon the remaining marinade on top of the pheasant and roast for 1½–2 hours, until tender. Baste frequently with the pan juices and with the white wine. Transfer the pheasant to a warmed serving platter, discarding the string and pancetta.

4 Tilt the pan and skim off the fat. Pour in the stock. Stir over medium heat, scraping up any sediment. Add the pheasant liver, if using. Bring to the boil; cook for 2–3 minutes. Strain into a pan.

5 Blend the butter to a paste with the flour. Stir into the liquid in the pan, a little at a time. Boil for 2–3 minutes, stirring until smooth. Remove from the heat, stir in the brandy and serve.

Pigeon Breasts with Pancetta

The robust, gamey flavour of wood pigeon is much appreciated in Italy.

Serves 4

4 whole pigeons
2 large onions
2 carrots, roughly chopped
1 celery stick, trimmed and
  roughly chopped

25g/1oz dried porcini mushrooms
150ml/¼ pint/⅔ cup hot water
25g/1oz/2 tbsp butter
30ml/2 tbsp olive oil
50g/2oz pancetta, diced
2 garlic cloves, crushed
150ml/¼ pint/⅔ cup red wine
salt and ground black pepper
flat leaf parsley, to garnish
cooked mushrooms, to serve

1 To prepare a pigeon, cut down the length of the bird, just to one side of the breastbone. Gradually cut away the meat from the breastbone until the breast comes away completely. Do the same on the other side. Repeat with the remaining pigeons.

2 Put the pigeon carcasses in a large pan. Halve one of the onions, leaving the skin on. Add to the pan with the carrots and celery and just cover with water. Bring to the boil, reduce the heat and simmer very gently, uncovered, for about 1½ hours to make a dark, rich stock. Leave to cool slightly, then strain through a large sieve (strainer) into a bowl.

3 Cover the dried mushrooms with the hot water and soak for 20 minutes. Peel and finely chop the remaining onion. Melt half the butter with the oil in a large frying pan. Add the onion and pancetta and fry very gently for 3 minutes. Add the pigeon breasts and fry for 2 minutes on each side to brown.

4 Add the mushrooms, with the soaking liquid, garlic, wine and 250ml/8fl oz/1 cup of the stock. Bring just to the boil, then reduce the heat and simmer gently for 5 minutes, until the pigeon breasts are tender, but still a little pink in the centre.

5 Lift out the pigeon breasts and keep them hot. Boil the sauce rapidly to reduce slightly. Gradually whisk in all the remaining butter and season with salt and pepper to taste. Serve the sauce with the pigeon, garnished with parsley and mushrooms.

Energy 546Kcal/2277kJ; Fat 33.2g; Saturated Fat 11.5g; Carbohydrate 9.1g; Fibre 0.5g

Energy 372Kcal/1549kJ; Fat 17.6g; Saturated Fat 4.3g; Carbohydrate 10.1g; Fibre 2.1g

Rabbit with Tomatoes

Rabbit is a popular ingredient in Italian cuisine and here it is used to create a hearty, flavourful dish.

Serves 4–5

675g/1½lb boned rabbit, cut into chunks
2 garlic cloves, thinly sliced
115g/4oz/½ cup thinly sliced pancetta or lean bacon
675g/1½lb tomatoes, peeled, seeded and roughly chopped
45ml/3 tbsp chopped fresh basil
60ml/4 tbsp olive oil
salt and ground black pepper

1 Preheat the oven to 200°C/400°F/Gas 6. Pat the rabbit pieces dry with kitchen paper. Place a thin slice of garlic on each piece, then wrap a slice of pancetta or bacon around it, making sure the garlic is held in place.

2 Place the tomatoes in a non-stick pan and cook them for a few minutes, until they give up some of their liquid and begin to dry out. Stir in the basil, then season with salt and pepper.

3 Place the tomatoes in a single layer in the bottom of a baking dish. Arrange the rabbit pieces on top of the tomatoes. Sprinkle with olive oil and place, uncovered, in the oven. Roast for 40–50 minutes.

4 Baste the rabbit occasionally with any fat in the dish. If the sauce seems to be too dry after the rabbit has cooked for about 25 minutes, the dish may be covered with foil for the remaining time.

Cook's Tip

Rabbit's meat is very pale and lean and the taste is somewhere between that of good-quality farmhouse chicken and veal. Wild rabbit has a stronger flavour, which combines well with robust flavours; farmed rabbit is very tender and much more delicate. If wished, chunks of chicken or turkey breast fillet could be used instead of rabbit in this recipe.

Energy 283Kcal/1178kJ; Fat 19.7g; Saturated Fat 5.4g; Carbohydrate 4g; Fibre 1.3g

Quail with Grapes

Tiny quail have a subtle, gamey flavour which is delicious combined with a fruity sauce. Use the tastiest grapes you can find.

Serves 4

6–8 fresh quail, gutted
60ml/4 tbsp olive oil
50g/2oz pancetta or bacon, cut into small dice
250ml/8fl oz/1 cup dry white wine
250ml/8fl oz/1 cup chicken stock, warmed
350g/12 oz green grapes
salt and ground black pepper

1 Wash the quail carefully inside and out with cold water, then pat dry thoroughly with kitchen paper. Season the cavities with a sprinkling of salt and pepper.

2 Heat the oil in a heavy frying pan or flameproof casserole large enough to hold all the quail in a single layer. Add the pancetta or bacon and cook over low heat for 5 minutes.

3 Increase the heat to medium to high and place the quail in the pan. Brown them evenly on all sides. Pour in the wine, and cook over medium heat, until it reduces by about half.

4 Turn the quail over. Cover the pan and cook for about 10–15 minutes. Add the chicken stock, turn the quail again, cover and cook for a further 15–20 minutes, or until the birds are tender.

5 Meanwhile, drop the grapes into a pan of boiling water, and blanch for about 3 minutes. Drain and reserve.

6 Using a slotted spoon, transfer the birds to a warmed serving platter and keep warm while the gravy is being finished. Strain the pan juices into a small cup. If bacon has been used, allow the fat to separate and rise to the top. Spoon off the fat and discard.

7 Pour the strained gravy into a small pan. Add the grapes and warm gently for 2–3 minutes. Spoon around the quail to serve.

Energy 509Kcal/2126kJ; Fat 29.4g; Saturated Fat 8.2g; Carbohydrate 13.9g; Fibre 0.6g

Fresh Orange Granita

A granita is like a water ice, but coarser and grainier in texture – hence its name. It makes a refreshing dessert after a rich main course, or a cooling treat on a hot summer's day.

Serves 4
4 large oranges
1 large lemon
150g/5oz/²⁄₃ cup sugar
dessert biscuits (cookies), to serve

1 Thinly pare the rind from the oranges and lemon, taking care to avoid the bitter white pith, and set aside. Cut the fruit in half and squeeze the orange and lemon juice into a jug. Set aside.

2 Heat the sugar and 475ml/16fl oz/2 cups water in a heavy pan, stirring over gentle heat, until the sugar dissolves. Bring to the boil, then boil without stirring for about 10 minutes, until a syrup forms.

3 Remove the syrup from the heat, and add most of the reserved pieces of orange and lemon rind but keep a few for decoration. Shake the pan. Cover and allow to cool.

4 Strain the sugar syrup into a shallow freezer container and add the fruit juice. Stir well to mix, then freeze, uncovered, for about 4 hours, until slushy.

5 Remove the half-frozen mixture from the freezer and mix with a fork, then return to the freezer and freeze again for another 4 hours, or until frozen hard.

6 To serve, turn into a bowl and allow to soften for about 10 minutes, then break up into small pieces with a fork again and pile the granita into long-stemmed glasses. Blanch the reserved strips of orange and lemon rind, and serve with dessert biscuits.

Cook's Tip
Almond-flavoured amaretti macaroons are perfect with this ice.

Energy 148Kcal/631kJ; Fat 0.1g; Saturated Fat 0g; Carbohydrate 37.5g; Fibre 2.3g

Coffee Granita

This refreshing granita is a regular sight in Italian cafés and gelaterias (ice cream stores), where you will often see the ice topped with a luxurious spoonful of whipped cream. Quite irresistible!

Serves 4–6
350ml/12fl oz/1¹⁄₂ cups hot
    strong espresso coffee
30ml/2 tbsp sugar
250ml/8fl oz/1 cup double
    (heavy) cream
10ml/2 tsp caster (superfine)
    sugar

1 Stir the sugar into the hot coffee until dissolved. Leave to cool, then chill. Pour into a shallow freezer container, cover and freeze for about 1 hour.

2 Mix in the frozen crust with a spoon. Return to the freezer for about 2¹⁄₂ hours, mixing and breaking up the ice every 30 minutes. Whip the cream with the caster sugar until stiff. Serve the granita in tall glasses, each topped with a spoonful of cream.

Lemon Granita

A classic Italian grainy ice, this tangy citrus granita is just the thing for cooling down – and it's easy to make.

Serves 4–5
115g/²⁄₃ cup sugar
grated rind of 1 lemon
juice of 2 large lemons

1 Heat 500ml/16fl oz/2 cups water with the sugar over low heat until the sugar dissolves. Bring to the boil. Remove from the heat, and allow to cool. Combine the lemon rind and juice with the sugar syrup. Pour into a shallow freezer container and freeze until solid.

2 Plunge the bottom of the frozen container in very hot water for a few seconds. Turn the frozen mixture out and chop it into large chunks. Place the mixture in a food processor fitted with metal blades and process until it forms small crystals. Spoon into serving glasses.

Top Energy 176Kcal/725kJ; Fat 16.8g; Saturated Fat 10.4g; Carbohydrate 5.9g; Fibre 0g
Above Energy 119Kcal/507kJ; Fat 0g; Carbohydrate 31.5g; Fibre 0g

Tiramisu

The name of this popular dessert translates as "pick me up", which is said to derive from the fact that it is so good that it literally makes you swoon when you eat it. There are many, many versions, and the recipe can be adapted to suit your own taste – you can vary the amount of mascarpone, eggs, sponge fingers, coffee and liqueur.

Serves 6–8

3 eggs, separated
450g/1lb/2 cups mascarpone
   cheese, at room temperature
1 sachet of vanilla sugar
175ml/6fl oz/¾ cup cold, very
   strong, black coffee
120ml/4fl oz/½ cup Kahlúa or
   other coffee-flavoured liqueur
18 savoiardi (Italian sponge
   fingers)
sifted unsweetened cocoa powder
   and grated dark (bittersweet)
   chocolate, to finish

1 Put the egg whites in a grease-free bowl and whisk with an electric mixer until stiff and in peaks.

2 Mix the mascarpone, vanilla sugar and egg yolks in a separate large bowl and whisk with the electric mixer until combined.

3 Fold in the egg whites, then put a few spoonfuls of the mixture in the bottom of a large serving bowl and spread it out evenly with the spoon.

4 Mix the coffee and liqueur together in a shallow dish. Dip a sponge finger in the mixture, turn it quickly so that it becomes saturated but does not disintegrate, and place it on top of the mascarpone mixture in the bowl. Add five more dipped sponge fingers, placing them side by side.

5 Spoon in about one-third of the remaining mascarpone mixture and spread it out. Make more layers in the same way, ending with mascarpone.

6 Level the surface, then sift cocoa powder all over the top. Cover and chill overnight. Before serving, sprinkle with more cocoa and grated chocolate.

Ricotta Pudding

The combination of ricotta cheese and candied fruits is popular in Sicily, where this delicious recipe originated. Easy to make, it offers a wonderfully rich and creamy way to finish a meal.

Serves 4–6

225g/8oz/1 cup ricotta cheese
50g/2oz/⅓ cup candied fruits
60ml/4 tbsp sweet Marsala
250ml/8fl oz/1 cup double
   (heavy) cream
50g/2oz/¼ cup caster (superfine)
   sugar, plus extra for dusting
finely grated rind of 1 orange
350g/12oz/2 cups fresh
   raspberries
strips of thinly pared orange rind,
   to decorate

1 Press the ricotta through a sieve (strainer) into a bowl to remove any lumps. Finely chop the candied fruits and stir into the sieved ricotta with half of the Marsala.

2 Put the cream, sugar and grated orange rind in another bowl and whip until the cream is standing in soft peaks.

3 Fold the whipped cream into the ricotta mixture. Spoon into individual glass serving bowls and top with the raspberries. Chill until ready to serve.

4 Just before serving, sprinkle with the remaining Marsala and dust the top of each bowl liberally with caster sugar. Decorate with the pared orange rind and serve immediately.

Cook's Tips
• This makes an ideal dessert for a dinner party as the creamy base can be made up to 24 hours ahead and chilled until ready to serve; add the raspberries just before serving and complete as described.
• Buy candied fruits in large pieces from a good delicatessen – tubs of chopped candied peel are too tough to eat raw, and should only be used in baking.

Energy 354Kcal/1472kJ; Fat 28.1g; Saturated Fat 17.4g; Carbohydrate 18.9g; Fibre 1.9g

Energy 215Kcal/894kJ; Fat 13.3g; Saturated Fat 5.9g; Carbohydrate 12.4g; Fibre 0.1g

Custard Ice Cream

Capture the divine experience of fine Italian ice cream with this classic recipe. The ice cream is soft in consistency and not over-sweet, making it truly melt-in-the-mouth.

Serves 6
750ml/1¼ pints/3½ cups milk
2.5ml/½ tsp grated lemon rind
6 egg yolks
150g/5oz/¾ cup granulated (white) sugar

1 To make the custard, heat the milk with the lemon rind in a small pan. Remove the pan from the heat as soon as small bubbles start to form on the surface. Do not let it boil.

2 Beat the egg yolks with a wire whisk or electric mixer. Gradually incorporate the sugar and continue beating for about 5 minutes, until the mixture is pale yellow. Strain the infused milk, then slowly beat it into the egg mixture drop by drop, making sure it is well incorporated.

3 When all the milk has been added, pour the mixture into the top of a double boiler or into a heatproof bowl placed over a pan of simmering water. Stir over medium heat, until the water in the pan is boiling and the custard thickens enough to lightly coat the back of a spoon. Remove from the heat and allow the custard to cool.

4 Freeze in an ice cream maker, following the manufacturer's instructions. The ice cream is ready when it is firm but still soft.

5 If you do not have an ice cream maker, pour the mixture into a metal or plastic freezer container and freeze for about 3 hours until set. Remove from the container and chop roughly into 7.5in/3in pieces. Place in the bowl of a food processor and process until smooth. Return to the freezer container, and freeze again until firm. Repeat the freezing-chopping process two or three times, until a smooth consistency is reached.

6 Allow the ice cream to soften slightly before scooping into individual glass dishes.

Chocolate Ice Cream

Nothing beats a good chocolate ice cream as a refreshing finish to a meal. Use good quality plain (semisweet) or cooking chocolate for the best flavour.

Serves 6
750ml/1¼ pints/3½ cups milk
10cm/4in piece vanilla pod (bean)
4 egg yolks
150g/5oz/¾ cup granulated (white) sugar
225g/8oz cooking chocolate

1 To make the custard, heat the milk with the vanilla pod in a small pan. Remove the pan from the heat as soon as small bubbles start to form on the surface. Do not let it boil.

2 Beat the egg yolks with a wire whisk or electric mixer. Gradually incorporate the sugar and continue beating for about 5 minutes, until the mixture is pale yellow. Strain the infused milk, then slowly beat it into the egg mixture drop by drop, making sure it is well incorporated.

3 Meanwhile, melt the chocolate in the top of a double boiler or in a heatproof bowl set over a pan of hot water.

4 Pour the custard into the top of the double boiler or bowl containing the melted chocolate. Stir over medium heat, until the custard thickens enough to lightly coat the back of a spoon. Remove from the heat and allow to cool.

5 Freeze in an ice cream maker, following the manufacturer's instructions. The ice cream is ready when it is firm but still soft.

6 If you do not have an ice cream maker, pour the mixture into a metal or plastic freezer container and freeze for about 3 hours until set. Remove from the container and chop roughly into 7.5in/3in pieces. Place in the bowl of a food processor and process until smooth. Return to the freezer container, and freeze again until firm. Repeat the freezing-chopping process two or three times, until a smooth consistency is reached.

7 Serve the ice cream in scoops in individual glass dishes.

Energy 238Kcal/1007kJ; Fat 7.16g; Saturated Fat 2.6g; Carbohydrate 39.5g; Fibre 0g

Energy 296Kcal/1243kJ; Fat 14.7g; Saturated Fat 7.7g; Carbohydrate 36.3g; Fibre 0.8g

Hazelnut Ice Cream

This popular flavour goes very well with scoops of chocolate and custard ice cream. Serve with wafers for an Italian iced treat.

Serves 4–6

75g/3oz/¹/₂ cup hazelnuts
475ml/16fl oz/2 cups milk
10cm/4in piece vanilla pod (bean)
4 egg yolks
75g/3oz granulated (white) sugar

1 Spread the hazelnuts out on a baking tray and place under a grill (broiler) for about 5 minutes, shaking the pan frequently to turn the nuts over. Cool the nuts slightly, then place on a clean dish towel and rub to remove the dark outer skin. Chop very finely, or grind in a food processor with 25g/1oz/2 tbsp sugar.

2 To make the custard, heat the milk with the vanilla pod in a small pan. Remove the pan from the heat as soon as small bubbles start to form on the surface. Do not let it boil.

3 Beat the egg yolks with a wire whisk or electric mixer. Gradually incorporate the sugar and continue beating for about 5 minutes until the mixture is pale yellow. Strain the infused milk, then slowly beat it into the egg mixture drop by drop.

4 Pour the mixture into the top of a double boiler or into a heatproof bowl placed over a pan of simmering water. Add the nuts. Stir over medium heat, until the water in the pan is boiling and the custard thickens enough to lightly coat the back of a spoon. Remove from the heat and allow to cool.

5 Freeze in an ice cream maker, following the manufacturer's instructions. The ice cream is ready when it is firm but still soft.

6 If you do not have an ice cream maker, pour the mixture into a metal or plastic freezer container and freeze for about 3 hours, until set. Remove from the container and chop roughly into 7.5in/3in pieces. Place in the bowl of a food processor and process until smooth. Return to the freezer container, and freeze again until firm. Repeat the freezing-chopping process two or three times, until a smooth consistency is reached.

Italian Fruit Salad & Ice Cream

If you visit Italy during the summer months, you will find little pavement fruit shops selling small dishes of macerated fresh soft fruits, which are delectable with a light ice.

juice of 6–8 oranges
juice of 1 lemon
15ml/1 tbsp liquid pear and
    apple concentrate
60ml/4 tbsp low-fat fromage frais
30ml/2 tbsp orange-flavoured
    liqueur (optional)
fresh mint sprigs, to decorate

Serves 6

900g/2lb/8 cups mixed ripe soft fruits, such as strawberries, raspberries, redcurrants, blueberries, peaches, apricots, plums and melons

1 Prepare the fruit according to type. Cut it into small pieces, but not so small that the mixture becomes a mush.

2 Put the fruit in a serving bowl and pour over enough orange juice to cover. Add the lemon juice, stir gently to mix, cover and chill in the refrigerator for 2 hours.

3 Set half the macerated fruit aside to serve as it is. Process the remainder in a blender or food process to form a purée. Pour the purée into a bowl.

4 Gently warm the pear and apple concentrate in a small pan and stir into the fruit purée. Whip the fromage frais or sour cream and fold into the fruit purée. Add the liqueur, if using.

5 Freeze in an ice cream maker, following the manufacturer's instructions. Alternatively, place in a shallow freezer container and freeze until ice crystals form around the edge. Beat the mixture in a chilled bowl until smooth. Repeat the process once or twice, then freeze until firm.

6 Soften slightly in the refrigerator before serving in scoops. Decorate with mint sprigs and serve with the macerated fruit.

Miniature Choc-ices

These little chocolate-coated ice creams make a fun alternative to the more familiar after-dinner chocolates, especially on hot summer evenings – although they need to be eaten quickly.

Makes about 25
750ml/1¼ pints/ 3 cups vanilla, chocolate or coffee ice cream
200g/7oz plain (semisweet) chocolate, broken into pieces
25g/1oz milk chocolate, broken into pieces
25g/1oz/¼ cup chopped hazelnuts, lightly toasted

1 Put a large baking sheet in the freezer for 10 minutes. Using a melon baller, scoop balls of ice cream and place these on the baking sheet. Freeze for at least 1 hour or until firm.

2 Line a second baking sheet with baking parchment and place in the freezer for 15 minutes. Melt the plain chocolate in a heatproof bowl set over a pan of gently simmering water. Melt the milk chocolate in a separate bowl over simmering water.

3 Using a metal spatula, transfer the ice cream scoops to the parchment-lined sheet. Spoon a little plain chocolate over one scoop so that most of it is coated.

4 Sprinkle immediately with chopped nuts, before the chocolate sets. Coat half the remaining scoops in the same way, sprinkling each one with nuts before the chocolate sets. Spoon the remaining plain chocolate over all the remaining scoops.

5 Using a teaspoon, carefully drizzle the melted milk chocolate over the choc-ices that are not topped with nuts. Freeze again until ready to serve.

> **Cook's Tip**
> *Serve the choc-ices in fluted paper sweet (candy) cases. If you can, buy gold cases as they will contrast very prettily with the dark chocolate coating.*

Gingered Semi-freddo

This Italian ice cream is rather like the original soft scoop ice cream. Made with a boiled sugar syrup rather than a traditional egg custard, and generously speckled with chopped stem ginger, this delicious ice cream will stay meltingly soft when frozen.

Serves 6
115g/4oz/generous ½ cup caster (superfine) sugar
4 egg yolks
300ml/½ pint/1¼ cups double (heavy) cream
115g/4oz/⅔ cup drained stem (preserved) ginger, finely chopped, plus extra, to decorate
chocolate cases, to serve

1 Mix the sugar and 120ml/4fl oz/½ cup cold water in a pan and heat gently, stirring occasionally, until the sugar has dissolved.

2 Increase the heat and boil for 4–5 minutes, without stirring, until the syrup registers 120°C/240°F on a sugar thermometer. Alternatively, test by dropping a little of the syrup into a cup of cold water; you should be able to mould the syrup into a ball.

3 Put the egg yolks in a large heatproof bowl and whisk until frothy. Place the bowl over a pan of simmering water and whisk in the sugar syrup. Continue whisking until the mixture is very thick. Remove from the heat and whisk until cool.

4 Whip the cream and lightly fold it into the egg yolk mixture with the chopped stem ginger. Pour into a freezer container and freeze for 1 hour.

5 Stir the semi-freddo to bring any ginger that has sunk up to the top, then return to freeze for 5–6 hours until firm. Scoop into chocolate cases. Decorate with slices of ginger and serve.

> **Cook's Tip**
> *To make chocolate cases, pour melted chocolate over squares of baking parchment, cool a little and then drape them over upturned glasses. Peel off the baking parchment when set.*

Energy 371Kcal/1540kJ; Fat 30.5g; Saturated Fat 17.7g; Carbohydrate 22.6g; Fibre 0.3g

Energy 117Kcal/488kJ; Fat 7.7g; Saturated Fat 4.3g; Carbohydrate 10.7g; Fibre 0.3g

Strawberry & Lavender Sorbet

A delightful hint of lavender transforms a familiar strawberry sorbet (sherbet) into a perfumed dinner-party dessert. It is important to buy plump, shiny fruit with a full flavour.

Serves 6
500g/1¼ lb/5 cups strawberries,
150g/5oz/¾ cup caster
   (superfine) sugar
6 fresh lavender flowers, plus
   extra to decorate
1 egg white

1 To hull the strawberries, prise out the leafy top with a sharp knife or a specially designed strawberry huller.

2 Place the sugar in a pan and pour in 300ml/½ pint/1¼ cups water. Bring to the boil, stirring until the sugar has dissolved.

3 Take the pan off the heat, add the lavender flowers and leave to infuse (steep) for 1 hour. If time permits, chill the syrup in the refrigerator before using.

4 Process the strawberries in a food processor or in batches in a blender, then press the purée through a large sieve (strainer) into a bowl.

5 Pour the purée into a freezer container, strain in the syrup, mix and freeze for 4 hours, or until mushy. Transfer to a food processor and process until smooth. Whisk the egg white until frothy, and stir into the mixture. Spoon the sorbet back into the container and freeze until firm.

6 Serve in scoops, piled into tall glasses, and decorated with sprigs of lavender flowers.

> **Cook's Tip**
> The size of the lavender flowers can vary; if they are very small, you may need to use eight. To double check, taste a little of the cooled lavender syrup. If you think the flavour is too mild, add two or three more flowers, reheat and cool again before using.

Lemon Sorbet

This is probably the most classic sorbet (sherbet) of all. Refreshingly tangy and yet deliciously smooth, it quite literally melts in the mouth.

Serves 6
200g/7oz/1 cup caster (superfine)
   sugar, plus extra
   for coating rind to decorate
4 lemons, well scrubbed
1 egg white

1 Put the sugar in a pan and pour in 300ml/½ pint/1¼ cups water. Bring to the boil, stirring occasionally until the sugar has just dissolved.

2 Using a swivel vegetable peeler, pare the rind thinly from two of the lemons so that it falls straight into the pan. Simmer for 2 minutes without stirring, then take the pan off the heat. Leave to cool, then chill in the refrigerator.

3 Squeeze the juice from all the lemons and add it to the syrup. Strain the syrup into a shallow freezer container, reserving the rind. Freeze the mixture for 4 hours, until mushy.

4 Spoon the sorbet into the bowl of a food processor and process until it is smooth. Lightly whisk the egg white with a fork until it is just frothy. Return the sorbet to the container, beat in the egg white and return the mixture to the freezer for 4 hours, or until it is firm.

5 Cut the reserved lemon rind into fine shreds and cook them in a small pan of boiling water for 5 minutes, or until tender. Drain, then place on a plate and sprinkle generously with caster sugar. Scoop the sorbet into bowls or glasses and decorate with the sugared lemon rind.

> **Cook's Tip**
> Try to buy unwaxed lemons for recipes such as this one where the lemon rind is used. The wax coating can adversely affect the flavour of the rind, which in turn alters the taste of the dish.

Energy 123Kcal/523kJ; Fat 0.1g; Saturated Fat 0g; Carbohydrate 31.1g; Fibre 0.9g

Energy 134Kcal/571kJ; Fat 0g; Saturated Fat 0g; Carbohydrate 35g; Fibre 0g

Iced Oranges

A colourful dessert that often features on menus in Italian eateries, this sorbet (sherbet) is not only totally refreshing, but also virtually fat-free.

Serves 8
150g/5oz/²⁄₃ cup caster
 (superfine) sugar
juice of I lemon
14 oranges, extra orange or
 orange juice if necessary
8 fresh bay leaves, to decorate

I Put the sugar in a heavy pan. Add half the lemon juice, then add 120ml/4fl oz/½ cup water. Cook over low heat, stirring until the sugar has dissolved. Bring to the boil and boil for 2–3 minutes, until the syrup is clear. Remove the pan from the heat and set aside.

2 Slice the tops off eight of the oranges to make lids. Scoop out the flesh of the oranges and reserve. Freeze the empty orange shells and lids until required.

3 Finely grate the rind of the remaining oranges and stir into the syrup. Squeeze the juice from the oranges and from the reserved flesh. There should be about 750ml/1¼ pints/3 cups of juice. If necessary, to make up to the correct quantity, squeeze another orange or add bought unsweetened orange juice.

4 Stir the orange juice and remaining lemon juice with 90ml/ 6 tbsp water into the syrup. Taste, adding more lemon juice or sugar as desired. Pour the mixture into a shallow freezer container and freeze for 3 hours.

5 Turn the orange sorbet mixture into a chilled bowl and whisk thoroughly to break up the ice crystals. Return to the container and freeze for a further 4 hours, until firm, but not solid.

6 Pack the frozen mixture into the hollowed-out orange shells, and set the lids on top. Freeze the sorbet-filled shells until ready to serve. Just before serving, push a skewer into the tops of the lids and push in a bay leaf, to decorate. Leave to stand for 15 minutes to allow the sorbet to soften slightly before serving.

Watermelon Sorbet

A slice of this refreshing Italian fruit sorbet (sherbet) is the perfect way to cool down on a hot sunny day. It also makes a mouthwatering summer appetizer with a difference.

Serves 6
½ small watermelon, weighing
 about 1kg/2¼lb
75g/3oz/½ cup caster (superfine)
 sugar
60ml/4 tbsp cranberry juice
 or water
30ml/2 tbsp lemon juice
fresh mint sprigs, to decorate

I Cut the watermelon into six equal-sized wedges. Scoop out the pink flesh from each wedge, discarding the seeds but reserving the shell.

2 Line a freezerproof bowl, about the same size as the melon, with clear film (plastic wrap). Arrange the melon skins in the bowl to re-form the shell, fitting them together snugly so that there are no gaps. Put in the freezer.

3 Put the sugar and cranberry juice or water in a pan and stir over low heat until the sugar has dissolved. Bring to the boil, then reduce the heat and simmer for 5 minutes. Remove the pan from the heat and set aside to cool.

4 Put the melon flesh and lemon juice in a blender or food processor and process to a smooth purée. Pour into a bowl, stir in the sugar syrup, then pour into a freezer container. Freeze the mixture for 3–3½ hours, or until slushy.

5 Turn the sorbet into a chilled freezerproof bowl and whisk well to break up the ice crystals. Return to the freezer for a further 30 minutes. Whisk again, then turn into the melon shell and freeze until solid.

6 Remove the sorbet from the freezer and leave to stand at room temperature for 15 minutes. Take the melon out of the bowl and cut into wedges with a warmed sharp knife. Serve decorated with fresh mint sprigs.

Energy 210Kcal/896kJ; Fat 0.4g; Saturated Fat 0g; Carbohydrate 50.8g; Fibre 6.3g

Energy 101Kcal/432kJ; Fat 0.5g; Saturated Fat 0.2g; Carbohydrate 24.9g; Fibre 0.2g

Peach Yogurt Ice

Juicy, ripe peaches are one of the delights of Italy. Here they are teamed up with yogurt to make a delicious yet healthy iced dessert.

Serves 6

500g/1¼lb ripe peaches
300ml/½ pint/1¼ cups low-fat
    peach or apricot yogurt
150ml/¼ pint/²⁄₃ cup Greek (US
    strained plain) yogurt
150ml/¼ pint/²⁄₃ cup low-fat
    natural yogurt
25–50g/1–2oz/2–4 tbsp caster
    (superfine) sugar
fresh mint sprigs, to decorate

1 Cut the peaches into quarters, remove the stones (pits) and peel off the skins. Chop the peach flesh.

2 Place the peach flesh in a blender or food processor and blend until smooth. Transfer to a bowl. Add all three yogurts and mix thoroughly.

3 Add enough of the sugar to sweeten to taste and stir to mix. Pour into a shallow freezer container. Cover and freeze for 1½–2 hours, until it is mushy in consistency. Turn the mixture into a chilled bowl and beat until smooth.

4 Return the mixture to the freezer container, cover and freeze until firm. Transfer the ice to the refrigerator about 30 minutes before serving, to allow it to soften a little. Serve in scoops, decorated with fresh mint sprigs.

> **Cook's Tip**
> Serve with crunchy amaretti for a lovely contrast in textures.

> **Variation**
> For an exotic flavour, use 450g/1lb chopped mango flesh instead of the peaches and substitute a mango yogurt.

Coffee & Chocolate Bombe

Known as zuccotto in Italy, this ice cream dessert is guaranteed to impress.

Serves 6–8

15–18 savoiardi (sponge fingers)
about 175ml/6fl oz/¾ cup sweet
    Marsala
75g/3oz amaretti
about 475ml/16fl oz/2 cups
    coffee ice cream, softened
about 475ml/16fl oz/2 cups
    vanilla ice cream, softened
50g/2oz dark (bittersweet) or
    plain (semisweet) chocolate,
    grated
chocolate curls and sifted cocoa
    powder or icing (confectioners')
    sugar, to decorate

1 Line a 1 litre/1¾ pint/4 cup deep bowl with a large piece of damp muslin, letting it hang over the top edge. Trim the savoiardi to fit the basin, if necessary. Pour the Marsala into a shallow dish. Dip a sponge finger in the Marsala, turning it quickly so that it becomes saturated but does not disintegrate. Stand it against the side of the bowl, sugared-side out.

2 Repeat with the remaining sponge fingers to line the bowl fully. Fill in the base and any gaps around the side with any trimmings and fingers cut to fit. Chill for about 30 minutes.

3 Put the amaretti in a large bowl and crush them with a rolling pin. Add the coffee ice cream and any remaining Marsala and beat until mixed. Spoon into the lined bowl.

4 Press the ice cream against the sponge to form an even layer with a hollow. Freeze for 2 hours. Beat the vanilla ice cream and grated chocolate together and spoon into the centre of the mould. Smooth the top, then cover with the overhanging muslin. Freeze overnight.

5 To serve, run a palette knife between the muslin and the bowl, then unfold the top of the muslin. Invert a chilled serving plate on top of the bombe, then invert the two so that the bombe is upside down on the plate. Carefully peel off the muslin. Decorate the bombe with the chocolate curls, then sift cocoa powder or icing sugar over. Serve at once.

Energy 147Kcal/623kJ; Fat 3.3g; Saturated Fat 1.7g; Carbohydrate 26.3g; Fibre 2g

Energy 433Kcal/1810kJ; Fat 22.6g; Saturated Fat 12.9g; Carbohydrate 46.1g; Fibre 0.5g

Fresh Fig, Apple & Date Dessert

Sweet Mediterranean figs
and dates combine
especially well with crisp
dessert apples to create this
appetizing dessert. A hint of
almond serves to unite the
flavours.

Serves 4
6 large apples
juice of ¹/₂ lemon
175g/6oz fresh dates
25g/1oz white marzipan
5ml/1 tsp orange flower water
60ml/4 tbsp natural yogurt
4 ripe green or purple fresh figs
4 whole almonds, toasted

1 Core the apples. Slice them thinly, then cut into thin
matchsticks. Put into a bowl, sprinkle with lemon juice to keep
them white and set aside.

2 Remove and discard the stones from the dates and cut the
flesh into thin strips, then combine with the apple slices. Toss
to mix.

3 In a small bowl, soften the marzipan with the orange flower
water and combine this with the yogurt. Mix well.

4 Pile the mixed apples and dates into the centre of four
plates. Remove and discard the stem from each of the figs and
cut the fruit into quarters without cutting right through the
base. Squeeze the base with the thumb and forefinger of each
hand to open up the fruit.

5 Place a fig in the centre of each apple and date salad, spoon
in some yogurt filling and decorate each portion with a toasted
almond. Serve.

Cook's Tip
When choosing fresh dates, select those that are fat and shiny,
with skins that are golden and smooth. You may wish to remove
the skin by squeezing the stem end, but the figs, however, have
thin skins that are edible.

Coffee Mascarpone Creams

These little desserts are rich
so you need a really robust
shot of coffee to achieve the
desired result. They are
good served with a glass of
liqueur or a cup of espresso.

Serves 4
115g/4oz/¹/₂ cup mascarpone
  cheese
45ml/3 tbsp espresso coffee
45ml/3 tbsp icing (confectioner's)
  sugar

1 Put the mascarpone in a bowl and add the coffee. Mix well
until smooth and creamy. Sift in the icing sugar and stir until
thoroughly combined.

2 Spoon the mixture into little china pots or ramekin dishes
and chill for 30 minutes before serving.

Figs with Ricotta Cream

Fresh, ripe figs are full of
natural sweetness and need
little adornment. This simple
Italian recipe makes the
most of their intense flavour
and creates a mouth-
watering low-fat dessert.

Serves 4
4 ripe, fresh figs
115g/4oz/¹/₂ cup ricotta or
  cottage cheese
45ml/3 tbsp crème fraîche
15ml/1 tbsp clear honey
2.5ml/¹/₂ tsp vanilla extract
freshly grated nutmeg, to decorate

1 Trim the stalks from the figs. Make four cuts through each fig
from the stalk end, cutting them almost through but leaving
them joined at the base.

2 Place the figs on serving plates and open them out.

3 In a bowl, mix together the ricotta or cottage cheese, crème
fraîche, honey and vanilla extract.

4 Spoon a little ricotta cream on to each plate and sprinkle
with grated nutmeg to decorate. Serve immediately.

Energy 178Kcal/759kJ; Fat 2.3g; Saturated Fat 0.2g; Carbohydrate 50.8g; Fibre 4.4g

Top Energy 146Kcal/604kJ; Fat 14g; Saturated Fat 9g; Carbohydrate 5g; Fibre 0g
Above Energy 128Kcal/536kJ; Fat 6g; Saturated Fat 3.7g; Carbohydrate 14.6g; Fibre 1.5g

Peaches with Amaretti Stuffing

Peaches are plentiful all over Italy. They are sometimes prepared hot, as here.

Serves 4
4 ripe fresh peaches
juice of ¹/₂ lemon
65g/2¹/₂oz/²/₃ cup crushed
  amaretti

30ml/2 tbsp Marsala, brandy or
  peach brandy
25g/1oz/2 tbsp butter, at room
  temperature
2.5ml/¹/₂ tsp vanilla extract
30ml/2 tbsp granulated sugar
1 egg yolk

1 Preheat the oven to 180°C/350°F/Gas 4. Wash the peaches. Cut them in half and remove the stones. Enlarge the hollow left by the stones by scooping out some of the peach with a small spoon. Sprinkle the peach halves with the lemon juice.

2 Soften the amaretti crumbs in the Marsala or brandy for a few minutes. Beat the butter until soft, and then stir in the amaretti mixture and all remaining ingredients.

3 Arrange the peach halves in a baking dish in a single layer, hollow-side upwards. Divide the amaretti mixture into 8 parts, and fill the hollows, mounding the stuffing up in the centre.

4 Bake for 35–40 minutes, until browned and bubbling. These peaches are delicious served hot or cold.

Cook's Tip
Amaretti are made from ground almonds, egg whites and sugar. They have a distinctive flavour, which comes from the addition of bitter almonds. They originated in Venice during the Renaissance and their English name of macaroons come from the Venetian macerone, meaning "fine paste". They come in many different forms, from the famous crunchy sugar-encrusted biscuits wrapped in pairs in twists of paper to soft-centred macaroons wrapped in foil. They are delicious dipped into hot coffee, and make a good filling for peaches when crumbled.

Italian Trifle

Known in Italy as "English Soup", this popular dessert is a kind of trifle that has little to do with England!

Serves 6–8
475ml/16fl oz/2 cups milk
grated rind of ¹/₂ lemon
4 egg yolks
75g/3oz/¹/₃ cup caster (superfine)
  sugar
50g/2oz/¹/₂ cup flour, sifted

15ml/1 tbsp rum or brandy
25g/1oz/2 tbsp butter
200g/7oz savoiardi (sponge
  fingers) or 300g/11oz sponge
  cake, sliced into 1cm/¹/₂ in
  slices
75ml/3fl oz/¹/₃ cup Kirsch or
  cherry brandy
75ml/3fl oz/¹/₃ cup Strega liqueur
45ml/3 tbsp apricot jam
fresh whipped cream, to garnish
chopped toasted nuts, to garnish

1 Heat the milk with the lemon rind in a small pan. Remove from the heat as soon as small bubbles form on the surface.

2 Beat the egg yolks in a large bowl with a wire whisk. Gradually incorporate the sugar, then continue beating until pale yellow. Beat in the flour. Stir in the milk very gradually, pouring it in through a sieve (strainer) to remove the lemon. When all the milk has been added, pour the mixture into a large, heavy pan.

3 Bring to the boil, stirring constantly with a whisk. Simmer for 5–6 minutes, stirring constantly. Remove from the heat and stir in the rum or brandy. Beat in the butter. Allow to cool to room temperature, stirring to prevent a skin from forming.

4 Brush the sponge fingers with the Kirsch or cherry brandy on one side, and the Strega liqueur on the other. Spread a thin layer of the custard over the bottom of a serving dish. Line the dish with a layer of sponge fingers. Cover with some of the custard. Add another layer of liqueur-brushed sponge fingers.

5 Heat the jam in a small pan with 30ml/2 tbsp water. When it is hot, brush evenly over the sponge. Continue with layers of custard and liqueur-brushed sponge, finishing with custard. Cover and chill for at least 2–3 hours. To serve, decorate the top of the trifle with whipped cream and chopped nuts.

Energy 309Kcal/1302kJ; Fat 8.9g; Saturated Fat 3.7g; Carbohydrate 46.5g; Fibre 0.6g

Energy 205Kcal/860kJ; Fat 9.3g; Saturated Fat 5.1g; Carbohydrate 25.4g; Fibre 1.7g

Fresh Fruit Salad

When peaches and strawberries are in season, combine them with apples and oranges to create this fresh-tasting salad.

Serves 4

2 eating apples
2 oranges
16–20 strawberries
2 peaches
30ml/2 tbsp lemon juice
15–30ml/1–2 tbsp orange flower water
icing (confectioners') sugar, to taste (optional)
a few fresh mint leaves, to decorate

1 Peel and core the apples and slice finely. Peel the oranges with a sharp knife, removing all the pith, then segment them, catching any juice in a bowl.

2 Hull half the strawberries and halve or quarter them, depending on size. Keep the remaining strawberries with their hulls intact for a pretty effect.

3 Blanch the peaches for about 1 minute in boiling water, then, using a knife, peel away the skin and cut the flesh into thick slices. Discard the stones. Place all the fruit in a large serving bowl. Toss lightly to mix.

4 Mix together the lemon juice, orange flower water and any leftover orange juice. Taste and add a little icing sugar to sweeten, if liked.

5 Pour the fruit juice mixture over the salad and serve, decorated with fresh mint leaves.

Variation
There are no rules with this fruit salad, and you can use almost any fruit that you like. Oranges, however, should form the base and are available all year round. Apples give a welcome contrast in texture.

Fresh & Dried Fruit Salad

This is a wonderful combination of fresh and dried fruit, and makes an excellent dessert throughout the year. Use frozen raspberries or blackberries in winter.

Serves 4

115g/4oz/½ cup dried apricots
115g/4oz/½ cup dried peaches
1 fresh pear
1 fresh apple
1 fresh orange
115g/4oz/⅔ cup mixed raspberries and blackberries
1 cinnamon stick
50g/2oz/¼ cup caster (superfine) sugar
15ml/1 tbsp clear honey
30ml/2 tbsp lemon juice

1 Soak the apricots and peaches in water for 1–2 hours, until plump, then drain. Cut into halves, quarters or thin slices.

2 Peel and core the pear and apple and cut them into cubes. Peel the orange with a sharp knife, removing all the pith, and cut into wedges.

3 Place all the fruit in a large pan with the raspberries and the blackberries. Add 600ml/1 pint/2 cups water, the cinnamon, sugar and honey and bring to the boil.

4 Cover and simmer very gently for 10–12 minutes. Remove the pan from the heat. Stir in the lemon juice. Allow to cool, then pour into a bowl and chill for 1–2 hours before serving.

Cook's Tip
Use ready-to-eat dried fruit and cut out the soaking time.

Variation
To vary the flavour of the fruit salad, try using cloves or preserved stem ginger instead of the cinnamon.

Energy 175Kcal/748kJ; Fat 0.5g; Saturated Fat 0g; Carbohydrate 42.3g; Fibre 5.1g

Energy 66Kcal/279kJ; Fat 0.2g; Saturated Fat 0g; Carbohydrate 15.2g; Fibre 2.9g

Banana & Mascarpone Creams

If you like cold banana custard, you will love this grown-up version. No one will guess that ready-made custard sauce is the key, although you can make your own if you have time.

Serves 4–6
250g/9oz generous 1 cup mascarpone cheese
300ml/½ pint/1¼ cups fresh ready-made custard sauce
150ml/¼ pint/⅔ cup Greek (US strained plain) yogurt
4 bananas
juice of 1 lime
50g/2oz/½ cup pecan nuts, coarsely chopped
120ml/4fl oz/½ cup maple syrup

1 Combine the mascarpone, custard sauce and yogurt in a large bowl and beat together until smooth. Make this mixture several hours ahead, if you like. Cover and chill, then stir well before using.

2 Peel the bananas, slice diagonally and place in a separate bowl. Pour the lime juice over the top and toss together until the bananas are coated in the juice.

3 Divide half of the custard mixture among four to six dessert glasses and top each portion with some of the banana slices, until you have used half of them.

4 Spoon the remaining custard mixture into the glasses and top with the remaining bananas. Scatter the nuts over the top. Drizzle maple syrup over each portion and chill for 30 minutes before serving.

> **Cook's Tip**
> Fresh custard sauce is now widely available from the chilled counters at larger supermarkets and makes an excellent base for this recipe. If you want to reduce the fat content slightly, use low-fat fromage frais or crème fraîche instead of mascarpone and a thick, low-fat yogurt instead of the Greek yogurt.

Bananas with Lime & Cardamom Sauce

Serve these bananas solo, with vanilla or custard ice cream, or spoon them over folded crêpes, or home-made biscotti.

Serves 4
6 small bananas
50g/2oz/¼ cup butter
seeds from 4 cardamom pods, crushed
50g/2oz/½ cup flaked (sliced) almonds
thinly pared rind and juice of 2 limes
50g/2oz/⅓ cup light muscovado (brown) sugar
30ml/2 tbsp dark rum (optional)
vanilla ice cream, to serve (optional)

1 Peel the bananas and cut them in half lengthways. Heat half the butter over low heat in a large non-stick frying pan. Add half the bananas and cook until the undersides are golden. Turn the bananas carefully, using a metal spatula. Cook until they are golden.

2 Transfer the cooked bananas to a heatproof serving dish and keep warm. Cook the remaining bananas in the same way.

3 Melt the remaining butter, then add the cardamom and almonds. Cook, stirring until golden.

4 Stir in the lime rind and juice, then the sugar. Cook, stirring, until the mixture is smooth, bubbling and slightly reduced. Stir in the rum, if using. Pour the sauce over the bananas and serve immediately, with vanilla ice cream, if you like.

> **Variations**
> • If you prefer not to use alcohol in your cooking, replace the rum with orange juice or even pineapple juice.
> • Try other soft fruits with this sauce, such as peaches, mangoes, pears or figs.

Energy 333Kcal/1395kJ; Fat 15.5g; Saturated Fat 5.6g; Carbohydrate 41.7g; Fibre 1.2g

Energy 363Kcal/1520kJ; Fat 17.6g; Saturated Fat 7.2g; Carbohydrate 45.4g; Fibre 2.3g

Baked Fruit Compote

Mixed dried fruits, combined with fruit juice and spices, then oven-baked, make a nutritious and warming Italian-style winter dessert.

Serves 6

115g/4oz/²/₃ cup ready-to-eat dried figs
115g/4oz/½ cup ready-to-eat dried apricots
50g/2oz/½ cup ready-to-eat dried apple rings
50g/2oz/¼ cup ready-to-eat prunes
50g/2oz/½ cup ready-to-eat dried pears
50g/2oz/½ cup ready-to-eat dried peaches
300ml/½ pint/1¼ cups unsweetened apple juice
300ml/½ pint/1¼ cups unsweetened orange juice
6 cloves
1 cinnamon stick
toasted flaked (sliced) almonds, to decorate (optional)

1 Preheat the oven to 180°C/350°F/Gas 4. Place the figs, apricots, apple rings, prunes, pears and peaches in a shallow ovenproof dish and stir to mix.

2 Mix together the apple and orange juices and pour over the fruit. Add the cloves and cinnamon stick and stir gently to mix.

3 Bake in the oven for about 30 minutes, until the fruit mixture is hot, stirring once or twice during cooking. Remove from the oven, set aside and leave to soak for 20 minutes, then remove and discard the cloves and cinnamon stick.

4 Spoon into serving bowls and serve warm or cold, decorated with toasted flaked almonds, if you like.

> **Cook's Tip**
> Whipped double (heavy) cream flavoured with orange liqueur and sweetened with a little icing (confectioners') sugar would make a luxurious accompaniment to this compote. Serve with crisp Italian biscuits (cookies) for a bit of crunch.

Grilled Nectarines with Amaretto

The luscious almond-flavoured liqueur from Italy adds a touch of luxury to these delicious low-fat grilled nectarines.

Serves 4

6 ripe nectarines
30ml/2 tbsp clear honey
60ml/4 tbsp Amaretto
half-fat crème fraîche, to serve (optional)

1 Cut the nectarines in half by running a small sharp knife down the side of each fruit from top to bottom, pushing the knife right through to the stone. Gently ease the nectarine apart and remove and discard the stone. Try not to handle the fruit too firmly as nectarines bruise easily.

2 Place the nectarines cut-side up in an ovenproof dish and drizzle 2.5ml/½ tsp honey and 5ml/1 tsp Amaretto over each nectarine half. Preheat the grill (broiler) until very hot and then grill the fruit until slightly charred. Serve warm with a little half-fat crème fraîche, if you like.

> **Cook's Tip**
> Sweet tasting Amaretto is actually made from apricot kernels, and is flavoured with almonds and aromatic extracts.

Fresh Figs with Honey & Wine

Any variety of figs can be used in this recipe. Choose ones that are plump and firm, and use them quickly as they do not store well.

Serves 6

450ml/¾ pint/1⅞ cups dry white wine
75g/3oz/⅓ cup clear honey
50g/2oz/¼ cup caster (superfine) sugar
1 small orange
8 whole cloves
450g/1lb fresh figs
1 cinnamon stick
mint sprigs, or bay leaves, to decorate

For the cream
300ml/½ pint/1¼ cups double cream
1 vanilla pod
5ml/1 tsp caster (superfine) sugar

1 Put the wine, honey and sugar in a heavy-based saucepan and heat gently until the sugar dissolves.

2 Stud the orange with the cloves and add to the syrup with the figs and cinnamon. Cover and simmer very gently for 5–10 minutes until the figs are softened. Transfer to a serving dish and leave to cool.

3 Put 150ml/¼ pint/⅔ cup of the cream in a small saucepan with the vanilla pod. Bring almost to the boil, then leave to cool and infuse for 30 minutes. Remove the vanilla pod and mix with the remaining cream and sugar in a bowl. Whip lightly and transfer to a serving dish. Decorate the figs, then serve immediately with the cream.

Energy 152Kcal/646kJ; Fat 0.7g; Saturated Fat 0g; Carbohydrate 36.1g; Fibre 4.4g

Top Energy 151Kcal/642kJ; Fat 0.2g; Saturated Fat 0g; Carbohydrate 30.9g; Fibre 2.7g
Above Energy 474Kcal/1976kJ; Fat 28g; Saturated Fat 17g; Carbohydrate 45g; Fibre 3.5g

Mixed Melon Salad

Combine several melon varieties with wild berries for a delicious fruit salad.

Serves 4
1 cantaloupe or charentais melon

1 Galia melon
900g/2lb watermelon
175g/6oz/1½ cups wild
   strawberries

1 Cut the cantaloupe or charentais melon, Galia melon and watermelon in half. Using a spoon, scoop out the seeds from all the melon. With a melon scoop, take out as many balls as you can from the three melons. Mix together in a large bowl, cover and chill for 2–3 hours.

2 Just before serving, add the wild strawberries and mix lightly.

Baked Apples with Marsala

The Marsala cooks down with the juice from the apples and the butter to make a rich, sticky sauce. Serve these tasty apples with a spoonful of thick cream.

Serves 6
4 medium cooking apples
50g/2oz/⅓ cup ready-to-eat
   dried figs
150ml/¼ pint/⅔ cup Marsala
50g/2oz/¼ cup butter, softened

1 Preheat the oven to 180°C/350°F/Gas 4. Using an apple corer, remove the cores from the apples and discard. Place the apples in a small, shallow baking tin (pan) and stuff the figs into the holes in the centre of each apple.

2 Top each apple with a quarter of the butter and pour over the Marsala. Cover the pan with foil and bake for 30 minutes.

3 Remove the foil from the apples and bake for a further 10 minutes, or until the apples are tender and the juices have reduced slightly. Serve immediately with any remaining pan juices drizzled over the top.

Stuffed Peaches with Mascarpone Cream

A thick velvety cream cheese, mascarpone is often used in Italian desserts. Here it harmonizes perfectly with baked peaches.

Serves 4
4 large peaches, halved and
   stoned
40g/1½oz amaretti, crumbled
30ml/2 tbsp ground almonds
45ml/3 tbsp sugar
15ml/1 tbsp unsweetened cocoa
   powder

150ml/¼ pint/⅔ cup sweet wine
25g/1oz/2 tbsp butter

For the mascarpone cream
30ml/2 tbsp caster (superfine)
   sugar
3 egg yolks
15ml/1 tbsp sweet wine
225g/8oz/1 cup mascarpone
   cheese
150ml/¼ pint/⅔ cup double
   (heavy) cream

1 Preheat the oven to 200°C/400°F/Gas 6. Using a teaspoon, scoop some of the flesh from the cavities in the peaches, to make a reasonable space for the stuffing. Chop the scooped-out peach flesh and place in a mixing bowl.

2 Add the amaretti, ground almonds, sugar and cocoa powder to the peach flesh and mix together. Stir in enough wine to make the mixture into a thick paste.

3 Place the peaches in a buttered ovenproof dish and fill them with the stuffing. Dot with the butter, then pour the remaining wine into the dish. Bake for 35 minutes.

4 To make the mascarpone cream, beat the sugar and egg yolks until thick and pale. Stir in the wine, then fold in the mascarpone. Whip the double cream to soft peaks and fold into the mixture.

5 Remove the peaches from the oven and leave to cool to room temperature. Transfer to individual dishes and serve topped with the mascarpone cream.

Top Energy 91Kcal/381kJ; Fat 0.7g; Saturated Fat 0g; Carbohydrate 0g; Fibre 2.7g
Above Energy 218Kcal/921kJ; Fat 6.4g; Saturated Fat 3.9g; Carbohydrate 36.8g; Fibre 2.1g

Energy 626Kcal/2607kJ; Fat 44g; Saturated Fat 23.5g; Carbohydrate 40.9g; Fibre 2.7g

Apple & Lemon Risotto with Poached Plums

Although it's entirely possible to cook this by the conventional risotto method – by adding the liquid slowly – it makes more sense to cook the rice with the milk in the same way as for a rice pudding.

Serves 4
1 cooking apple
15g/½oz/1 tbsp butter
175g/6oz/scant 1 cup risotto rice
600ml/1 pint/2½ cups creamy milk
about 50g/2oz/¼ cup caster (superfine) sugar
1.5ml/¼ tsp ground cinnamon

30ml/2 tbsp lemon juice
45ml/3 tbsp double (heavy) cream
grated rind of 1 lemon, to decorate

For the poached plums
50g/2oz/¼ cup light muscovado (brown) sugar
200ml/7fl oz/scant 1 cup apple juice
3 star anise
cinnamon stick
6 plums, halved and sliced

1 Peel and core the apple. Cut it into large chunks. Put these in a large, non-stick pan and add the butter. Heat gently, until the butter melts.

2 Add the rice and milk and stir well. Bring to the boil over medium heat, then simmer very gently for 20–25 minutes, stirring occasionally.

3 To make the poached plums, dissolve the sugar in 150ml/¼ pint/⅔ cup apple juice in a pan. Add the spices and bring to the boil. Boil for 2 minutes. Add the plums and simmer for 2 minutes. Set aside until ready to serve.

4 Stir the sugar, cinnamon and lemon juice into the risotto. Cook for 2 minutes, stirring all the time, then stir in the cream. Taste and add more sugar if necessary. Decorate with the lemon rind and serve with the poached plums.

Chocolate Risotto

If you've never tasted a sweet risotto, there's a treat in store. Chocolate risotto is delectable, and children of all ages love it.

Serves 4–6
175g/6oz/scant 1 cup risotto rice
600ml/1 pint/2½ cups creamy milk
75g/3oz plain (semisweet) chocolate, broken into pieces

25g/1oz/2 tbsp butter
about 50g/2oz/¼ cup caster (superfine) sugar
pinch of ground cinnamon
60ml/4 tbsp double (heavy) cream
fresh raspberries and chocolate caraque (see below), to decorate
chocolate sauce, to serve

1 Put the rice in a non-stick pan. Pour in the milk and bring to the boil over low to medium heat. Reduce the heat to the lowest setting and simmer very gently for about 20 minutes, stirring occasionally, until the rice is very soft.

2 Stir in the chocolate, butter and sugar. Cook, stirring all the time over very gentle heat for 1–2 minutes, until the chocolate has melted.

3 Remove the pan from the heat and stir in the ground cinnamon and double cream. Cover the pan and leave to stand for a few minutes.

4 Spoon the risotto into individual dishes or dessert plates, and decorate with fresh raspberries and chocolate caraque. Serve with chocolate sauce.

> **Cook's Tip**
> To make chocolate caraque, melt some chocolate in a heat-proof bowl set over a pan of simmering water, then pour the chocolate in a thin layer on to a cold baking sheet and leave to set hard. Holding a large knife sideways, push the blade at an angle across the surface of the chocolate to roll off long curls.

Zabaglione

This sumptuous warm dessert is very quick and easy to prepare, but needs to be made at the last minutes. Serve with savoiardi, the Italian sponge fingers.

Serves 6
4 egg yolks
65 g/2½ oz/⅓ cup caster
   (superfine) sugar
120 ml/4 fl oz/½ cup dry
   Marsala

1 Half fill a pan with water and bring it to simmering point. Put the egg yolks and sugar in a large heatproof bowl and beat with a hand-held electric mixer until pale and creamy.

2 Put the bowl over the pan and gradually pour in the Marsala, whisking until it is very thick and has increased in volume.

3 Remove the bowl from the water and pour the zabaglione into tall glasses. Serve immediately.

Warm Chocolate Zabaglione

Once you've tasted this sensuous dessert, you'll never regard cocoa in quite the same way again. Serve with mini amaretti or other small, crisp sweet biscuits.

Serves 6
6 egg yolks
150g/5oz/¾ cup caster
   (superfine) sugar
45ml/3 tbsp unsweetened cocoa
   powder, plus extra for dusting
200ml/7fl oz/scant 1 cup
   Marsala

1 Half fill a pan with water and bring it to simmering point. Put the egg yolks and sugar in a large heatproof bowl and beat with a hand-held electric mixer until pale and creamy.

2 Add the cocoa and Marsala, then place the bowl over the simmering water. Beat with a hand-held electric mixer until the mixture is smooth, thick and foamy. Pour quickly into tall glasses, dust lightly with cocoa and serve immediately.

Lovers' Knots

The irresistible treats are known as cenci in Italian, which literally translates as "rags and tatters", but they are often referred to by the more endearing term of lovers' knots. They are eaten at carnival time in February.

Makes 24
150g/5oz/1¼ cups plain
   (all-purpose) flour
2.5ml/½ tsp baking powder
pinch of salt
30ml/2 tbsp caster (superfine)
   sugar, plus extra for dusting
1 egg, beaten
about 25ml/1½ tbsp rum
vegetable oil, for deep frying

1 Sift the flour, baking powder and salt into a bowl, then stir in the sugar. Add the egg. Stir with a fork until it is evenly mixed with the flour, then add the rum gradually and continue mixing until the dough draws together.

2 Knead the dough on a lightly floured surface until it is smooth. Divide the dough into quarters.

3 Roll each piece out to a 15 x 7.5cm/6 x 3in rectangle and trim to make the sides straight. Cut each rectangle lengthways into six strips, 1cm/½in wide, and carefully tie each strip into a simple knot.

4 Heat the oil in a deep-fat fryer to a temperature of 190°C/375°F. Deep fry the knots in batches for 1–2 minutes, until crisp and golden.

5 Transfer the knots to kitchen paper with a slotted spoon. Serve warm, dusted with sugar.

> **Cook's Tip**
> If you do not have a deep-fat fryer with a built-in thermostat, or a deep-fat thermometer, test the temperature of the oil before deep frying by dropping in a scrap of the dough trimmings – it should turn crisp and golden in about 30 seconds.

Top Energy 111Kcal/464kJ; Fat 3.7g; Saturated Fat 1.1g; Carbohydrate 12.7g; Fibre 0g
Above Energy 233Kcal/979kJ; Fat 7.5g; Saturated Fat 2.7g; Carbohydrate 29.5g; Fibre 1g

Energy 56Kcal/236kJ; Fat 3.1g; Saturated Fat 0.4g; Carbohydrate 6.2g; Fibre 0.2g

Baked Ricotta Cakes with Red Sauce

These honey-flavoured desserts take only minutes to make from a few ingredients. The fragrant fruity sauce provides a contrast of both colour and flavour. The red berry sauce can be made a day in advance and chilled until ready to use.

Serves 4
250g/9oz/generous 1 cup ricotta cheese
2 egg whites, beaten
60ml/4 tbsp scented honey, plus extra to taste
450g/1lb/4 cups mixed fresh or frozen fruit, such as strawberries, raspberries, blackberries and cherries

1 Preheat the oven to 180°C/350°F/Gas 4. Place the ricotta cheese in a bowl and break up with a wooden spoon. Add the beaten egg whites and honey, and mix thoroughly until smooth and well combined.

2 Lightly grease four ramekins. Spoon the ricotta mixture into the prepared ramekins and level the tops. Bake for 20 minutes, or until the ricotta cakes are risen and golden.

3 Meanwhile, make the fruit sauce. Reserve about one-quarter of the fruit for decoration. Place the rest of the fruit in a pan, with a little water if the fruit is fresh, and heat gently until softened. Leave to cool slightly and remove any stones (pits) if using cherries.

4 Press the fruit through a sieve (strainer), then taste and sweeten with honey if it is too tart. Serve the sauce, warm or cold, with the ricotta cakes and decorate each serving with the reserved whole mixed fruit.

> **Cook's Tip**
> If using frozen fruit, you will not need to add extra water, as the fruit usually yields its juice easily on thawing.

Energy 128Kcal/534kJ; Fat 6.1g; Saturated Fat 3.8g; Carbohydrate 13.4g; Fibre 0.8g

Eggy Bread Panettone

The light texture and deliciously spiced flavour of the Italian speciality bread panettone transforms an old favourite into a memorable dessert. Serve with a selection of summer fruits for a great finale to a meal.

Serves 4
2 large (US extra large) eggs
50g/2oz/¼ cup butter or 30ml/2 tbsp sunflower oil
4 large panettone slices
30ml/2 tbsp caster (superfine) sugar
450g/1lb/4 cups mixed fresh summer fruit, such as strawberries, raspberries and blackcurrants

1 Break the eggs into a bowl and beat with a fork, then transfer to a shallow dish. Dip the panettone slices into the beaten egg, turning them to coat evenly.

2 Heat the butter or oil in a large non-stick frying pan and add the panettone slices: you will probably have to do this in batches, depending on the size of the pan. Fry the panettone slices over medium heat for 2–3 minutes on each side, until golden brown.

3 Remove the panettone slices from the pan and drain on kitchen paper. Cut the slices in half diagonally and dust with the sugar. Serve immediately with the mixed summer fruit.

> **Cook's Tip**
> Panettone, which literally translates as "big bread", is a light-textured, spiced yeast bread containing sultanas (golden raisins) and candied fruit. Originally a speciality of Milan, it is now sold all over Italy as a Christmas delicacy and is traditionally given as a gift. Panettoni are widely exported these days, and you can usually buy them from specialist food shops and delicatessens. Packed attractively in pastel-coloured dome-shaped boxes, they can vary in size from small to enormous. Panettone is usually served sliced into wedges and eaten like cake.

Energy 465Kcal/1934kJ; Fat 33g; Saturated Fat 11g; Carbohydrate 37g; Fibre 0.5g

Apricot Panettone Pudding

Slices of light-textured panettone are layered with dried apricots and cooked in a creamy coffee custard for a satisfying dessert.

Serves 4

50g/2oz/4 tbsp unsalted
  butter, softened
6 x 1cm/½in thick slices (about
  400g/14oz) panettone
  containing candied fruit

175g/6oz/¾ cup ready-to-eat
  dried apricots, chopped
400ml/14fl oz/1⅔ cups milk
250ml/8fl oz/1 cup double
  (heavy) cream
60ml/4 tbsp mild-flavoured
  ground coffee
90g/3½oz/½ cup caster
  (superfine) sugar
3 eggs
30ml/2 tbsp demerara (raw) sugar
pouring cream or crème fraîche,
  to serve

1 Preheat the oven to 160°C/325°F/Gas 3. Brush a 2 litre/3½ pint/8 cup oval baking dish with 15g/½oz/1 tbsp of the butter. Spread the panettone with the remaining butter and arrange in the dish. Cut to fit and scatter the apricots over the layers.

2 Heat the milk and cream into a pan until almost boiling. Pour the milk mixture over the coffee; leave to infuse (steep) for 10 minutes. Strain through a fine sieve, discarding the coffee grounds.

3 Lightly beat the caster sugar and eggs together, then whisk in the warm coffee-flavoured milk. Slowly pour the mixture over the panettone. Leave it to soak for 15 minutes.

4 Sprinkle the top of the pudding with demerara sugar and place the dish in a large roasting tin (pan). Pour in enough boiling water to come halfway up the sides of the baking dish. Bake for 40–45 minutes, until the top is golden and crusty, but the middle still slightly wobbly. Remove from the oven, but leave the dish in the hot water for 10 minutes. Serve warm.

> **Cook's Tip**
> This recipe works well with chocolate-flavoured panettone.

Hot Chocolate Rum Soufflés

Light as air, melt-in-the-mouth soufflés are always impressive, yet they are surprisingly easy to make. For an indulgent touch, serve the soufflés with whipped cream flavoured with dark rum and grated orange rind.

Serves 6

50g/2oz/½ cup unsweetened
  cocoa powder
65g/2½oz/5 tbsp caster
  (superfine) sugar, plus extra
  caster or icing (confectioners')
  sugar, for dusting
butter, for greasing
30ml/2 tbsp dark rum
6 egg whites

1 Preheat the oven to 190°C/375°F/Gas 5. Place a baking sheet in the oven to heat up.

2 Mix 15ml/1 tbsp of the cocoa powder with 15ml/1 tbsp of the caster sugar in a bowl. Grease six 250ml/8fl oz/1 cup ramekins. Pour some of the cocoa and sugar mixture into each of the dishes in turn, rotating them so that the sides and bottoms are evenly coated.

3 Mix together the remaining cocoa powder with the dark rum in a small bowl.

4 Whisk the egg whites in a clean, grease-free bowl until they form stiff peaks. Whisk in the remaining sugar. Stir a generous spoonful of the whites into the cocoa mixture to lighten it, then fold in the remaining whites.

5 Divide the mixture among the prepared dishes. Place on the hot baking sheet and bake for 13–15 minutes, or until well risen. Serve immediately, dusted with caster or icing sugar.

> **Cook's Tip**
> When serving the soufflés at the end of a dinner party, prepare them just before the meal is served. Put them in the oven when the main course is finished and serve steaming hot.

Baked Sweet Ravioli

These delicious sweet ravioli have a luscious ricotta and chocolate filling.

Serves 4
225g/8oz/2 cups plain (all-purpose) flour
65g/2½oz/⅓ cup caster (superfine) sugar
90g/3½oz/scant ½ cup butter
1 egg
5ml/1 tsp finely grated lemon rind

For the filling
175g/6oz/¾ cup ricotta cheese
50g/2oz/¼ cup caster (superfine) sugar
4ml/¾ tsp vanilla extract
1 medium egg yolk
15ml/1 tbsp mixed candied fruits or mixed peel
25g/1oz dark (bittersweet) chocolate, finely chopped or grated
1 small egg, beaten

1 Put the flour and sugar into a food processor and, on full speed, add the butter in pieces until fully worked into the mixture. With the food processor still running, add the egg and lemon rind. The mixture should form a dough which just holds together. Scrape the dough on to a sheet of clear film (plastic wrap), cover with another sheet, flatten and chill until needed.

2 To make the filling, push the ricotta through a sieve (strainer) into a bowl. Stir in the sugar, vanilla, egg yolk, peel and chocolate.

3 Allow the pastry to come to room temperature. Divide the pastry in half and roll each half between sheets of clear film to make strips, measuring 15 x 56cm/6 x 22in. Preheat the oven to 180°C/350°F/Gas 4.

4 Arrange heaped tablespoons of the filling in two rows along one of the pastry strips, ensuring there is at least 2.5cm/1in clear space around each spoonful. Brush the pastry between the filling with beaten egg. Place the second strip of pastry on top and press down between each mound of filling to seal.

5 Using a 6 cm/2½in plain pastry cutter, cut around each mound of filling to make circular ravioli. Lift each one and, with your fingertips, seal the edges. Place the ravioli on a greased baking sheet and bake for 15 minutes until golden brown.

Apple Cake

This moist cake is best served warm. It comes from Genoa, home of the whisked sponge. When whipping the cream, try adding grated lemon rind – it tastes delicious.

Serves 6
675g/1½lb eating apples
finely grated rind and juice of 1 large lemon
4 eggs
150g/5oz/¾ cup caster (superfine) sugar
150g/5oz/1¼ cups plain (all-purpose) flour
5ml/1 tsp baking powder
pinch of salt
115g/4oz/½ cup butter, melted and cooled, plus extra for greasing
1 sachet of vanilla sugar, for sprinkling
very finely pared strips of citrus rind, to decorate
whipped cream, to serve

1 Preheat the oven to 180°C/350°F/Gas 4. Brush a 23cm/9in springform cake tin (pan) with melted butter and line the base with non-stick baking parchment. Quarter, core and peel the apples, then slice thinly. Put the apple slices in a bowl and pour over the lemon juice.

2 Put the eggs, sugar and lemon rind in a bowl and whisk with a hand-held electric mixture until the mixture is thick and mousse-like. The whisk should leave a trail.

3 Sift half the flour, all the baking powder and the salt over the egg mousse, then fold in gently with a large metal spoon. Slowly drizzle in the melted butter from the side of the bowl and fold it in gently with the spoon. Sift over the remaining flour, fold it in gently, then add the apples and fold these in equally gently.

4 Spoon into the prepared tin and level the surface. Bake for 40 minutes, or until a skewer comes out clean. Leave to settle in the tin for about 10 minutes, then invert on a wire rack.

5 Turn the cake the right way up and sprinkle with vanilla sugar. Decorate with the citrus rind. Serve warm, with cream.

Energy 612Kcal/2569kJ; Fat 29.4g; Saturated Fat 17.2g; Carbohydrate 79.9g; Fibre 2g

Energy 415Kcal/1743kJ; Fat 19.9g; Saturated Fat 11.1g; Carbohydrate 55.7g; Fibre 2.6g

Chocolate Salami

This after-dinner sweetmeat resembles a salami in shape, hence its curious name. It is very rich so slice it thinly.

Serves 8–12

24 Petit Beurre biscuits
(cookies), broken
350g/12oz plain (bittersweet)
chocolate, broken into squares

225g/8oz/1 cup unsalted butter,
softened
60ml/4 tbsp amaretto liqueur
2 egg yolks
50g/2oz/1/2 cup flaked (sliced)
almonds, lightly toasted and
thinly shredded lengthways
25g/1oz/1/4 cup ground almonds

1 Place the biscuits in a food processor fitted with a metal blade and process until coarsely crushed.

2 Place the chocolate in a large heatproof bowl over a pan of barely simmering water, add a small chunk of butter and all the liqueur and heat until the chocolate melts, stirring occasionally.

3 Remove the bowl from the heat, allow the chocolate to cool for a minute or two, then stir in the egg yolks followed by the remaining butter, a little at a time. Add most of the crushed biscuits, reserving a good handful, and stir well to mix. Stir in the shredded almonds. Leave the mixture in a cold place for about 1 hour until it begins to stiffen.

4 Process the reserved crushed biscuits in the food processor until they are very finely ground. Turn into a bowl and mix with the ground almonds. Cover and set aside until ready to serve.

5 Turn the biscuit mixture on to a sheet of lightly oiled greaseproof (wax) paper, then shape into a 35cm/14in sausage with a metal spatula, tapering the ends so that the roll looks like a salami. Wrap in the paper and freeze for 4 hours until solid.

6 To serve, unwrap the "salami". Spread the ground biscuits and almonds out on a clean sheet of greaseproof paper and roll the salami in them until evenly coated. Transfer to a board and leave to stand for about 1 hour before serving in slices.

Apricot Parcels

Apricots, mincemeat and marzipan layered with filo pastry make a delicious end to a meal and an impressive dinner party sweetmeat.

Makes 8

350g/12oz filo pastry, thawed
if frozen

50g/2oz/1/4 cup butter, melted
8 apricots, halved and stoned
60ml/4 tbsp luxury mincemeat
12 ratafias, crushed
30ml/2 tbsp grated marzipan
icing (confectioners') sugar, for
dusting

1 Preheat the oven to 200°C/400°F/Gas 6. Spread the filo pastry on to a flat surface. Cut into 32 × 18cm/7in squares.

2 Brush four of the squares with a little melted butter and stack them one on top of the other, giving each layer a quarter turn so that the stack acquires a star shape. Repeat the process to make eight stars.

3 Place an apricot half, hollow up, in the centre of each pastry star. Mix together the mincemeat, crushed ratafias and marzipan, and spoon a little of the mixture into the hollow in each apricot.

4 Top with another apricot half, then bring the corners of each pastry together and squeeze to make a gathered purse. Place the purses on a baking sheet and brush each with a little melted butter. Bake for 15–20 minutes, or until the pastry is golden and crisp.

5 Lightly dust with icing sugar to serve.

> **Cook's Tips**
> • Whipped cream, flavoured with a little brandy or rum, makes an ideal accompaniment.
> • Vin Santo, a port-like sweet drink from Tuscany, would be an excellent after dinner wine to serve with these parcels.

Pine Nut Tart

Strange though it may seem, this traditional tart is an Italian version of the humble Bakewell tart from England.

Serves 8

115g/4oz/8 tbsp butter, softened
115g/4oz/generous ¹/₂ cup caster (superfine) sugar
1 egg
2 egg yolks
150g/5oz/1¹/₄ cups ground almonds
115g/4oz/1 cup pine nuts
60ml/4 tbsp seedless raspberry jam

icing (confectioners') sugar, for dusting
whipped cream, to serve (optional)

For the pastry

175g/6oz/1¹/₂ cups plain (all-purpose) flour
65g/2¹/₂oz/¹/₃ cup caster (superfine) sugar
1.5ml/¹/₄ tsp baking powder
pinch of salt
115g/4oz/¹/₂ cup chilled butter, diced
1 egg yolk

1 To make the pastry, sift the flour, sugar, baking powder and salt on to a cold work surface. Make a well in the centre and put in the diced butter and egg yolk. Gradually work the flour into the butter and egg yolk, using your fingertips.

2 Gather the dough together and press into a 23cm/9in fluted tart tin (pan) with a removable base. Chill for 30 minutes.

3 Meanwhile, make the filling. Cream the butter and sugar together with an electric mixer until light and fluffy, then beat in the egg and egg yolks a little at a time, alternating them with the ground almonds. Beat in the pine nuts.

4 Preheat the oven to 160°C/325°F/Gas 3. Spread the jam over the pastry case, then spoon in the filling. Bake for 30–35 minutes, or until a skewer inserted in the centre of the tart comes out clean.

5 Transfer to a wire rack and leave to cool, then carefully remove the side of the tin, leaving the tart on the tin base. Dust with icing sugar and serve with whipped cream, if you like.

Ricotta Cheesecake

The firm texture of low-fat ricotta makes it ideal for this Sicilian-style dessert.

Serves 8

450g/1lb/2 cups low-fat ricotta cheese
120ml/4fl oz/¹/₂ cup double (heavy) cream
2 eggs
1 egg yolk
75g/3oz/¹/₃ cup caster (superfine) sugar

finely grated rind of 1 orange
finely grated rind of 1 lemon

For the pastry

175g/6oz/1¹/₂ cups plain (all-purpose) flour
45ml/3 tbsp caster (superfine) sugar
pinch of salt
115g/4oz/¹/₂ cup chilled butter, diced
1 egg yolk

1 To make the pastry, sift the flour, sugar and salt on to a cold work surface. Make a well in the centre and put in the diced butter and egg yolk. Gradually work the flour into the diced butter and egg yolk, using your fingertips.

2 Gather the dough together, reserve about a quarter for the lattice, then press the rest into a 23cm/9in fluted tart tin (pan) with a removable base. Chill the pastry case for 30 minutes.

3 Meanwhile, preheat the oven to 190°C/375°F/Gas 5 and make the filling. Put all the ricotta, cream, eggs, egg yolk, sugar and orange and lemon rinds in a large bowl and beat together.

4 Prick the bottom of the pastry case, then line with foil and fill with baking beans. Bake blind for 15 minutes. Transfer to a wire rack, remove the foil and beans and allow to cool in the tin.

5 Spoon the cheese and cream filling into the pastry case and level the surface. Roll out the reserved dough and cut into strips. Arrange the strips on the top of the filling in a lattice pattern, sticking them in place with water.

6 Bake for 30–35 minutes, until golden and set. Transfer to a wire rack and leave to cool, then carefully remove the tins sides.

Energy 415Kcal/1732kJ; Fat 26.7g; Saturated Fat 16.1g; Carbohydrate 35g; Fibre 0.7g

Energy 502Kcal/2093kJ; Fat 33.3g; Saturated Fat 16.1g; Carbohydrate 46.9g; Fibre 1.7g

Yellow Plum Tart

A lovely tart – glazed yellow plums arranged on a delectable almond filling.

Serves 8

175g/6oz/1½ cups plain (all-purpose) flour
pinch of salt
75g/3oz/6 tbsp butter, chilled
30ml/2 tbsp caster (superfine) sugar
a few drops of pure vanilla extract
45ml/3 tbsp iced water

45ml/3 tbsp apricot jam, sieved
cream or custard, to serve

For the filling

75g/3oz/6 tbsp caster (superfine) sugar
75g/3oz/6 tbsp butter, softened
75g/3oz/¾ cup ground almonds
1 egg, beaten
30ml/2 tbsp plain (all-purpose) flour
450g/1lb yellow plums or greengages, halved and stoned

1 Sift the flour and salt into a bowl, then rub in the butter until the mixture resembles fine breadcrumbs. Stir in the sugar, vanilla extract and enough of the iced water to form a soft dough.

2 Knead the dough gently on a lightly floured surface until smooth. Wrap in clear film (plastic wrap); chill for 10 minutes.

3 Preheat the oven to 200°C/400°F/Gas 6. Roll out the pastry and line a 23cm/9in fluted flan tin (tart pan), allowing any excess pastry to overhang the top. Prick the base with a fork and line with non-stick baking parchment and baking beans.

4 Bake blind for 10 minutes, remove the paper and beans, then return the pastry case to the oven for 10 minutes. Remove and allow to cool. Trim off any excess pastry with a sharp knife.

5 To make the filling, beat together all the ingredients except the plums. Spread on the base of the pastry case. Arrange the plums on top, cut-side down. To make a glaze, heat the jam with 15ml/1 tbsp water, then brush a little over the fruit.

6 Bake the plum tart for about 50 minutes, until the almond filling is cooked and the plums are tender. Warm any remaining jam glaze and brush over the top. Serve with cream or custard.

Nectarine Amaretto Cake

This deliciously moist Italian-style cake is a real treat.

Serves 10

3 eggs, separated
175g/6oz/generous ¾ cup caster (superfine) sugar
finely grated rind and juice of 1 lemon
50g/2oz/⅓ cup semolina
40g/1½ oz/⅓ cup ground almonds

25g/1oz/¼ cup plain (all-purpose) flour
2 nectarines or peaches, halved, stoned and sliced

For the glaze and syrup

45ml/3 tbsp apricot jam
5–10ml/1–2 tsp lemon juice
75g/3oz/6 tbsp caster (superfine) sugar
30ml/2 tbsp Amaretto liqueur

1 Preheat the oven to 180°C/350°F/Gas 4. Lightly grease a 20cm/8in round loose-based cake tin (pan). Whisk the egg yolks, caster sugar, lemon rind and juice in a bowl until thick, pale and creamy. Fold in the semolina, almonds and flour.

2 Whisk the egg whites in a separate bowl until fairly stiff. Using a metal spoon, stir a generous spoonful of the whisked egg whites into the semolina mixture to lighten it, then fold in the remaining egg whites. Spoon into cake tin and level the surface.

3 Bake for 30–35 minutes, until the centre of the cake springs back when lightly pressed. Remove the cake from the oven and loosen around the edge with a palette knife. Prick the top of the cake with a skewer and leave to cool slightly in the tin.

4 Meanwhile, make the glaze. Melt the apricot jam with the lemon juice, then pass through a sieve (strainer). Keep the glaze warm. To make the syrup, heat the sugar and 90ml/6 tbsp water in a small pan, stirring until dissolved, then boil without stirring for 2 minutes. Stir in the Amaretto, then drizzle the syrup over the top of the cake in the tin.

5 Remove the cake from the tin and place it on a serving plate. Arrange the nectarines or peaches over the top of the cake and brush with the warm apricot glaze. Serve warm or cold.

Energy 195Kcal/827kJ; Fat 4.1g; Saturated Fat 0.7g; Carbohydrate 37.1g; Fibre 0.8g

Energy 366Kcal/1531kJ; Fat 21.7g; Saturated Fat 10.4g; Carbohydrate 39.5g; Fibre 2.4g

Chestnut Pudding

Sweet chestnuts, gathered in the mountainous regions of Italy during October and November, are turned into irresistible desserts, such as this creamy pudding.

Serves 4–5
450g/1lb fresh sweet chestnuts
300ml/½ pint/1¼ cups milk
115/4oz/½ cup sugar
2 eggs, separated, at room
  temperature
25g/1oz/¼ cup unsweetened
  cocoa powder
2.5ml/½ tsp pure vanilla extract
50g/2oz/⅓ cup icing
  (confectioners') sugar, sifted
butter, for greasing
fresh whipped cream and
  marrons glacés, cut into small
  pieces, to decorate

1 Cut a cross in the side of the chestnuts and drop them into a pan of boiling water. Cook for 5–6 minutes. Remove with a slotted spoon, then peel while still warm.

2 Place the peeled chestnuts in a heavy or non-stick pan with the milk and half of the sugar. Cook over low heat, stirring occasionally, until soft. Remove from the heat and allow to cool. Press the contents of the pan through a sieve (strainer).

3 Preheat the oven to 180°C/350°F/Gas 4. Beat the egg yolks with the remaining sugar until the mixture is pale yellow and fluffy. Beat in the cocoa powder and the vanilla.

4 In a separate bowl, whisk the egg whites with a wire whisk or electric mixer until they form soft peaks. Gradually beat in the sifted icing sugar and continue beating until the mixture forms stiff peaks.

5 Fold the chestnut and egg yolk mixtures together. Fold in the egg whites. Turn the mixture into one large or several individual buttered pudding moulds. Place on a baking sheet and bake in the oven for 12–20 minutes until firm, depending on the size.

6 Remove from the oven and allow to cool for 10 minutes before unmoulding. Serve decorated with whipped cream and marrons glacés.

Choux Pastries with Two Custards

Italian pastry shops are filled with displays of sweetly scented pastries like these.

Makes about 48
115g/4oz/½ cup butter
2.5cm/1in piece vanilla pod (bean)
pinch of salt
150g/5oz/1¼ cups flour
5 eggs

For the custard fillings
50g/2oz dark (bittersweet)
  chocolate
300ml/½ pint/1¼ cups milk
4 egg yolks
65g/2½oz/scant ⅓ cup
  granulated (white) sugar
40g/1½oz/generous ⅓ cup flour
5ml/1 tsp pure vanilla extract
300ml/½ pint/1¼ cups whipping
  cream
unsweetened cocoa powder and
  icing (confectioners') sugar, to
  decorate

1 Preheat the oven to 190°C/375°F/Gas 5. Heat 200ml/7fl oz/ scant 1 cup water with the butter, vanilla and salt. When the butter has melted, beat in the flour. Cook over low heat, stirring constantly, for about 8 minutes. Remove from the heat.

2 Mix the eggs into the flour mixture, one at a time. Remove the vanilla pod.

3 Butter a baking sheet. Spoon the mixture into a pastry bag fitted with a round nozzle and squeeze out small walnut-sized balls of the mixture onto the sheet, leaving space between the rows. Bake for 20–25 minutes or until the pastries are golden brown. Remove from the oven and allow to cool.

4 Meanwhile, make the fillings. Melt the chocolate in the top half of a double boiler or in a bowl set over a pan of simmering water. Heat the milk in a small pan, taking care not to let it boil.

5 Beat the egg yolks with a wire whisk or electric mixer. Gradually incorporate the sugar and continue beating until the mixture is pale yellow. Beat in the flour. Beat in the hot milk very gradually, pouring it in through a sieve (strainer).

6 Pour into a heavy medium pan and bring to the boil. Simmer for 5–6 minutes, stirring constantly. Remove from the heat and divide the custard between two bowls. Add the melted chocolate to one and the vanilla to the other. Allow to cool.

7 Whip the cream. Fold half of it carefully into each of the custards. Fill two pastry bags fitted with round nozzles with the custards. Fill half of the choux pastries with the chocolate custard, and the rest with the vanilla custard, making a little hole and piping the filling in through the side of each pastry. Dust the tops of the chocolate-filled pastries with cocoa powder and the rest with icing sugar. Serve immediately.

Variation
The choux pastries may be filled with fresh whipped cream flavoured with 5ml/1 tsp vanilla extract or 30–45ml/2–3 tbsp spirit such as brandy or rum.

Jam Tart

Jam tarts are popular in northern Italy, where they are traditionally decorated with pastry strips.

Serves 6–8

200g/7oz/1³⁄₄ cups flour
pinch of salt
50g/2oz/¹⁄₄ cup granulated
 (white) sugar
115g/4oz/¹⁄₂ cup butter or
 margarine, chilled
1 egg
1.5ml/¹⁄₄ tsp grated lemon rind
350g/12oz/1¹⁄₄ cups fruit jam,
 such as raspberry or apricot
1 egg, lightly beaten with 30ml/
 2 tbsp whipping cream, for
 glazing

1 To make the pastry, place the flour, salt and sugar in a mixing bowl. Using a pastry blender or two knives, cut the butter or margarine into the dry ingredients as quickly as possible until the mixture resembles coarse breadcrumbs. Beat the egg with the lemon rind in a cup and pour it over the flour mixture. Combine with a fork until the dough holds together. If it is too crumbly, mix in 15–30ml/1–2 tbsp of water.

2 Gather the dough into 2 balls, one slightly larger than the other, then flatten into discs. Wrap in baking parchment, and chill in the refrigerator for at least 40 minutes.

3 Lightly grease a shallow 23cm/9in flan tin (tart pan), preferably with a removable bottom. Roll out the larger disc of pastry on a lightly floured surface to about 3mm/¹⁄₈in thick. Roll the pastry around the rolling pin and transfer to the prepared tin. Trim the edges evenly with a small knife. Prick the bottom with a fork. Chill for at least 30 minutes.

4 Preheat the oven to 190°C/375°F/Gas 5. Spread the jam evenly over the base of the pastry. Roll out remaining pastry.

5 Cut the pastry into strips about 1cm/¹⁄₂in wide. Arrange them over the jam in a lattice pattern. Trim the edges of the strips even with the edge of the pan, pressing them lightly on to the pastry shell. Brush the pastry with the egg and cream glaze. Bake for 35 minutes, or until the crust is golden brown.

Energy 260Kcal/1092kJ; Fat 12.8g; Saturated Fat 7.7g; Carbohydrate 35.5g; Fibre 0.2g

Chocolate Nut Tart

This is a luxurious relative of the simple jam tart.

Serves 6–8

200g/7oz/1³⁄₄ cups flour
pinch of salt
50g/2oz/¹⁄₄ cup granulated
 (white) sugar
115g/4oz/¹⁄₂ cup butter or
 margarine, chilled
1 egg
15ml/1 tbsp Marsala
1.5ml/¹⁄₄ tsp grated lemon rind

For the filling

200g/7oz/1³⁄₄ cups amaretti
100g/3¹⁄₂oz/³⁄₄ cup blanched
 almonds
50g/2oz/¹⁄₂ cup blanched
 hazelnuts
45ml/3 tbsp sugar
200g/7oz plain (bittersweet)
 cooking chocolate
45ml/3 tbsp milk
50g/2oz/¹⁄₄ cup butter
45ml/3 tbsp liqueur, such as
 amaretto or brandy
30ml/2 tbsp single (light) cream

1 Make the pastry as for the Jam Tart, beating the Marsala with the egg and lemon rind and mixing into the dry ingredients.

2 Lightly grease a shallow 26cm/10in flan tin (tart pan), preferably with a removable bottom. Roll out the pastry on a lightly floured surface to about 3mm/¹⁄₈in thick . Transfer the pastry to the prepared tin. Trim the edges evenly and prick the bottom with a fork. Chill for at least 30 minutes.

3 Grind the amaretti to crumbs in a food processor. Transfer to a mixing bowl. Set 8 whole almonds aside and place the rest in the food processor with the hazelnuts and sugar. Grind to a medium texture. Add the nuts to the amaretti and mix well.

4 Preheat the oven to 190°C/375°F/Gas 5. Melt the chocolate with the milk and butter in a bowl over a pan of simmering water. Stir until smooth. Pour the chocolate mixture into the ground amaretti and nuts. Mix well. Add the liqueur and cream.

5 Spread the chocolate and nut filling evenly in the pastry shell. Bake for about 35 minutes, until the filling has puffed up and is beginning to darken. Cool to room temperature. Split the remaining almonds in half and use them to decorate the tart.

Energy 556Kcal/2320kJ; Fat 35.5g; Saturated Fat 16.5g; Carbohydrate 54.2g; Fibre 2.5g

Cassata

In this version of the famous Italian dessert, chocolate-flavoured ricotta is wickedly layered with rum- and coffee-soaked fingers. For best results, try to find authentic savoiardi biscuits.

Serves 8
500g/1¼lb/2½ cups ricotta cheese
75g/3oz/¾ cup icing (confectioners') sugar, plus extra for dusting

2.5ml/½ tsp pure vanilla extract
grated rind and juice of 1 small orange
50g/2oz dark (bittersweet) chocolate, grated
250g/9oz/1½ cups mixed candied fruits, such as orange, pineapple, citron, cherries and angelica
250ml/8fl oz/1 cup freshly brewed strong black coffee
120ml/4fl oz/½ cup rum
24 savoiardi (sponge fingers)
geranium leaves, to decorate

1 Line the base and sides of a 20cm/8in round cake tin (pan) with clear film (plastic wrap). Put the ricotta in a bowl. Sift in the icing sugar, then add the vanilla extract with the orange rind and juice. Beat until smooth, then stir in the chocolate.

2 Cut the candied fruits into small pieces, then stir into the ricotta to distribute well.

3 Mix the coffee and rum. Line the bottom of the tin with sponge fingers, dipping each in the coffee mixture first. Cut the remaining fingers in half, dip them in the liquid and arrange around the sides.

4 Spoon the cassata mixture into the centre and level the top. Cover with more clear film, then place a plate on top that fits exactly inside the rim of the tin. Weight this with a bag of dried beans or sugar, then chill overnight until firm.

5 To serve, remove the weights and the top layer of clear film, then turn out on to a plate, shaking the tin firmly, if necessary, and tugging the clear film gently. Lift the clear film off. Dust the top of the cassata with a little sifted icing sugar and serve in wedges, decorated with geranium leaves.

Sicilian Ricotta Cake

A glorious dessert of layered sponge, ricotta cheese and candied peel, steeped in alcohol.

Serves 8–10
675g/1½lb/3 cups ricotta cheese
finely grated rind of 1 orange
2 sachets of vanilla sugar
75ml/5 tbsp orange-flavoured liqueur
115g/4oz candied peel
8 trifle sponge cakes
60ml/4 tbsp freshly squeezed orange juice
extra candied peel, to decorate

1 Push the ricotta cheese through a sieve (strainer) into a bowl, add the orange rind, vanilla sugar and 15 ml/1 tbsp of the liqueur and beat well to mix. Transfer about one-third of the mixture to another bowl, cover and chill until serving time.

2 Finely chop the candied peel and beat into the remaining ricotta cheese mixture until evenly mixed. Set aside.

3 Line the base of a 1.2 litre/2 pint/5 cup loaf tin (pan) with non-stick baking parchment. Cut the trifle sponges in half horizontally. Arrange four pieces of sponge side by side in the bottom of the loaf tin and sprinkle with 15ml/1 tbsp each of liqueur and orange juice.

4 Put one-third of the ricotta and fruit mixture in the tin and spread out. Cover with four more pieces of sponge and sprinkle with 15ml/1 tbsp each liqueur and orange juice as before.

5 Repeat the alternate layers of ricotta mixture and sponge until all the ingredients are used, ending with soaked sponge. Cover with a piece of non-stick baking parchment.

6 Cut a piece of card to fit inside the tin, place on top of the baking parchment and weight down evenly. Chill for 24 hours.

7 To serve, run a palette knife down the sides of the cassata then turn out on to a plate. Peel off the lining paper. Spread the chilled ricotta mixture over the cake to cover completely, then decorate the top with candied peel. Serve chilled.

Energy 219Kcal/917kJ; Fat 10.6g; Saturated Fat 6.3g; Carbohydrate 22.4g; Fibre 0.7g

Energy 380Kcal/1598kJ; Fat 13.3g; Saturated Fat 7.3g; Carbohydrate 50.7g; Fibre 1.9g

Spicy Fruit Cake from Siena

This delicious flat cake, known as panforte, has a wonderful spicy flavour. It is very rich, so it should be cut into small wedges.

Serves 12–14
butter, for greasing
175g/6oz/1 cup hazelnuts, roughly chopped
75g/3oz/1/2 cup whole almonds, roughly chopped
225g/8oz/1 1/3 cups mixed candied fruits, diced
1.5ml/1/4 tsp ground coriander
4ml/3/4 tsp ground cinnamon
1.5ml/1/4 tsp ground cloves
1.5ml/1/4 tsp grated nutmeg
50g/2oz/1/2 cup plain (all-purpose) flour
115g/4oz/1/3 cup honey
115g/4oz/generous 1 cup granulated (white) sugar
icing (confectioners') sugar, for dusting

1 Preheat the oven to 180°C/350°F/Gas 4. Grease a 20cm/8in round cake tin (pan). Line the base with baking parchment.

2 Spread the nuts on a baking sheet and lightly toast in the oven for about 10 minutes. Remove and set aside. Lower the oven temperature to 150°C/300°F/Gas 2.

3 In a large mixing bowl, mix the candied fruits with all the spices and the flour. Add the nuts and stir in thoroughly.

4 In a small heavy pan, stir together the honey and sugar, then bring to the boil. Cook until it reaches 138°C/280°F on a sugar thermometer or when a small amount spooned into iced water forms a hard ball when pressed between the fingertips.

5 At this stage, immediately pour the sugar syrup into the dry ingredients and stir until evenly coated. Pour into the prepared tin. Dip a spoon into water and use the back of the spoon to press the mixture firmly into the tin. Bake for 1 hour.

6 When ready, the cake will still feel quite soft, but will harden as it cools. Cool completely in the tin and then turn out on to a plate. Cut into wedges and dust with icing sugar to serve.

Lemon Ricotta Cake

This luscious lemony cake from Sardinia is quite different from a traditional cheesecake.

Serves 6–8
75g/3oz/6 tbsp butter
150g/5oz/3/4 cup granulated (white) sugar
75g/3oz/generous 1/3 cup ricotta
3 eggs, separated
175g/6oz/1 1/2 cups flour
grated rind of 1 lemon
45ml/3 tbsp fresh lemon juice
7ml/1 1/2 tsp baking powder
icing (confectioners') sugar, for dusting

1 Grease a 23cm/9in round cake or springform tin (pan). Line the bottom with baking parchment. Grease the paper. Dust with flour. Set aside. Preheat the oven to 180°F/350°F/Gas 4.

2 Put the butter and sugar in a mixing bowl and cream together until smooth. Beat in the ricotta.

3 Beat in the egg yolks, one at a time. Add 30ml/2 tbsp of the flour, with the lemon rind and juice. Sift the remaining flour with the baking powder and beat into the batter until just blended.

4 Whisk the egg whites with a hand-held whisk or electric mixer until they form stiff peaks. Fold a tablespoon into the batter to lighten, then carefully fold the rest into the batter.

5 Turn the mixture into the prepared cake tin. Bake for 45 minutes, or until a cake tester inserted in the centre of the cake comes out clean.

6 Allow the cake to cool for 10 minutes before turning it out onto a rack to cool. Dust the cake generously with icing sugar before serving.

Cook's Tip
Make sure the bowl in which the whites are whisked is completely grease-free as any grease will affect the volume.

Ladies' Kisses

These old-fashioned Piedmontese biscuits (cookies) make pretty petits fours.

Makes 20

150g/5oz/10 tbsp butter, softened

115g/4oz/½ cup caster (superfine) sugar
1 egg yolk
2.5 ml/½ tsp almond extract
115g/4oz/1 cup ground almonds
175g/6oz/1½ cups plain (all-purpose) flour
50g/2oz plain (bittersweet) chocolate

1 Cream the butter and sugar together with an electric mixer until light and fluffy, then beat in the egg yolk, almond extract, ground almonds and flour until evenly mixed. Chill for about 2 hours until the mixture is firm.

2 Preheat the oven to 160°C/325°F/Gas 3. Line 3–4 baking sheets with non-stick baking parchment.

3 Break off small pieces of dough and roll into balls with your hands, making 40 altogether. Place the balls on the baking sheets, spacing them out as they will spread in the oven.

4 Bake the biscuits (cookies) for 20 minutes, or until golden. Remove the baking sheets from the oven, carefully lift off the paper with the biscuits still in place, then put on wire racks. Leave the biscuits to cool on the paper. Repeat with the remaining mixture.

5 When the biscuits are cold, lift them off the paper. Melt the chocolate in a bowl set over a pan of hot water. Sandwich the biscuits in pairs, with the melted chocolate. Leave to cool and set before serving.

> **Cook's Tip**
> These biscuits look extra dainty served in frilly petit four cases, and sprinkled with icing (confectioners') sugar.

Biscotti

These lovely, crunchy Italian biscuits (cookies) are part-baked, sliced to reveal a feast of mixed nuts and then baked again until crisp and golden. Traditionally they're served dipped in Vin Santo, a sweet dessert wine – perfect for rounding off an Italian meal.

Makes 24

50g/2oz/¼ cup unsalted butter, softened, plus extra for greasing

115g/4oz/½ cup caster (superfine) sugar
175g/6oz/1½ cups self-raising (self-rising) flour
1.5ml/¼ tsp salt
10ml/2 tsp baking powder
5ml/1 tsp ground coriander
finely grated rind of 1 lemon
50g/2oz/½ cup polenta
1 egg, lightly beaten
10ml/2 tsp brandy or orange-flavoured liqueur
50g/2oz/½ cup unblanched almonds
50g/2oz/½ cup pistachio nuts

1 Preheat the oven to 160°C/325°F/Gas 3. Lightly grease a baking sheet. Cream together the butter and sugar.

2 Sift all the flour, salt, baking powder and coriander into the bowl. Add the lemon rind, polenta, egg and brandy or liqueur and mix together to make a soft dough.

3 Stir in the nuts until evenly combined. Halve the mixture. Shape each half into a flat sausage about 23cm/9in long and 6cm/2½in wide. Place on the baking sheet and bake for about 30 minutes, until risen and just firm. Remove from the oven.

4 When cool, cut each sausage diagonally into 12 thin slices. Return to the baking sheet and cook for a further 10 minutes, until crisp. Transfer to a wire rack to cool completely. Store in an airtight container for up to 1 week.

> **Cook's Tip**
> Make sure you use a sharp, serrated knife to slice the cooled biscuits, otherwise they will crumble.

Chocolate Amaretti

A chocolate version of the famous Italian macaroons.

Makes about 24

150g/5oz/1 cup blanched whole almonds
90g/3½oz/½ cup caster (superfine) sugar
15ml/1 tbsp unsweetened cocoa powder
30ml/2 tbsp icing (confectioners') sugar
2 egg whites
pinch of cream of tartar
5ml/1 tsp almond extract
15g/½oz flaked (sliced) almonds, to decorate

1 Preheat the oven to 180°C/350°F/Gas 4. Place the whole almonds on a baking sheet and bake in the oven for 10–12 minutes, stirring occasionally, until golden brown. Remove from the oven and set aside to cool to room temperature. Reduce the oven temperature to 160°C/325°F/Gas 3.

2 Line a large baking sheet with baking parchment and set aside. Using a food processor fitted with a metal blade, process the toasted almonds with 45g/1¾oz/½ cup sugar until the almonds are finely ground. Transfer to a medium bowl and sift in the cocoa powder and icing sugar; stir to mix. Set aside.

3 In a mixing bowl, beat the egg whites and cream of tartar together, using an electric mixer, until stiff peaks form. Sprinkle in the remaining 45g/1¾oz/¼ cup sugar, a tablespoon at a time, beating well after each addition, and continue beating until the egg whites are glossy and stiff. Beat in the almond extract.

4 Sprinkle the almond-sugar mixture over the whisked egg whites and gently fold them in until just blended. Spoon the mixture into a large piping bag fitted with a plain 1cm/½in nozzle. Pipe the mixture into 4cm/1½in rounds about 2.5cm/1in apart on the baking sheet. Press an almond into each one.

5 Bake the amaretti in the oven for 12–15 minutes or until crisp. Place the baking sheets on a wire rack and cool for 10 minutes. Remove the amaretti and place on a wire rack to cool completely. When cool, store in an airtight container.

Apricot & Almond Bars

These moist apricot and almond fingers are an irresistible low-fat snack or treat for all to enjoy.

Makes 18

225g/8oz/2 cups self-raising (self-rising) flour
115g/4oz/⅔ cup light muscovado (brown) sugar
50g/2oz/⅓ cup semolina
175g/6oz/1 cup ready-to-eat dried apricots, chopped
2 eggs
30ml/2 tbsp malt extract
30ml/2 tbsp clear honey
60ml/4 tbsp skimmed milk
60ml/4 tbsp sunflower oil
few drops of almond extract
30ml/2 tbsp flaked almonds

1 Preheat the oven to 160°C/325°F/Gas 3. Lightly grease and line a 28 × 18cm/11 × 7in shallow baking tin (pan) and set aside. Sift the flour into a bowl and add the semolina, dried apricots, eggs, malt extract, honey, milk, oil and almond extract. Mix well until smooth.

2 Turn the mixture into the prepared tin, spread to the edges and sprinkle with the flaked almonds.

3 Bake in the oven for 30–35 minutes, or until the centre of the cake springs back when lightly pressed. Turn out onto a wire rack and allow to cool.

4 Remove and discard the paper; place the cake on a board and cut it into 18 slices with a sharp knife.

> **Cook's Tip**
> These cake bars will keep for a few days in an airtight container. They make a great snack for lunch boxes.

> **Variation**
> Use dates instead of the dried apricots and add two pinches of cinnamon powder instead of the almond extract.

Energy 65Kcal/270kJ; Fat 4g; Saturated Fat 0.4g; Carbohydrate 5.8g; Fibre 0.6g

Energy 146Kcal/616kJ; Fat 4.6g; Saturated Fat 0.6g; Carbohydrate 24.7g; Fibre 1.2g

Sultana Cornmeal Biscuits

These little yellow biscuits (cookies) come from the Veneto region of Italy. The cornmeal gives them their delightful flavour and texture. Excellent served with a glass of wine.

Makes about 48

75g/3oz/½ cup sultanas (golden raisins)
115g/4oz/¾ cup finely ground yellow cornmeal
175g/6oz/1½ cups plain (all-purpose) flour
7ml/1½ tsp baking powder
pinch of salt
225g/8oz/1 cup butter
225g/8oz/1 cup sugar
2 eggs
15ml/1 tbsp Marsala or 5ml/1 tsp vanilla extract

1 Soak the sultanas in a small bowl of warm water for 15 minutes. Drain. Preheat the oven to 180°C/350°F/Gas 4.

2 Sift the cornmeal, flour, baking powder and the salt together into a bowl.

3 Cream the butter and sugar together until light and fluffy. Beat in the eggs, one at a time. Beat in the Marsala or vanilla extract. Add the dry ingredients to the batter, beating until well blended. Stir in the sultanas.

4 Drop heaped teaspoons of batter onto a greased baking sheet in rows about 5cm/2in apart. Bake for 7–8 minutes, or until the biscuits are golden brown at the edges. Transfer to a wire rack to cool.

Cook's Tip
Space the mounds of batter well to allow for expansion.

Variation
Instead of the Marsala or vanilla, use 5ml/1 tsp finely grated orange or lemon rind for a citrus flavour.

Amaretti

Make your own version of the famous Italian almond biscuits (cookies). In Italy bitter almonds are used, but sweet almonds can be substituted successfully.

Makes about 36

175g/6oz/1½ cups sweet almonds
225g/8oz/1 cup caster (superfine) sugar
2 egg whites
2.5ml/½ tsp almond extract or 5ml/1 tsp vanilla extract
icing (confectioners') sugar, for dusting

1 Preheat the oven to 160°C/325°F/Gas 3. To remove the skins from the almonds, first drop them into a pan of boiling water for 1–2 minutes. Drain well, then rub off the skins with a cloth.

2 Place the almonds on a baking sheet and let them dry out in the oven for 10–15 minutes without browning. Remove from the oven and allow to cool. Turn the oven off.

3 Grind the almonds with half of the sugar in a food processor.

4 Using an electric mixer or wire whisk, beat the egg whites until they form soft peaks. Sprinkle half of the remaining sugar over them and continue beating until stiff peaks are formed. Gently fold in the remaining sugar, the almond or vanilla extract and the almonds.

5 Spoon the almond mixture into a pastry bag with a smooth nozzle. Line a baking sheet with baking parchment. Dust the paper lightly with flour.

6 Pipe out the mixture in rounds the size of a walnut. Sprinkle lightly with the icing sugar and leave to stand for 2 hours. Near the end of this time, turn the oven on again and preheat to 180°C/350°F/Gas 4.

7 Bake the amaretti for 15 minutes, or until light golden. Remove from the oven and cool on a rack. When completely cool, the cookies may be stored in an airtight container.

Hazelnut Bites

Serve these sweet little nut cookies as petits fours with after-dinner coffee.

Makes about 26
115g/4oz/¹/₂ cup butter, softened
75g/3oz/³/₄ cup icing
 (confectioners') sugar, sifted
115g/4oz/1 cup plain (all-
 purpose) flour
75g/3oz/³/₄ cup ground hazelnuts
1 egg yolk
blanched whole hazelnuts, to
 decorate
icing (confectioners') sugar, to
 finish

1 Preheat the oven to 180°C/350°F/Gas 4. Line 3–4 baking sheets with non-stick baking parchment.

2 Cream the butter and sugar together with an electric mixer until light and fluffy. Beat in the flour with the ground hazelnuts and egg yolk until evenly mixed.

3 Take a teaspoonful of the mixture at a time and shape it into a round with your fingers. Place the rounds well apart on the baking paper and press a whole hazelnut into the centre of each one.

4 Bake the biscuits, one tray at a time, for about 10 minutes, or until golden brown, then transfer to a wire rack and sift over icing sugar to cover. Leave to cool.

Cook's Tip
Don't worry that the biscuits are still soft at the end of the baking time – they will harden as they cool.

Variation
For almond bites, use ground almonds instead of the hazelnuts and decorate with blanched almonds.

Tea Biscuits

These dainty little biscuits (cookies) are very quick and easy to make. Candied peel is a favoured ingredient in Italian sweet bakes and desserts.

Makes 20

150g/5oz/10 tbsp butter,
 softened
75g/3oz/³/₄ cup icing
 (confectioners') sugar, sifted
1 egg, beaten
a few drops of almond extract
225g/8oz/2 cups plain
 (all-purpose) flour
2–3 large pieces of candied peel

1 Preheat the oven to 230°C/450°F/Gas 8. Line two baking sheets with non-stick baking parchment.

2 Cream the butter and sugar with an electric mixer until light and fluffy, then beat in the egg, almond extract and flour until evenly mixed.

3 Spoon the mixture into a piping bag fitted with a star nozzle and pipe 10 rosette shapes on each of the baking sheets.

4 Cut the candied peel into small diamond shapes and press one diamond into the centre of each biscuit, to decorate. Bake for 5 minutes, or until golden. Transfer the biscuits with the baking paper to a wire rack and leave to cool. Lift the biscuits off the paper when cool.

Cook's Tip
If you would rather not pipe the mixture, simply spoon it on to the baking paper and press it down with a fork.

Variation
Use 10 red glacé cherries instead of the candied peel. Cut them in half and press one half, cut side down, into the centre of each piped biscuit.

Energy 113Kcal/471kJ; Fat 6.6g; Saturated Fat 4g; Carbohydrate 12.7g; Fibre 0.4g

Energy 68Kcal/283kJ; Fat 6g; Saturated Fat 2.7g; Carbohydrate 3.2g; Fibre 0.2g

Sicilian Scroll

A pale yellow loaf, enhanced with a nutty flavour from the sesame seeds.

Makes 1 loaf
450g/1lb finely ground semolina
115g/4oz/1 cup unbleached strong white bread flour, plus extra for dusting

10ml/2 tsp salt
20g/¾oz fresh yeast
360ml/12½ fl oz/generous 1½ cups lukewarm water
30ml/2 tbsp extra virgin olive oil
30ml/2 tbsp sesame seeds, for sprinkling

1 Lightly grease a baking sheet (cookie sheet) and set aside. Mix the semolina, white bread flour and salt together in a large bowl and make a well in the centre.

2 In a jug, cream the yeast with half the water, then stir in the remaining water. Add the creamed yeast to the centre of the semolina mixture with the olive oil. Gradually incorporate the semolina and flour to form a firm dough.

3 Turn the dough out on to a lightly floured surface. Knead for 8–10 minutes, until smooth and elastic. Place in a lightly oiled bowl, cover with lightly oiled clear film (plastic wrap) and leave to rise in a warm place for 1–1½ hours, or until the dough has doubled in bulk.

4 Turn out on to a lightly floured surface and knock back. Knead, then shape the dough into a fat roll about 50cm/20in long. Form into an "S" shape. Transfer to the prepared baking sheet, cover with oiled clear film and leave to rise in a warm place for 30–45 minutes, or until doubled in size.

5 Meanwhile, preheat the oven to 220°C/425°F/Gas 7. Brush the top of the scroll with water and sprinkle with the sesame seeds. Bake for 10 minutes. Spray the inside of the oven with water twice during this time.

6 Reduce the oven temperature to 200°C/400°F/Gas 6 and bake for a further 25–30 minutes until golden. Cool on a rack.

Energy 293Kcal/1240kJ; Fat 6.1g; Saturated Fat 0.7g; Carbohydrate 54.8g; Fibre 1.9g

Prosciutto Loaf

This savoury bread from Parma is spiked with the local dried ham.

Makes 1 loaf
350g/12oz/3 cups unbleached strong white bread flour, plus extra for dusting

7.5ml/1½ tsp salt
15g/½ oz fresh yeast
250ml/8fl oz/1 cup lukewarm water
40g/1½ oz prosciutto, torn into small pieces
5ml/1 tsp ground black pepper

1 Lightly grease a baking sheet and set aside. Sift the flour and salt into a bowl and make a well in the centre. In a small bowl, cream the yeast with 30ml/2 tbsp of the water, then gradually mix in the rest. Pour into the centre of the flour.

2 Gradually beat in most of the flour to make a batter. When most of the flour is incorporated, mix in the rest with your hand to form a moist dough. Knead on a lightly floured surface for 5 minutes until smooth and elastic. Place in an oiled bowl, cover with lightly oiled clear film (plastic wrap) and leave to rise in a warm place for 1½ hours, or until doubled in bulk.

3 Turn the dough out on to a lightly floured surface, knock back and knead for 1 minute. Flatten to a round, then sprinkle with half the prosciutto and pepper. Fold in half and repeat with the remaining ham and pepper. Roll up, tucking in the sides.

4 Place on the baking sheet, cover with oiled clear film. Leave to rise in a warm place for 30 minutes. Turn out on to a lightly floured surface, roll into an oval, fold in half and seal the edges. Flatten and fold again. Seal and fold again to make a long loaf.

5 Roll into a stubby long loaf. Draw out the edges by rolling the dough under the palms of your hands. Place back on the prepared baking sheet, cover with oiled clear film and leave to rise in a warm place for 45 minutes, or until the loaf has doubled in bulk. Preheat the oven to 200°C/400°F/Gas 6. Make 3–4 slashes in the top and bake for 30 minutes, or until golden. Transfer to a wire rack to cool. Serve in slices.

Energy 206Kcal/876kJ; Fat 1g; Saturated Fat 0.2g; Carbohydrate 45.4g; Fibre 1.8g

Prosciutto & Parmesan Bread

This nourishing Italian bread is particularly good served in slices and topped with grilled vegetables: ideal for a tasty lunch or supper.

Makes 1 loaf
225g/8oz/2 cups self-raising (self-rising) wholemeal (whole-wheat) flour
225g/8oz/2 cups self-raising (self-rising) white flour, plus extra for dusting
5ml/1 tsp baking powder
5ml/1 tsp salt
5ml/1 tsp ground black pepper
75g/3oz prosciutto, chopped
25g/1oz/2 tbsp grated fresh Parmesan cheese
30ml/2 tbsp chopped fresh parsley
45ml/3 tbsp Meaux mustard
350ml/12fl oz/1½ cups buttermilk
skimmed milk, to glaze

1 Preheat the oven to 200°C/400°F/Gas 6. Flour a baking sheet and set aside. Place the wholemeal flour in a bowl and sift in the white flour, baking powder and salt.

2 Add the pepper and ham. Set aside about 15ml/1 tbsp of the grated Parmesan and stir the rest into the flour mixture. Stir in the parsley. Make a well in the centre of the mixture.

3 Mix the mustard and buttermilk together in a jug, pour into the flour mixture and quickly mix to a soft dough. Turn the dough out on to a lightly floured surface and knead briefly.

4 Shape the dough into an oval loaf, brush with milk and sprinkle with the remaining cheese. Place the loaf on the prepared baking sheet. Bake in the oven for 25–30 minutes, or until golden brown. Transfer to a wire rack to cool. Serve in slices.

> **Variation**
> For a vegetarian loaf, replace the prosciutto with sun-dried tomatoes in oil, drained and chopped, and use 15ml/1 tbsp tomato purée (paste) instead of the mustard.

Energy 231Kcal/980kJ; Fat 3.1g; Saturated Fat 1g; Carbohydrate 42.2g; Fibre 4g

Olive & Herb Bread

Olive breads are popular all over Italy. This delicious version is enhanced with chopped fresh herbs and is perfect with pasta and salads.

Makes 2 loaves
2 red onions, thinly sliced
30ml/2 tbsp olive oil
225g/8oz/1½ cups pitted black or green olives
800g/1¾lb/7 cups strong white bread flour, plus extra for dusting
7.5ml/1½ tsp salt
20ml/4 tsp easy-blend (rapid-rise) dried yeast
45ml/3 tbsp roughly chopped fresh parsley, coriander (cilantro) or mint
475ml/16fl oz/2 cups hand-hot water

1 Fry the onions in the oil in a pan until soft. Remove the pan from the heat and set aside. Roughly chop the black or green olives and set aside.

2 Put the flour, salt, yeast and chopped fresh herbs in a large bowl with the olives and fried onions and pour in the water. Mix to a dough using a round-bladed knife, adding a little more water if the mixture feels dry.

3 Turn out on to a lightly floured surface and knead for about 10 minutes, until smooth and elastic. Put in a clean bowl, cover with clear film (plastic wrap) and leave in a warm place until doubled in bulk.

4 Preheat the oven to 220°C/425°F/Gas 7. Lightly grease two baking sheets. Turn the dough out on to a lightly floured surface and cut in half. Shape into two rounds. Place on the prepared baking sheets, cover loosely with lightly oiled clear film and leave until doubled in bulk.

5 Slash the tops of the loaves with a sharp knife, then bake in the oven for about 40 minutes, or until they sound hollow when tapped underneath. Transfer to a wire rack to cool. Serve warm or cold, in slices.

Energy 166Kcal/702kJ; Fat 2.9g; Saturated Fat 0.4g; Carbohydrate 32.7g; Fibre 2g

Tuscany Bread

This Tuscan bread is made without salt and probably originates from the days when salt was heavily taxed. To compensate for the lack of salt, serve with salty foods such as olives.

Makes 1 loaf
500g/1¼lb/4½ cups unbleached strong white bread flour, plus extra for dusting
350ml/12fl oz/1½ cups boiling water
15g/½oz fresh yeast
60ml/4 tbsp lukewarm water

1 Sift 175g/6oz/1½ cups of the flour into a large bowl. Pour over the boiling water, leave for a couple of minutes, then mix well. Cover the bowl with a damp dish towel. Stand for 10 hours.

2 Lightly flour a baking sheet and set aside. In a bowl, cream the yeast with the lukewarm water. Mix well into the flour mixture. Gradually add the remaining flour and mix to form a dough. Turn out on to a lightly floured surface and knead for 5–8 minutes, until smooth and elastic.

3 Place in a lightly oiled bowl, cover with lightly oiled clear film (plastic wrap) and leave to rise in a warm place for 1–1½ hours, or until doubled in bulk.

4 Turn the dough out on to a lightly floured surface, knock back and shape into a round. Fold the sides of the round into the centre and seal. Place seam-side up on the prepared baking sheet. Cover with oiled clear film and leave to rise in a warm place for 30–45 minutes, or until doubled in bulk.

5 Flatten the loaf to about half its risen height and flip over. Cover with a large upturned bowl and leave to rise again in a warm place for 30 minutes.

6 Meanwhile, preheat the oven to 220°C/425°F/Gas 7. Slash the top of the loaf, using a sharp knife, if wished. Bake for 30–35 minutes, or until golden. Transfer to a wire rack to cool. Serve in slices or wedges.

Energy 214Kcal/911kJ; Fat 0.8g; Saturated Fat 0.1g; Carbohydrate 48.6g; Fibre 1.9g

Polenta Bread

Polenta is combined with pine nuts in this tasty bread.

Makes 1 loaf
50g/2oz/⅓ cup polenta
300ml/½ pint/1¼ cups luke-warm water
15g/½oz fresh yeast
2.5ml/½ tsp clear honey
225g/8oz/2 cups unbleached strong white bread flour, plus extra for dusting
25g/1oz/2 tbsp butter
30ml/2 tbsp pine nuts
7.5ml/1½ tsp salt
1 egg yolk, mixed with 15ml/1 tbsp water

1 Lightly grease a baking sheet and set aside. Mix the polenta and 250ml/8fl oz/1 cup of the water in a pan and bring to the boil, stirring continuously. Reduce the heat and simmer for 2–3 minutes. Remove from the heat and set aside for 10 minutes.

2 In a small bowl, mix the yeast with the remaining water and honey until creamy. Sift 115g/4oz/1 cup of the flour into a large bowl. Gradually beat in the yeast mixture, then gradually stir in the polenta mixture. Turn out on to a lightly floured surface and knead for 5 minutes, until smooth and elastic. Cover the bowl with oiled clear film (plastic wrap). Leave the dough to rise in a warm place for about 2 hours, or until it has doubled in bulk.

3 Meanwhile, melt the butter in a small pan, add the pine nuts and cook over medium heat, stirring, until pale golden. Set aside.

4 Add the remaining flour and the salt to the polenta dough and mix to form a soft dough. Knead in the pine nuts. Turn out on to a floured surface and knead for 5 minutes, until smooth and elastic. Place in an oiled bowl, cover with clear film and leave to rise in a warm place for 1 hour, until doubled in size.

5 Knock back the dough and turn it out on to a floured surface. Cut into two pieces and roll each piece into a fat sausage about 40cm/15in long. Plait together and place on the baking sheet. Cover with oiled clear film and leave to rise in a warm place for 45 minutes. Preheat the oven to 200°C/400°F/Gas 6. Brush with the egg yolk mixture and bake for 30 minutes until golden.

Energy 177Kcal/742kJ; Fat 6.4g; Saturated Fat 2.1g; Carbohydrate 26.8g; Fibre 1.1g

Olive & Oregano Bread

Tangy black olives, punchy onion and fragrant oregano give this delicious bread a truly Italian feel.

Makes I loaf
300ml/½ pint/1¼ cups
   lukewarm water
5ml/1 tsp active dried yeast
pinch of sugar
15ml/1 tbsp olive oil

1 onion, chopped
450g/1lb/4 cups white bread
   flour, plus extra for dusting
5ml/1 tsp salt
1.5ml/¼ tsp ground black pepper
75g/3oz/½ cup pitted black
   olives, rough chopped
15ml/1tbsp black olive paste
15ml/1tbsp chopped fresh
   oregano
15ml/1tbsp chopped fresh parsley

1 Put half the warm water in a small bowl. Sprinkle the yeast on top, add the sugar and mix well. Set aside for 10 minutes.

2 Heat the oil in a frying pan and fry the onion until golden, stirring occasionally. Remove the pan from the heat. Set aside.

3 Sift the flour into a mixing bowl with the salt and pepper. Make a well in the centre. Add the yeast mixture, the onions (with the oil), the olives, olive paste, oregano and parsley and remaining water. Gradually mix in the flour to a soft dough.

4 Transfer the dough to a lightly floured surface and knead for 5 minutes until smooth and elastic. Place in a mixing bowl, cover with a damp dish towel and leave to rise in a warm place for about 2 hours, until the dough has doubled in bulk. Lightly grease a baking sheet and set aside.

5 Transfer the dough to a lightly floured surface and knead for a few minutes. Shape into a 20cm/8in round and place on the prepared baking sheet. Make criss-cross cuts on top of the dough. Cover and leave in a warm place for 30 minutes, until well risen. Preheat the oven to 220°C/425°F/Gas 7.

6 Dust the loaf with a little flour. Bake for 10 minutes, then lower the oven to 200°C/400°F/Gas 6. Bake for another 20 minutes, or until the loaf sounds hollow. Cool on a wire rack.

Sultana & Walnut Bread

This versatile bread is delicious with savoury dishes, but also tastes good with lashings of jam.

Makes I loaf
300g/11oz/2¾ cups strong white
   flour, plus extra for dusting
2.5ml/½ tsp salt

15ml/1 tbsp butter
7.5ml/1½ tsp easy-blend (rapid-
   rise) dried yeast
175ml/6fl oz/¾ cup warm water
115g/4oz/scant 1 cup sultanas
   (golden raisins)
75g/3oz/½ cup walnuts, roughly
   chopped
melted butter, for brushing

1 Sift the flour and salt into a bowl, cut in the butter with a knife, then stir in the yeast.

2 Gradually add the warm water to the flour mixture, stirring with a spoon at first, then forming the dough with your hands.

3 Turn the dough out on to a floured surface and knead for about 10 minutes until smooth and elastic. Knead the sultanas and walnuts into the dough until they are evenly distributed. Shape into a rough oval, place on a lightly oiled baking sheet and cover with oiled clear film (plastic wrap).

4 Leave to rise in a warm place for 1–2 hours, or until doubled in size. Preheat the oven to 220°C/425°F/Gas 7.

5 Uncover the loaf and bake in the oven for 10 minutes, then reduce the oven temperature to 190°C/375°F/Gas 5 and bake for a further 20–25 minutes.

6 Transfer to a wire rack, brush with melted butter and cover with a dish towel. Cool before slicing.

> **Cook's Tip**
> *Easy-blend dried yeast is sold in sachets at most supermarkets. It is a real boon for the busy cook because it cuts out the need to let the dough rise before shaping.*

Energy 172Kcal/727kJ; Fat 2.3g; Saturated Fat 0.4g; Carbohydrate 35.4g; Fibre 1.7g

Energy 1967Kcal/8283kJ; Fat 68g; Saturated Fat 12.6g; Carbohydrate 315; Fibre 14.2g

Italian Bread Sticks

Grissini, the typically Italian bread sticks, are especially good when hand-made. For an attractive finish and extra flavour, try rolling them lightly in poppy, linseed or sesame seeds before baking.

Makes about 30

15g/½ oz/1 tbsp fresh bread yeast or 7g/¼ oz/½ tbsp active dried yeast
120ml/4fl oz/½ cup lukewarm water
pinch of sugar
5ml/1 tsp salt
200–225g/7–8oz/1¾–2 cups unbleached white bread flour, plus extra for dusting

1 Place the yeast in a warm bowl and pour on the warm water. Stir in the sugar, mix with a fork and stand for 5–10 minutes until the yeast has dispersed and starts to foam.

2 Using a wooden spoon, stir in the salt and about one-third of the flour. Mix in another third of the flour, stirring until the mixture begins to pull away from the sides of the bowl. Turn the dough on to a surface dusted with some flour. Knead, working in the remaining flour a little at a time. Knead for 8–10 minutes until elastic and smooth. Form into a ball.

3 Tear off a walnut-sized ball from the dough. Roll lightly between your hands into a small sausage shape. Set aside on a lightly floured surface. Repeat this process to make 30 pieces.

4 Place one piece of dough on a clean smooth work surface without any flour on it. Roll the dough under the spread-out fingers of both hands, moving your hands backwards and forwards to lengthen and thin the dough into a long strand about 1cm/½in thick. Transfer to a very lightly greased baking tray. Repeat this process to make evenly sized bread sticks.

5 Preheat the oven to 200°C/400°F/Gas 6. Cover the tray with a cloth and place the grissini in a warm place to rise for 10–15 minutes. Bake for 8–10 minutes. Turn the grissini over and return to the oven for 6–7 minutes. Do not let them brown. Allow to cool and serve while still crisp.

Energy 23Kcal/99kJ; Fat 0.1g; Saturated Fat 0g; Carbohydrate 5.3g; Fibre 0.2g

Ciabatta

This classic Italian bread gained its name because its shape resembles an old shoe.

Makes 3 loaves
For the biga starter
7g/¼oz fresh yeast
175–200ml/6–7fl oz/scant 1 cup lukewarm water
350g/12oz/3 cups unbleached plain flour, plus extra for dusting

For the dough
15g/½oz fresh yeast
400ml/14fl oz/1⅔ cups lukewarm water
60ml/4 tbsp lukewarm semi-skimmed (low-fat) milk
500g/1¼lb/4½ cups unbleached strong white bread flour
10ml/2 tsp salt
45ml/3 tbsp extra virgin olive oil

1 To make the biga, cream the yeast with a little of the water. Sift the flour into a bowl. Gradually mix in the yeast mixture and enough of the remaining water to form a firm dough.

2 Turn out on to a lightly floured surface and knead for about 5 minutes, until smooth. Return the dough to the bowl and cover with oiled clear film (plastic wrap). Leave in a warm place for 12–15 hours, or until dough has risen and is starting to collapse.

3 Sprinkle three baking sheets with flour. Mix the yeast for the dough with a little of the water until creamy, then mix in the remaining water. Add the yeast mixture to the biga and mix well. Beat in the milk with a wooden spoon. Mix in the flour by hand for 15 minutes, lifting the dough to form a very wet mixture.

4 Beat in the salt and oil. Cover with oiled clear film and leave to rise in a warm place for 1½–2 hours, or until doubled in size.

5 Using a spoon, turn one-third of the dough at a time on to each prepared baking sheet, trying to avoid knocking back the dough in the process. Using floured hands, shape into oblong loaves, about 2.5cm/1in thick. Flatten slightly. Sprinkle with flour and leave to rise in a warm place for 30 minutes. Meanwhile, preheat the oven to 220°C/425°F/Gas 7. Bake the loaves for 25–30 minutes, or until golden. Transfer to a wire rack to cool.

Energy 269Kcal/1139kJ; Fat 3.8g; Saturated Fat 0.6g; Carbohydrate 55.3g; Fibre 2.2g

Ham & Tomato Scones

The intense flavour of sun-dried tomatoes permeates these delicious savoury scones, which are wonderful spread with butter or goat's cheese and served with a hot bowl of soup.

Makes 12

225g/8oz/2 cups self-raising (self-rising) flour, plus extra for dusting
5ml/1 tsp dry mustard
5ml/1 tsp paprika, plus extra for sprinkling
2.5ml/½ tsp salt
25g/1oz/2 tbsp margarine
15ml/1 tbsp chopped fresh basil
50g/2oz/1 cup dry sun-dried tomatoes, soaked in warm water, drained and chopped
50g/2oz cooked lean ham, chopped
90–120ml/3–4fl oz/6 tbsp–½ cup skimmed milk, plus extra for brushing

1 Preheat the oven to 200°C/400°F/Gas 6. Lightly flour a large greased baking sheet and set aside. Sift the flour, dry mustard, paprika and salt into a large bowl. Rub in the margarine until the mixture resembles breadcrumbs.

2 Stir in the chopped basil, sun-dried tomatoes and cooked ham, and mix lightly. Pour in enough skimmed milk to mix to a soft dough.

3 Turn out on to a lightly floured surface, knead briefly and roll out to a 20 × 15cm/8 × 6in rectangle. Cut into 5cm/2in squares and arrange on the baking sheet.

4 Brush the tops lightly with milk, sprinkle with paprika and bake in the oven for about 12–15 minutes or until golden brown. Transfer to a wire rack to cool. Serve warm or cold – the scones are best eaten fresh on the day they are made.

> **Variation**
> *For a slightly different flavour, use chopped prosciutto instead of the cooked ham. The ham can be replaced by a lightly fried, chopped red onion, for a vegetarian alternative.*

Mixed Olive Bread

Mixed black and green olives and good-quality fruity olive oil combine to make this strongly flavoured and irresistible Italian bread, ideal as an accompaniment to soups and salad.

Makes 1 loaf

275g/10oz/2½ cups unbleached strong white bread flour, plus extra for dusting
50g/2oz/½ cup strong wholemeal (wholewheat) bread flour
10g/¼ oz sachet easy-blend (rapid-rise) dried yeast
2.5ml/½ tsp salt
210ml/7½fl oz/scant 1 cup lukewarm water
15ml/1 tbsp extra virgin olive oil, plus 15ml/1 tbsp olive oil for brushing
115g/4oz/⅔ cup mixed pitted black and green olives, coarsely chopped

1 Lightly grease a baking sheet and set aside. Mix the flours, yeast and salt in a bowl and make a well in the centre.

2 Add the water and 15ml/1 tbsp oil to the centre of the flour and mix to form a soft dough. Knead the dough on a lightly floured surface for 8–10 minutes, until smooth and elastic. Place in a lightly oiled bowl, cover with lightly oiled clear film (plastic wrap) and leave to rise, in a warm place for 1 hour, or until doubled in size.

3 Turn the dough out on to a lightly floured surface and knock back. Flatten out and sprinkle over the olives. Knead to distribute the olives evenly throughout the dough. Leave to rest for 5 minutes, then shape into an oval loaf. Place on the prepared baking sheet.

4 Make six deep cuts in the top of the dough and gently push the sections over. Cover with oiled clear film and leave to rise in a warm place for 30–45 minutes, or until doubled in size.

5 Meanwhile, preheat the oven to 200°C/400°F/Gas 6. Brush the top of the bread with olive oil and bake in the oven for 35 minutes, until golden. Transfer to a wire rack to cool. Serve warm or cold in slices.

Energy 166Kcal/700kJ; Fat 3.5g; Saturated Fat 0.5g; Carbohydrate 31.6g; Fibre 1.7g

Energy 81Kcal/345kJ; Fat 1.4g; Saturated Fat 0.4g; Carbohydrate 15.2g; Fibre 0.6g

Focaccia with Green Peppercorns & Rock Salt

There's something irresistible about a loaf of freshly baked focaccia with its dimpled surface and fabulous flavour. This peppery version just proves the point.

Makes 1 loaf
350g/12oz/3 cups white bread flour, plus extra for dusting
2.5ml/½ tsp salt
10ml/2 tsp easy-blend (rapid-rise) dried yeast
10ml/2 tsp drained green peppercorns in brine, lightly crushed
25ml/5 tsp extra virgin olive oil
about 250ml/8fl oz/1 cup lukewarm water
20ml/4 tsp roughly crushed rock salt, for the topping
fresh basil leaves, to garnish

1 Sift the flour and salt into a mixing bowl. Stir in the yeast and peppercorns. Make a well in the centre and add 15ml/1 tbsp of the oil, with half the water. Mix, gradually incorporating the flour and adding more water to make a soft dough.

2 Knead the dough on a lightly floured surface for 10 minutes. Return to the clean, oiled bowl, and cover with oiled clear film (plastic wrap). Leave in a warm place, until doubled in size.

3 Knock down the dough and knead lightly for 2–3 minutes. Place on an oiled baking sheet and pat out to an oval. Cover with lightly oiled clear film and leave for 30 minutes.

4 Preheat the oven to 190°C/375°F/Gas 5. Make a few dimples in the surface of the dough with your fingers. Drizzle with the remaining oil and sprinkle with the salt. Bake for 25–30 minutes, until pale gold. Scatter with basil leaves and serve warm.

> **Cook's Tip**
> *Kneading is a vital step in bread-making as it develops the gluten in the flour. Press and stretch the dough, using the heel of your hand and turning the dough frequently.*

Saffron Focaccia

A dazzling yellow bread that is both light in texture and distinctive in flavour. The olive oil drizzled over the top makes the bread moist and it keeps well.

Makes one loaf
a pinch of saffron threads
150ml/¼ pint/⅔ cup boiling water
225g/8oz/2 cups strong white bread flour
2.5ml/½ tsp salt
5ml/1 tsp easy-blend (rapid-rise) dried yeast
15ml/1 tbsp olive oil

For the topping
2 garlic cloves, sliced
1 red onion, cut into thin wedges
rosemary sprigs
12 black olives, pitted and coarsely chopped
15ml/1 tbsp olive oil

1 Place the saffron in a heatproof jug (pitcher) and pour in the boiling water. Leave to infuse (steep) until lukewarm.

2 Place the flour, salt, yeast and olive oil in a food processor. Turn on and gradually add the saffron and its liquid. Process until the dough forms a ball. Alternatively, use your hands to incorporate the liquid into the flour.

3 Turn out on to a floured surface and knead for 10–15 minutes. Place in a bowl, cover with clear film (plastic wrap) and leave to rise until doubled in size, about 30–40 minutes.

4 Knock back the dough and roll into an oval shape about 1cm/½in thick. Place on a lightly greased baking sheet and leave to rise for 30 minutes.

5 Preheat the oven to 200°C/400°F/Gas 6. With your fingers, press indentations over the surface of the bread.

6 To make the topping cover the dough with the sliced garlic, onion wedges, rosemary sprigs and chopped olives.

7 Brush lightly with olive oil and bake for 25 minutes, or until the loaf sounds hollow when tapped on the base. Leave to cool on a wire rack.

Sun-dried Tomato Bread

This tasty bread, flavoured with chopped onion and sun-dried tomatoes, is a gem from the Italian kitchen.

Makes 4 small loaves
675g/1½ lb/6 cups strong plain flour, plus extra for dusting
10ml/2 tsp salt
25g/1oz/2 tbsp caster (superfine) sugar
25g/1oz fresh yeast
400–475ml/14–16fl oz/1⅔– 2 cups lukewarm milk
15ml/1 tbsp tomato purée (paste)
75g/3oz/¾ cup sun-dried tomatoes in oil, drained and chopped, plus 75ml/5 tbsp oil from the jar
75ml/5 tbsp extra virgin olive oil
1 large onion, chopped

1 Sift the flour, salt and sugar into a bowl and make a well in the centre. Crumble the yeast into a jug, mix with 150ml/ ¼ pint/⅔ cup of the milk and pour into the well in the flour.

2 Stir the tomato purée into the remaining milk, then add to the well in the flour, with the tomato oil and olive oil.

3 Mix the liquid ingredients, then gradually incorporate the surrounding flour to make a dough. Knead on a floured surface for about 10 minutes, then return the dough to the clean bowl, cover with lightly oiled clear film (plastic wrap) and leave to rise in a warm place for about 2 hours.

4 Knock back the dough and add the tomatoes and onion. Knead until evenly distributed. Shape into four rounds and place on two greased baking sheets. Cover each pair with a dish towel and leave to rise again for about 45 minutes.

5 Preheat the oven to 190°C/375°F/Gas 5. Bake the bread for 45 minutes, or until the loaves sound hollow when you tap them underneath. Cool on a wire rack.

Cook's Tip
Use a pair of sharp kitchen scissors to cut up the tomatoes.

Warm Herb Bread

This mouthwatering Italian-style bread, flavoured with basil, rosemary, olive oil and sun-dried tomatoes, is absolutely delicious served warm with fresh salads.

Makes 3 loaves
1.3kg/3lb/12 cups white bread flour, plus extra for dusting
15ml/1 tbsp salt
5ml/1 tsp caster (superfine) sugar
7g/¼oz sachet easy-blend (rapid-rise) dried yeast
about 900ml/1½ pints/3¾ cups lukewarm water
75g/3oz/1½ cups sun-dried tomatoes in oil, drained and roughly chopped
150ml/¼ pint/⅔ cup extra virgin olive oil
75ml/5 tbsp chopped mixed fresh basil and rosemary

To finish
extra virgin olive oil
rosemary leaves
sea salt flakes

1 Sift the flour and salt into a bowl. Stir in the sugar and yeast. Make a well in the centre and add the water, tomatoes, oil and herbs. Beat well, gradually incorporating the surrounding flour.

2 As the mixture becomes stiffer, bring it together with your hands. Mix to a soft but not sticky dough, adding a little extra water if needed.

3 Knead the dough on a lightly floured surface for about 10 minutes, then return it to the bowl, cover loosely with oiled clear film (plastic wrap) and put in a warm place for 30–40 minutes, or until doubled in size.

4 Knead the dough again until smooth and elastic, then cut it into three pieces. Shape each into an oval loaf about 18cm/7in long and place each on an oiled baking sheet. Slash the top of each loaf in a criss-cross pattern. Cover loosely and leave in a warm place for 15–20 minutes, until well risen.

5 Preheat the oven to 220°C/425°F/Gas 7. Brush the loaves with a little olive oil and sprinkle with the rosemary leaves and salt flakes. Cook for about 25 minutes, until golden brown. The bases should sound hollow when tapped.

Index

NOTES

Notes

Notes

NOTES

NOTES

NOTES